Natsume's
BOOK of FRIENDS

Shojo Beat

Natsume's BOOK of FRIENDS

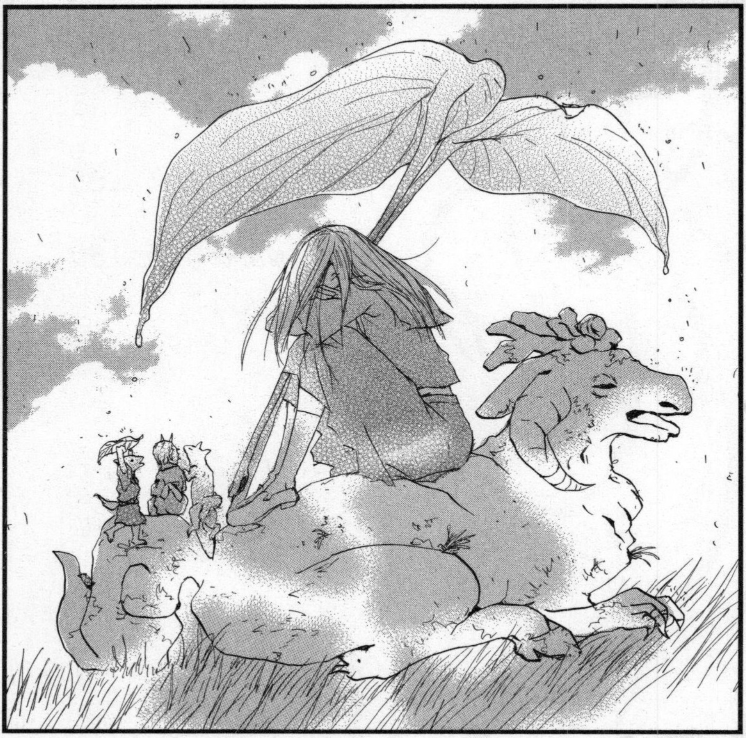

STORY and ART by
Yuki Midorikawa

VOLUME 19

Natsume's BOOK of FRIENDS

VOLUME 19 CONTENTS

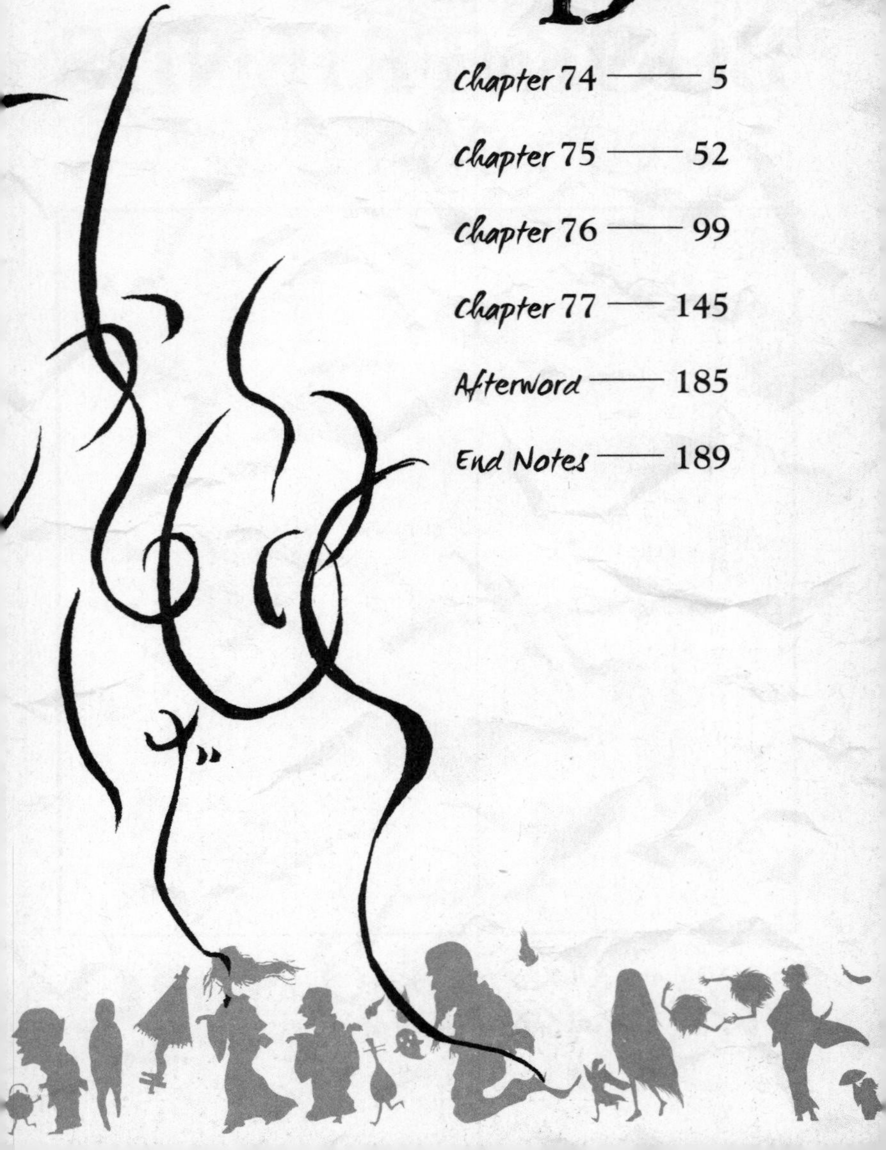

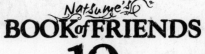

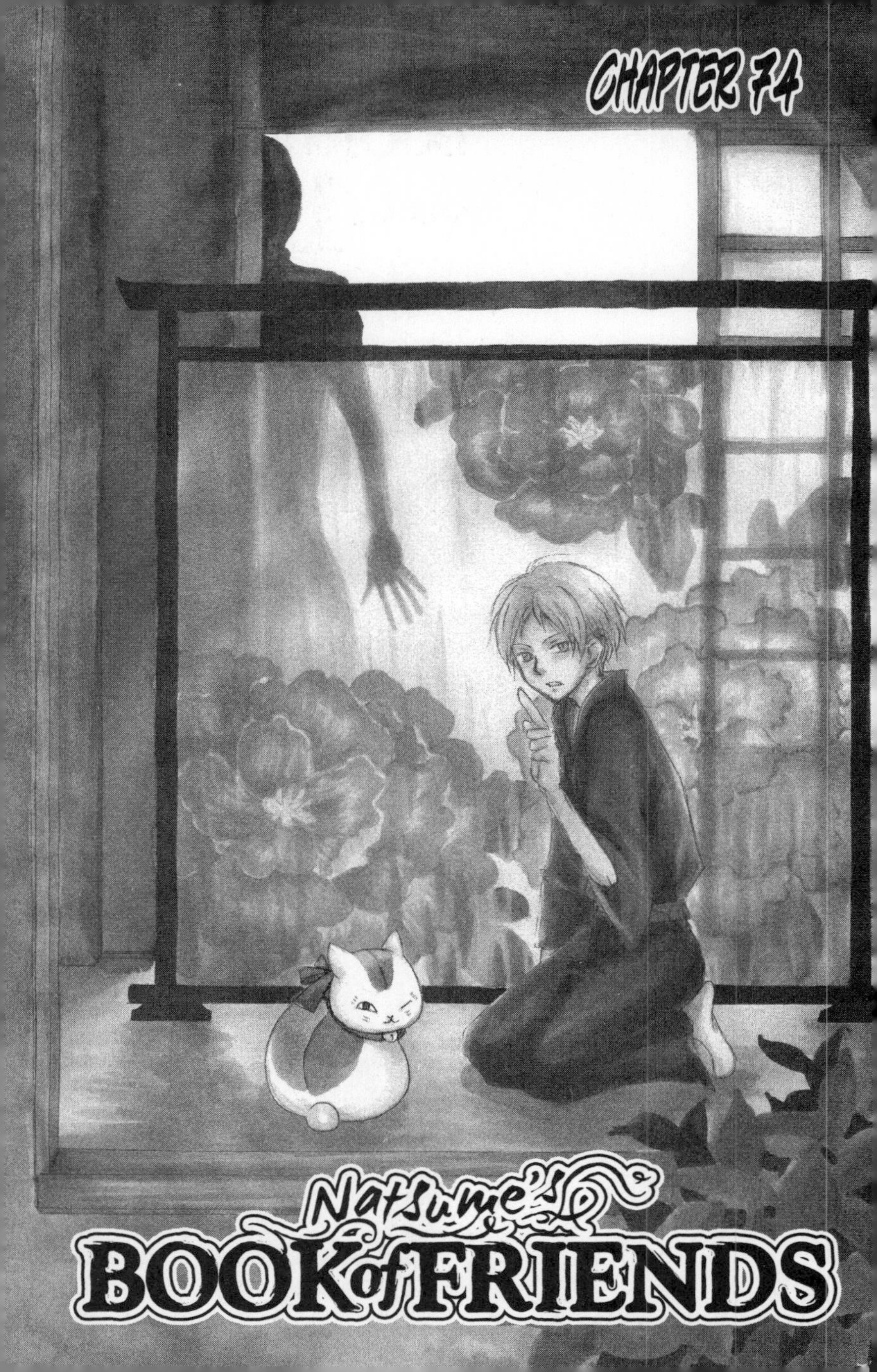
CHAPTER 74
Natsume's
BOOK of FRIENDS

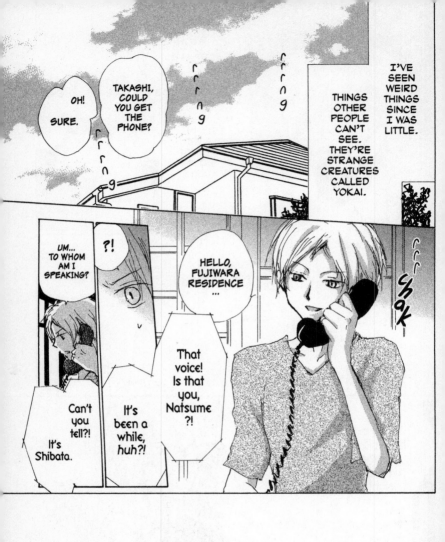

I'VE SEEN WEIRD THINGS SINCE I WAS LITTLE.
THINGS OTHER PEOPLE CAN'T SEE. THEY'RE STRANGE CREATURES CALLED YOKAI.
rrrng
rrrng
TAKASHI, COULD YOU GET THE PHONE?
rrrng
OH! SURE.
shak
HELLO, FUJIWARA RESIDENCE...
That voice! Is that you, Natsume?!
?!
It's been a while, huh?!
UM... TO WHOM AM I SPEAKING?
Can't you tell?! It's Shibata.

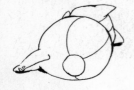

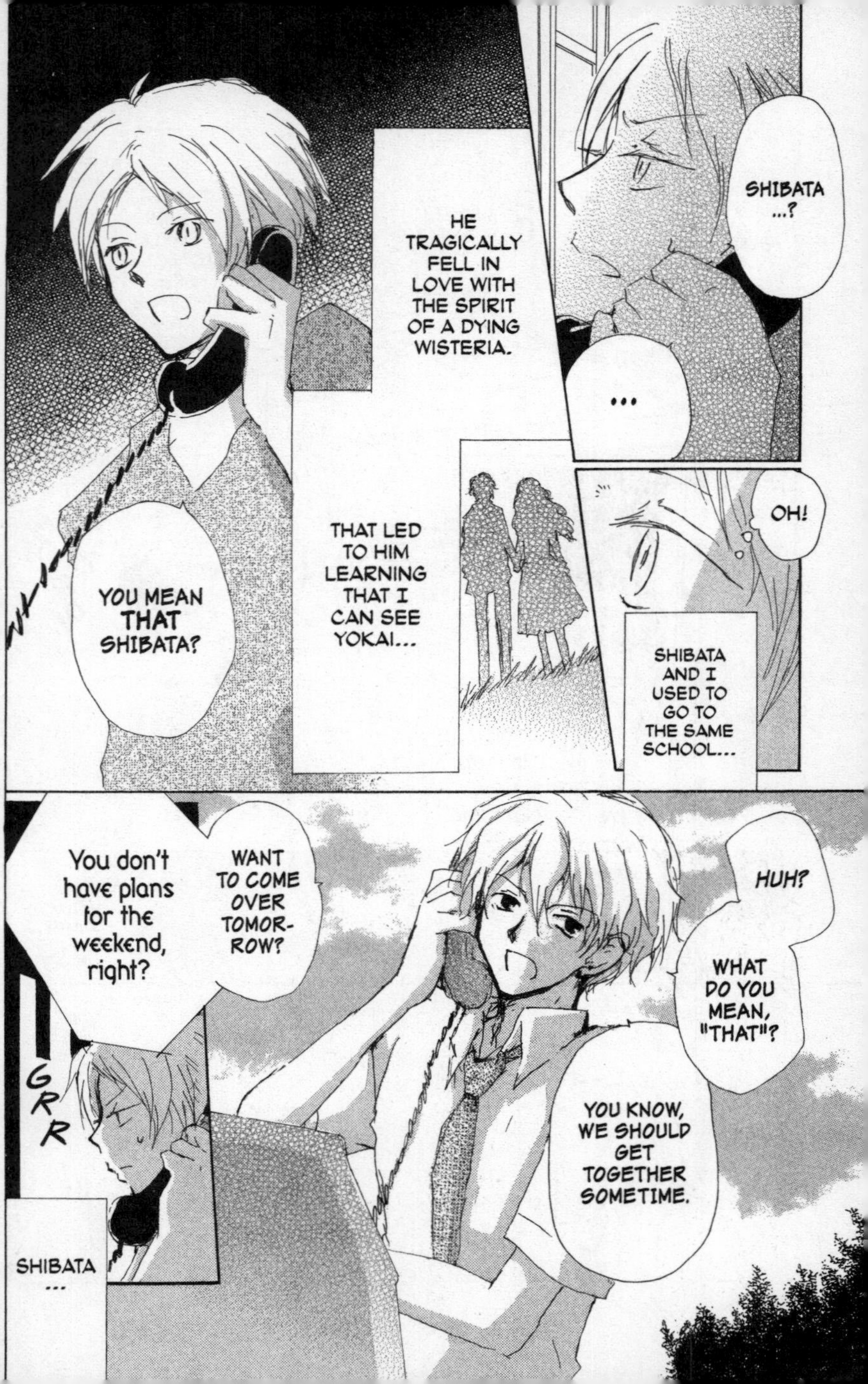
SHIBATA ...?
...
OH!
SHIBATA AND I USED TO GO TO THE SAME SCHOOL...
HE TRAGICALLY FELL IN LOVE WITH THE SPIRIT OF A DYING WISTERIA.
THAT LED TO HIM LEARNING THAT I CAN SEE YOKAI...
YOU MEAN THAT SHIBATA?
HUH?
WHAT DO YOU MEAN, "THAT"?
YOU KNOW, WE SHOULD GET TOGETHER SOMETIME.
WANT TO COME OVER TOMOR-ROW?
You don't have plans for the weekend, right?
GRR
SHIBATA ...

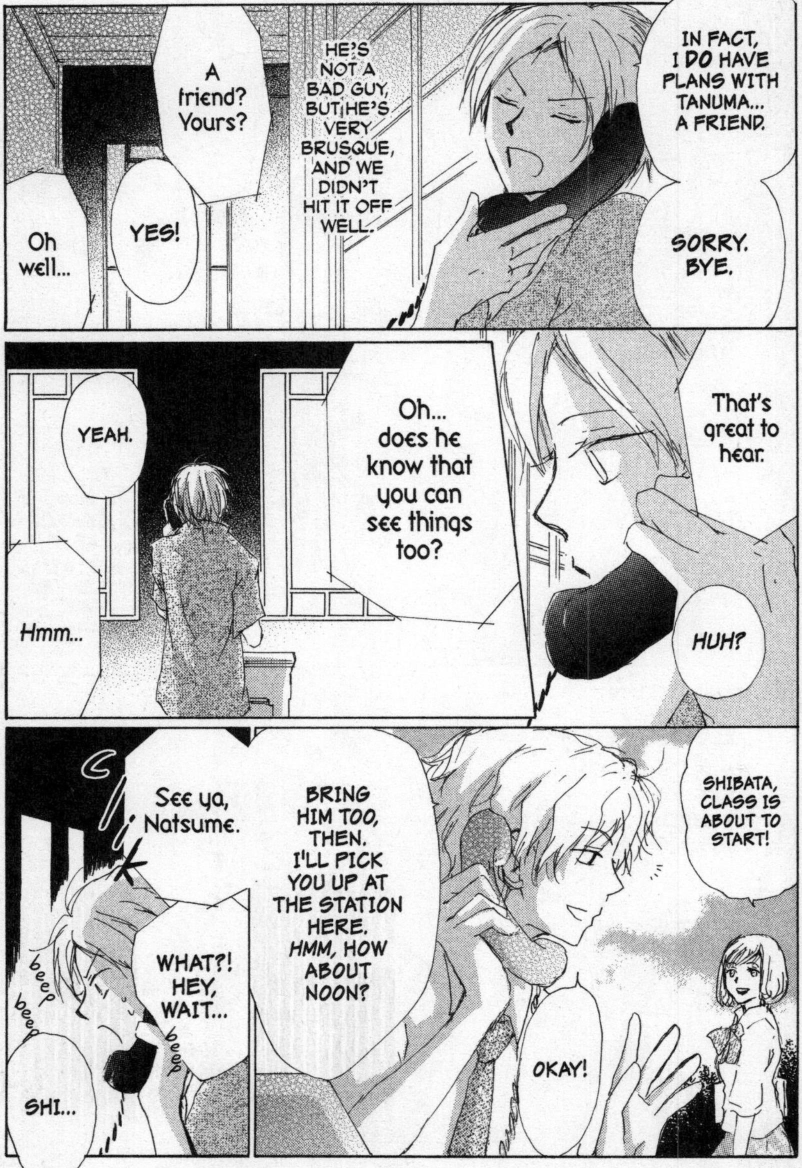
IN FACT, I DO HAVE PLANS WITH TANUMA... A FRIEND.
SORRY. BYE.
HE'S NOT A BAD GUY, BUT HE'S VERY BRUSQUE, AND WE DIDN'T HIT IT OFF WELL.
A friend? Yours?
YES!
Oh well...
That's great to hear.
HUH?
Oh... does he know that you can see things too?
YEAH.
Hmm...
SHIBATA, CLASS IS ABOUT TO START!
OKAY!
BRING HIM TOO, THEN. I'LL PICK YOU UP AT THE STATION HERE. HMM, HOW ABOUT NOON?
See ya, Natsume.
Cli
WHAT?! HEY, WAIT...
beep
beep
beep
SHI...

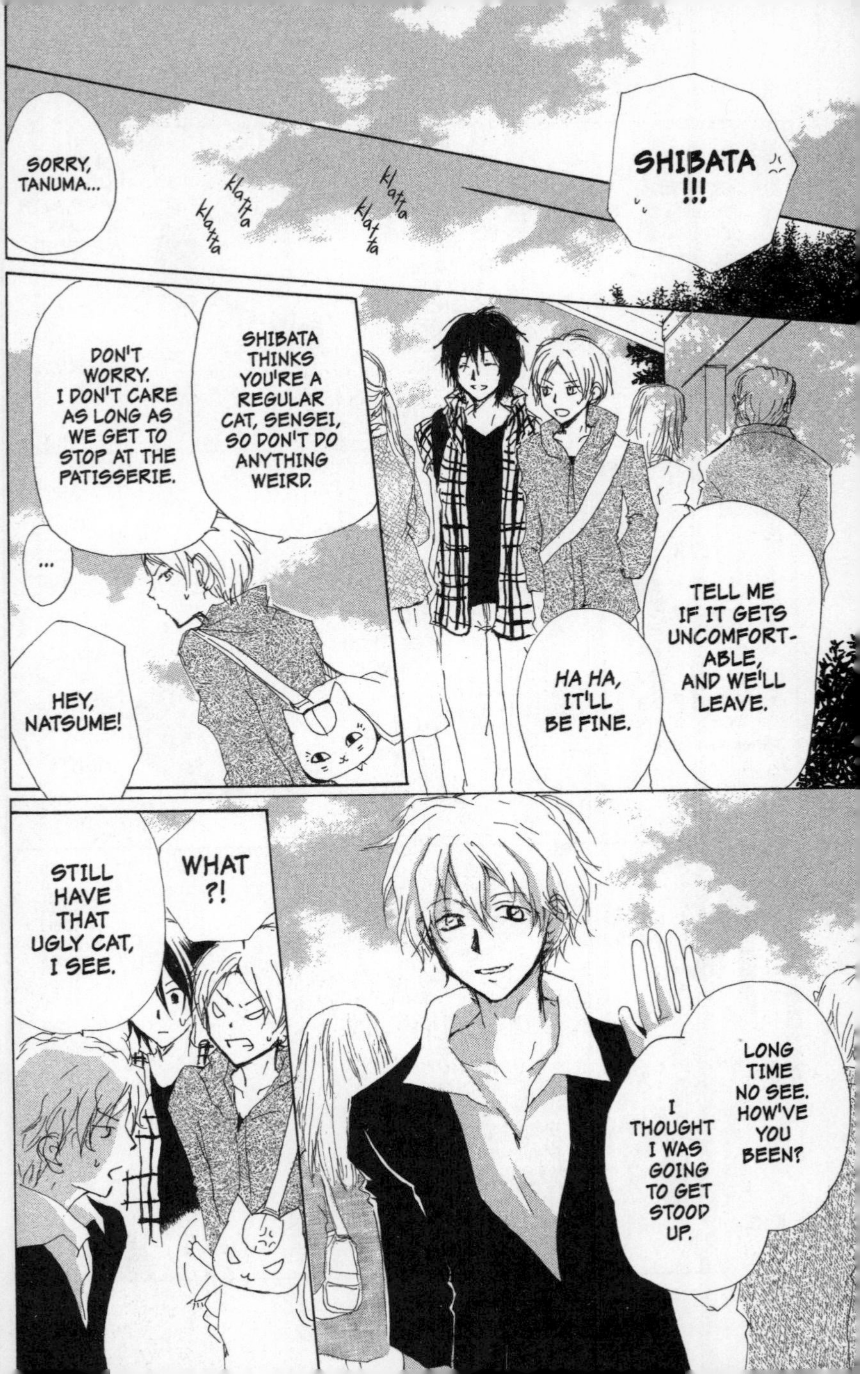
SHIBATA !!!
klatta klatta
klatta klatta
SORRY, TANUMA...
TELL ME IF IT GETS UNCOMFORT-ABLE, AND WE'LL LEAVE.
HA HA, IT'LL BE FINE.
SHIBATA THINKS YOU'RE A REGULAR CAT, SENSEI, SO DON'T DO ANYTHING WEIRD.
DON'T WORRY. I DON'T CARE AS LONG AS WE GET TO STOP AT THE PATISSERIE.
...
HEY, NATSUME!
LONG TIME NO SEE. HOW'VE YOU BEEN?
I THOUGHT I WAS GOING TO GET STOOD UP.
WHAT ?!
STILL HAVE THAT UGLY CAT, I SEE.

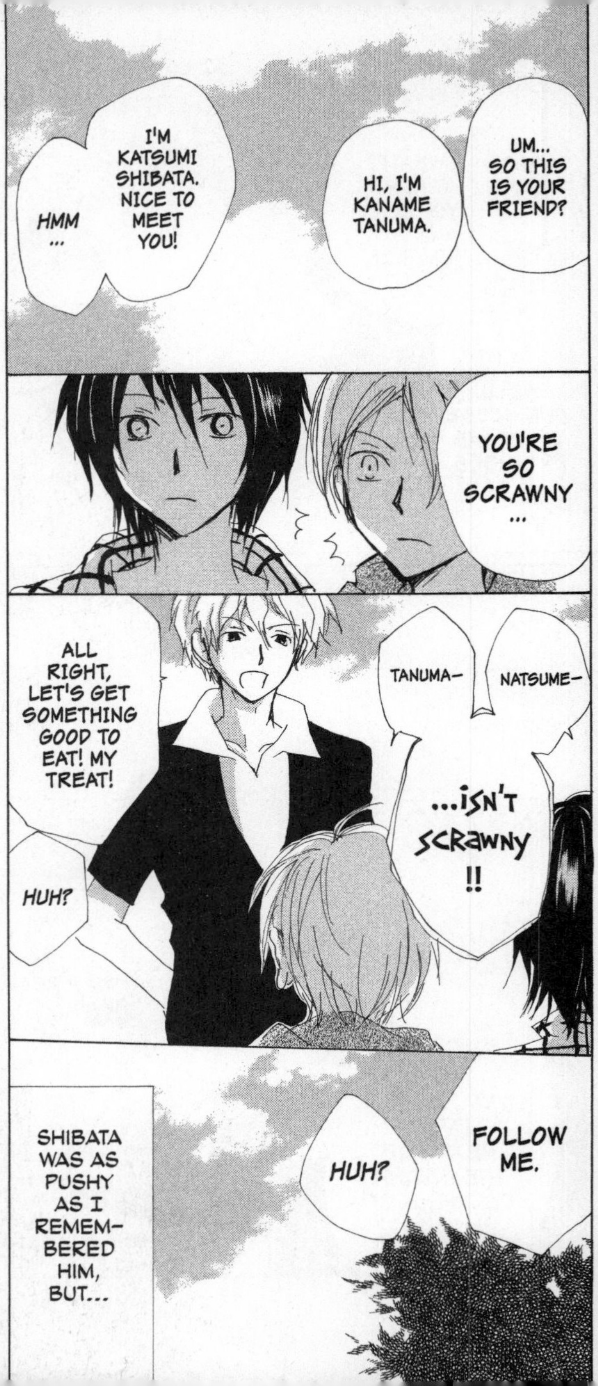
UM... SO THIS IS YOUR FRIEND?
HI, I'M KANAME TANUMA.
I'M KATSUMI SHIBATA. NICE TO MEET YOU!
HMM ...
YOU'RE SO SCRAWNY ...
NATSUME-
TANUMA-
...ISN'T SCRAWNY !!
ALL RIGHT, LET'S GET SOMETHING GOOD TO EAT! MY TREAT!
HUH?
FOLLOW ME.
HUH?
SHIBATA WAS AS PUSHY AS I REMEMBERED HIM, BUT...

01

Hello, Midorikawa here. Natsume's Book of Friends has reached the 19th volume.

I appreciate the joys of getting to work on a long series. I'll keep reaffirming my goals and the nature of my characters, and yet incorporate gradual changes.

Maybe because I've been working on this a long time, I often think back to the time I first started drawing Natsume. There are things I can now do that I was unable to in the beginning, and there are also things that Natsume could've done back then that he wouldn't do anymore. It's quite emotional, partly fun and partly sad.

I'll work hard so you'll stick around.

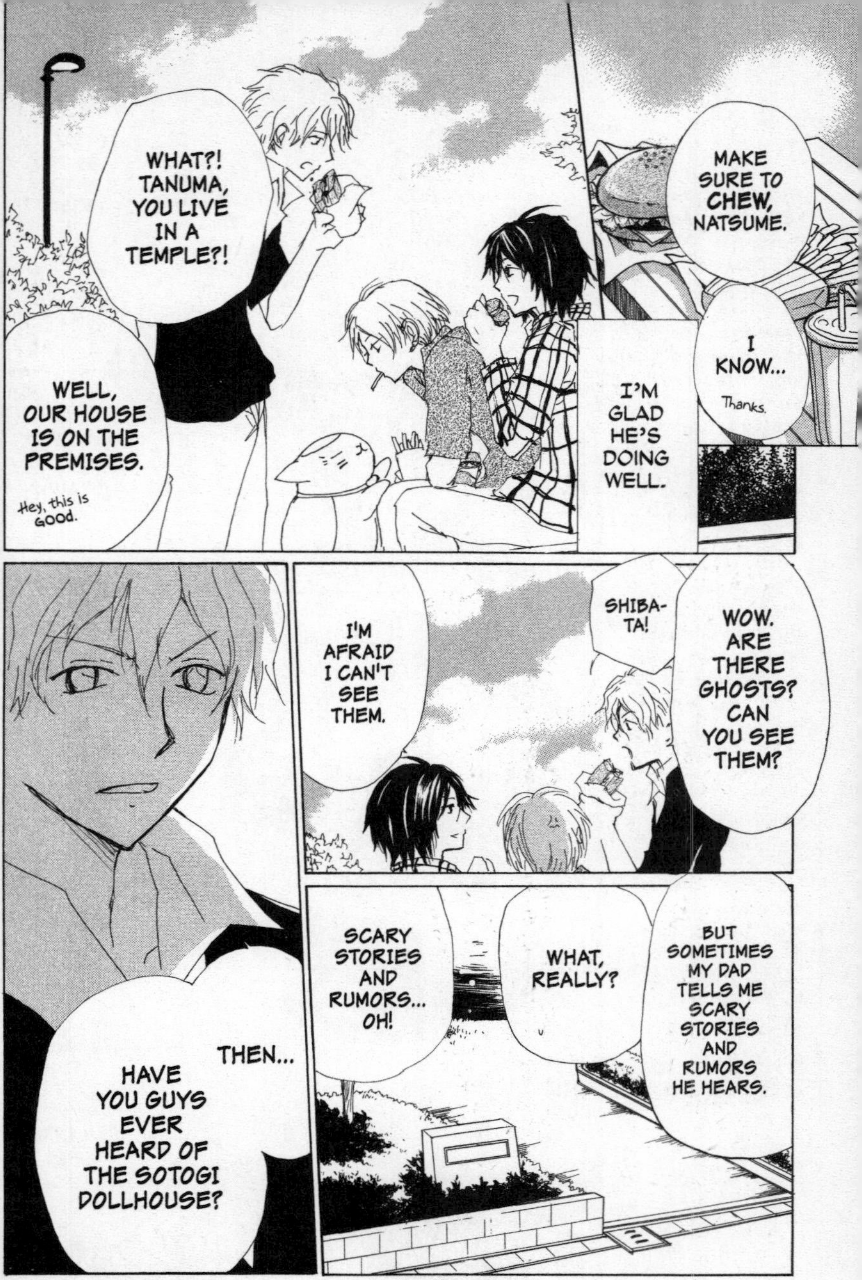

MAKE SURE TO CHEW, NATSUME.
I KNOW...
Thanks.
I'M GLAD HE'S DOING WELL.
WHAT?! TANUMA, YOU LIVE IN A TEMPLE?!
WELL, OUR HOUSE IS ON THE PREMISES.
Hey, this is good.
WOW. ARE THERE GHOSTS? CAN YOU SEE THEM?
SHIBATA!
I'M AFRAID I CAN'T SEE THEM.
BUT SOMETIMES MY DAD TELLS ME SCARY STORIES AND RUMORS HE HEARS.
WHAT, REALLY?
SCARY STORIES AND RUMORS... OH!
THEN...
HAVE YOU GUYS EVER HEARD OF THE SOTOGI DOLLHOUSE?

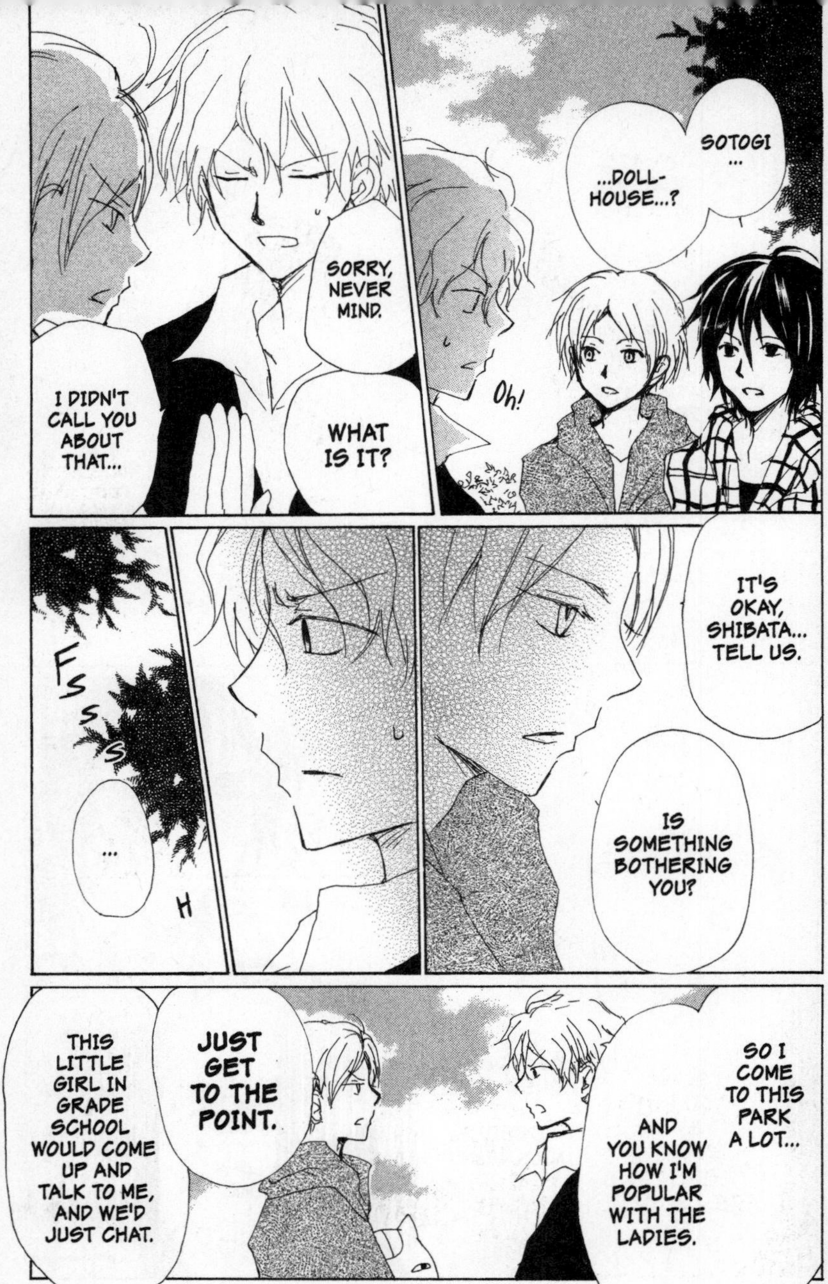
SOTOGI ...
...DOLL-HOUSE...?
Oh!
SORRY, NEVER MIND.
WHAT IS IT?
I DIDN'T CALL YOU ABOUT THAT...
IT'S OKAY, SHIBATA... TELL US.
IS SOMETHING BOTHERING YOU?
FSSSH
...
SO I COME TO THIS PARK A LOT...
AND YOU KNOW HOW I'M POPULAR WITH THE LADIES.
JUST GET TO THE POINT.
THIS LITTLE GIRL IN GRADE SCHOOL WOULD COME UP AND TALK TO ME, AND WE'D JUST CHAT.

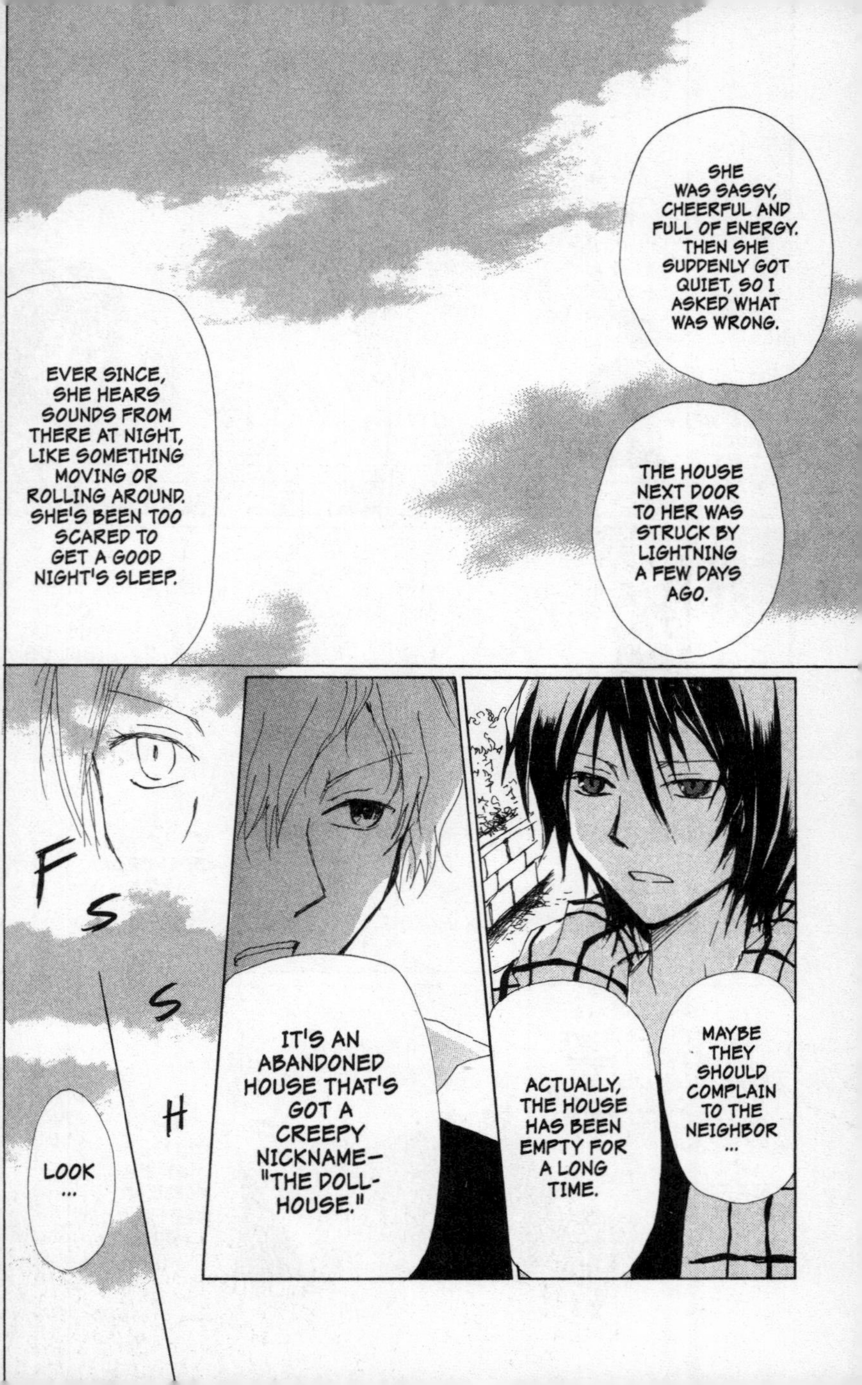
SHE WAS SASSY, CHEERFUL AND FULL OF ENERGY. THEN SHE SUDDENLY GOT QUIET, SO I ASKED WHAT WAS WRONG.
THE HOUSE NEXT DOOR TO HER WAS STRUCK BY LIGHTNING A FEW DAYS AGO.
EVER SINCE, SHE HEARS SOUNDS FROM THERE AT NIGHT, LIKE SOMETHING MOVING OR ROLLING AROUND. SHE'S BEEN TOO SCARED TO GET A GOOD NIGHT'S SLEEP.
MAYBE THEY SHOULD COMPLAIN TO THE NEIGHBOR ...
ACTUALLY, THE HOUSE HAS BEEN EMPTY FOR A LONG TIME.
IT'S AN ABANDONED HOUSE THAT'S GOT A CREEPY NICKNAME— "THE DOLL-HOUSE."
LOOK ...
FSSH

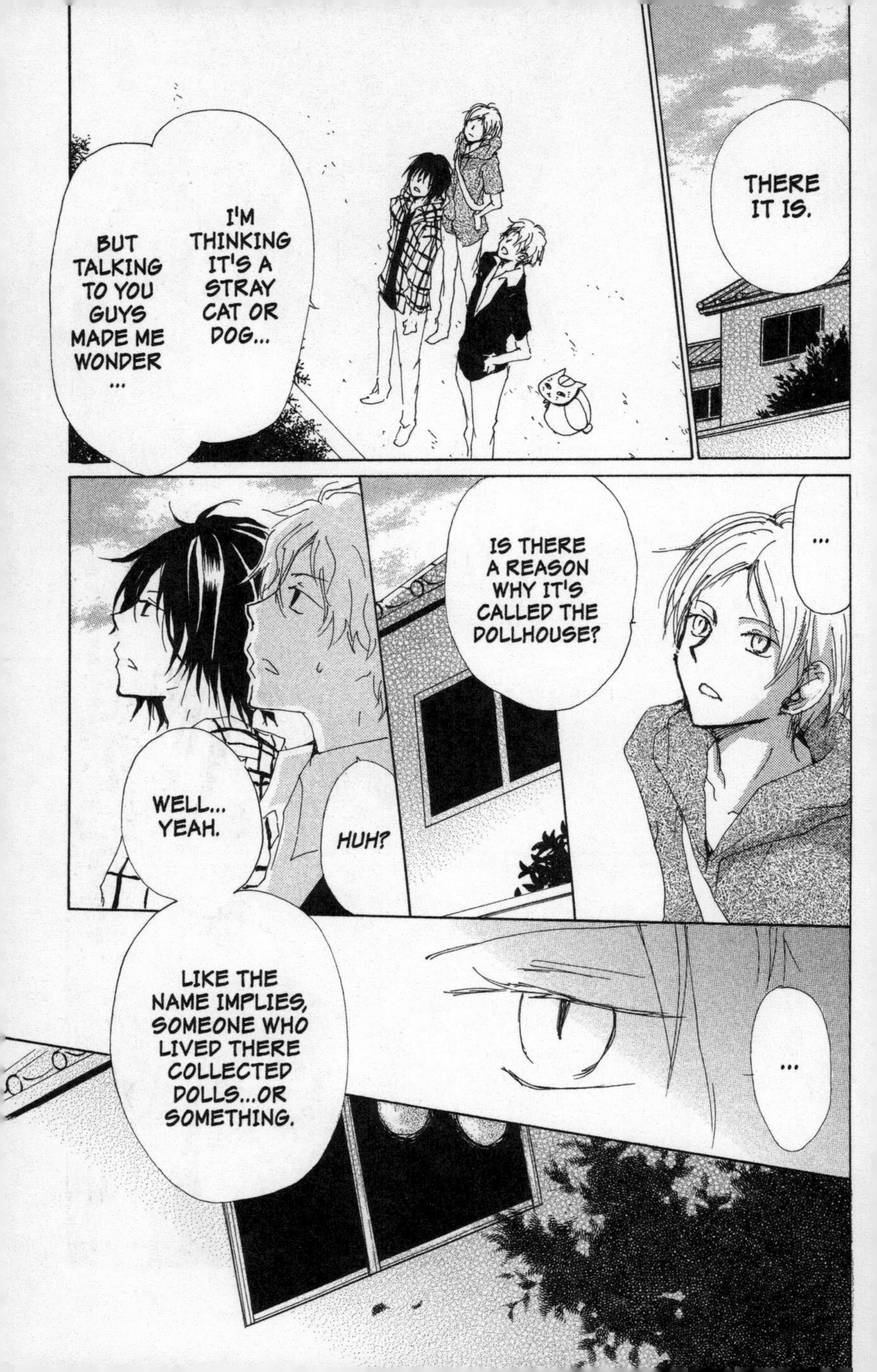
THERE IT IS.
I'M THINKING IT'S A STRAY CAT OR DOG...
BUT TALKING TO YOU GUYS MADE ME WONDER...
...
IS THERE A REASON WHY IT'S CALLED THE DOLLHOUSE?
HUH?
WELL... YEAH.
...
LIKE THE NAME IMPLIES, SOMEONE WHO LIVED THERE COLLECTED DOLLS...OR SOMETHING.

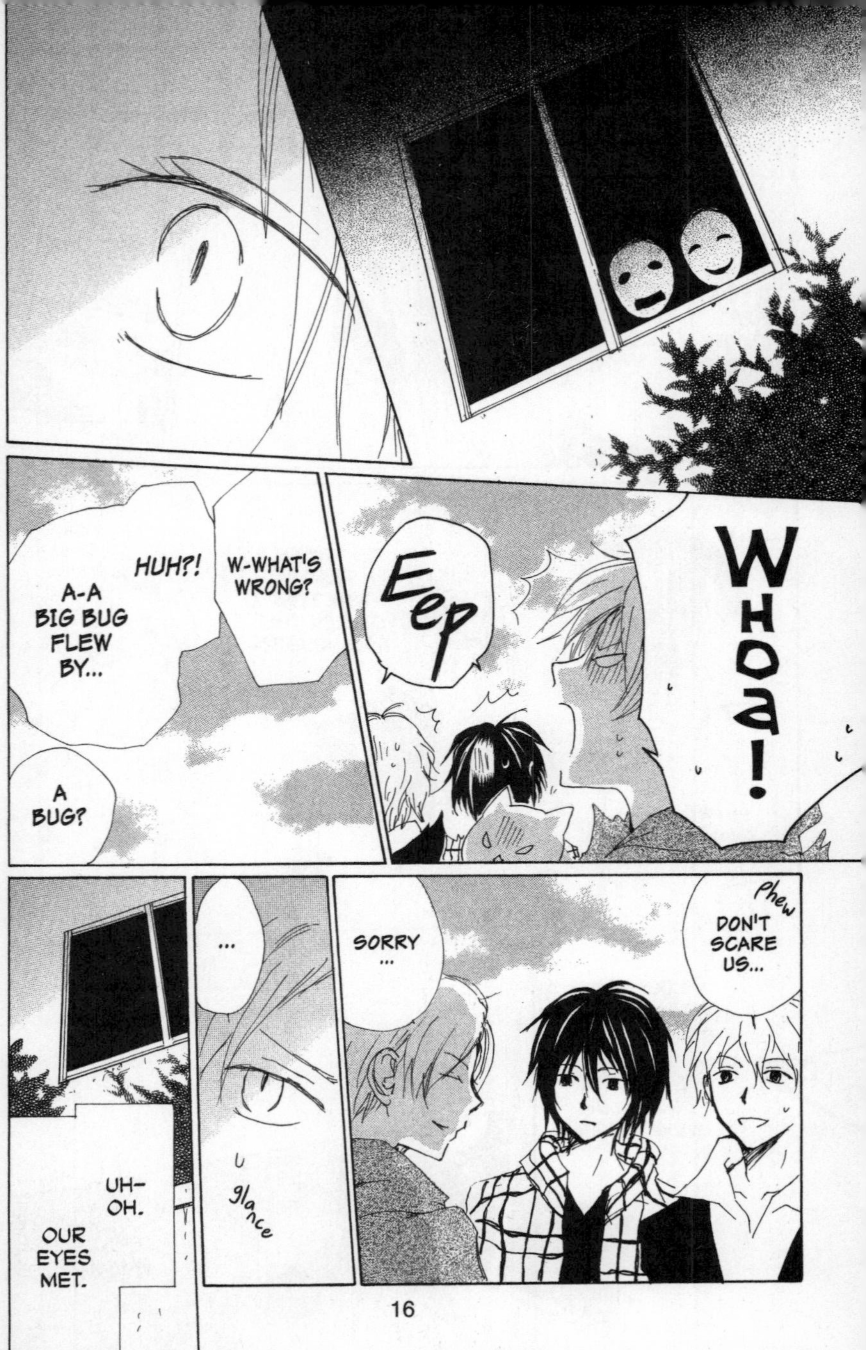
WHOA!
EEP
W-WHAT'S WRONG?
HUH?!
A-A BIG BUG FLEW BY...
A BUG?
PHEW
DON'T SCARE US...
SORRY...
...
GLANCE
UH-OH.
OUR EYES MET.

02

❋ Here comes Nyanko Sensei!

Miss Junko Kanechiku is drawing a cute and fun comic strip based on Natsume's Book of Friends on Hakusensha's Lala Online website!

The characters who are usually serious or taciturn are drawn so adorably and playfully here, sometimes going wild and crazy and having a blast, showing a side they never do. It's such a fun strip, and I look forward to it all the time. I was ecstatic when I heard they're going to anthologize it in a graphic novel. It's a world that's a little different, fun and exciting, like you're peeking into a chest of toys. Please check it out.

Miss Kanechiku, I love you! Thank you so much!

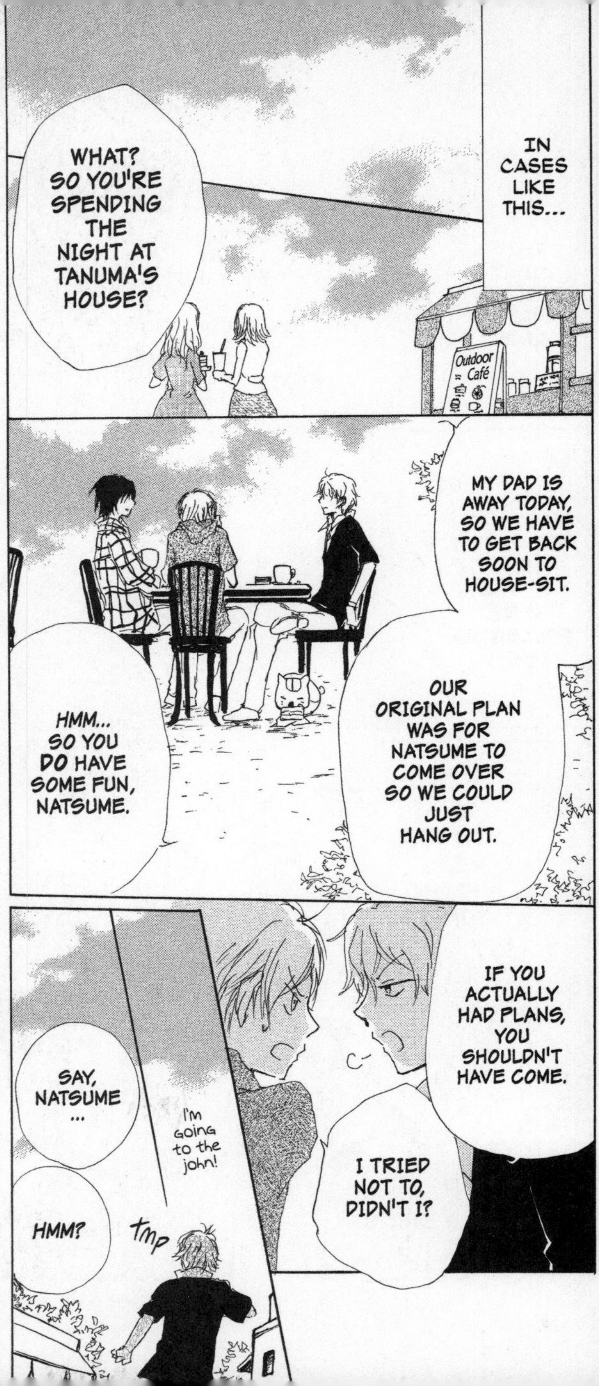
IN CASES LIKE THIS...
WHAT? SO YOU'RE SPENDING THE NIGHT AT TANUMA'S HOUSE?
Outdoor Café
MY DAD IS AWAY TODAY, SO WE HAVE TO GET BACK SOON TO HOUSE-SIT.
OUR ORIGINAL PLAN WAS FOR NATSUME TO COME OVER SO WE COULD JUST HANG OUT.
HMM... SO YOU DO HAVE SOME FUN, NATSUME.
IF YOU ACTUALLY HAD PLANS, YOU SHOULDN'T HAVE COME.
I TRIED NOT TO, DIDN'T I?
I'm going to the john!
SAY, NATSUME...
HMM?
tmp

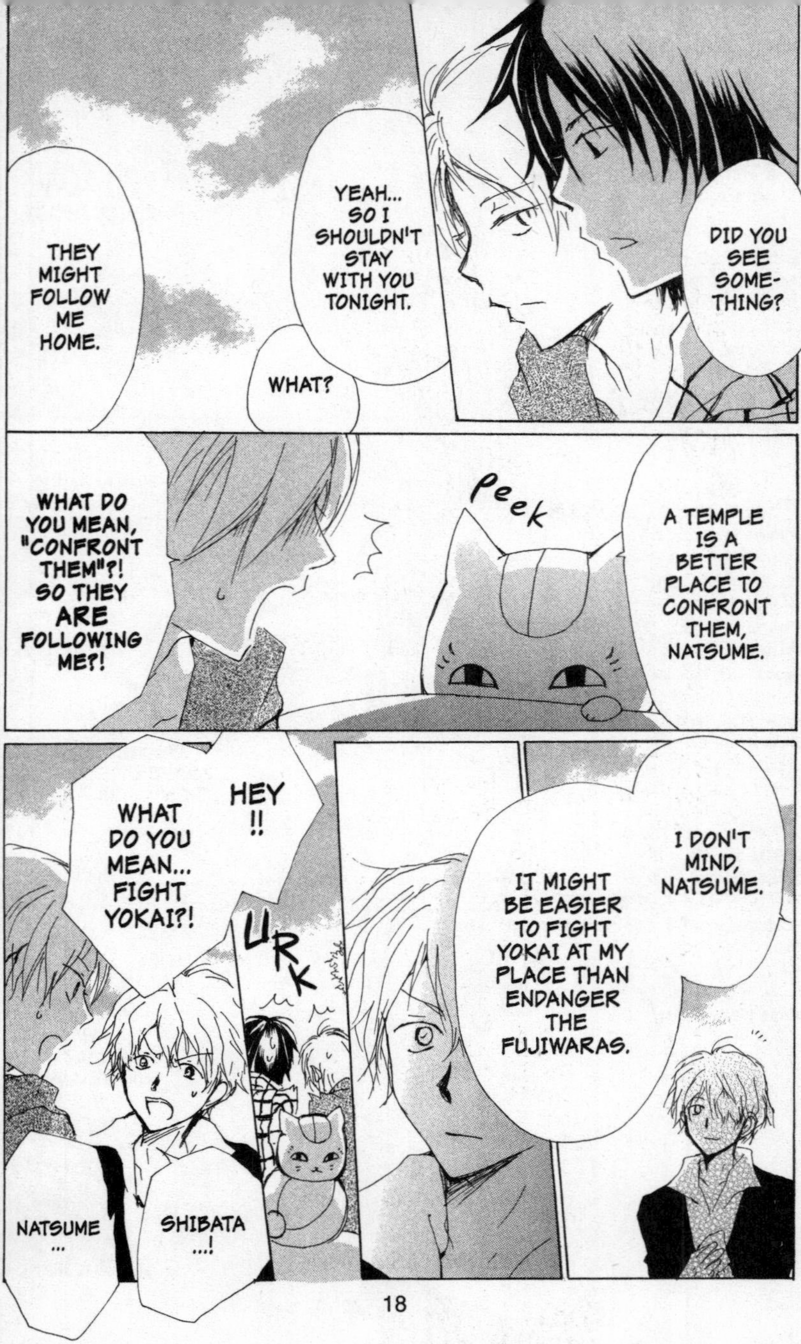
DID YOU SEE SOME-THING?
YEAH... SO I SHOULDN'T STAY WITH YOU TONIGHT.
THEY MIGHT FOLLOW ME HOME.
WHAT?
A TEMPLE IS A BETTER PLACE TO CONFRONT THEM, NATSUME.
Peek
WHAT DO YOU MEAN, "CONFRONT THEM"?! SO THEY ARE FOLLOWING ME?!
I DON'T MIND, NATSUME.
IT MIGHT BE EASIER TO FIGHT YOKAI AT MY PLACE THAN ENDANGER THE FUJIWARAS.
HEY !!
WHAT DO YOU MEAN... FIGHT YOKAI?!
URK
SHIBATA ...!
NATSUME ...

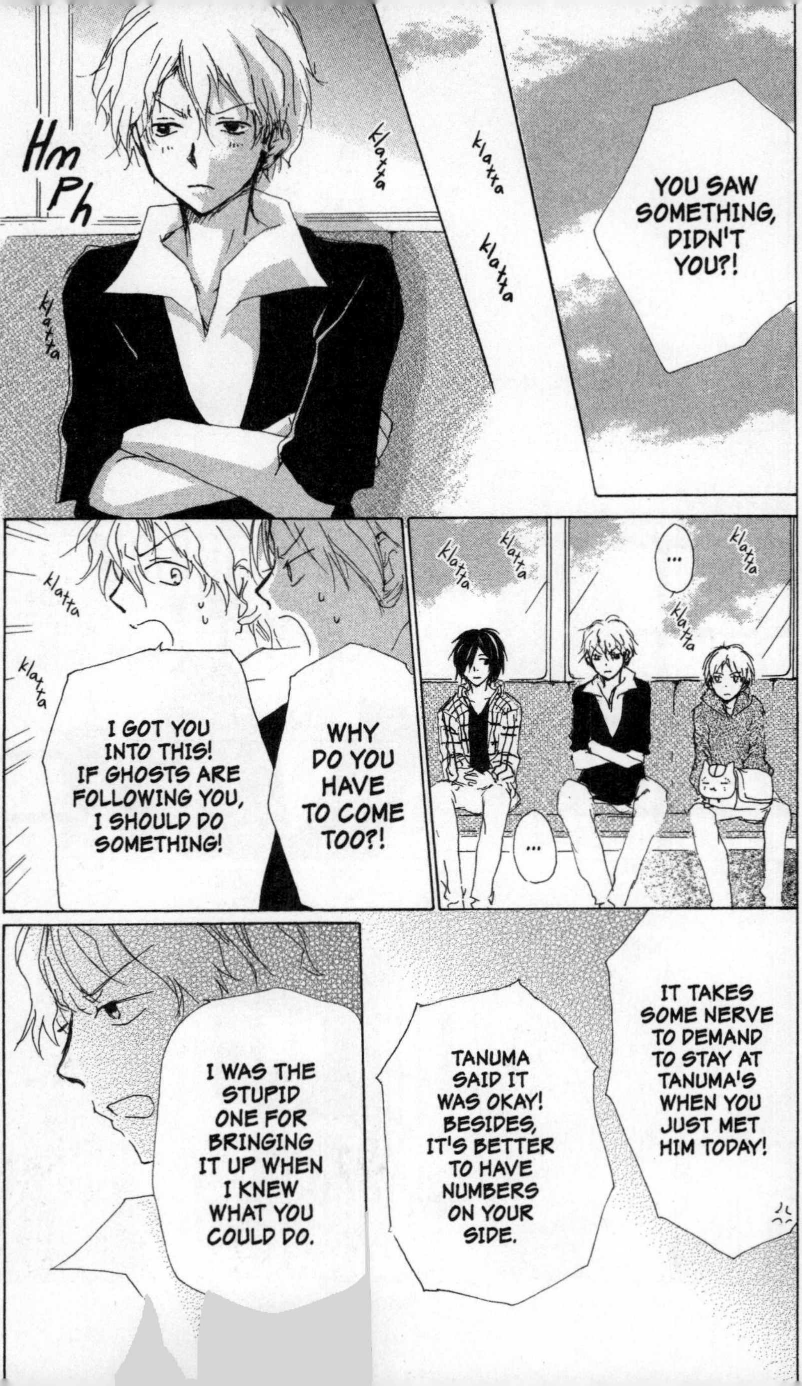
YOU SAW SOMETHING, DIDN'T YOU?!
klatta
klatta
klatta
Hm Ph
klatta
klatta
...
klatta
klatta
klatta
...
WHY DO YOU HAVE TO COME TOO?!
I GOT YOU INTO THIS! IF GHOSTS ARE FOLLOWING YOU, I SHOULD DO SOMETHING!
klatta
klatta
IT TAKES SOME NERVE TO DEMAND TO STAY AT TANUMA'S WHEN YOU JUST MET HIM TODAY!
TANUMA SAID IT WAS OKAY! BESIDES, IT'S BETTER TO HAVE NUMBERS ON YOUR SIDE.
I WAS THE STUPID ONE FOR BRINGING IT UP WHEN I KNEW WHAT YOU COULD DO.

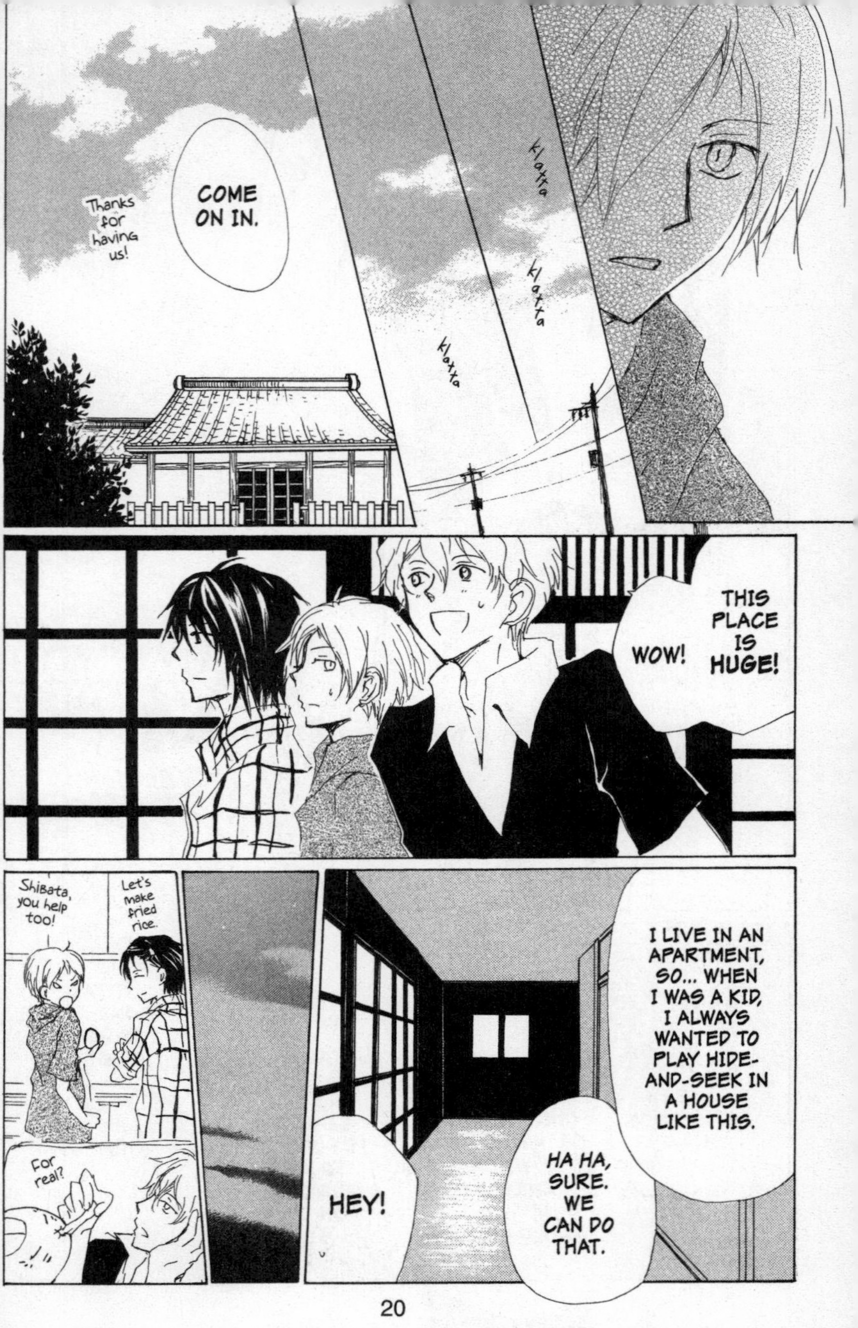
klatta
klatta
klatta
COME ON IN.
Thanks for having us!
WOW! THIS PLACE IS HUGE!
I LIVE IN AN APARTMENT, SO... WHEN I WAS A KID, I ALWAYS WANTED TO PLAY HIDE-AND-SEEK IN A HOUSE LIKE THIS.
HA HA, SURE. WE CAN DO THAT.
HEY!
Let's make fried rice.
Shibata, you help too!
For real?

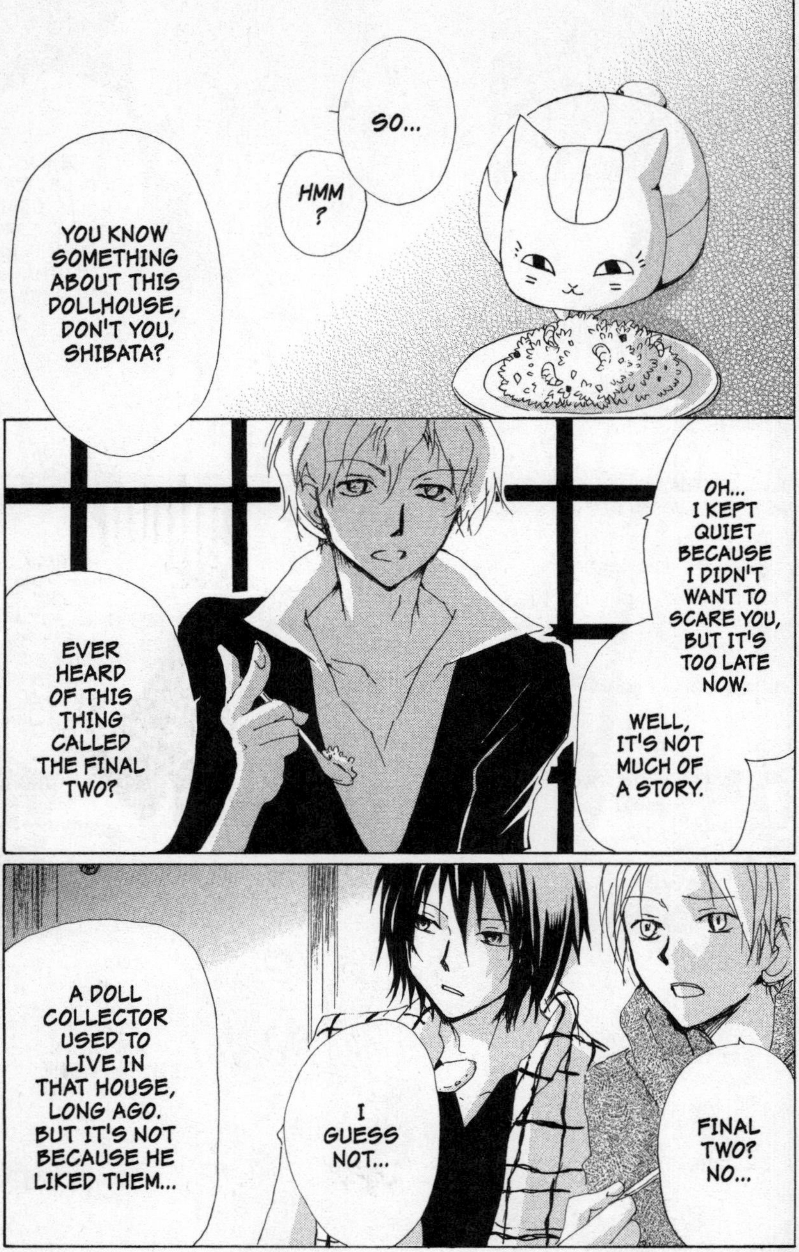
SO...
HMM ?
YOU KNOW SOMETHING ABOUT THIS DOLLHOUSE, DON'T YOU, SHIBATA?
OH... I KEPT QUIET BECAUSE I DIDN'T WANT TO SCARE YOU, BUT IT'S TOO LATE NOW.
WELL, IT'S NOT MUCH OF A STORY.
EVER HEARD OF THIS THING CALLED THE FINAL TWO?
FINAL TWO? NO...
I GUESS NOT...
A DOLL COLLECTOR USED TO LIVE IN THAT HOUSE, LONG AGO. BUT IT'S NOT BECAUSE HE LIKED THEM...

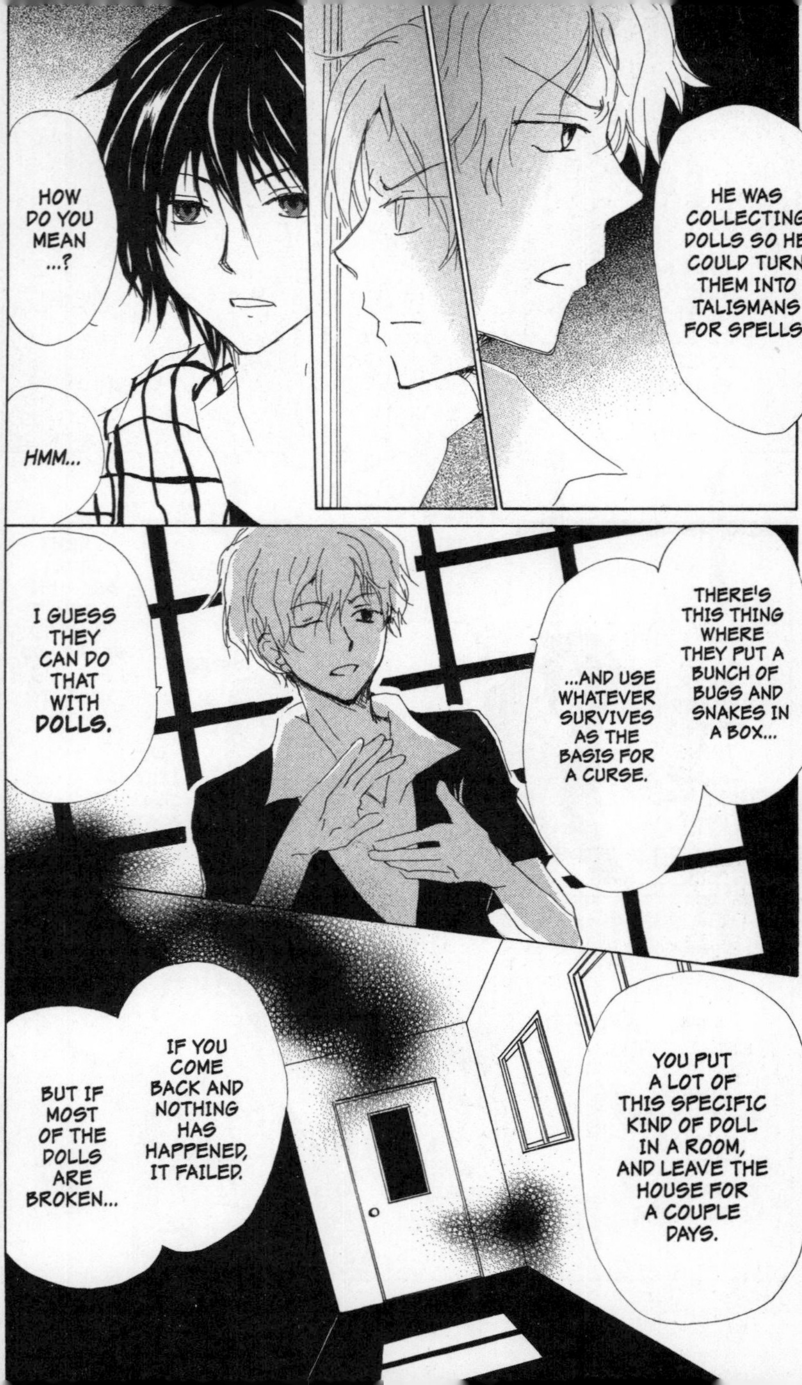
HE WAS COLLECTING DOLLS SO HE COULD TURN THEM INTO TALISMANS FOR SPELLS.
HOW DO YOU MEAN ...?
HMM...
THERE'S THIS THING WHERE THEY PUT A BUNCH OF BUGS AND SNAKES IN A BOX...
...AND USE WHATEVER SURVIVES AS THE BASIS FOR A CURSE.
I GUESS THEY CAN DO THAT WITH DOLLS.
YOU PUT A LOT OF THIS SPECIFIC KIND OF DOLL IN A ROOM, AND LEAVE THE HOUSE FOR A COUPLE DAYS.
IF YOU COME BACK AND NOTHING HAS HAPPENED, IT FAILED.
BUT IF MOST OF THE DOLLS ARE BROKEN...

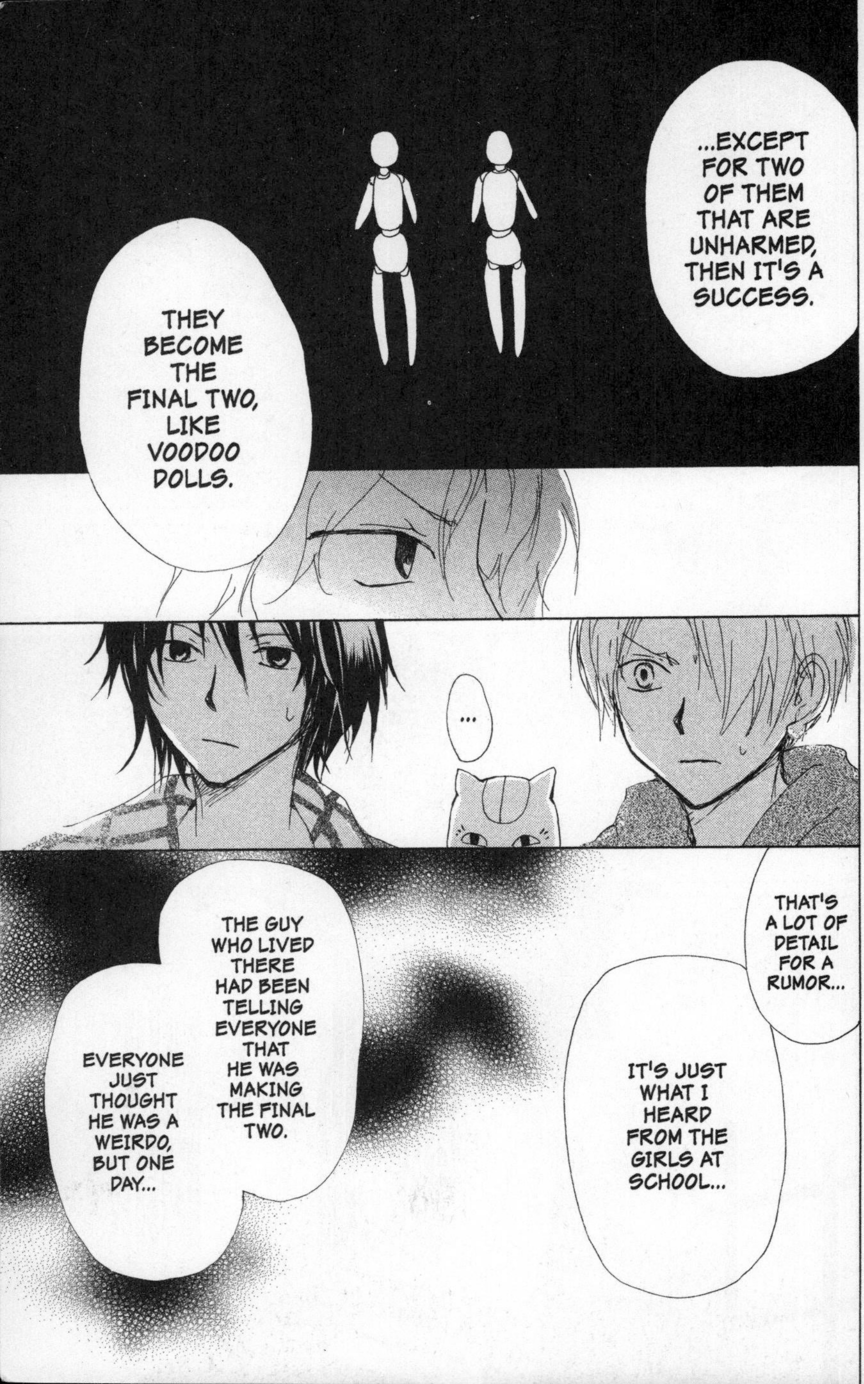
...EXCEPT FOR TWO OF THEM THAT ARE UNHARMED, THEN IT'S A SUCCESS.
THEY BECOME THE FINAL TWO, LIKE VOODOO DOLLS.
...
THAT'S A LOT OF DETAIL FOR A RUMOR...
IT'S JUST WHAT I HEARD FROM THE GIRLS AT SCHOOL...
THE GUY WHO LIVED THERE HAD BEEN TELLING EVERYONE THAT HE WAS MAKING THE FINAL TWO.
EVERYONE JUST THOUGHT HE WAS A WEIRDO, BUT ONE DAY...

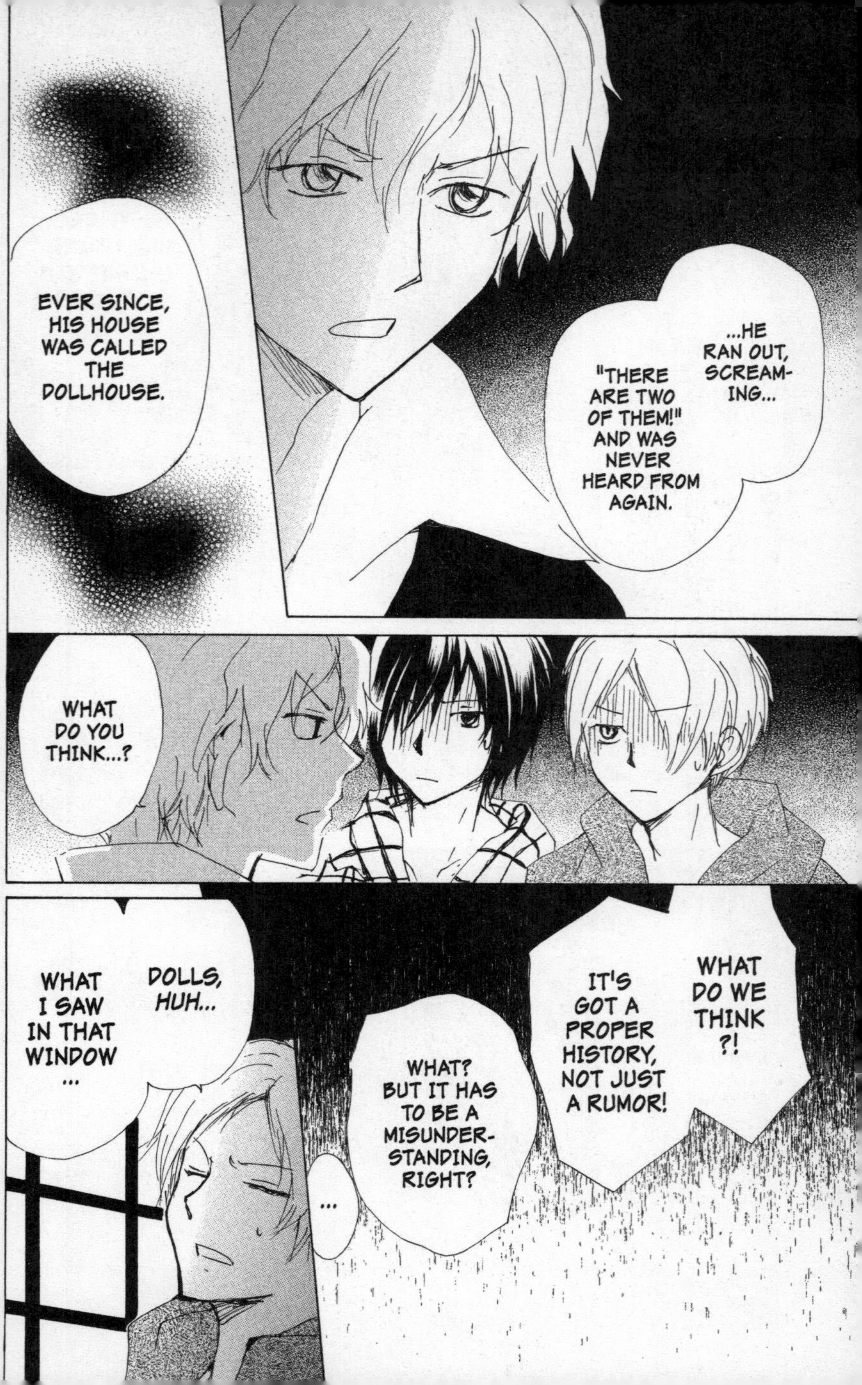

...HE RAN OUT, SCREAMING...
"THERE ARE TWO OF THEM!" AND WAS NEVER HEARD FROM AGAIN.
EVER SINCE, HIS HOUSE WAS CALLED THE DOLLHOUSE.
WHAT DO YOU THINK...?
WHAT DO WE THINK?!
IT'S GOT A PROPER HISTORY, NOT JUST A RUMOR!
WHAT? BUT IT HAS TO BE A MISUNDERSTANDING, RIGHT?
...
DOLLS, HUH...
WHAT I SAW IN THAT WINDOW...

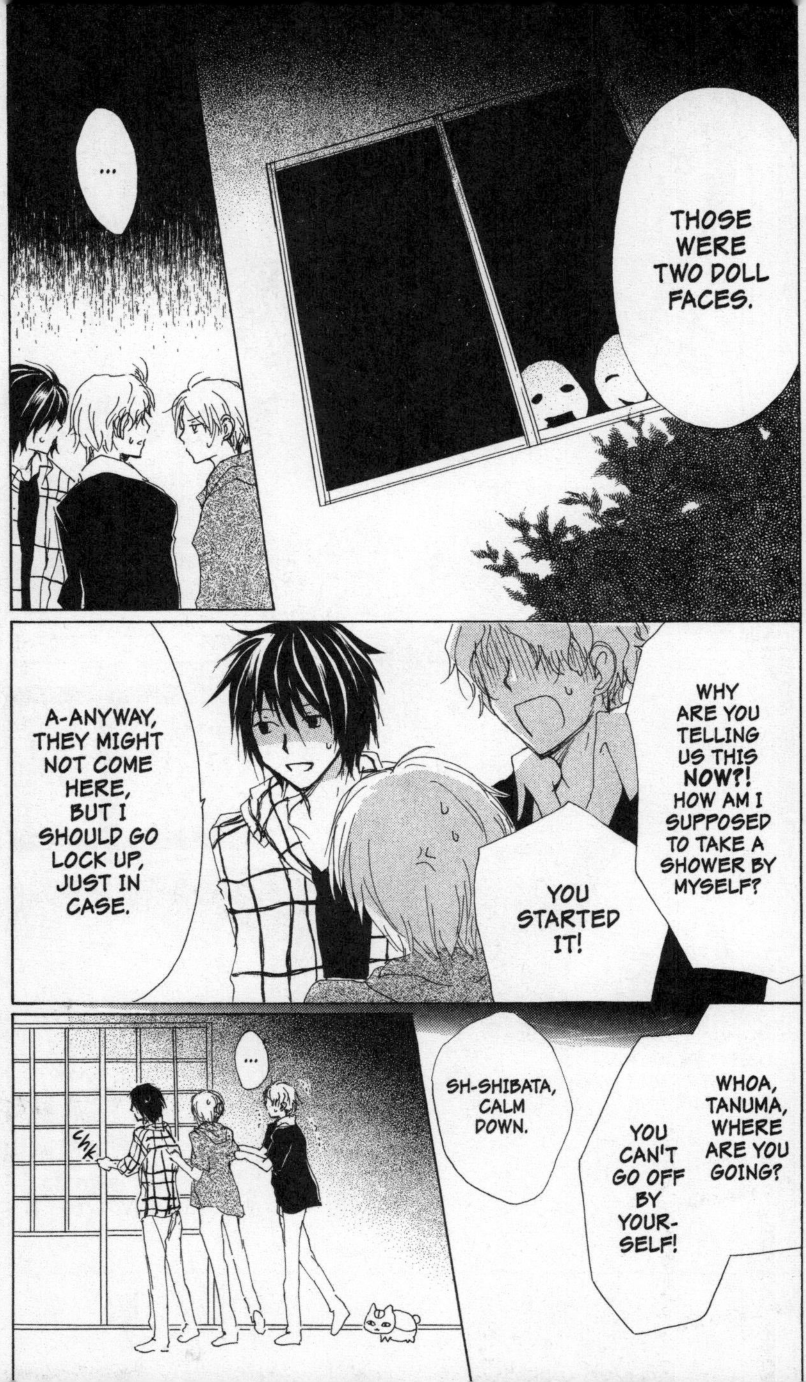
THOSE WERE TWO DOLL FACES.
...
WHY ARE YOU TELLING US THIS NOW?! HOW AM I SUPPOSED TO TAKE A SHOWER BY MYSELF?
YOU STARTED IT!
A-ANYWAY, THEY MIGHT NOT COME HERE, BUT I SHOULD GO LOCK UP, JUST IN CASE.
WHOA, TANUMA, WHERE ARE YOU GOING?
YOU CAN'T GO OFF BY YOUR-SELF!
SH-SHIBATA, CALM DOWN.
...
CHK

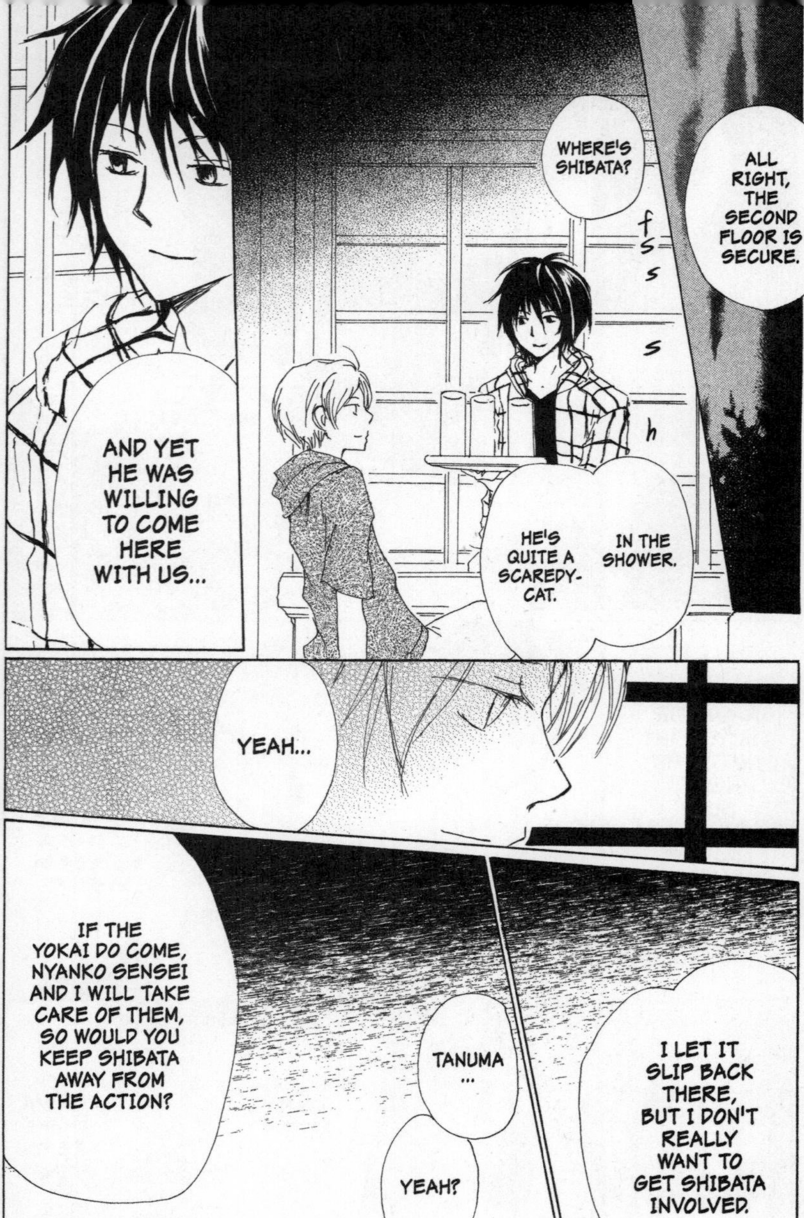
ALL RIGHT, THE SECOND FLOOR IS SECURE.
WHERE'S SHIBATA?
fsssh
IN THE SHOWER.
HE'S QUITE A SCAREDY-CAT.
AND YET HE WAS WILLING TO COME HERE WITH US...
YEAH...
I LET IT SLIP BACK THERE, BUT I DON'T REALLY WANT TO GET SHIBATA INVOLVED.
TANUMA...
YEAH?
IF THE YOKAI DO COME, NYANKO SENSEI AND I WILL TAKE CARE OF THEM, SO WOULD YOU KEEP SHIBATA AWAY FROM THE ACTION?

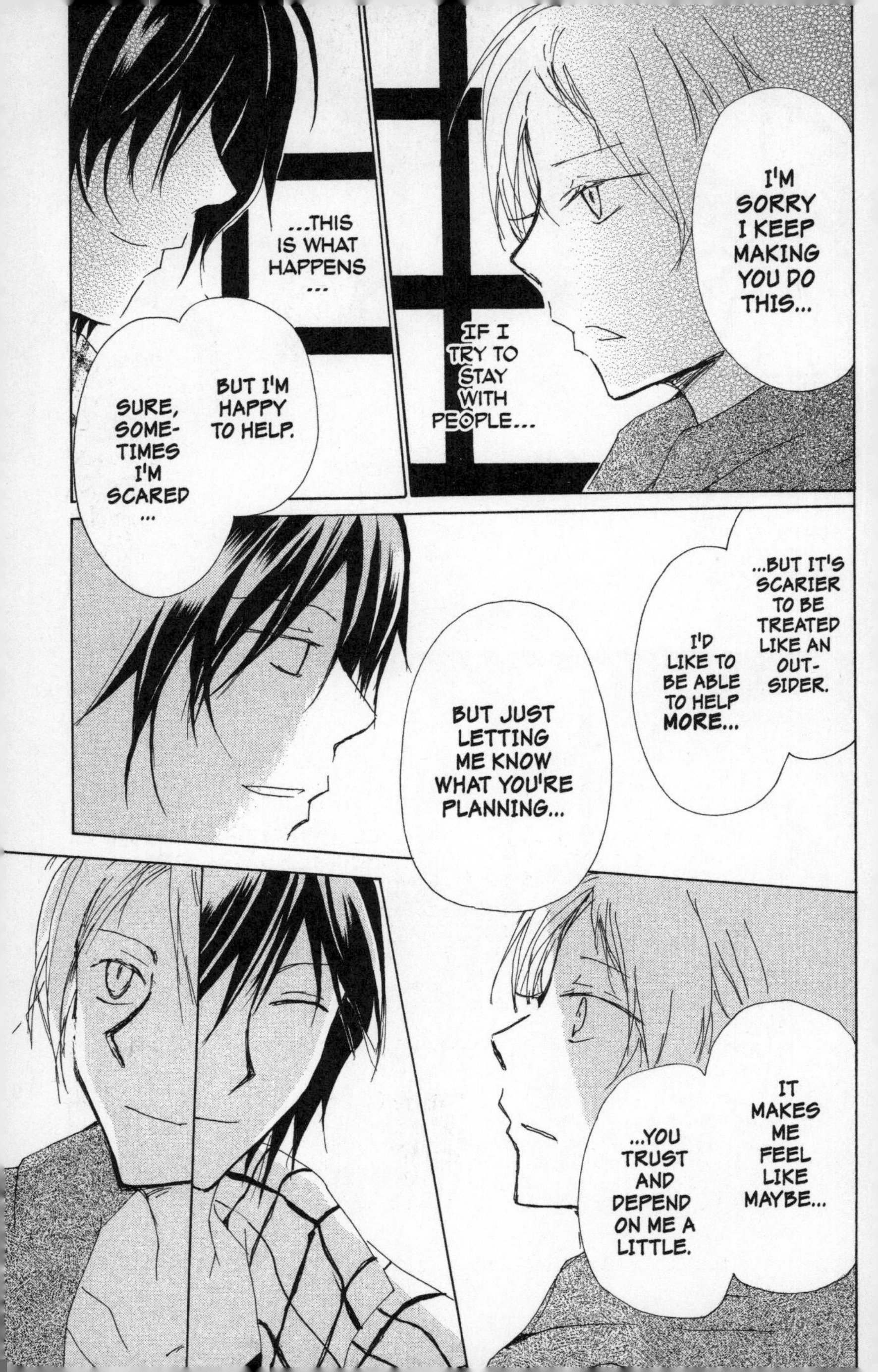
I'M SORRY I KEEP MAKING YOU DO THIS...
IF I TRY TO STAY WITH PEOPLE...
...THIS IS WHAT HAPPENS...
BUT I'M HAPPY TO HELP.
SURE, SOMETIMES I'M SCARED...
...BUT IT'S SCARIER TO BE TREATED LIKE AN OUT-SIDER.
I'D LIKE TO BE ABLE TO HELP MORE...
BUT JUST LETTING ME KNOW WHAT YOU'RE PLANNING...
IT MAKES ME FEEL LIKE MAYBE...
...YOU TRUST AND DEPEND ON ME A LITTLE.

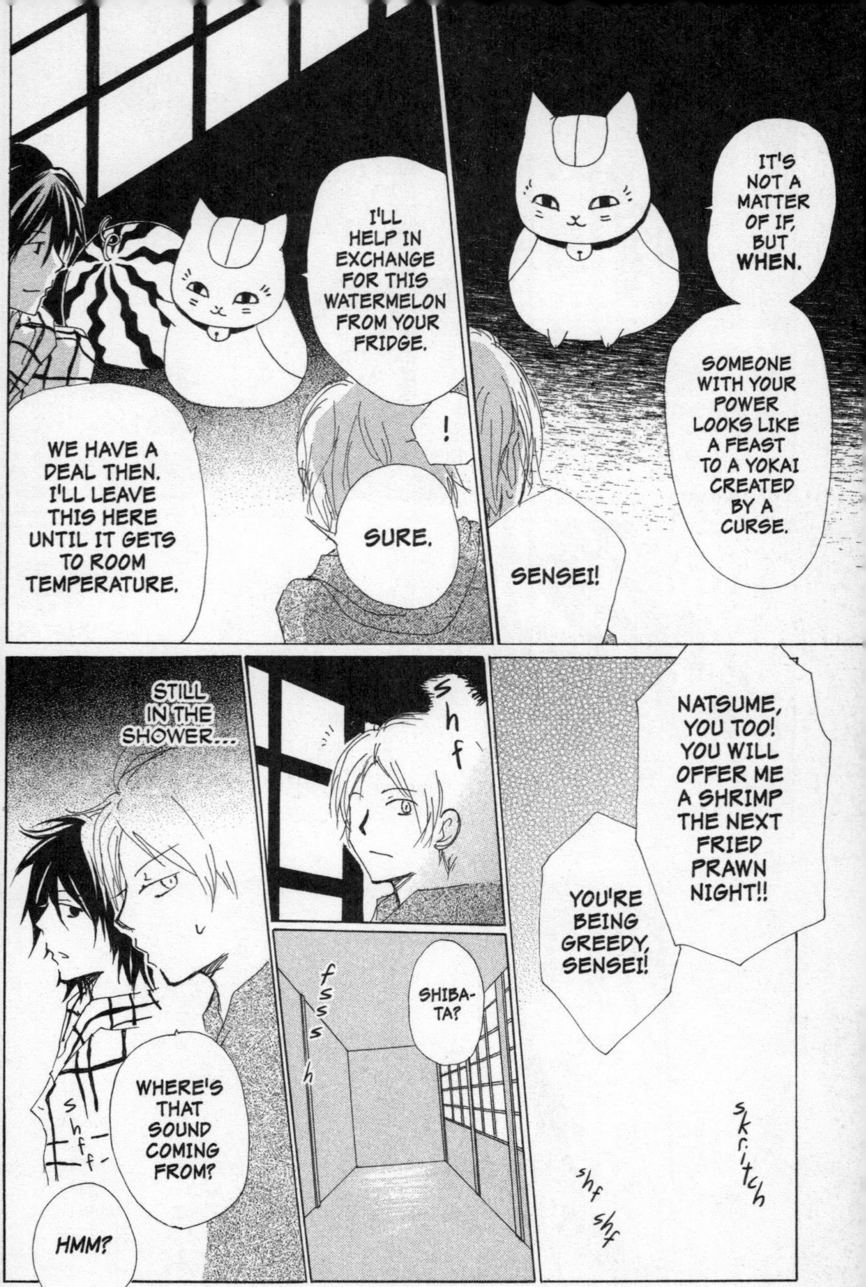
IT'S NOT A MATTER OF IF, BUT WHEN.
SOMEONE WITH YOUR POWER LOOKS LIKE A FEAST TO A YOKAI CREATED BY A CURSE.
SENSEI!
I'LL HELP IN EXCHANGE FOR THIS WATERMELON FROM YOUR FRIDGE.
!
SURE.
WE HAVE A DEAL THEN. I'LL LEAVE THIS HERE UNTIL IT GETS TO ROOM TEMPERATURE.
NATSUME, YOU TOO! YOU WILL OFFER ME A SHRIMP THE NEXT FRIED PRAWN NIGHT!!
YOU'RE BEING GREEDY, SENSEI!
skritch
shf shf
shf
SHIBA-TA?
fsssh
STILL IN THE SHOWER...
WHERE'S THAT SOUND COMING FROM?
shf f
HMM?

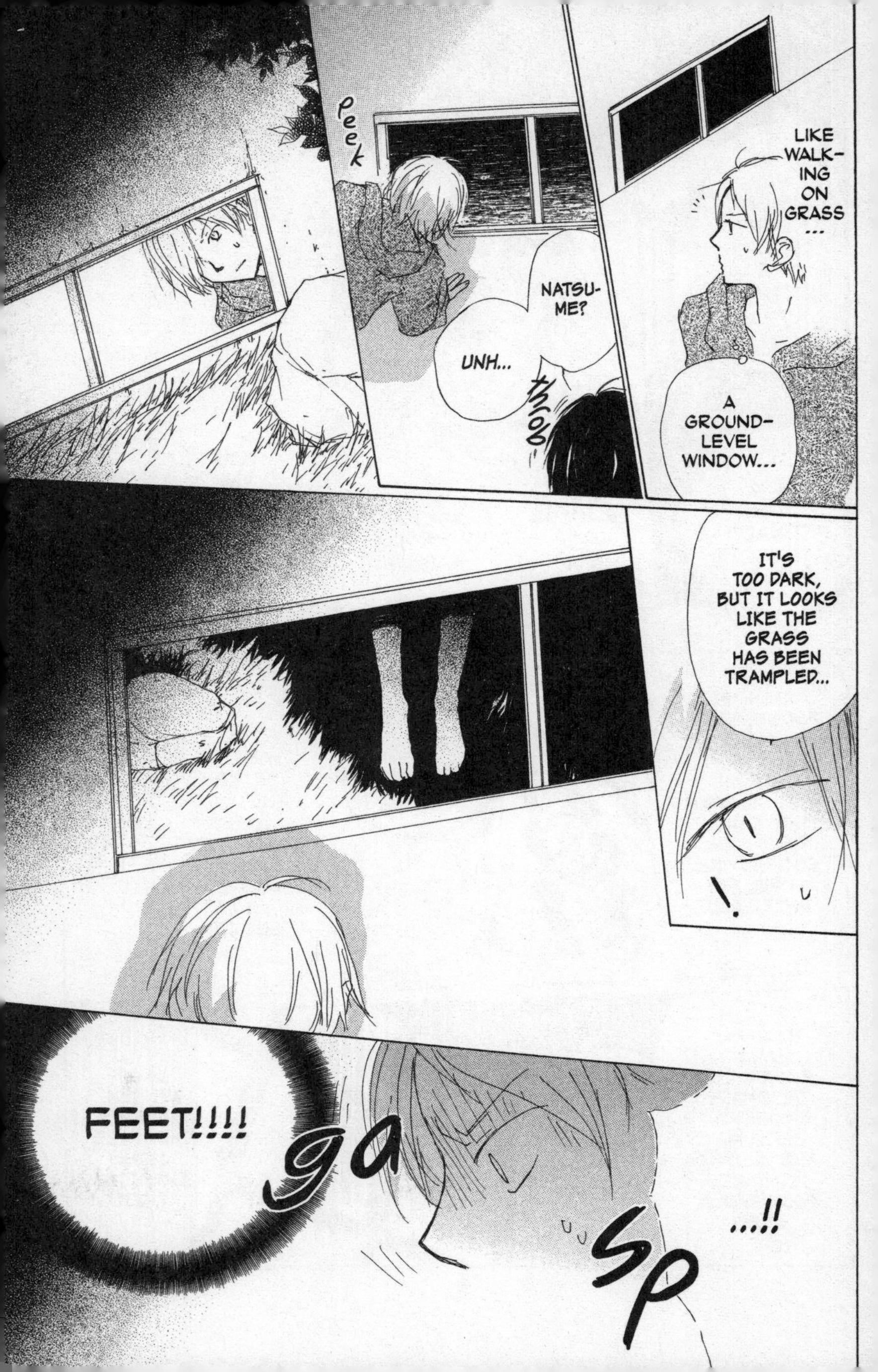
LIKE WALKING ON GRASS...
A GROUND-LEVEL WINDOW...
Peek
NATSUME?
UNH...
throb
IT'S TOO DARK, BUT IT LOOKS LIKE THE GRASS HAS BEEN TRAMPLED...
!
...!!
gasp
FEET!!!!!

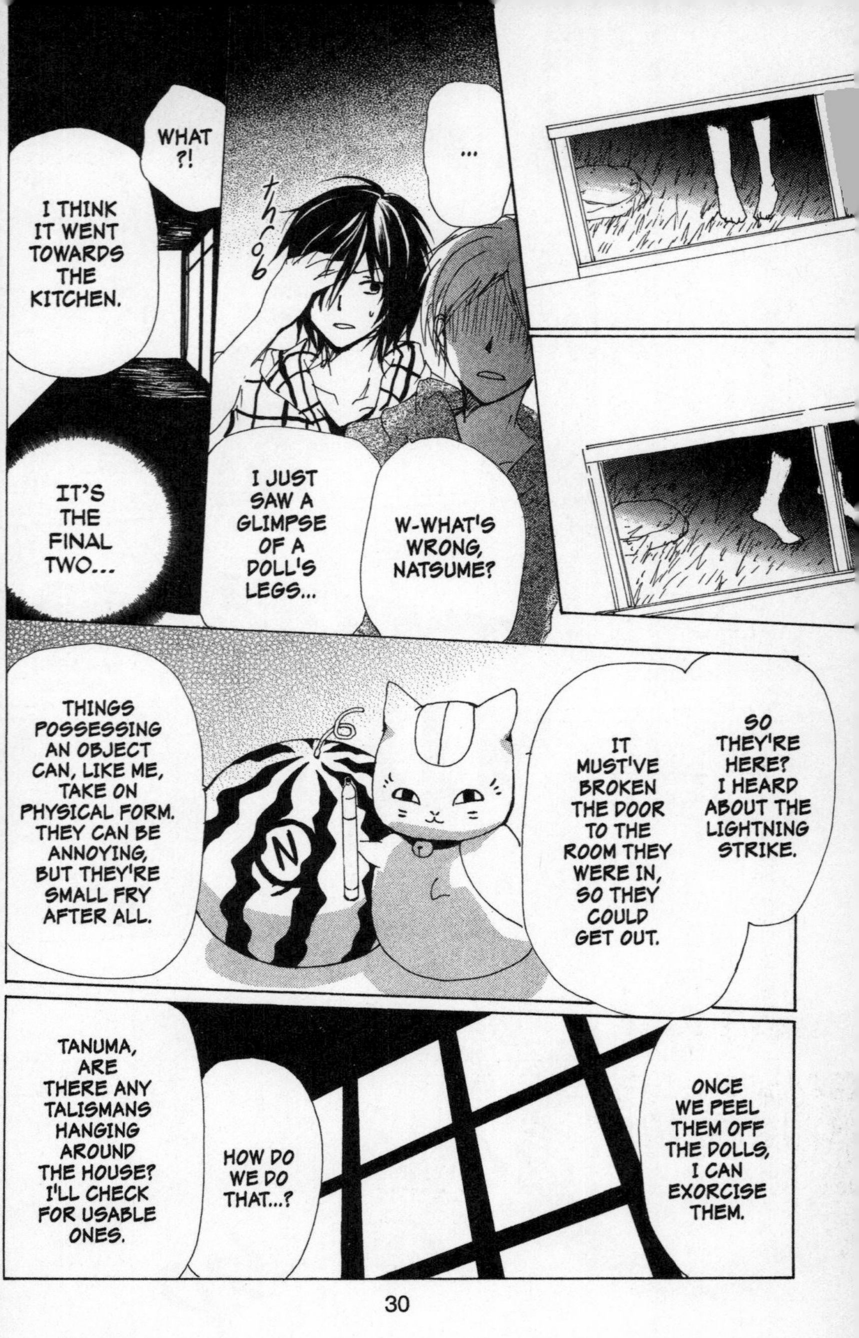
...
throb
W-WHAT'S WRONG, NATSUME?
I JUST SAW A GLIMPSE OF A DOLL'S LEGS...
WHAT?!
I THINK IT WENT TOWARDS THE KITCHEN.
IT'S THE FINAL TWO...
SO THEY'RE HERE? I HEARD ABOUT THE LIGHTNING STRIKE.
IT MUST'VE BROKEN THE DOOR TO THE ROOM THEY WERE IN, SO THEY COULD GET OUT.
THINGS POSSESSING AN OBJECT CAN, LIKE ME, TAKE ON PHYSICAL FORM. THEY CAN BE ANNOYING, BUT THEY'RE SMALL FRY AFTER ALL.
ONCE WE PEEL THEM OFF THE DOLLS, I CAN EXORCISE THEM.
HOW DO WE DO THAT...?
TANUMA, ARE THERE ANY TALISMANS HANGING AROUND THE HOUSE? I'LL CHECK FOR USABLE ONES.

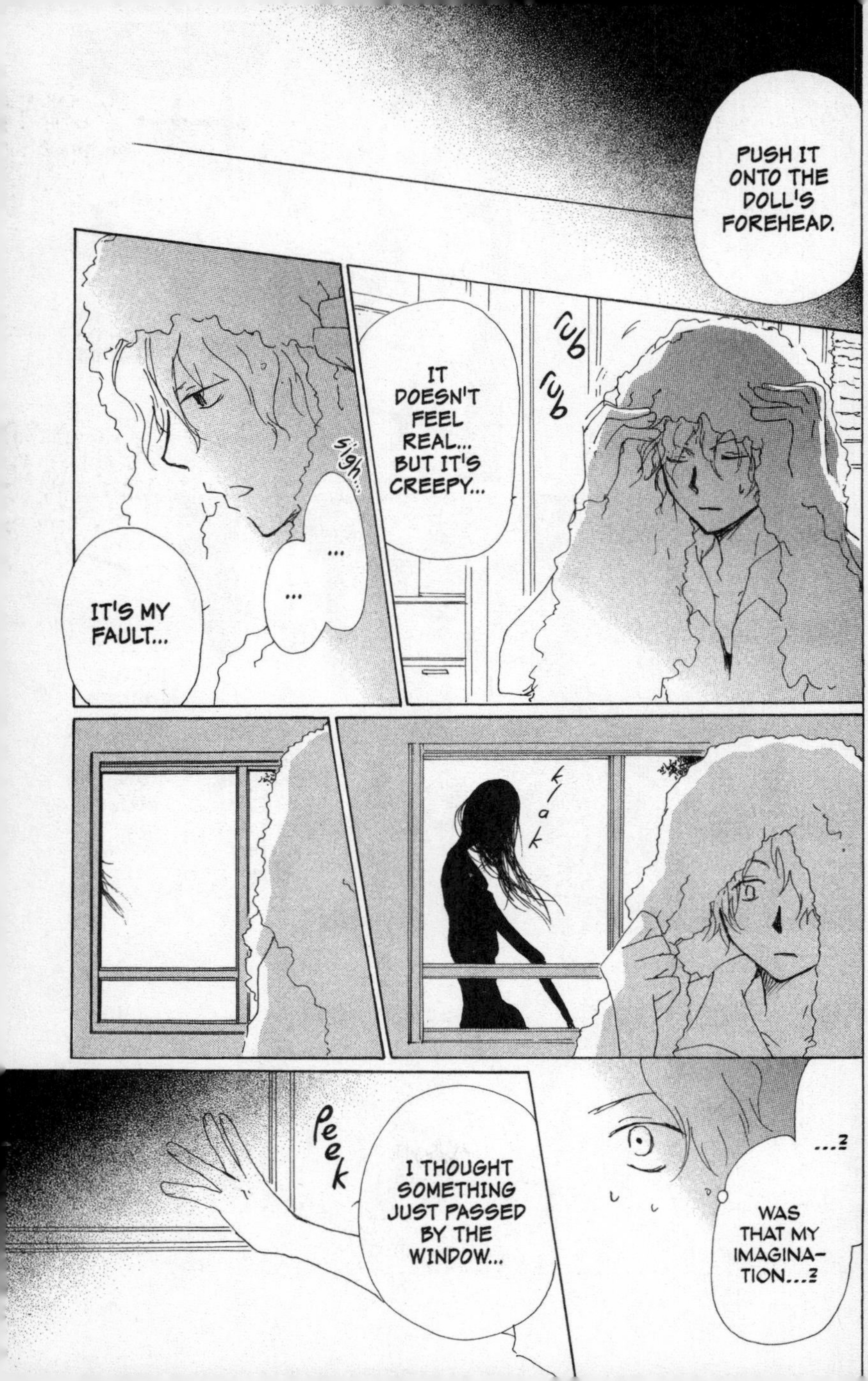
PUSH IT ONTO THE DOLL'S FOREHEAD.
rub rub
IT DOESN'T FEEL REAL... BUT IT'S CREEPY...
sigh...
...
...
IT'S MY FAULT...
klak
...?
WAS THAT MY IMAGINATION...?
Peek
I THOUGHT SOMETHING JUST PASSED BY THE WINDOW...

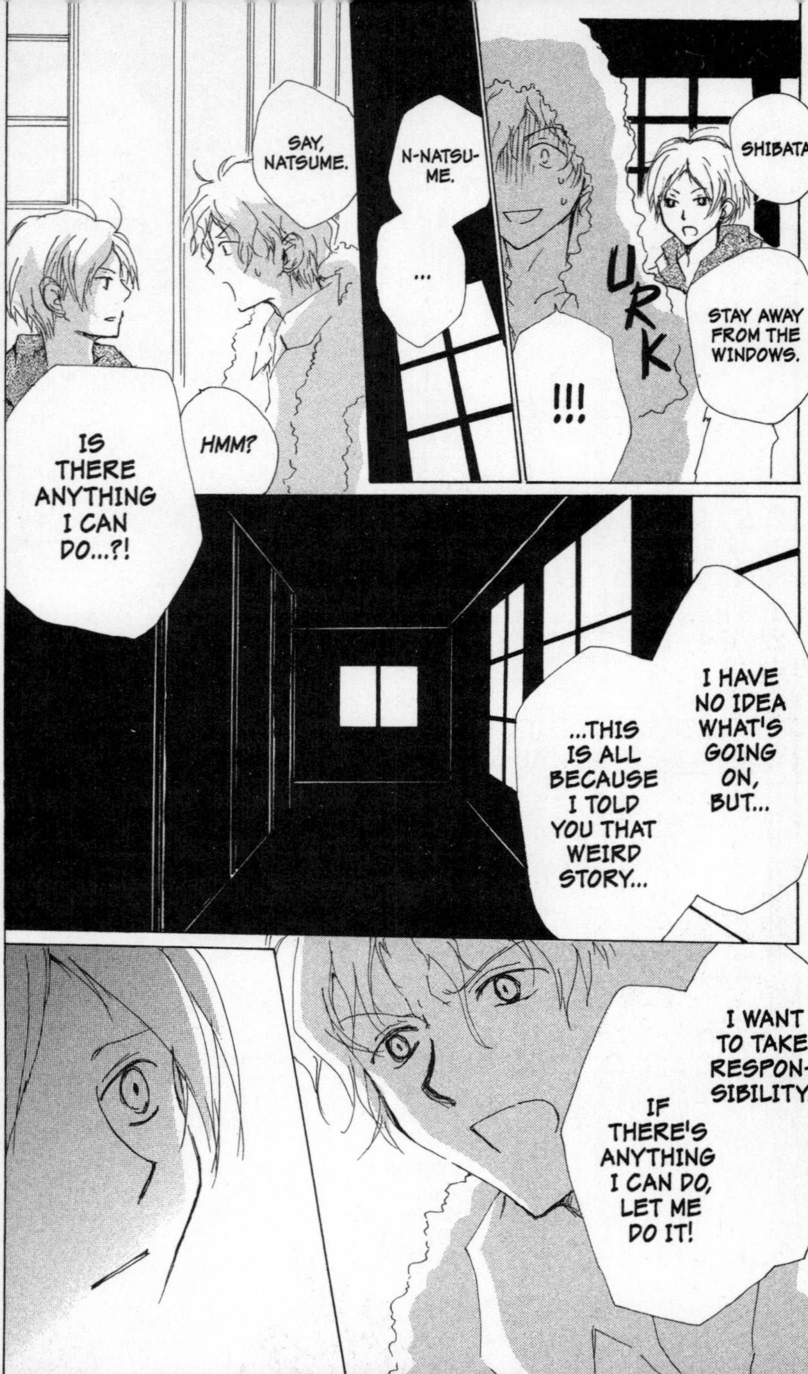
SHIBATA.
STAY AWAY FROM THE WINDOWS.
URK
!!!
N-NATSU-ME.
...
SAY, NATSUME.
HMM?
IS THERE ANYTHING I CAN DO...?!
I HAVE NO IDEA WHAT'S GOING ON, BUT...
...THIS IS ALL BECAUSE I TOLD YOU THAT WEIRD STORY...
I WANT TO TAKE RESPON-SIBILITY.
IF THERE'S ANYTHING I CAN DO, LET ME DO IT!

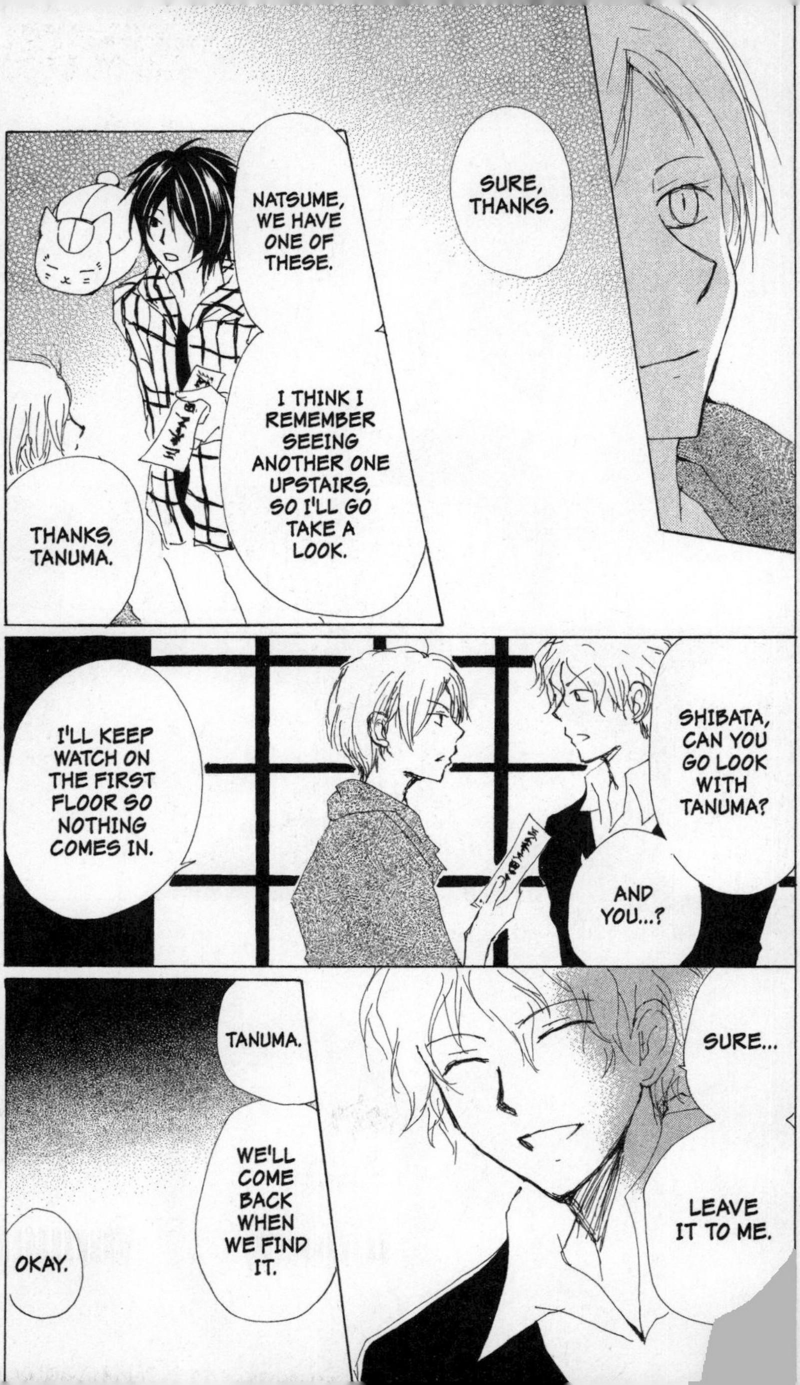
SURE, THANKS.
NATSUME, WE HAVE ONE OF THESE.
I THINK I REMEMBER SEEING ANOTHER ONE UPSTAIRS, SO I'LL GO TAKE A LOOK.
THANKS, TANUMA.
SHIBATA, CAN YOU GO LOOK WITH TANUMA?
AND YOU...?
I'LL KEEP WATCH ON THE FIRST FLOOR SO NOTHING COMES IN.
SURE...
LEAVE IT TO ME.
TANUMA.
WE'LL COME BACK WHEN WE FIND IT.
OKAY.

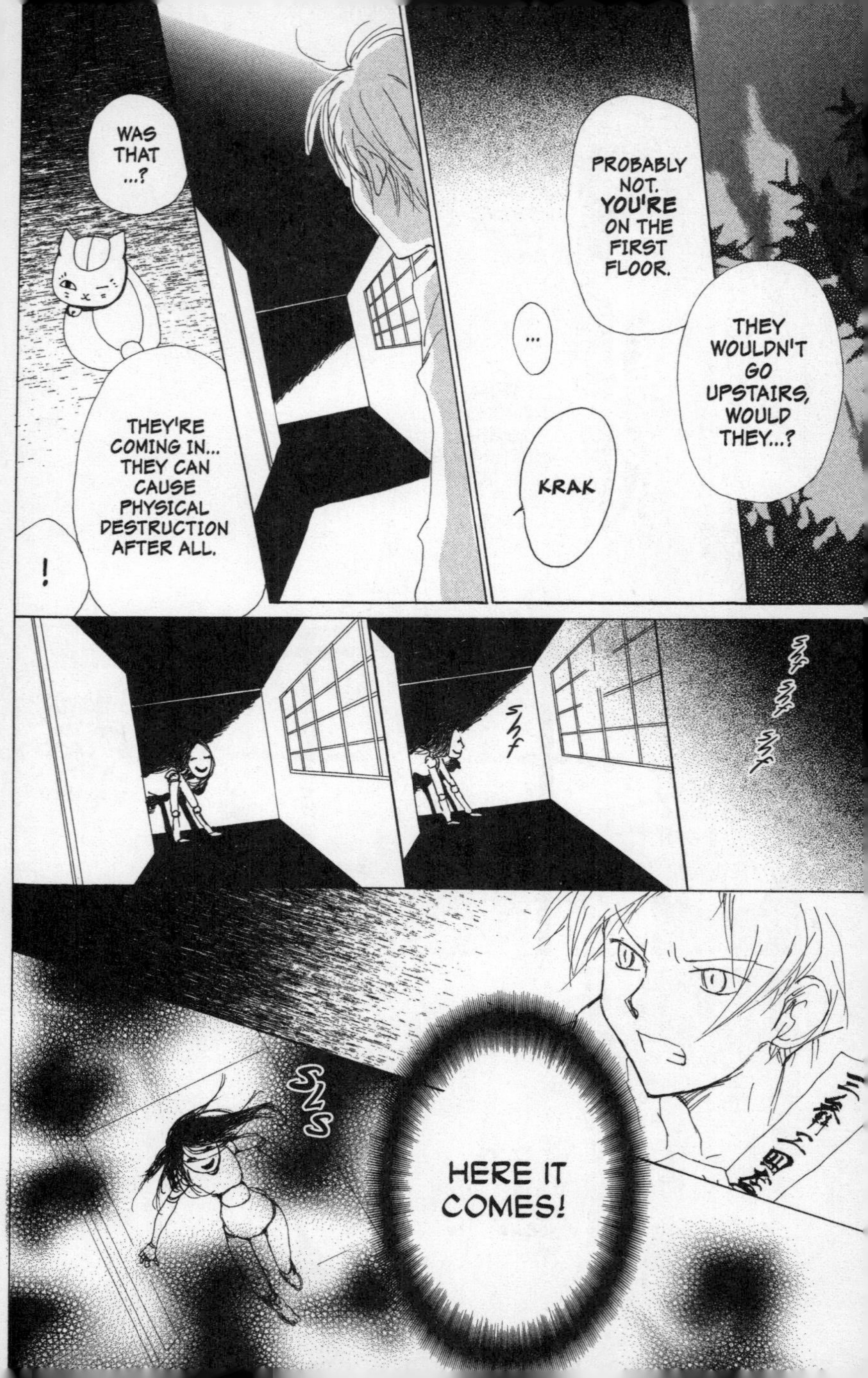
THEY WOULDN'T GO UPSTAIRS, WOULD THEY...?
PROBABLY NOT. YOU'RE ON THE FIRST FLOOR.
...
KRAK
WAS THAT ...?
THEY'RE COMING IN... THEY CAN CAUSE PHYSICAL DESTRUCTION AFTER ALL.
!
SFF SFF SFF
SFF
HERE IT COMES!
SLS

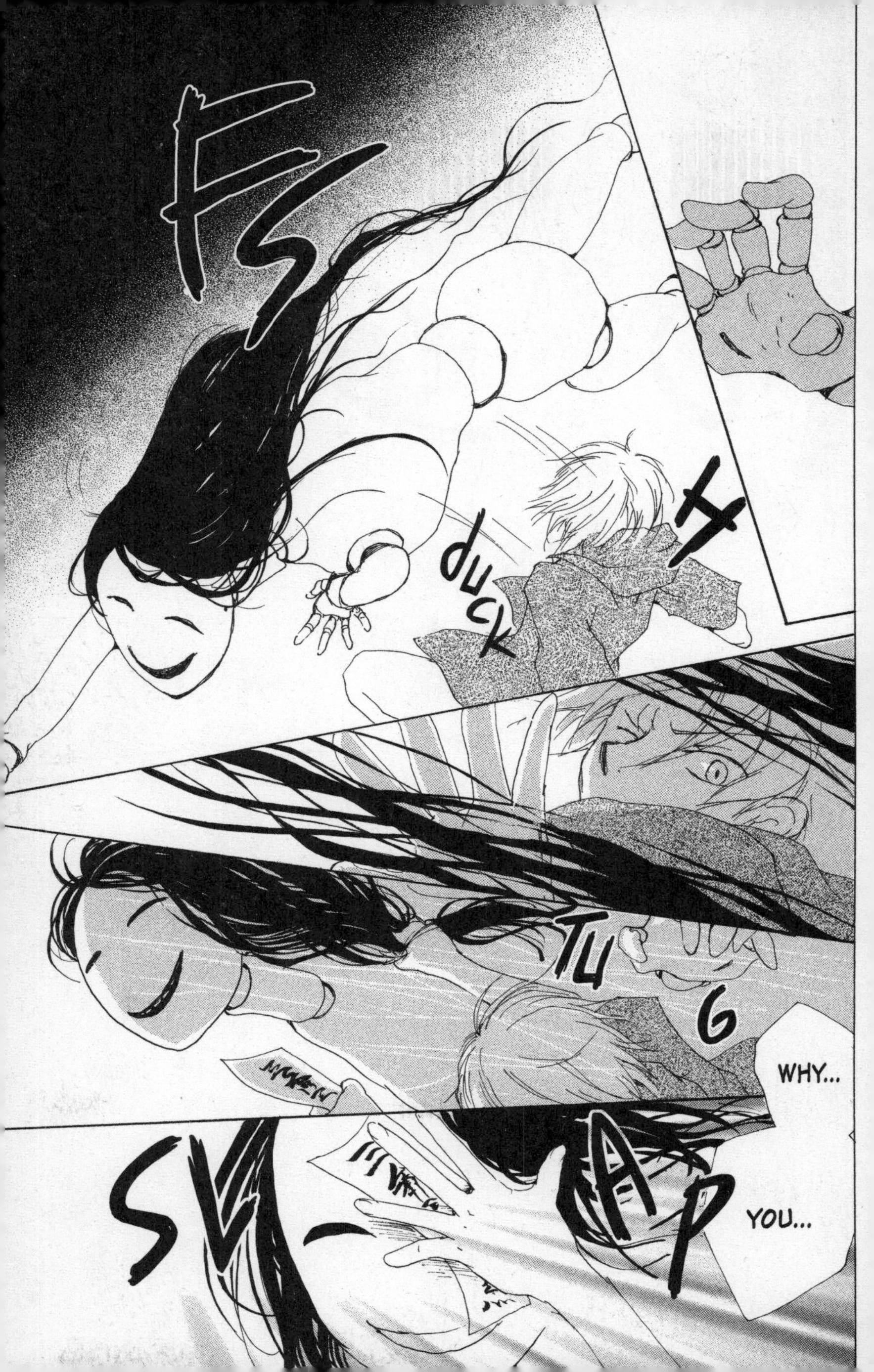
H
duck
FS
TUG
WHY...
SWAP
YOU...

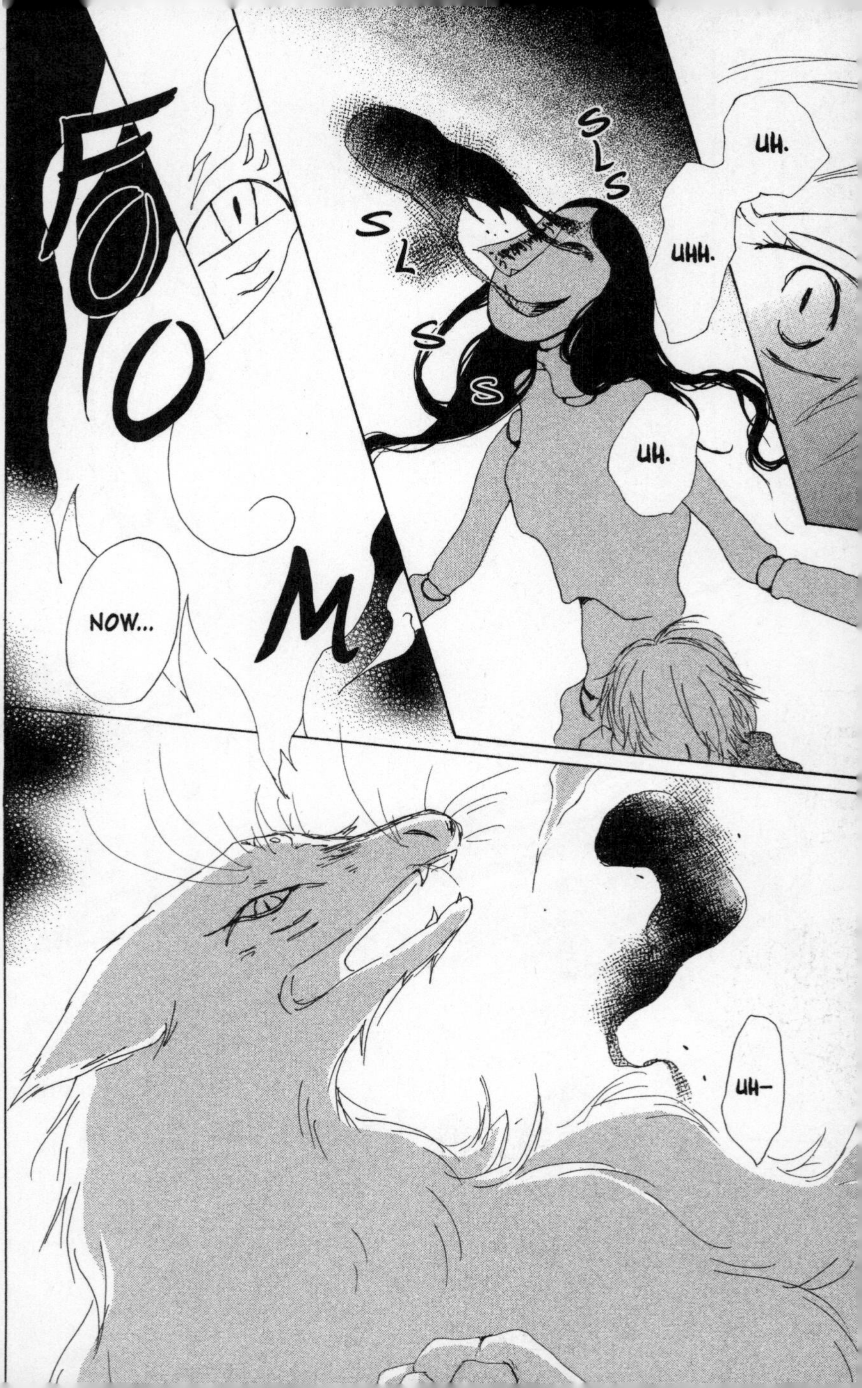
UH.
UHH.
SLS
SL
SS
UH.
FOOOM
NOW...
UH–

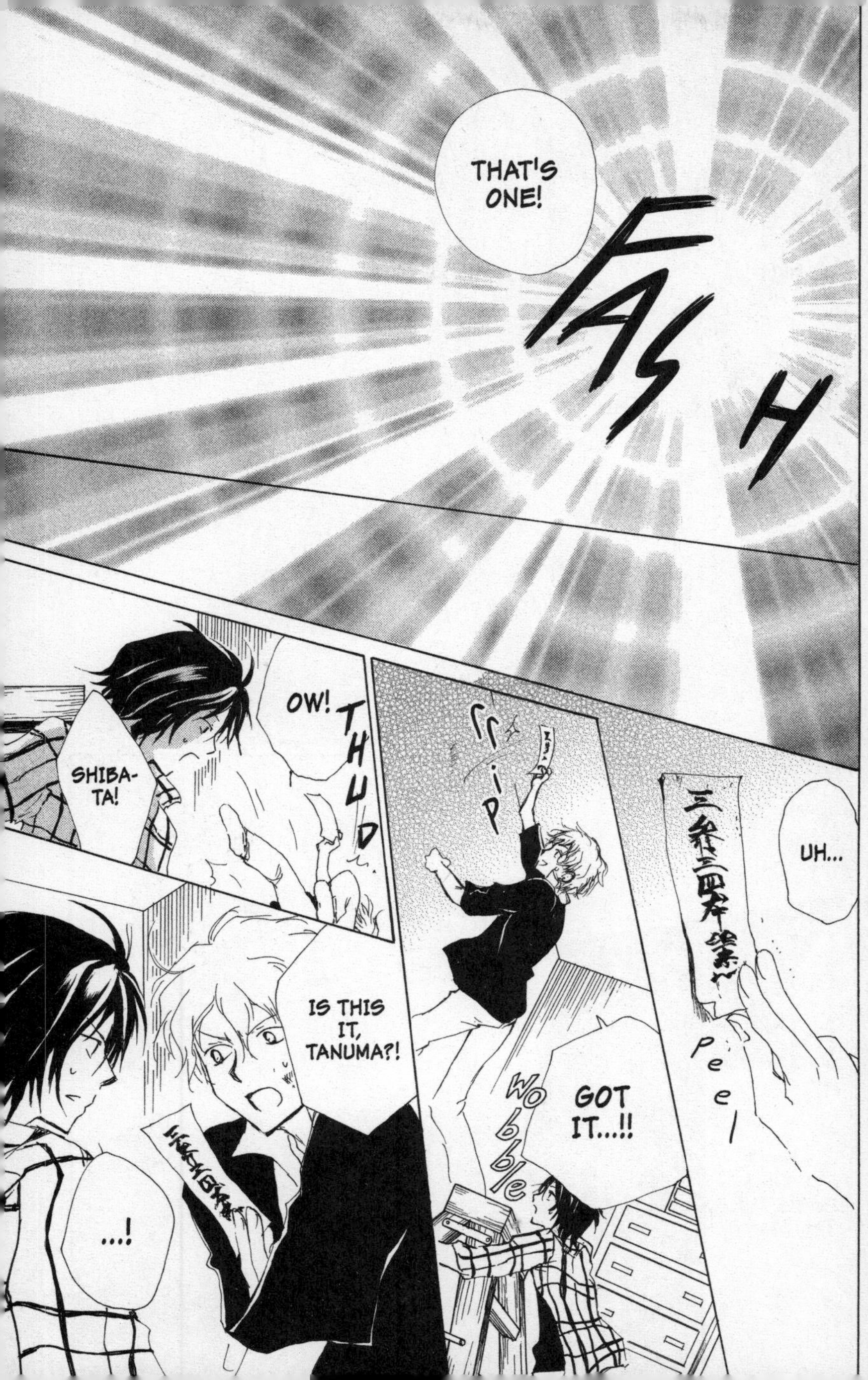
THAT'S ONE!
FASH
UH...
Peel
GOT IT...!!
wobble
rip
OW!
THUD
SHIBA-TA!
IS THIS IT, TANUMA?!
...!

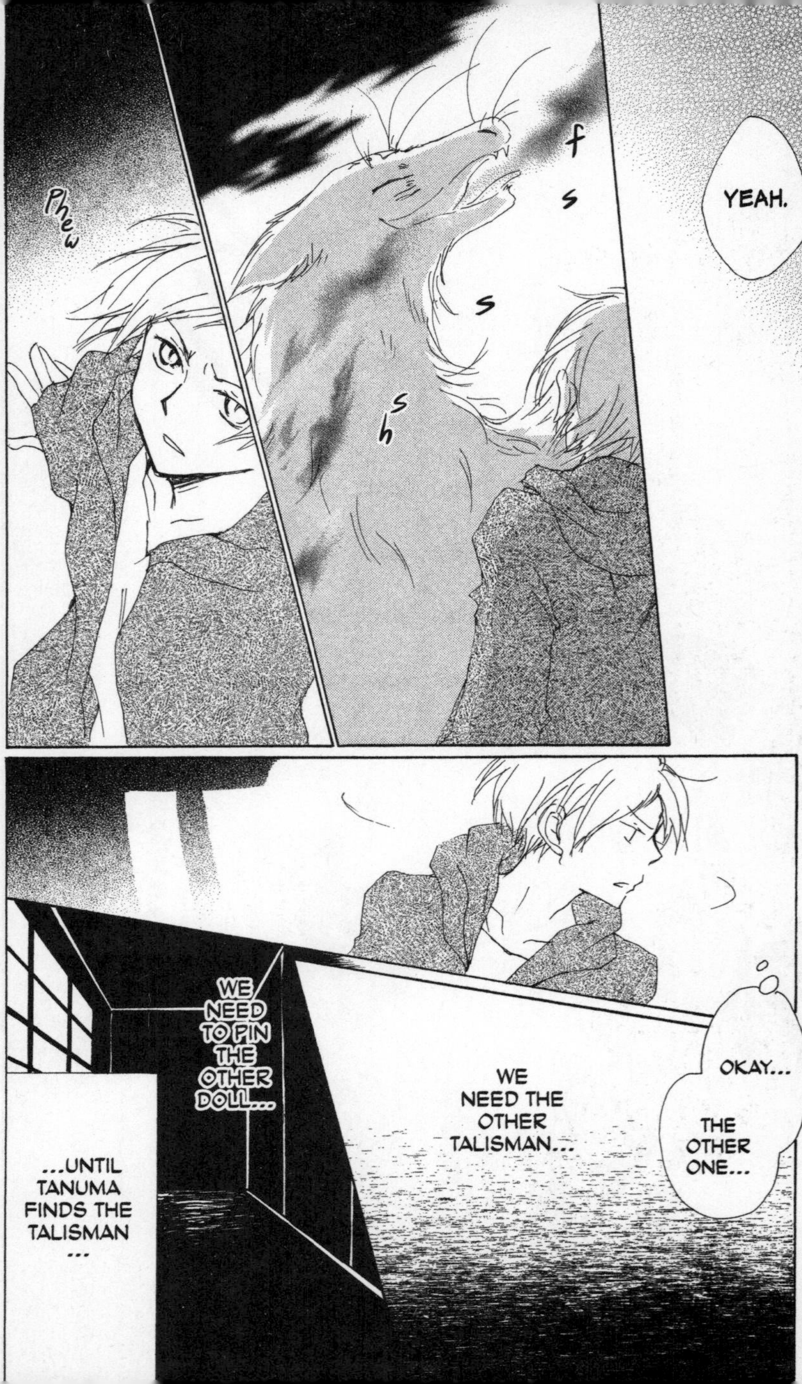
YEAH.
fsssh
Phew
OKAY... THE OTHER ONE...
WE NEED THE OTHER TALISMAN...
WE NEED TO PIN THE OTHER DOLL...
...UNTIL TANUMA FINDS THE TALISMAN...

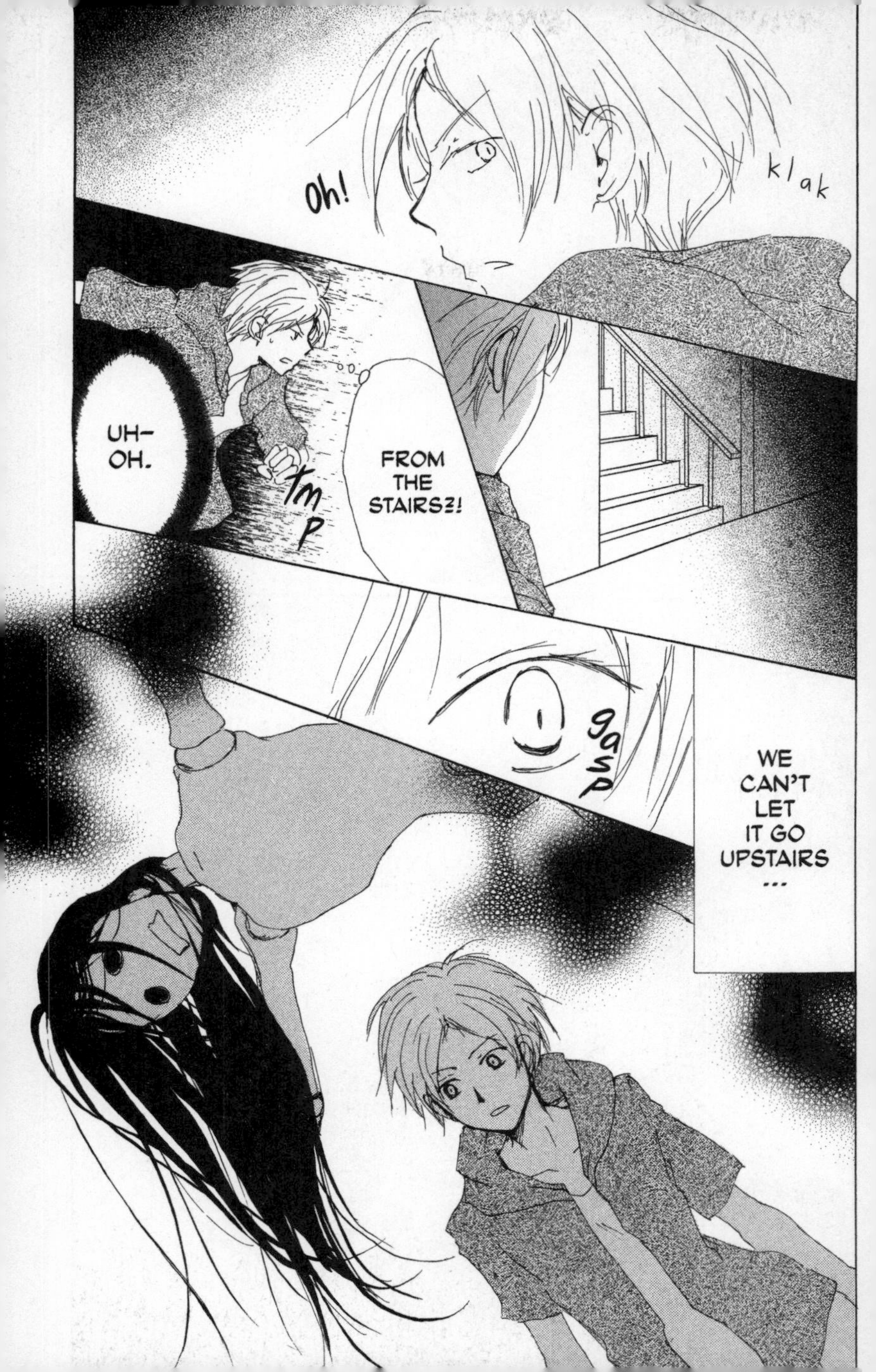
klak
Oh!
FROM THE STAIRS?!
tmp
UH-OH.
gasp
WE CAN'T LET IT GO UPSTAIRS...

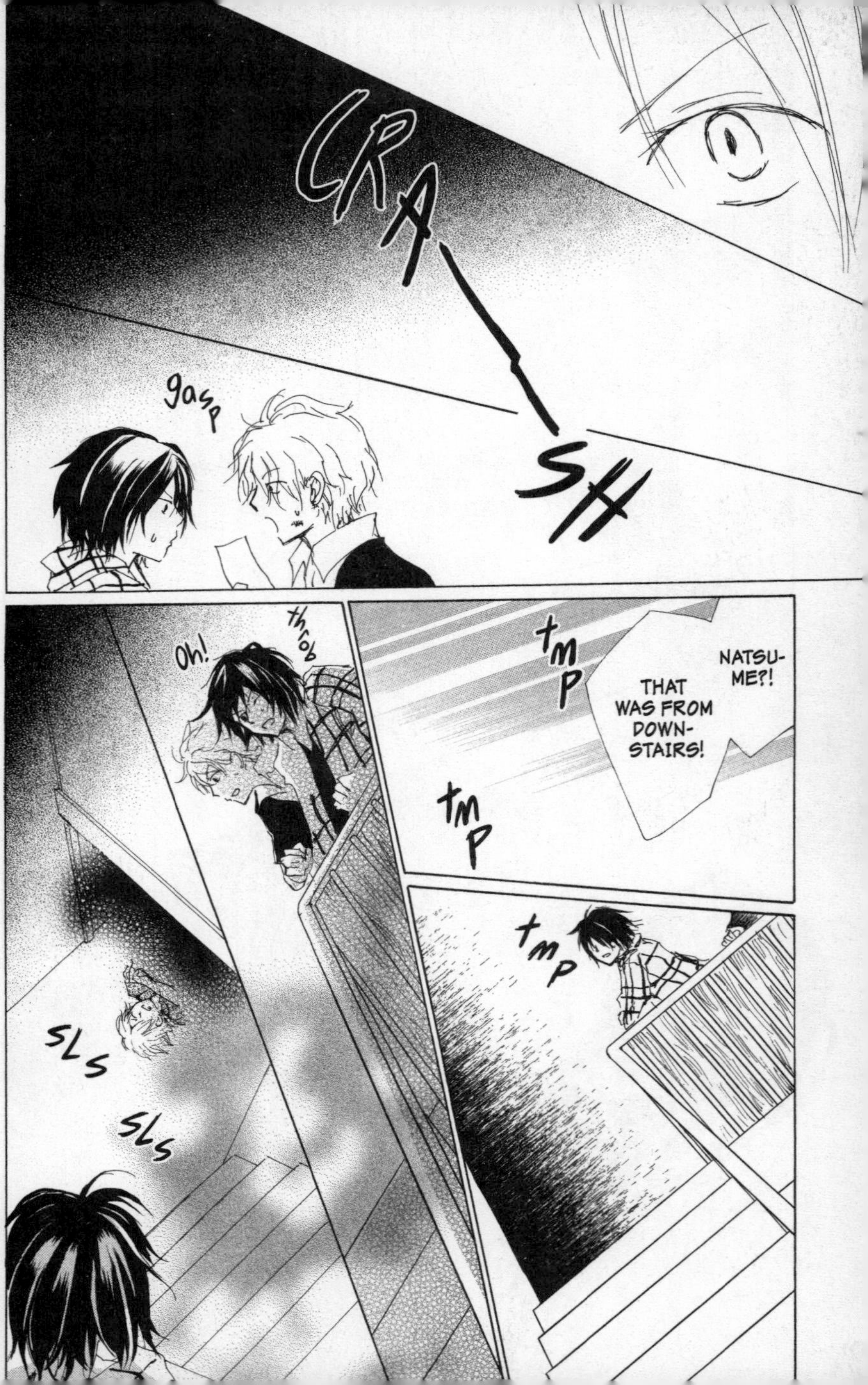
CRA—SH
gasp
tmp
NATSUME?!
THAT WAS FROM DOWNSTAIRS!
tmp
tmp
throb
Oh!
sls
sls

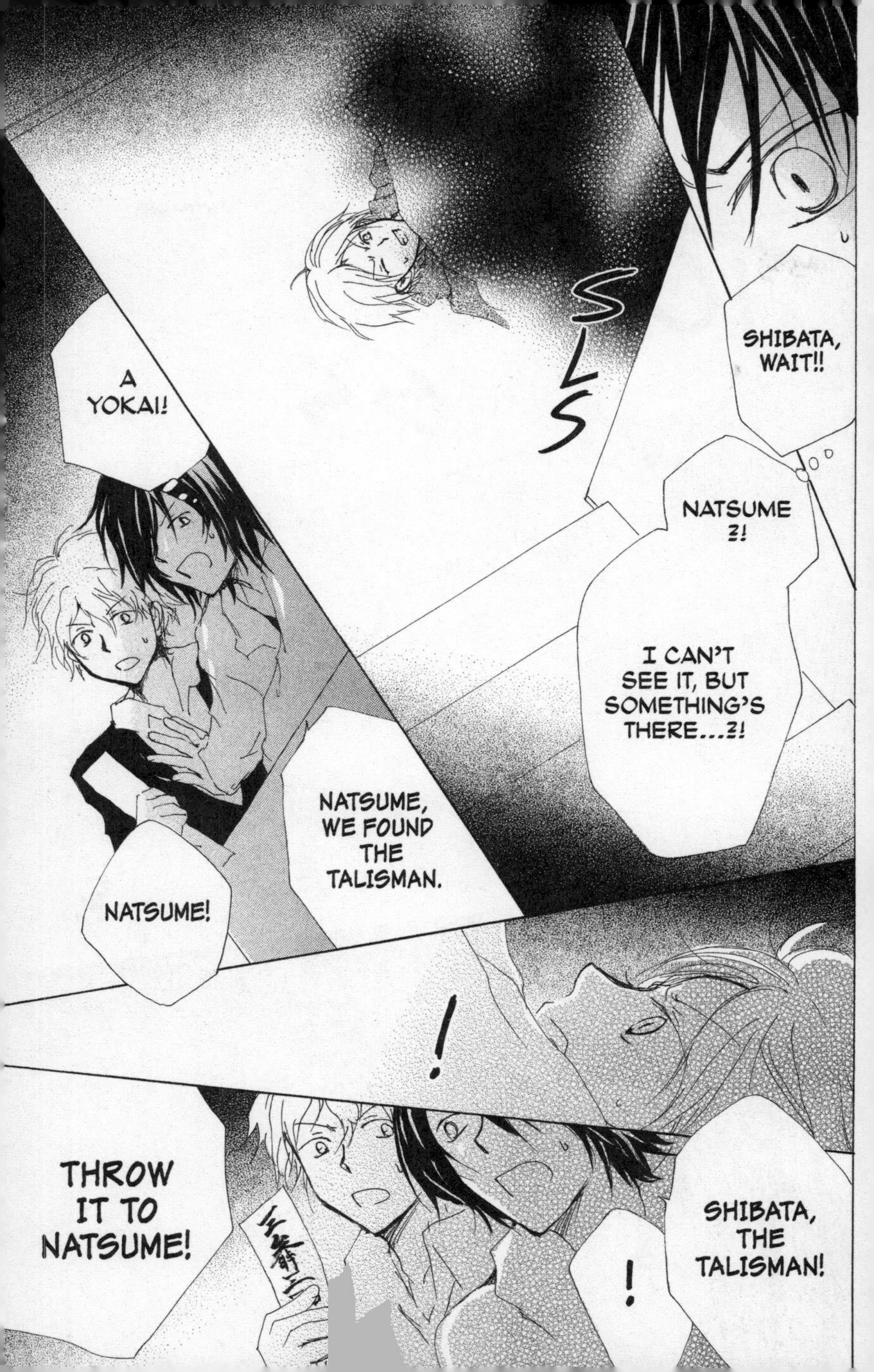
SHIBATA, WAIT!!
NATSUME ?!
I CAN'T SEE IT, BUT SOMETHING'S THERE...?!
SLS
A YOKAI!
NATSUME, WE FOUND THE TALISMAN.
NATSUME!
!
SHIBATA, THE TALISMAN!
!
THROW IT TO NATSUME!

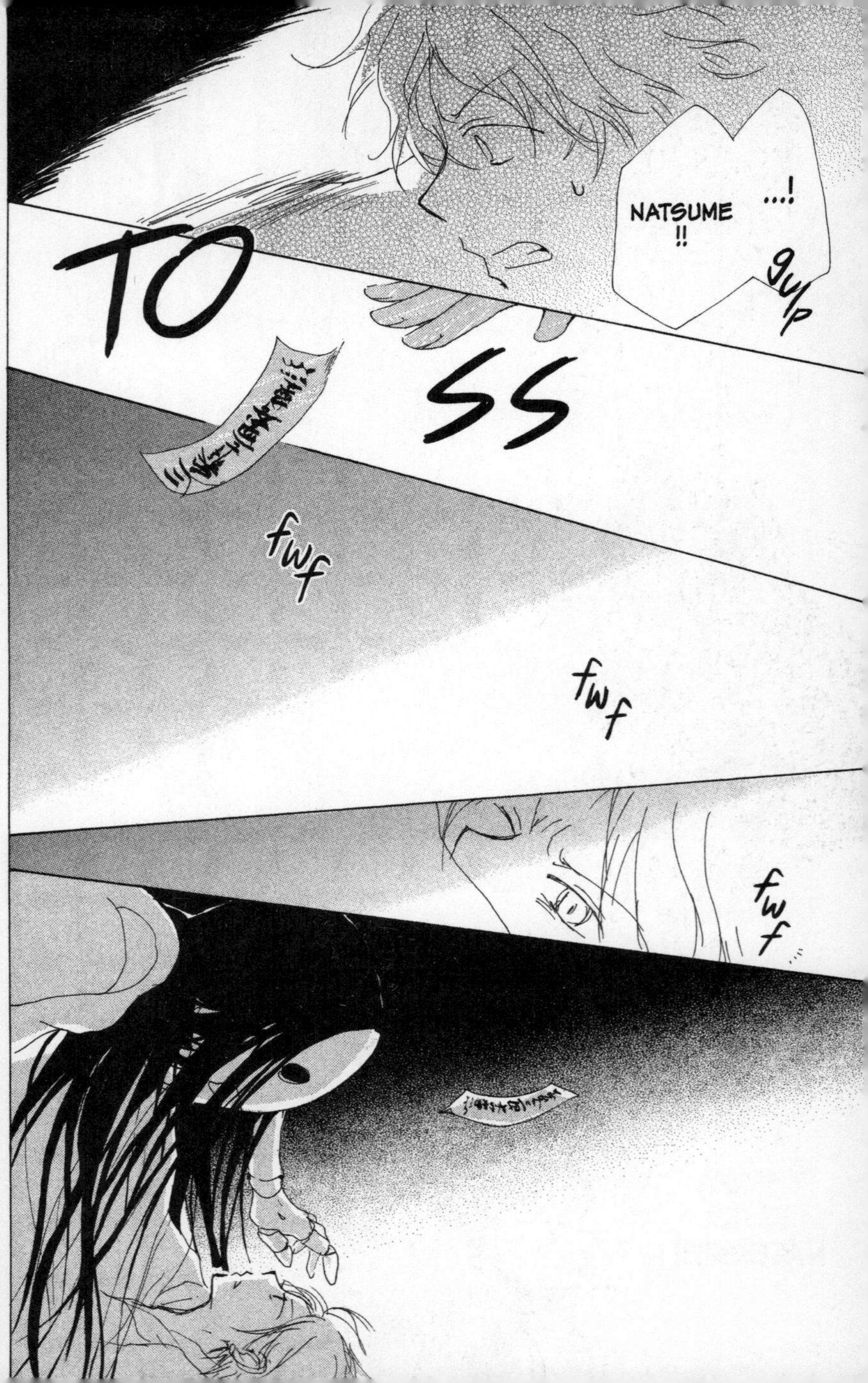
...!
NATSUME !!
gulp
TOSS
fwf
fwf
fwf...

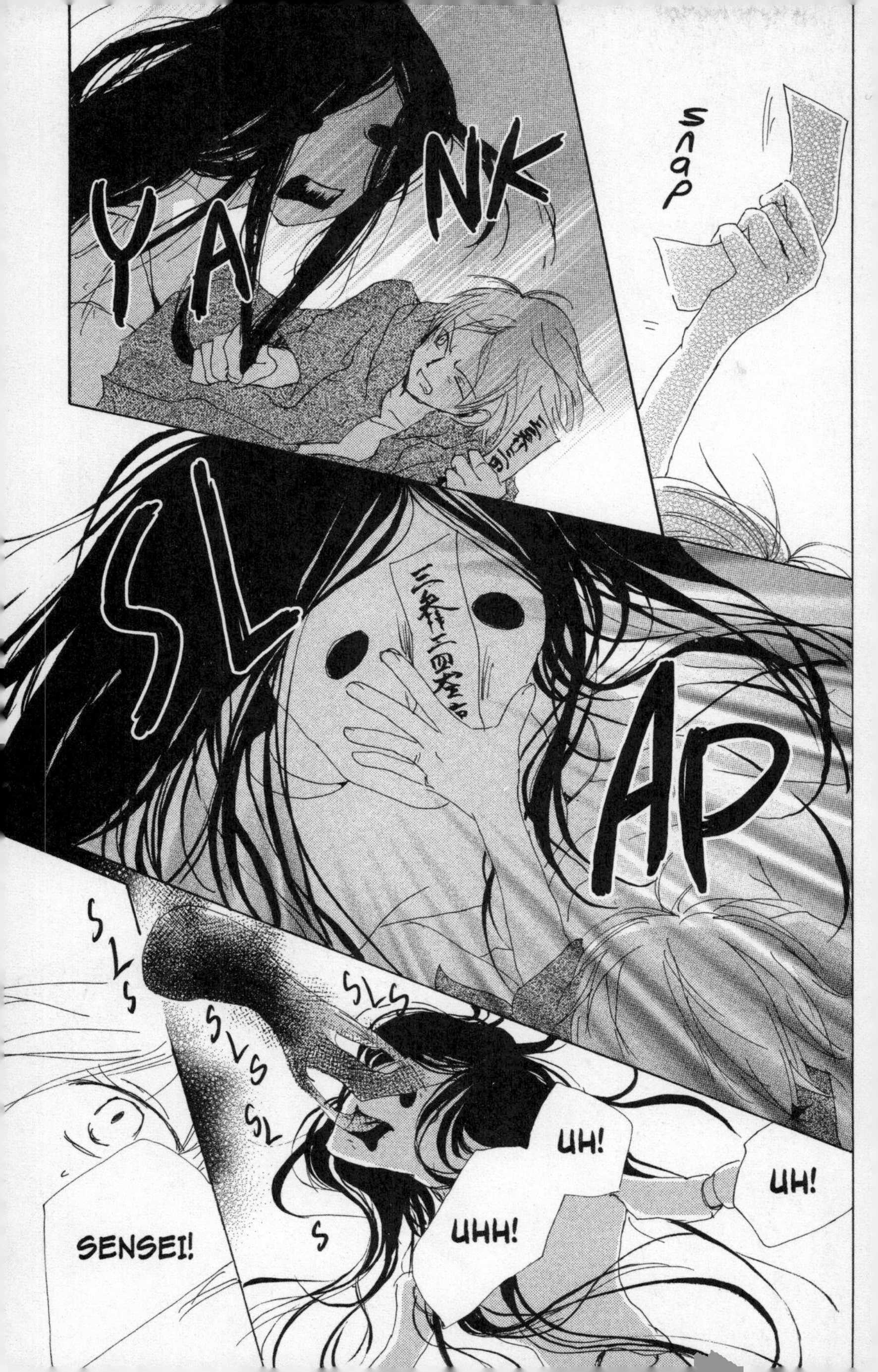
snap
YANK
SLAP
UH!
UH!
SLS
SLS
SLS
SL
UHH!
S
SENSEI!

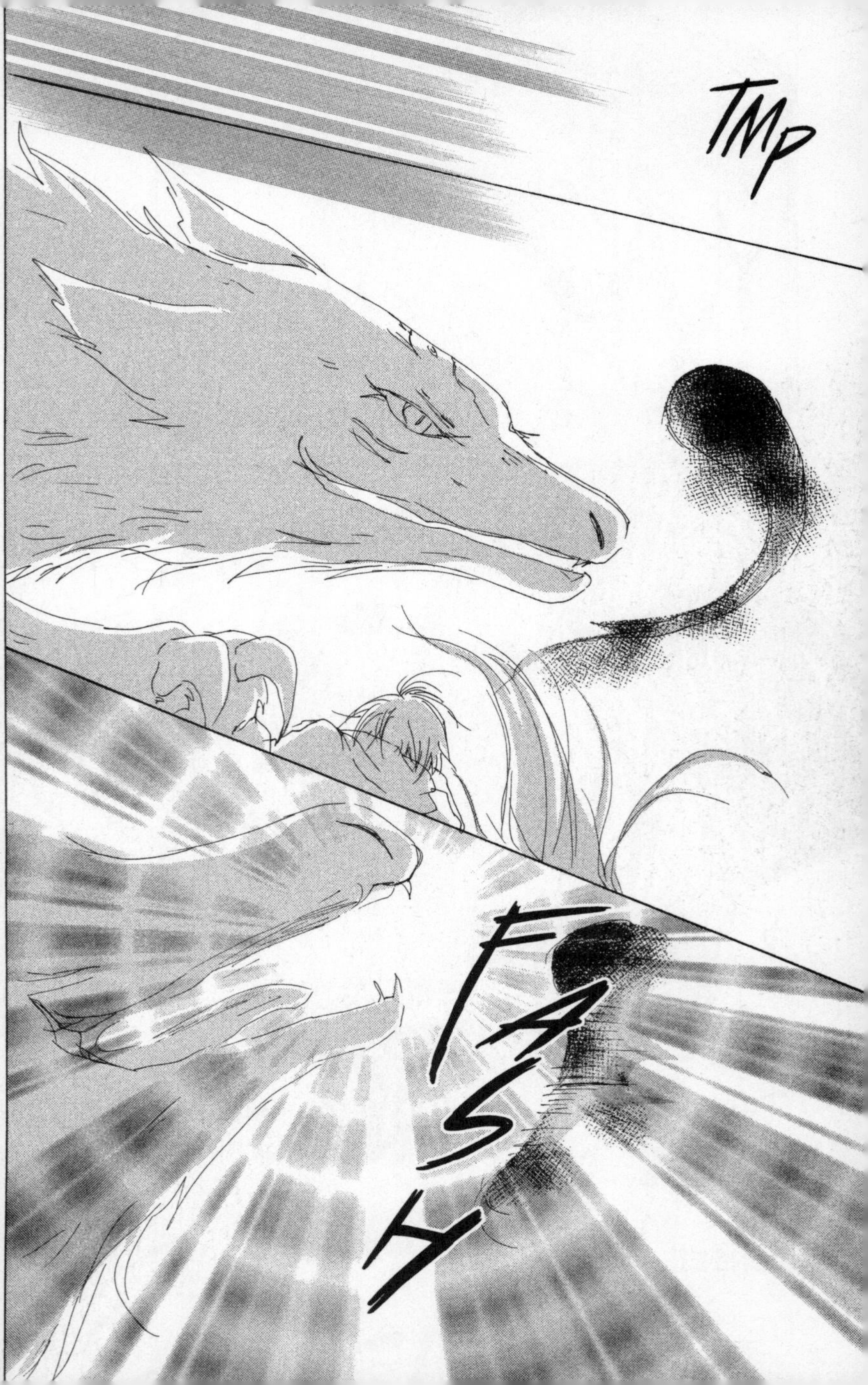
TMP
FASH

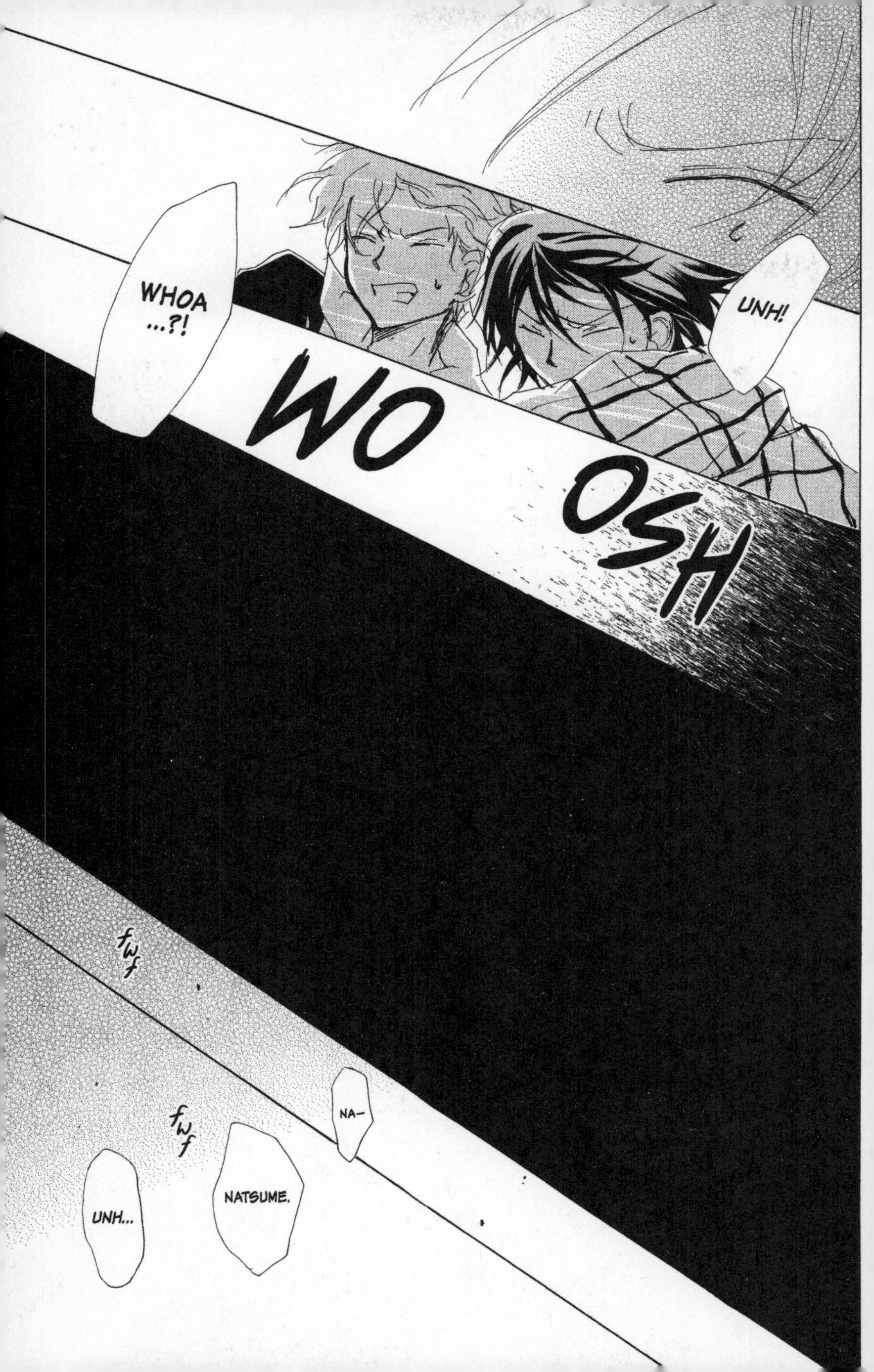
UNH!
WHOA ...?!
WOOSH
NA—
NATSUME.
fwf
fwf
UNH...

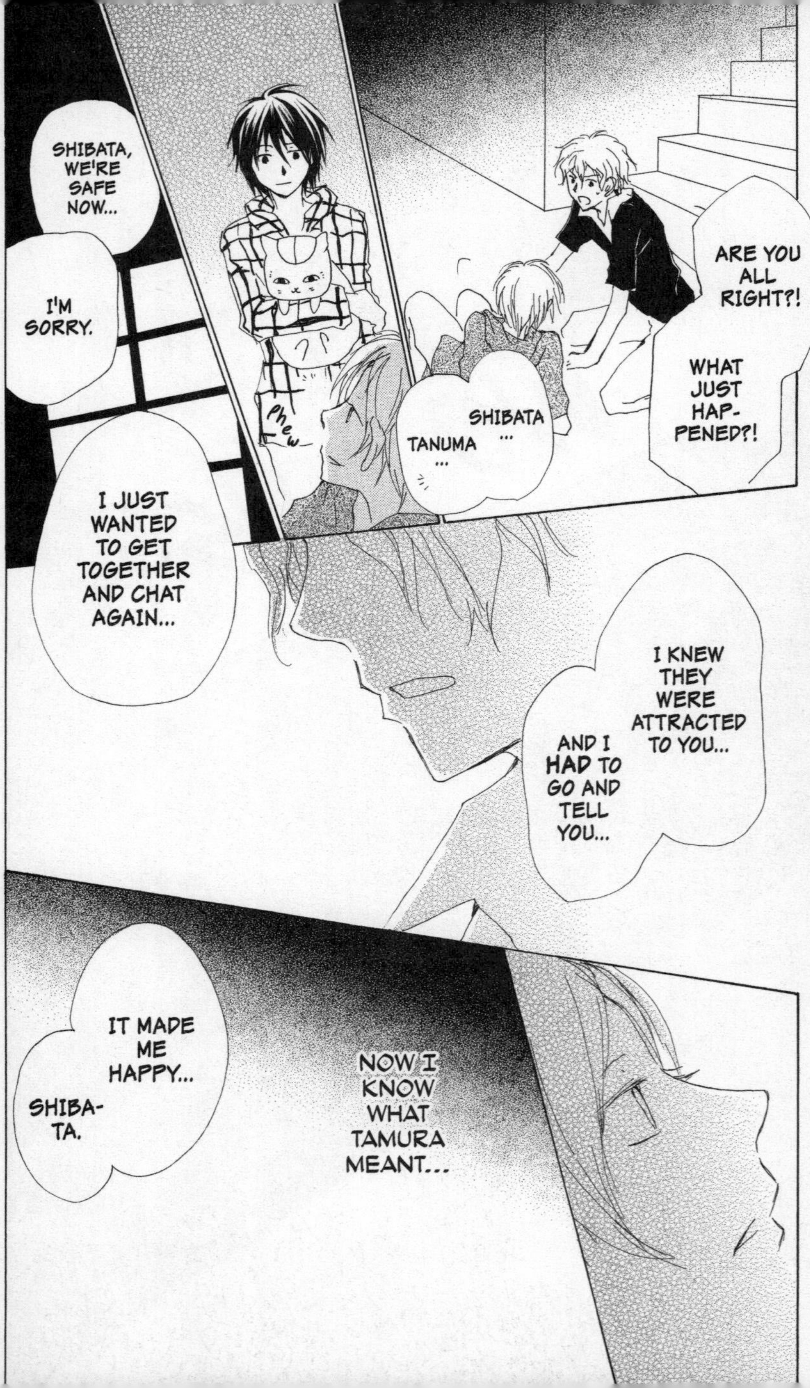
ARE YOU ALL RIGHT?!
WHAT JUST HAP-PENED?!
SHIBATA ...
TANUMA ...
Phew
SHIBATA, WE'RE SAFE NOW...
I'M SORRY.
I JUST WANTED TO GET TOGETHER AND CHAT AGAIN...
I KNEW THEY WERE ATTRACTED TO YOU...
AND I **HAD** TO GO AND TELL YOU...
NOW I KNOW WHAT TAMURA MEANT...
IT MADE ME HAPPY...
SHIBA-TA.

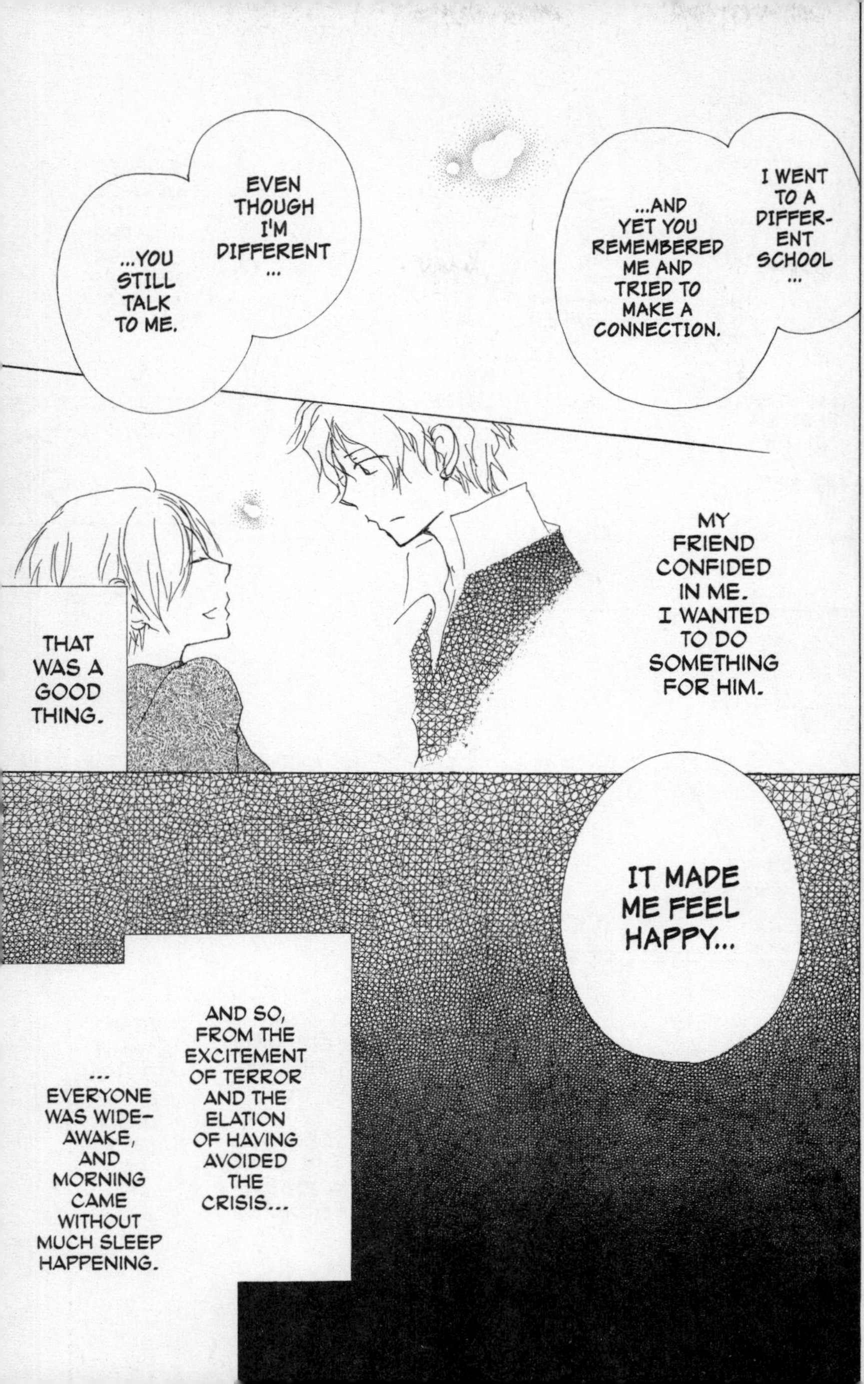
I WENT TO A DIFFER-ENT SCHOOL ...
...AND YET YOU REMEMBERED ME AND TRIED TO MAKE A CONNECTION.
EVEN THOUGH I'M DIFFERENT ...
...YOU STILL TALK TO ME.
MY FRIEND CONFIDED IN ME. I WANTED TO DO SOMETHING FOR HIM.
THAT WAS A GOOD THING.
IT MADE ME FEEL HAPPY...
AND SO, FROM THE EXCITEMENT OF TERROR AND THE ELATION OF HAVING AVOIDED THE CRISIS...
... EVERYONE WAS WIDE-AWAKE, AND MORNING CAME WITHOUT MUCH SLEEP HAPPENING.

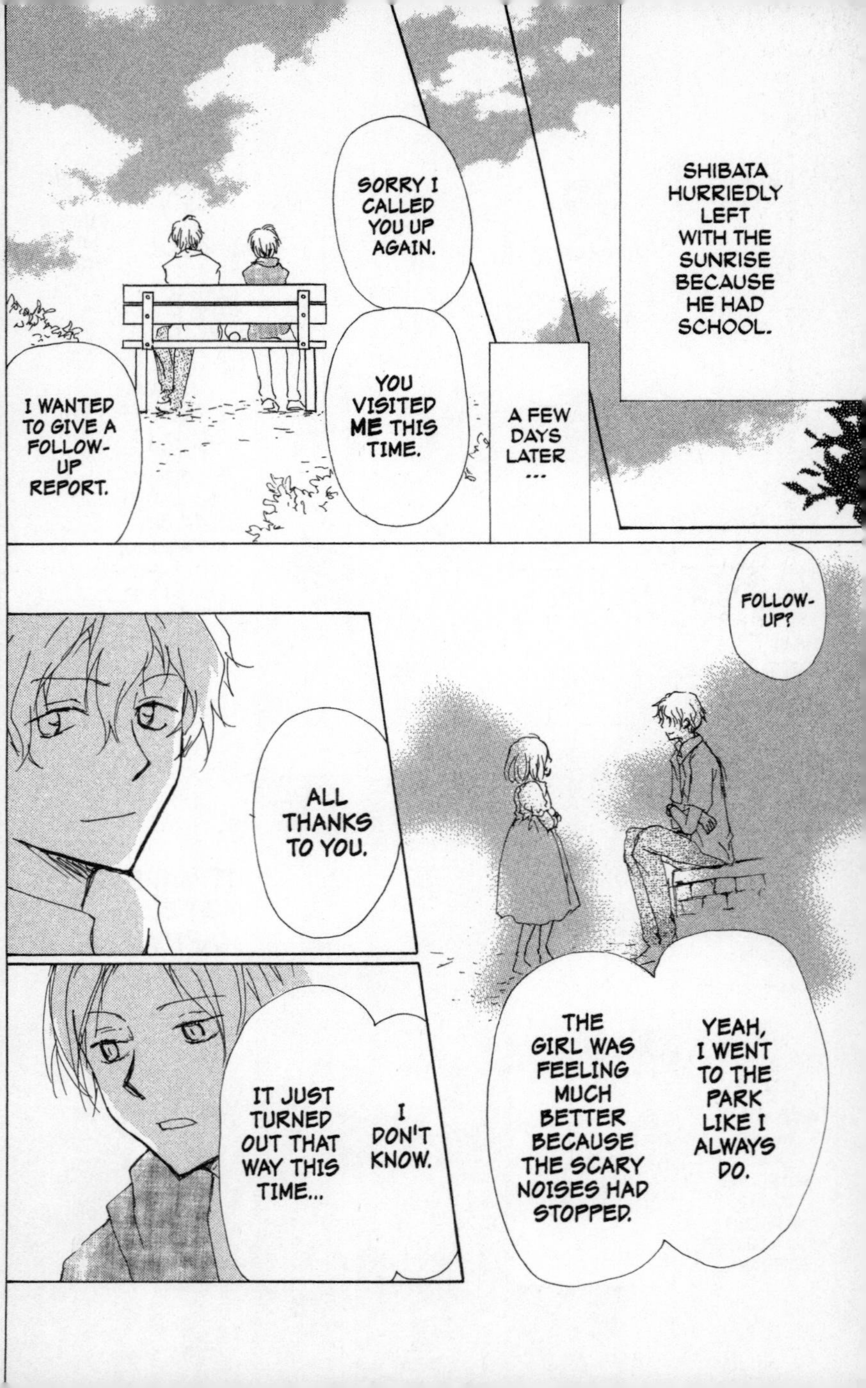
SHIBATA HURRIEDLY LEFT WITH THE SUNRISE BECAUSE HE HAD SCHOOL.
A FEW DAYS LATER ...
SORRY I CALLED YOU UP AGAIN.
YOU VISITED ME THIS TIME.
I WANTED TO GIVE A FOLLOW-UP REPORT.
FOLLOW-UP?
YEAH, I WENT TO THE PARK LIKE I ALWAYS DO.
THE GIRL WAS FEELING MUCH BETTER BECAUSE THE SCARY NOISES HAD STOPPED.
ALL THANKS TO YOU.
I DON'T KNOW.
IT JUST TURNED OUT THAT WAY THIS TIME...

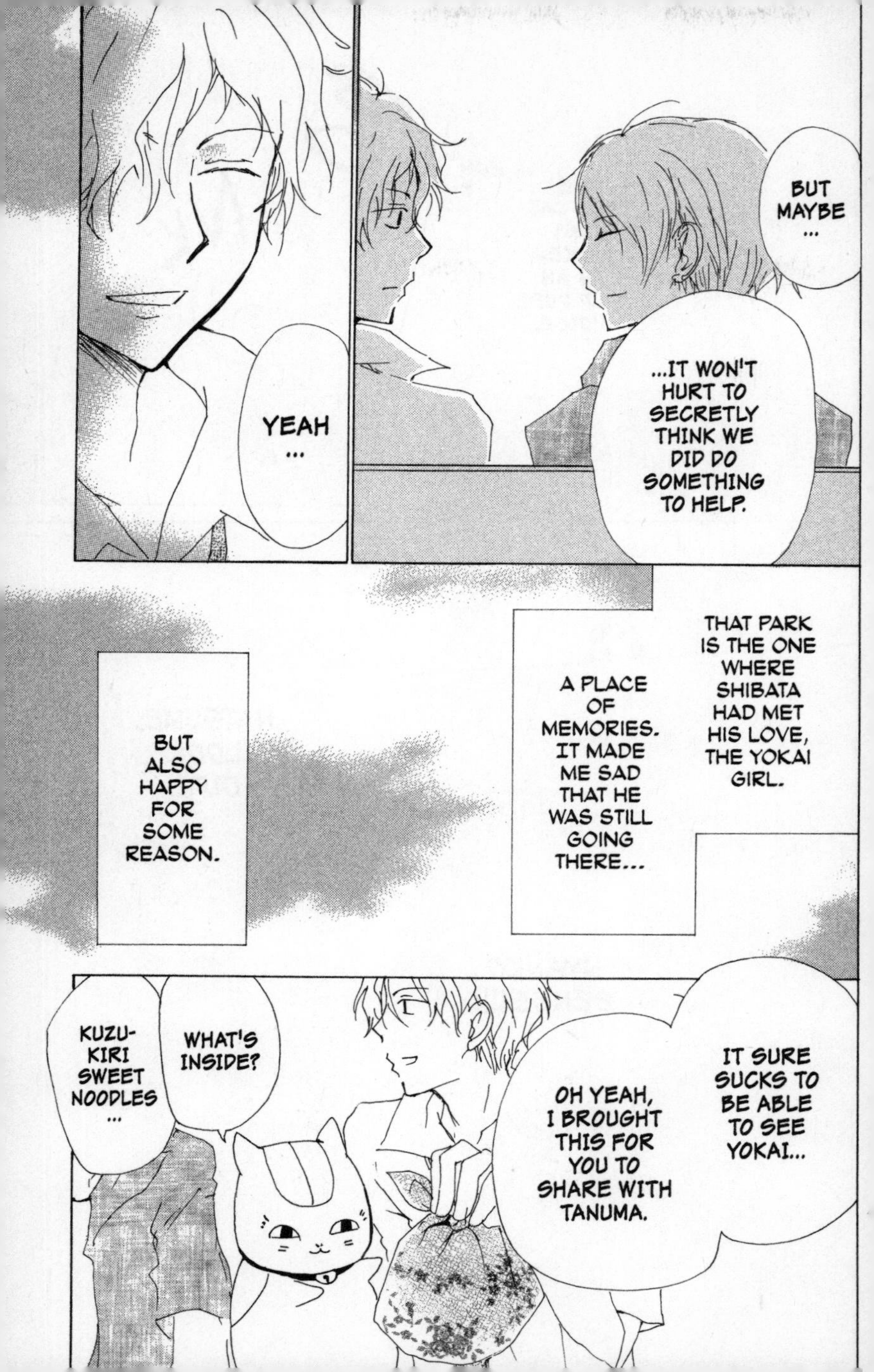
BUT MAYBE ...
...IT WON'T HURT TO SECRETLY THINK WE DID DO SOMETHING TO HELP.
YEAH ...
THAT PARK IS THE ONE WHERE SHIBATA HAD MET HIS LOVE, THE YOKAI GIRL.
A PLACE OF MEMORIES. IT MADE ME SAD THAT HE WAS STILL GOING THERE...
BUT ALSO HAPPY FOR SOME REASON.
IT SURE SUCKS TO BE ABLE TO SEE YOKAI...
OH YEAH, I BROUGHT THIS FOR YOU TO SHARE WITH TANUMA.
WHAT'S INSIDE?
KUZU-KIRI SWEET NOODLES ...

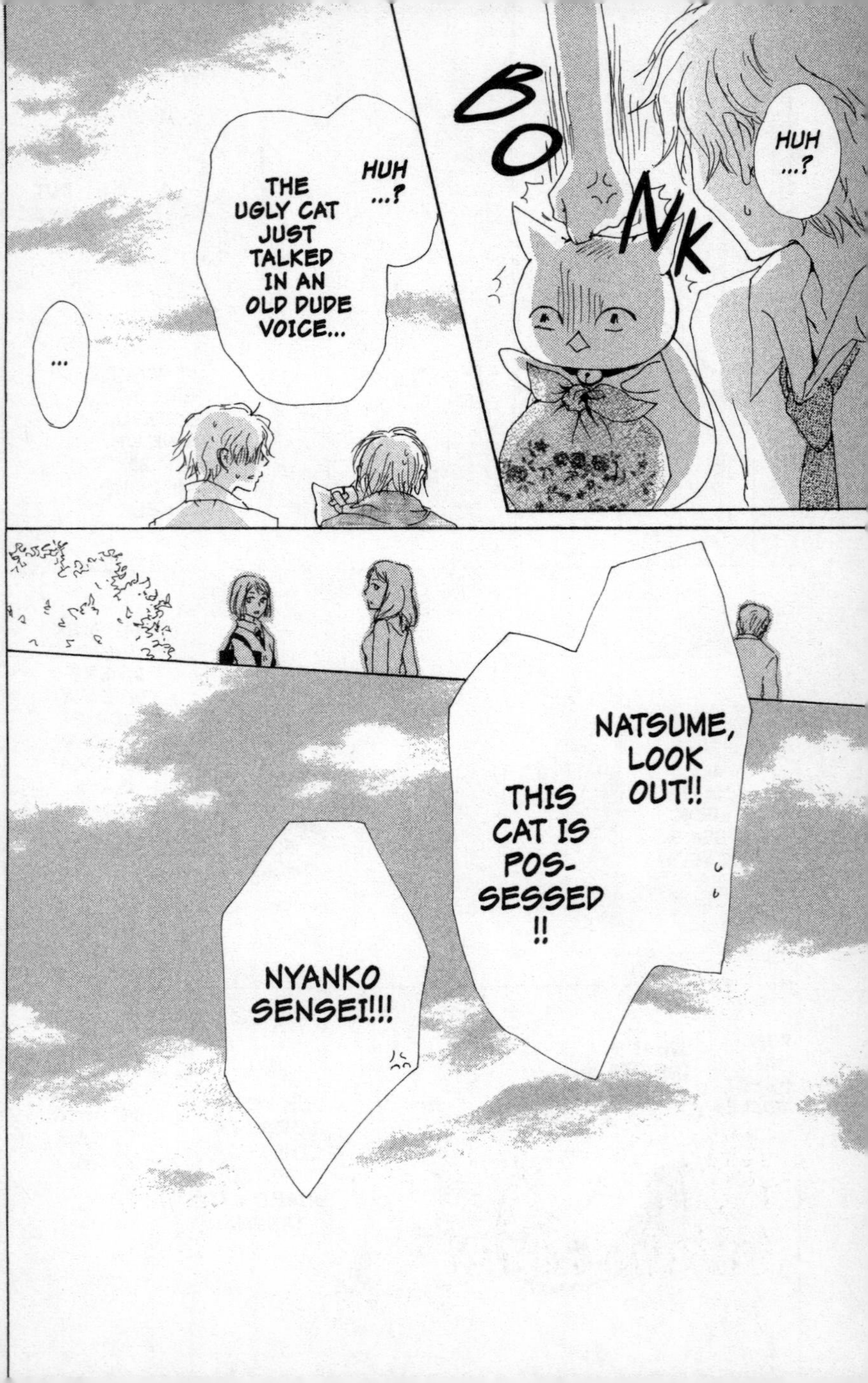
BONK
HUH ...?
HUH ...?
THE UGLY CAT JUST TALKED IN AN OLD DUDE VOICE...
...
NATSUME, LOOK OUT!!
THIS CAT IS POS-SESSED !!
NYANKO SENSEI!!!

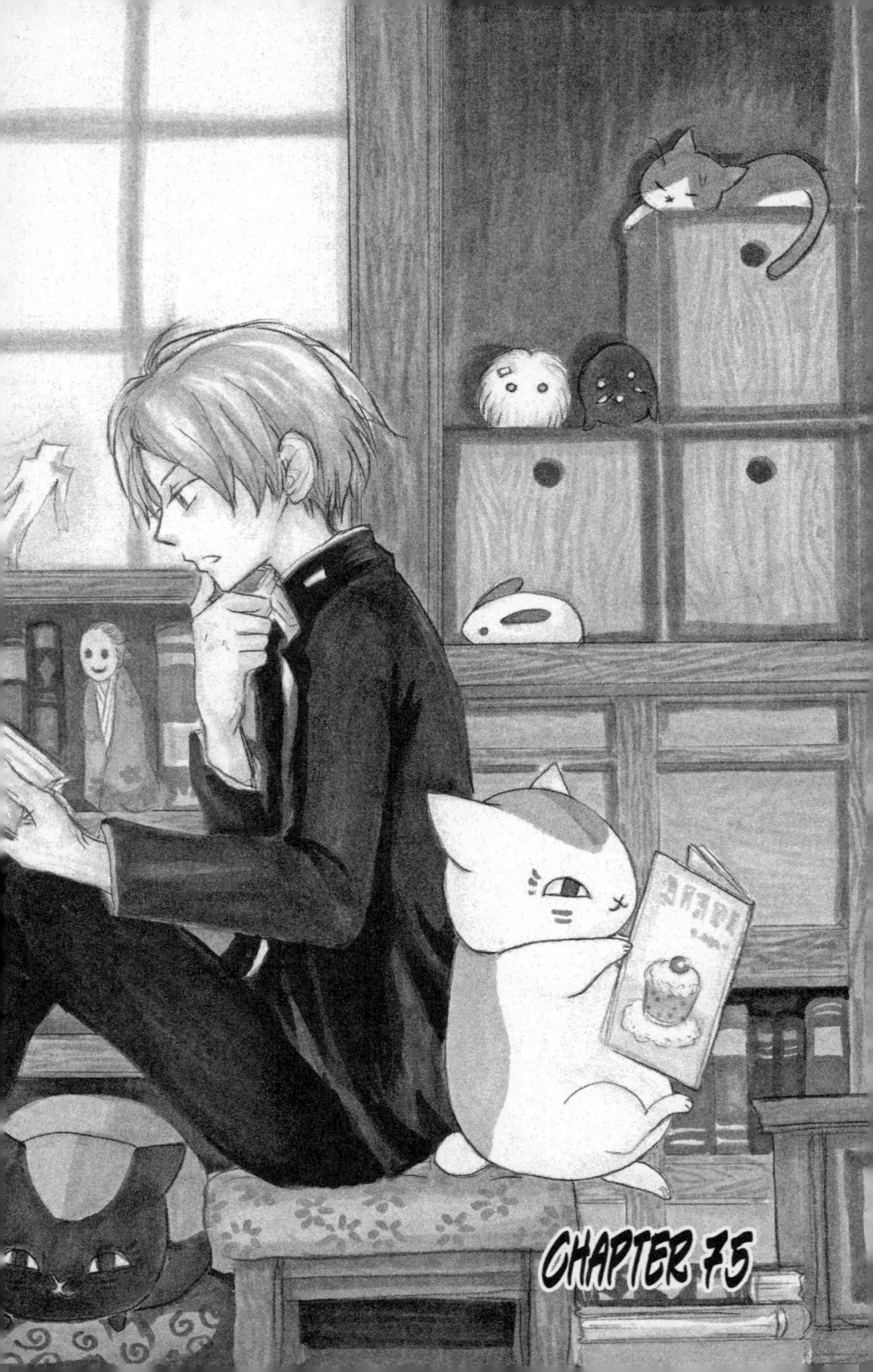
CHAPTER 75

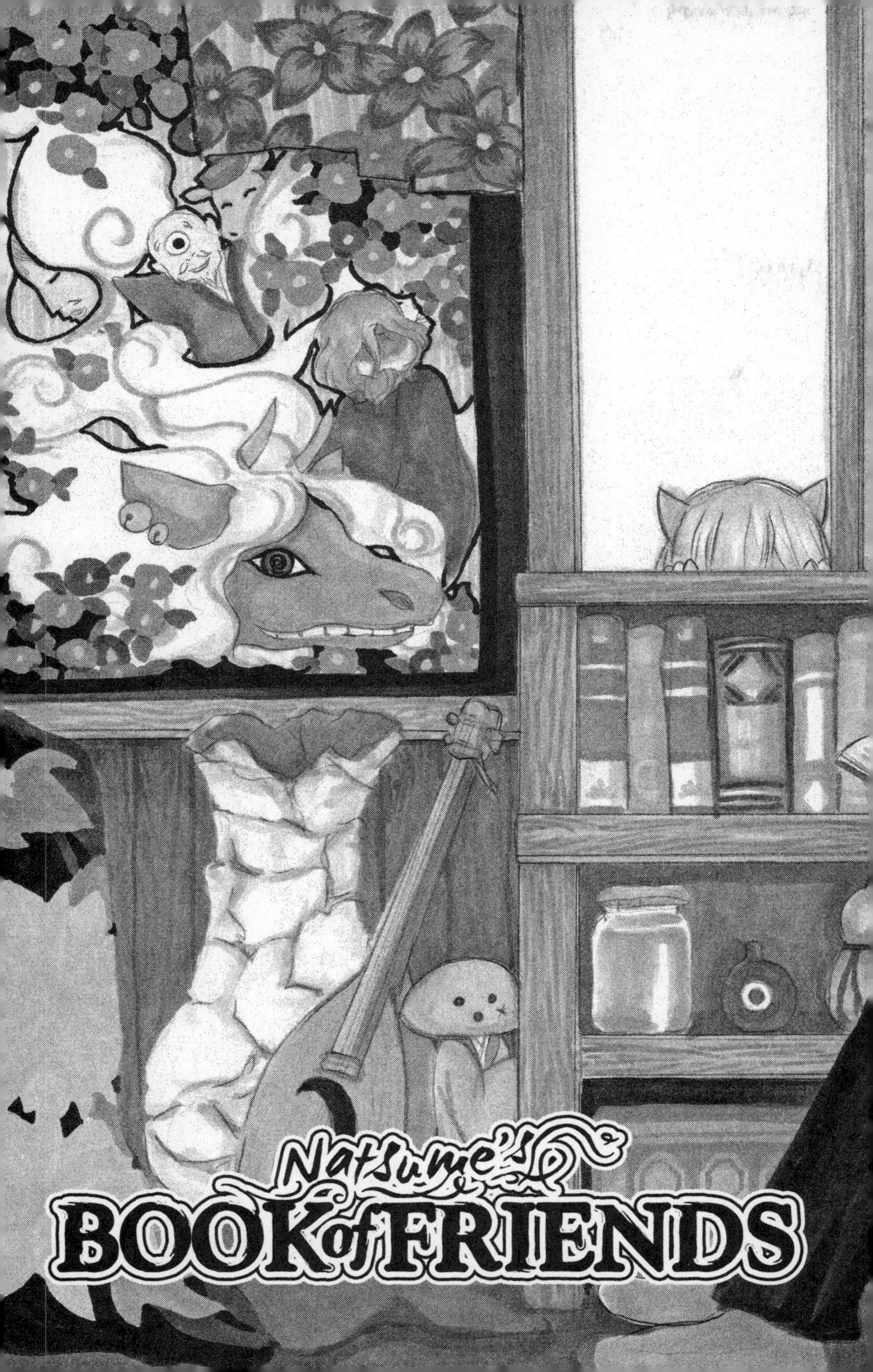
Natsume's
BOOK of FRIENDS

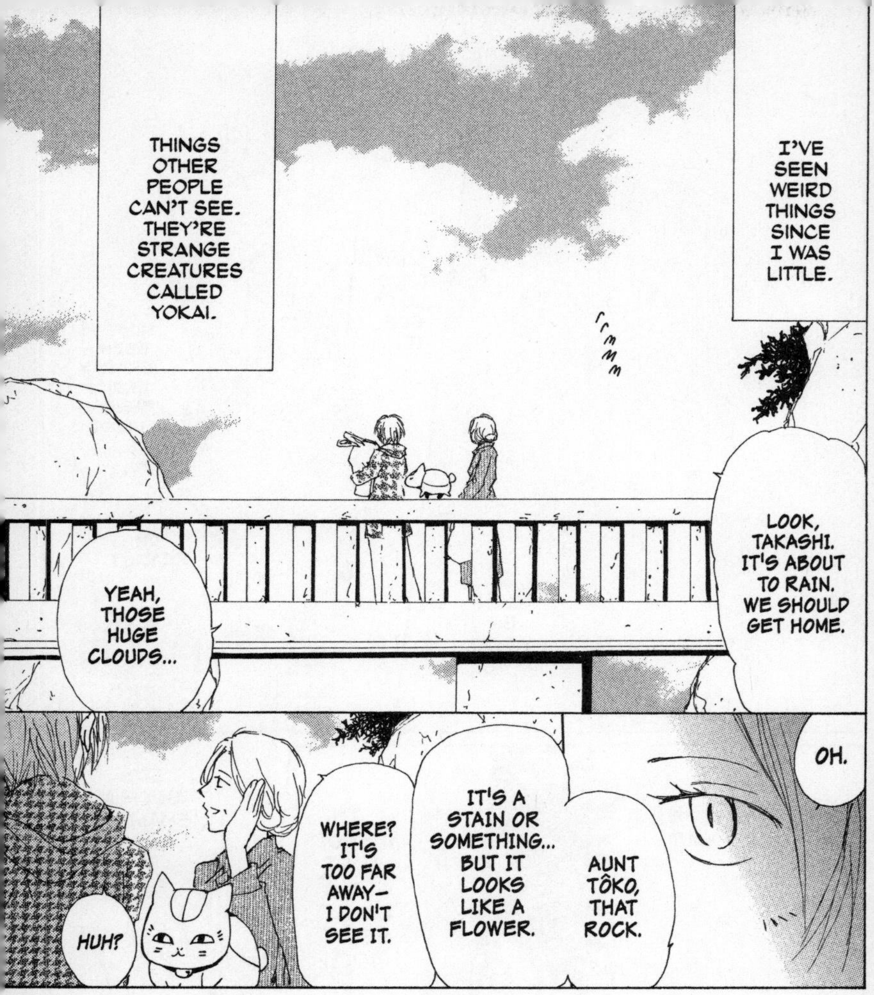
I'VE SEEN WEIRD THINGS SINCE I WAS LITTLE.
THINGS OTHER PEOPLE CAN'T SEE. THEY'RE STRANGE CREATURES CALLED YOKAI.
rrmmm
LOOK, TAKASHI. IT'S ABOUT TO RAIN. WE SHOULD GET HOME.
YEAH, THOSE HUGE CLOUDS...
OH.
AUNT TÔKO, THAT ROCK.
IT'S A STAIN OR SOMETHING... BUT IT LOOKS LIKE A FLOWER.
WHERE? IT'S TOO FAR AWAY— I DON'T SEE IT.
HUH?
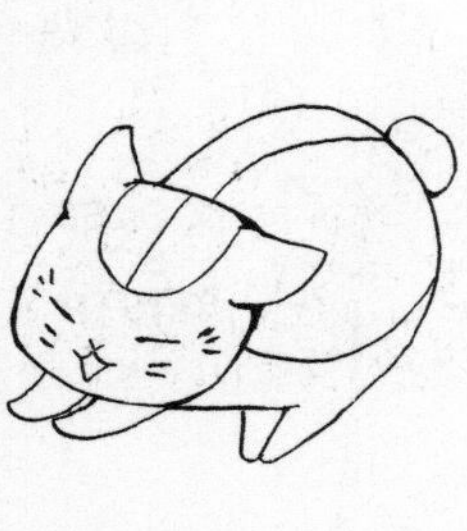

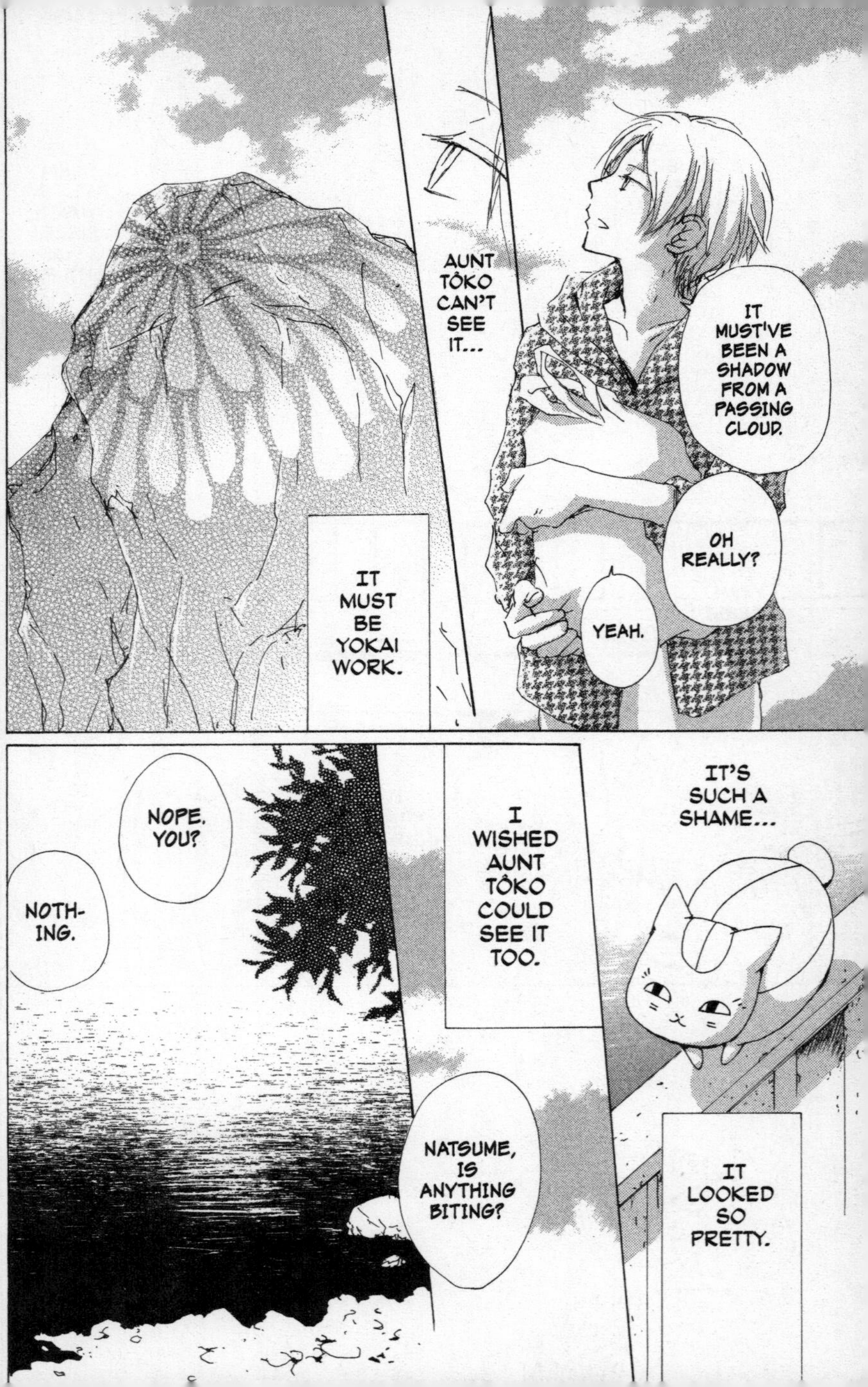
IT MUST'VE BEEN A SHADOW FROM A PASSING CLOUD.
OH REALLY?
YEAH.
AUNT TÔKO CAN'T SEE IT...
IT MUST BE YOKAI WORK.
IT'S SUCH A SHAME...
IT LOOKED SO PRETTY.
I WISHED AUNT TÔKO COULD SEE IT TOO.
NATSUME, IS ANYTHING BITING?
NOPE. YOU?
NOTH-ING.

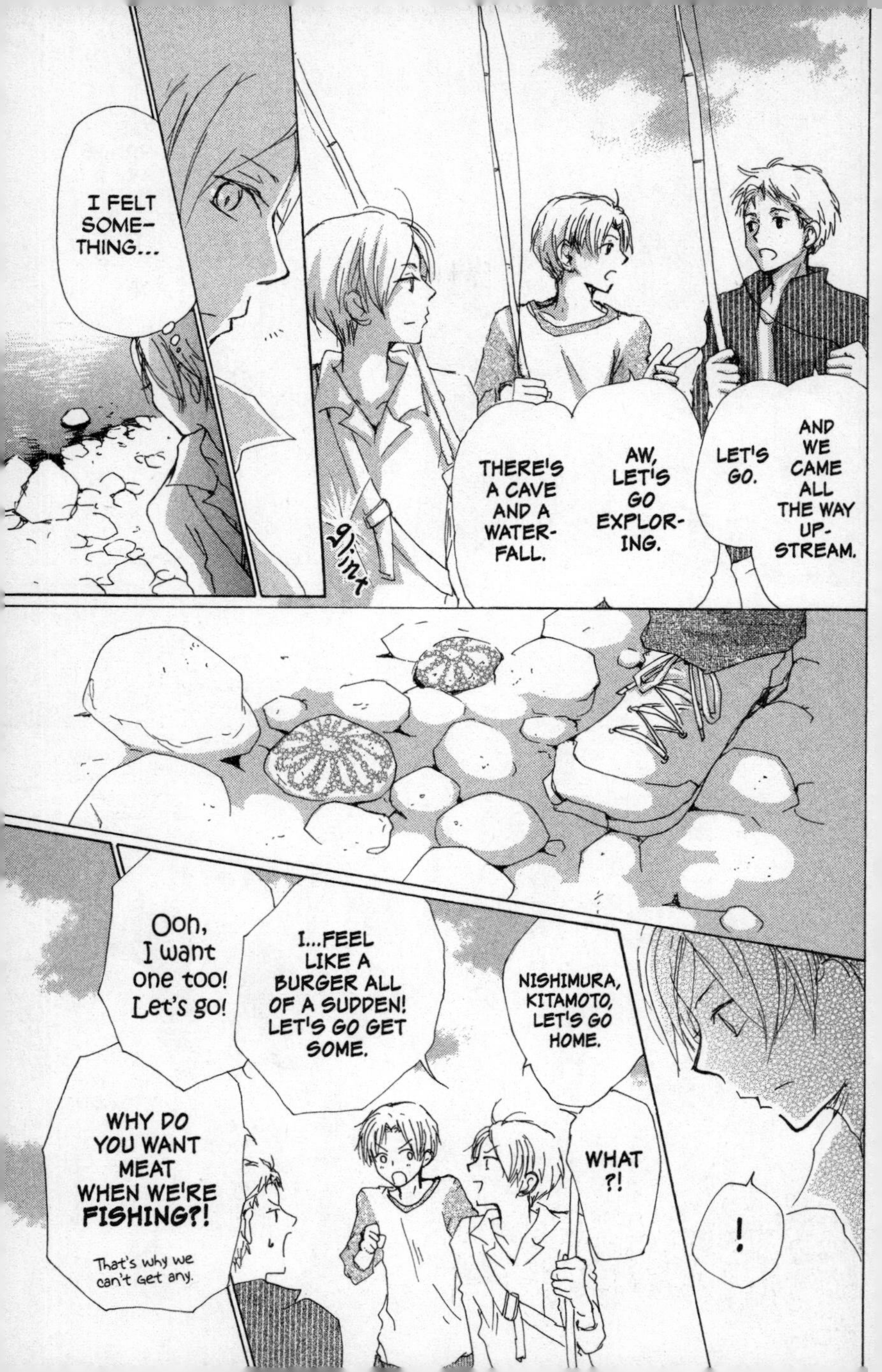
AND WE CAME ALL THE WAY UPSTREAM.
LET'S GO.
AW, LET'S GO EXPLORING.
THERE'S A CAVE AND A WATERFALL.
glint
I FELT SOMETHING...
!
NISHIMURA, KITAMOTO, LET'S GO HOME.
WHAT?!
I...FEEL LIKE A BURGER ALL OF A SUDDEN! LET'S GO GET SOME.
Ooh, I want one too! Let's go!
WHY DO YOU WANT MEAT WHEN WE'RE **FISHING?!**
That's why we can't get any.

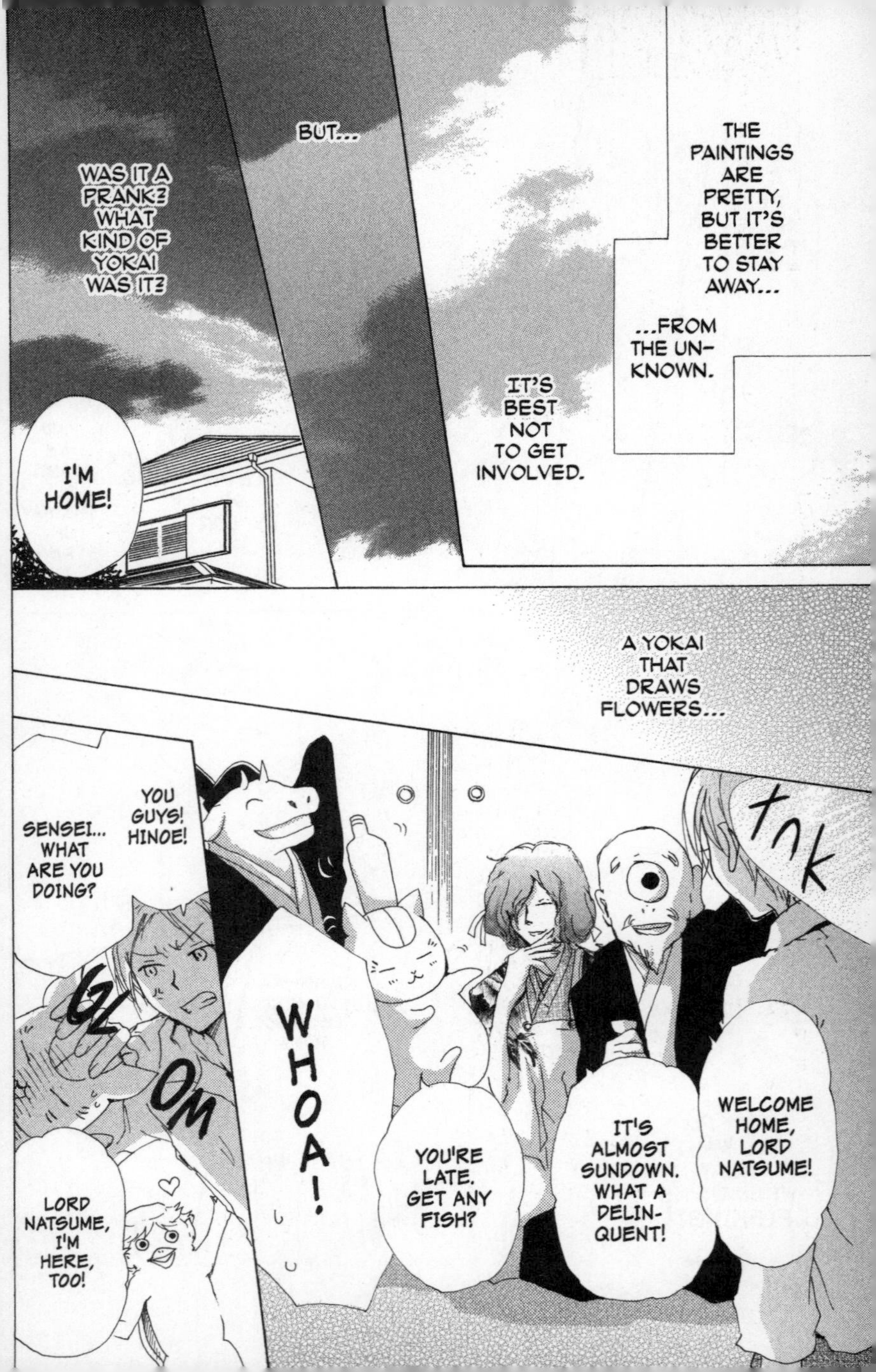
THE PAINTINGS ARE PRETTY, BUT IT'S BETTER TO STAY AWAY...
...FROM THE UN-KNOWN.
IT'S BEST NOT TO GET INVOLVED.
BUT...
WAS IT A PRANK? WHAT KIND OF YOKAI WAS IT?
I'M HOME!
A YOKAI THAT DRAWS FLOWERS...
TNK
WELCOME HOME, LORD NATSUME!
IT'S ALMOST SUNDOWN. WHAT A DELIN-QUENT!
YOU'RE LATE. GET ANY FISH?
WHOA!
YOU GUYS! HINOE!
SENSEI... WHAT ARE YOU DOING?
GLOOM
LORD NATSUME, I'M HERE, TOO!

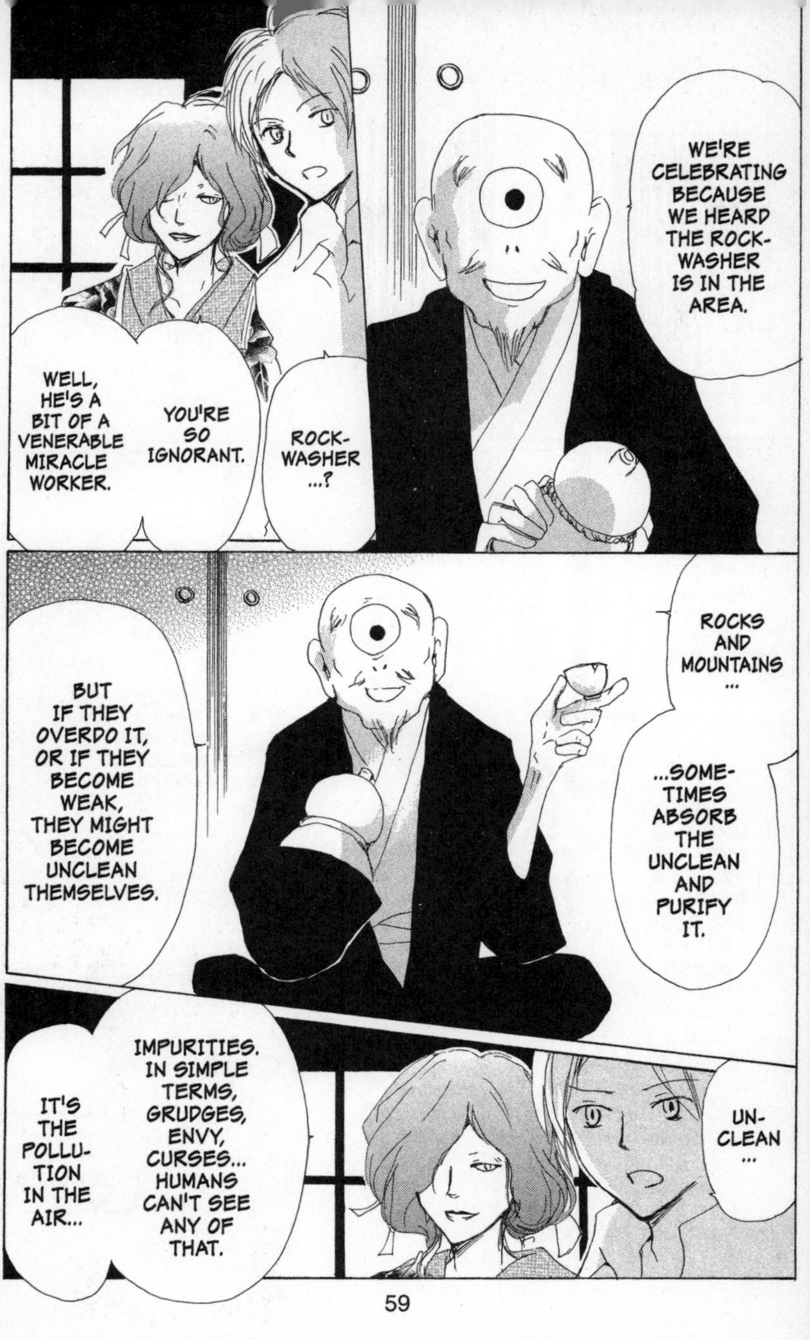
WE'RE CELEBRATING BECAUSE WE HEARD THE ROCK-WASHER IS IN THE AREA.
ROCK-WASHER ...?
YOU'RE SO IGNORANT.
WELL, HE'S A BIT OF A VENERABLE MIRACLE WORKER.
ROCKS AND MOUNTAINS ...
...SOME-TIMES ABSORB THE UNCLEAN AND PURIFY IT.
BUT IF THEY OVERDO IT, OR IF THEY BECOME WEAK, THEY MIGHT BECOME UNCLEAN THEMSELVES.
UN-CLEAN ...
IMPURITIES. IN SIMPLE TERMS, GRUDGES, ENVY, CURSES... HUMANS CAN'T SEE ANY OF THAT.
IT'S THE POLLU-TION IN THE AIR...

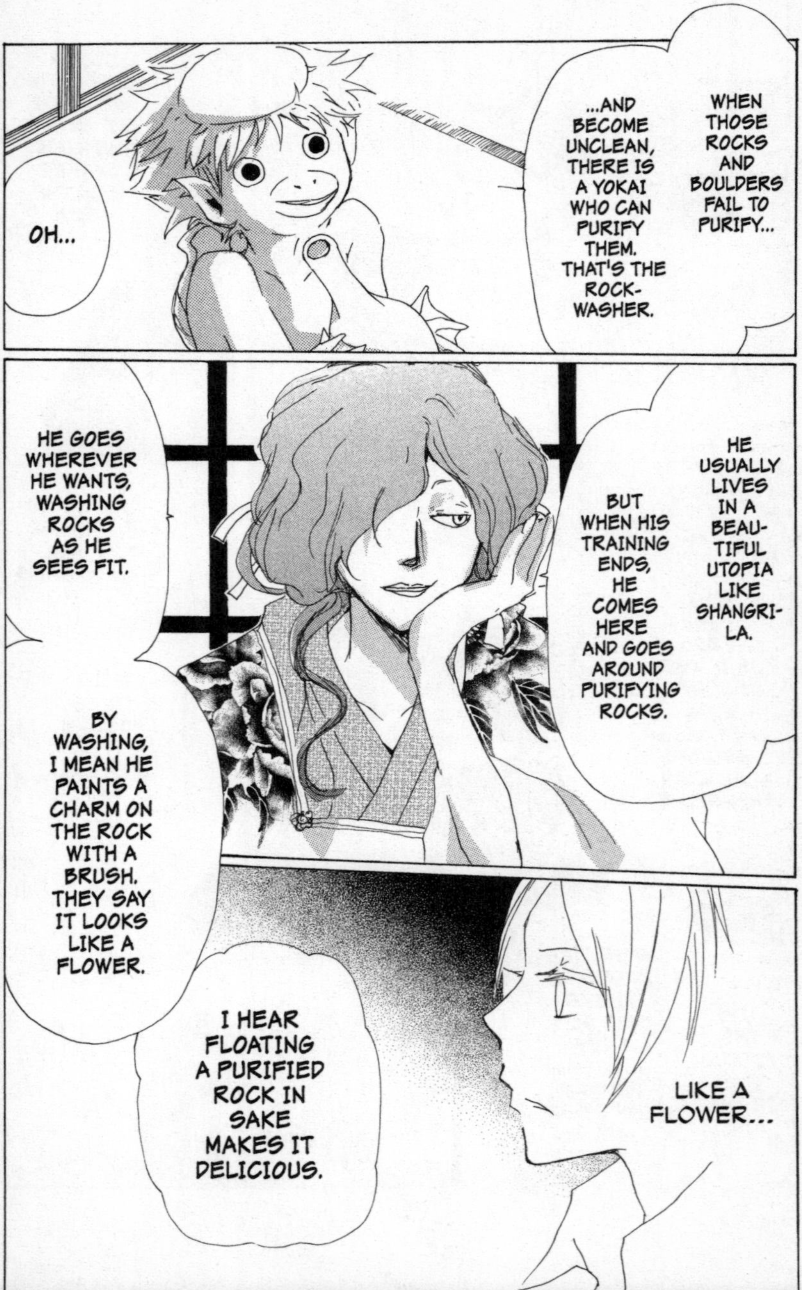
WHEN THOSE ROCKS AND BOULDERS FAIL TO PURIFY...
...AND BECOME UNCLEAN, THERE IS A YOKAI WHO CAN PURIFY THEM. THAT'S THE ROCK-WASHER.
OH...
HE USUALLY LIVES IN A BEAUTIFUL UTOPIA LIKE SHANGRI-LA.
BUT WHEN HIS TRAINING ENDS, HE COMES HERE AND GOES AROUND PURIFYING ROCKS.
HE GOES WHEREVER HE WANTS, WASHING ROCKS AS HE SEES FIT.
BY WASHING, I MEAN HE PAINTS A CHARM ON THE ROCK WITH A BRUSH. THEY SAY IT LOOKS LIKE A FLOWER.
I HEAR FLOATING A PURIFIED ROCK IN SAKE MAKES IT DELICIOUS.
LIKE A FLOWER...

03

❋Sendai Gallery

I'm a little late in reporting it, but the gallery show they held in Sendai to commemorate Natsume's tenth anniversary is now over. Thank you so much to everyone who helped out and to all who visited.

It was a little embarrassing for me to see the illustrations and pages on which I spent so much time worrying over the colors. It's hard to express it, but when they put the art up, it felt exciting, like being able to get close to the readers. The organizers made each exhibit hall a wonderful place, and I will cherish the memories for the rest of my life. I was immersed in happiness when I read the notes people had written in the guestbook for the occasion. It'll be a keepsake. Thank you so much.

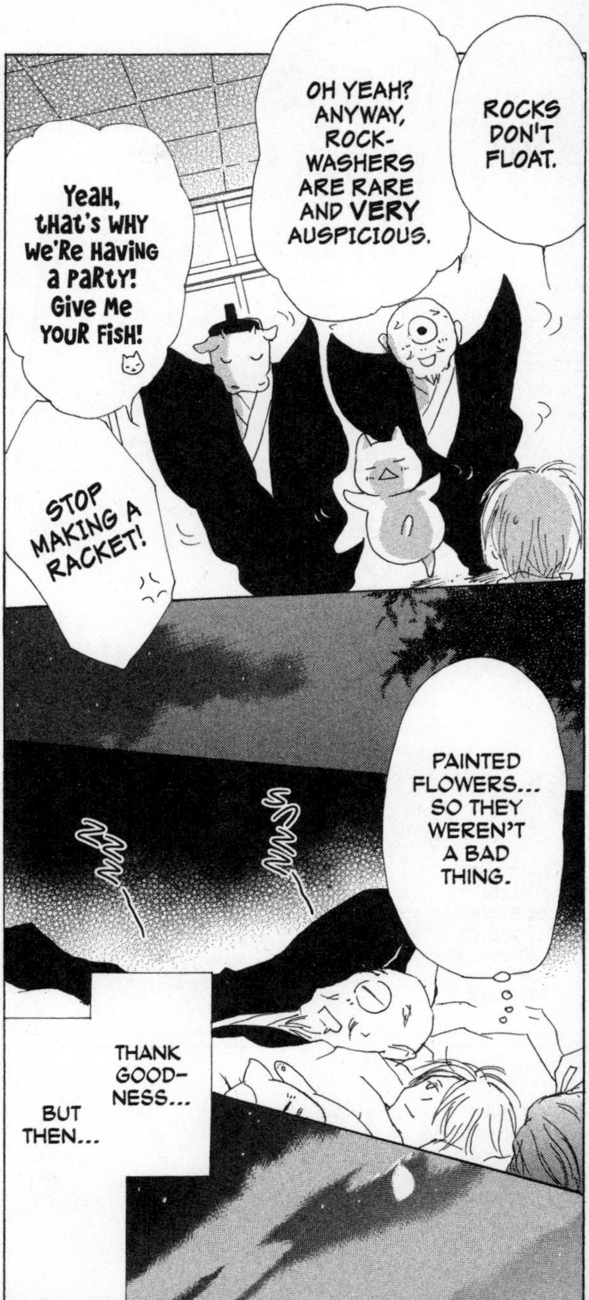
ROCKS DON'T FLOAT.
OH YEAH? ANYWAY, ROCK-WASHERS ARE RARE AND VERY AUSPICIOUS.
Yeah, that's WHY we're having a party! Give me your fish!
STOP MAKING A RACKET!
PAINTED FLOWERS... SO THEY WEREN'T A BAD THING.
THANK GOODNESS...
BUT THEN...

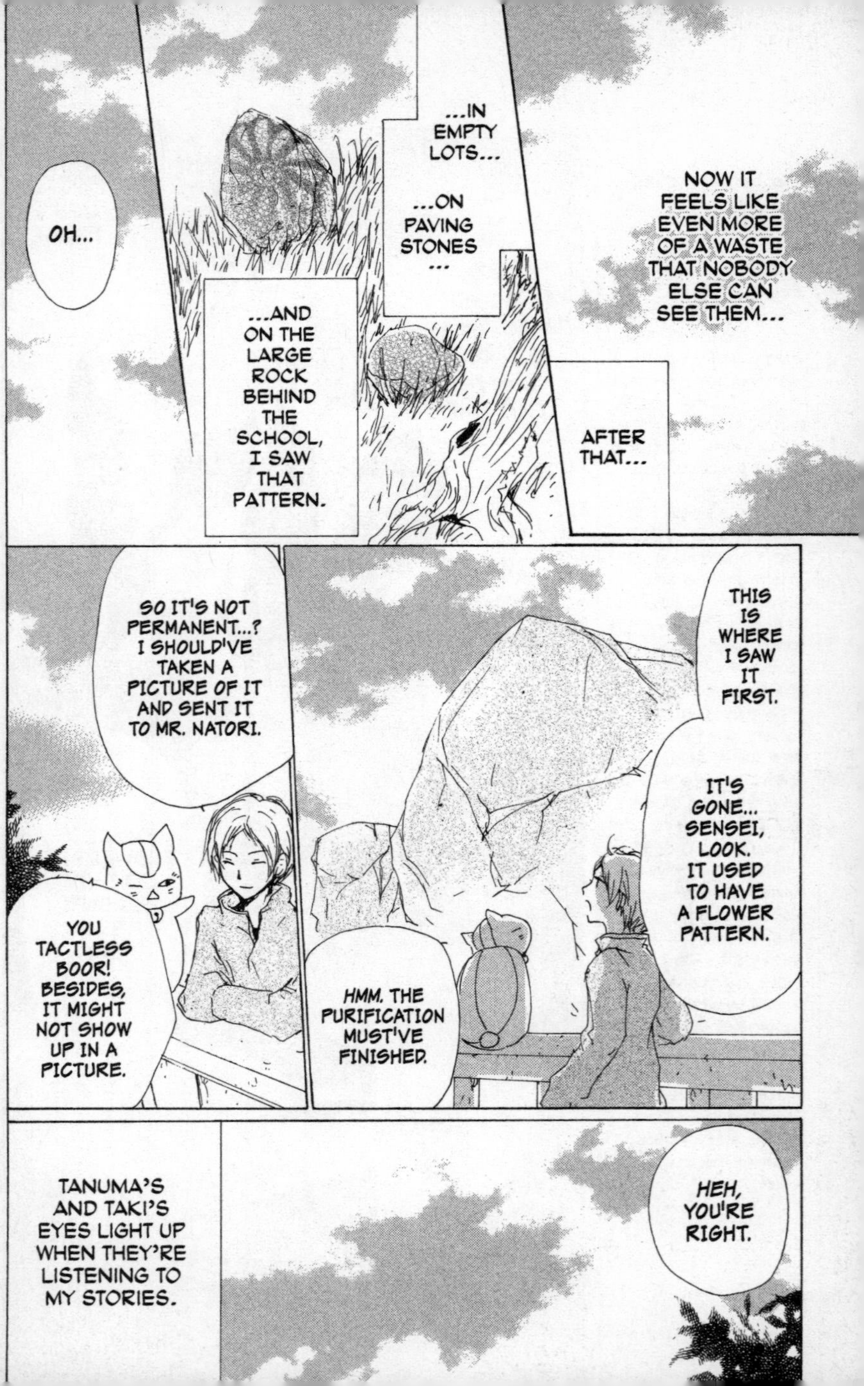
NOW IT FEELS LIKE EVEN MORE OF A WASTE THAT NOBODY ELSE CAN SEE THEM...
AFTER THAT...
...IN EMPTY LOTS...
...ON PAVING STONES...
...AND ON THE LARGE ROCK BEHIND THE SCHOOL, I SAW THAT PATTERN.
OH...
THIS IS WHERE I SAW IT FIRST.
IT'S GONE... SENSEI, LOOK. IT USED TO HAVE A FLOWER PATTERN.
HMM. THE PURIFICATION MUST'VE FINISHED.
SO IT'S NOT PERMANENT...? I SHOULD'VE TAKEN A PICTURE OF IT AND SENT IT TO MR. NATORI.
YOU TACTLESS BOOR! BESIDES, IT MIGHT NOT SHOW UP IN A PICTURE.
HEH, YOU'RE RIGHT.
TANUMA'S AND TAKI'S EYES LIGHT UP WHEN THEY'RE LISTENING TO MY STORIES.

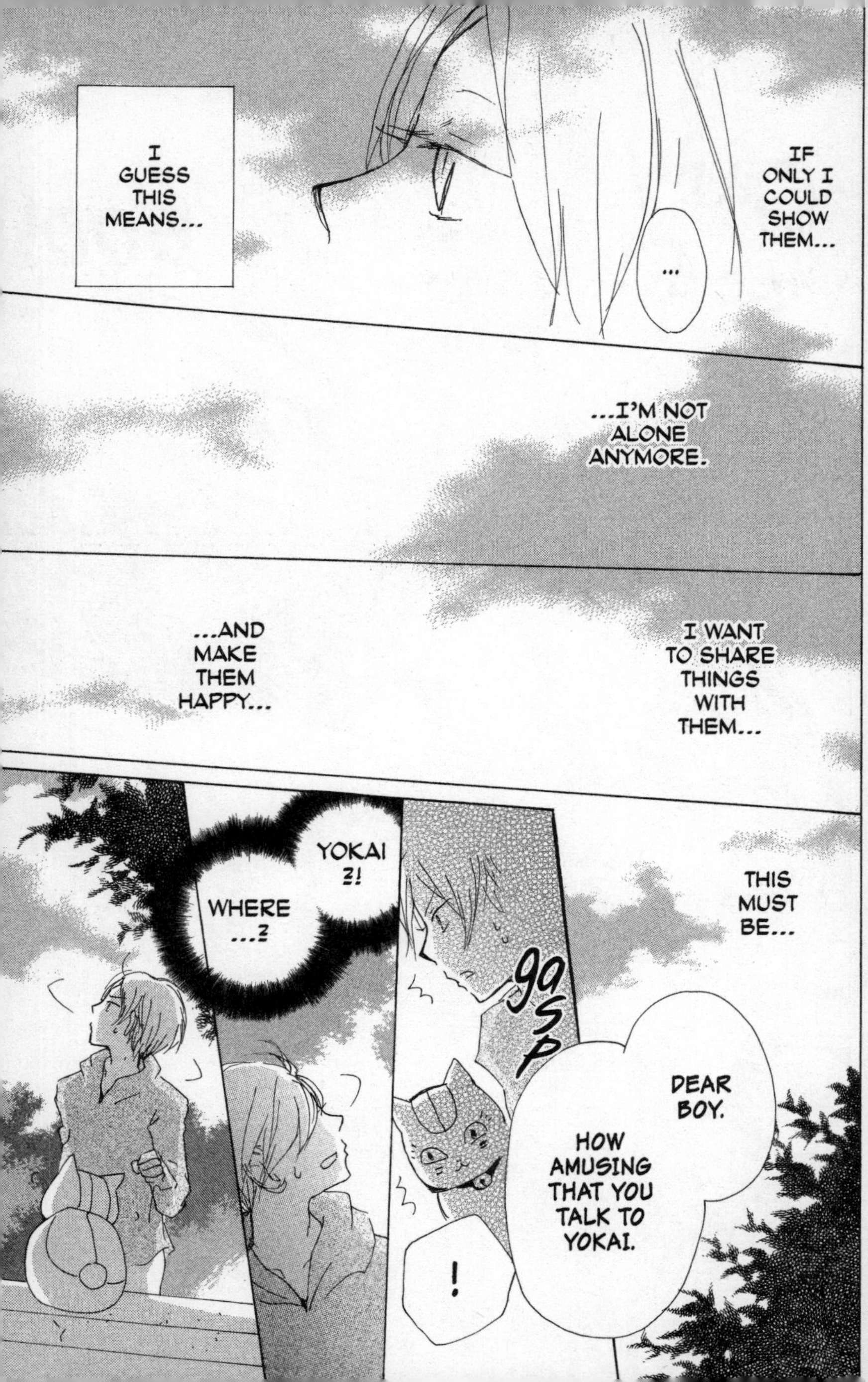
IF ONLY I COULD SHOW THEM...
...
I GUESS THIS MEANS...
...I'M NOT ALONE ANYMORE.
I WANT TO SHARE THINGS WITH THEM...
...AND MAKE THEM HAPPY...
THIS MUST BE...
gasp
DEAR BOY.
HOW AMUSING THAT YOU TALK TO YOKAI.
!
YOKAI?!
WHERE...?

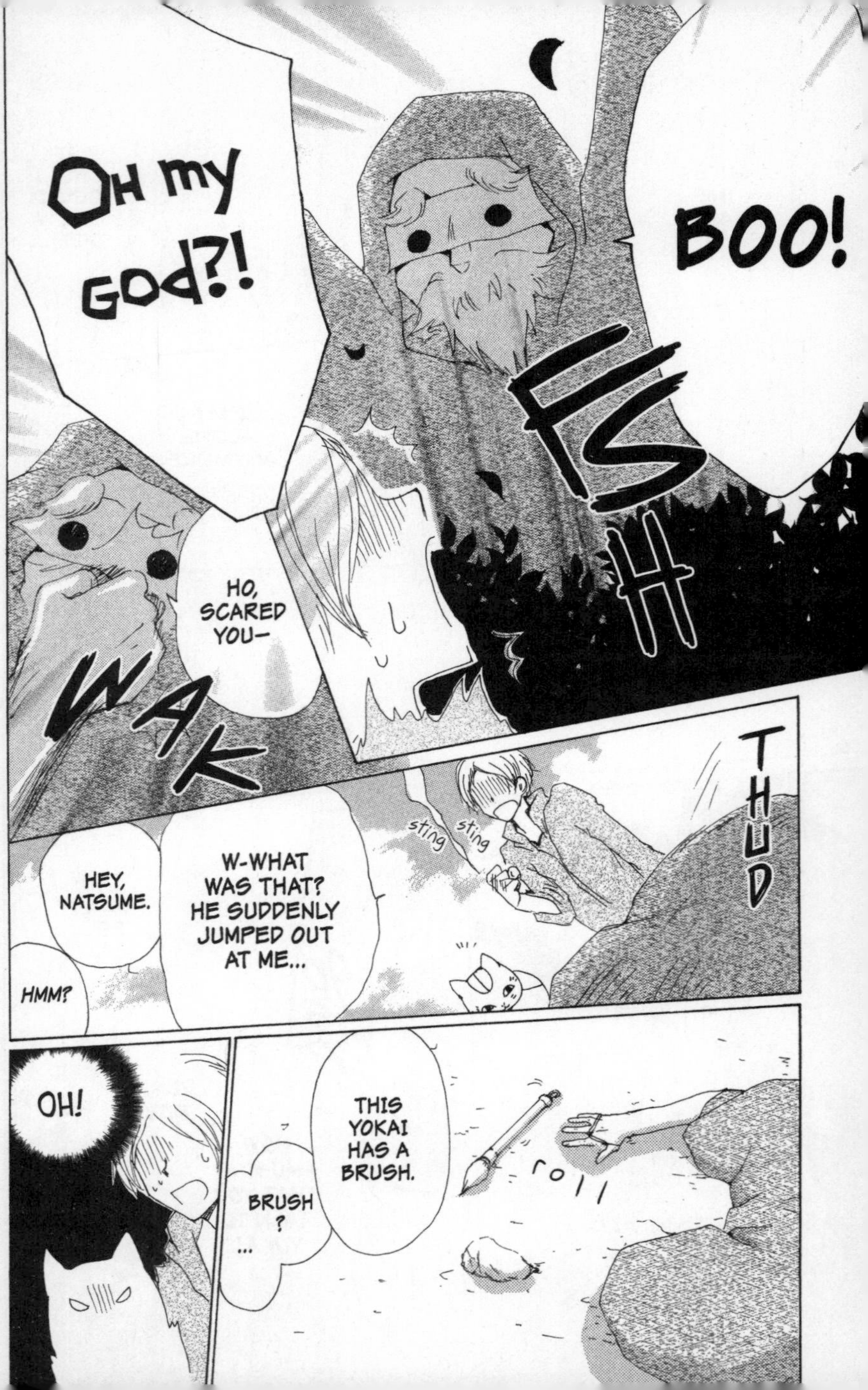
BOO!
OH my GOD?!
FSH
HO, SCARED YOU—
WAK
THUD
sting sting
W-WHAT WAS THAT? HE SUDDENLY JUMPED OUT AT ME...
HEY, NATSUME.
HMM?
roll
THIS YOKAI HAS A BRUSH.
BRUSH?
...
OH!

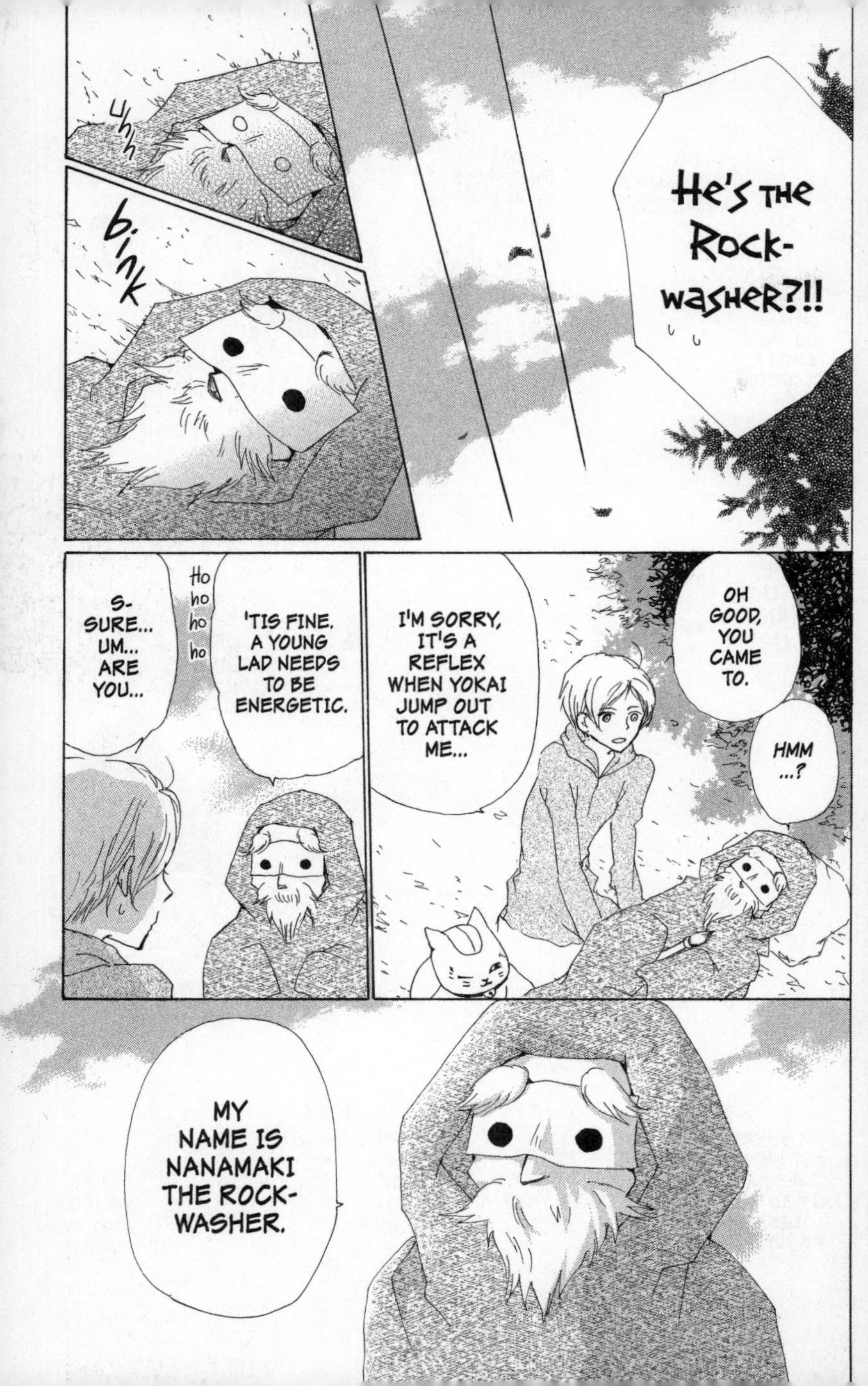
He's the Rock-washer?!!
uhh
bink
OH GOOD, YOU CAME TO.
HMM ...?
I'M SORRY, IT'S A REFLEX WHEN YOKAI JUMP OUT TO ATTACK ME...
'TIS FINE. A YOUNG LAD NEEDS TO BE ENERGETIC.
Ho ho ho ho
S-SURE... UM... ARE YOU...
MY NAME IS NANAMAKI THE ROCK-WASHER.

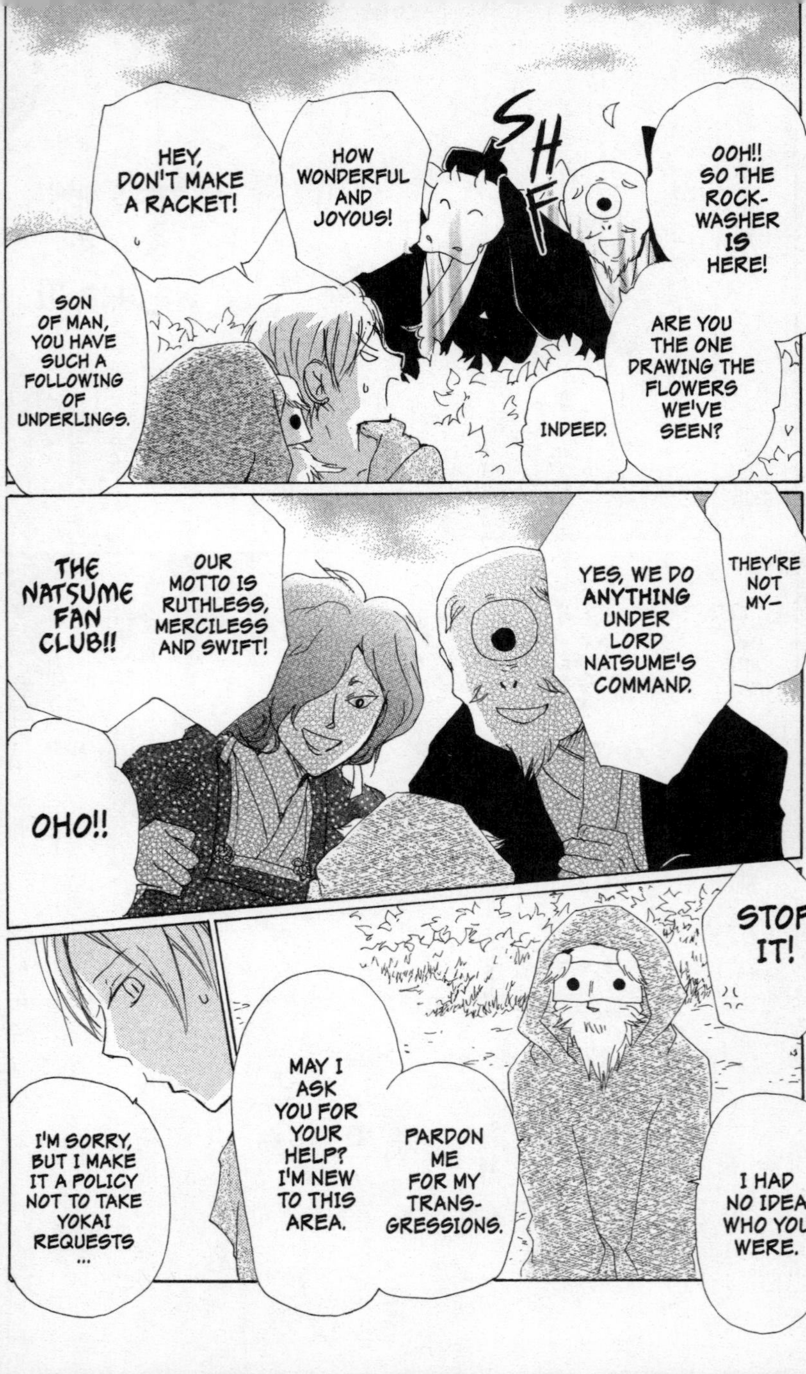
OOH!! SO THE ROCK-WASHER IS HERE!
SHF
HOW WONDERFUL AND JOYOUS!
HEY, DON'T MAKE A RACKET!
ARE YOU THE ONE DRAWING THE FLOWERS WE'VE SEEN?
INDEED.
SON OF MAN, YOU HAVE SUCH A FOLLOWING OF UNDERLINGS.
THEY'RE NOT MY—
YES, WE DO ANYTHING UNDER LORD NATSUME'S COMMAND.
OUR MOTTO IS RUTHLESS, MERCILESS AND SWIFT!
THE NATSUME FAN CLUB!!
OHO!!
STOP IT!
I HAD NO IDEA WHO YOU WERE.
PARDON ME FOR MY TRANSGRESSIONS.
MAY I ASK YOU FOR YOUR HELP? I'M NEW TO THIS AREA.
I'M SORRY, BUT I MAKE IT A POLICY NOT TO TAKE YOKAI REQUESTS ...

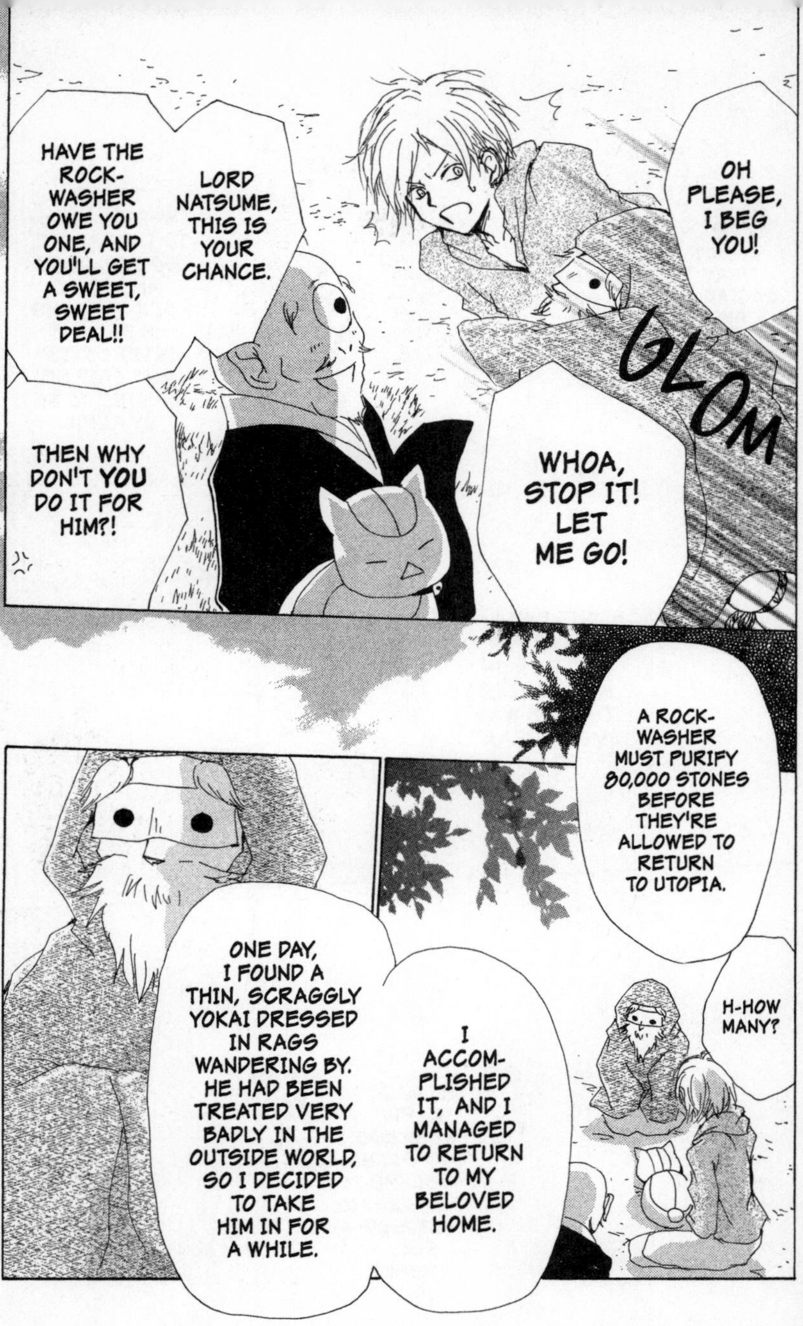
OH PLEASE, I BEG YOU!
GLOM
WHOA, STOP IT! LET ME GO!
LORD NATSUME, THIS IS YOUR CHANCE.
HAVE THE ROCK-WASHER OWE YOU ONE, AND YOU'LL GET A SWEET, SWEET DEAL!!
THEN WHY DON'T YOU DO IT FOR HIM?!
A ROCK-WASHER MUST PURIFY 80,000 STONES BEFORE THEY'RE ALLOWED TO RETURN TO UTOPIA.
H-HOW MANY?
I ACCOMPLISHED IT, AND I MANAGED TO RETURN TO MY BELOVED HOME.
ONE DAY, I FOUND A THIN, SCRAGGLY YOKAI DRESSED IN RAGS WANDERING BY. HE HAD BEEN TREATED VERY BADLY IN THE OUTSIDE WORLD, SO I DECIDED TO TAKE HIM IN FOR A WHILE.

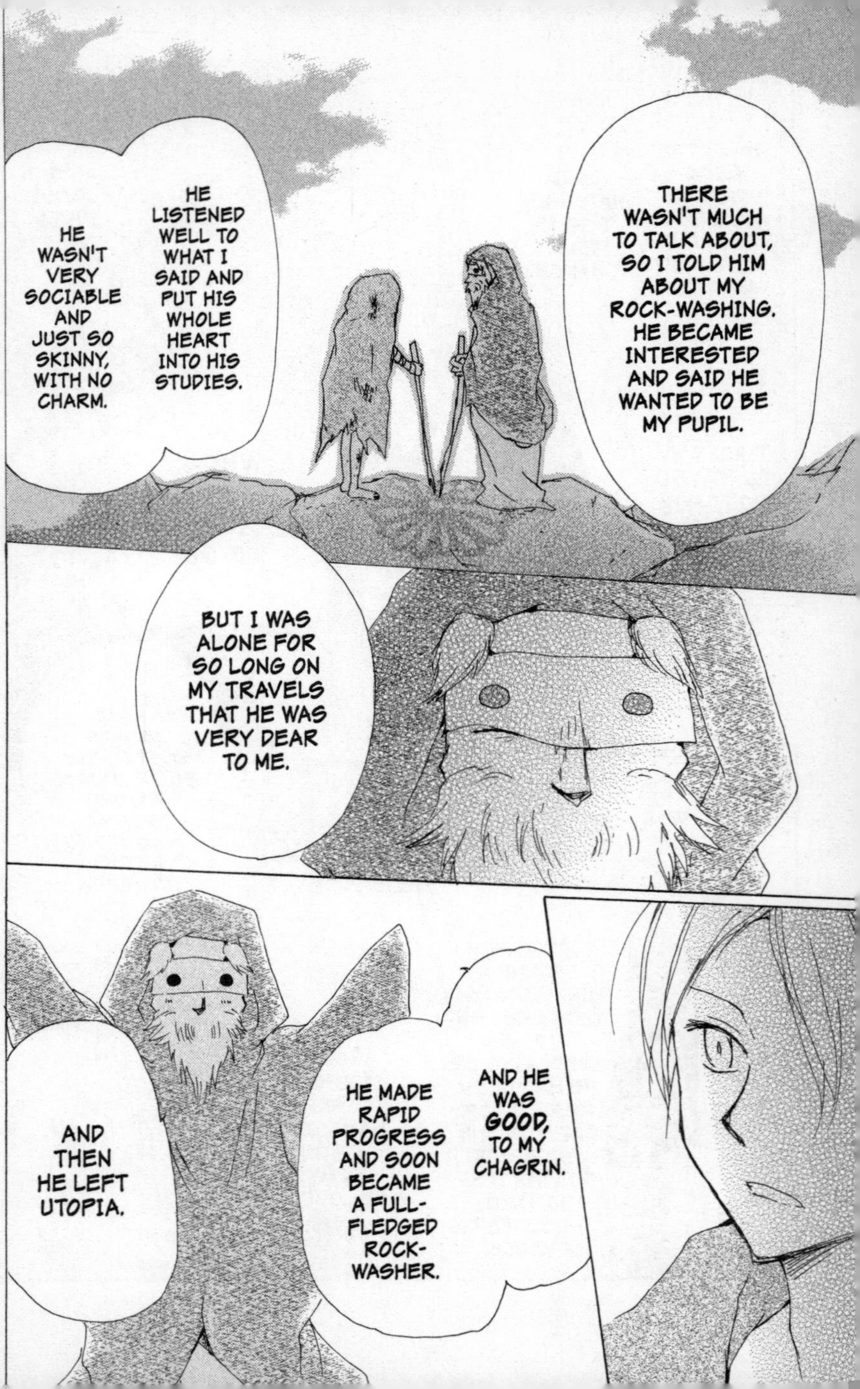
THERE WASN'T MUCH TO TALK ABOUT, SO I TOLD HIM ABOUT MY ROCK-WASHING. HE BECAME INTERESTED AND SAID HE WANTED TO BE MY PUPIL.
HE LISTENED WELL TO WHAT I SAID AND PUT HIS WHOLE HEART INTO HIS STUDIES.
HE WASN'T VERY SOCIABLE AND JUST SO SKINNY, WITH NO CHARM.
BUT I WAS ALONE FOR SO LONG ON MY TRAVELS THAT HE WAS VERY DEAR TO ME.
AND HE WAS GOOD, TO MY CHAGRIN.
HE MADE RAPID PROGRESS AND SOON BECAME A FULL-FLEDGED ROCK-WASHER.
AND THEN HE LEFT UTOPIA.

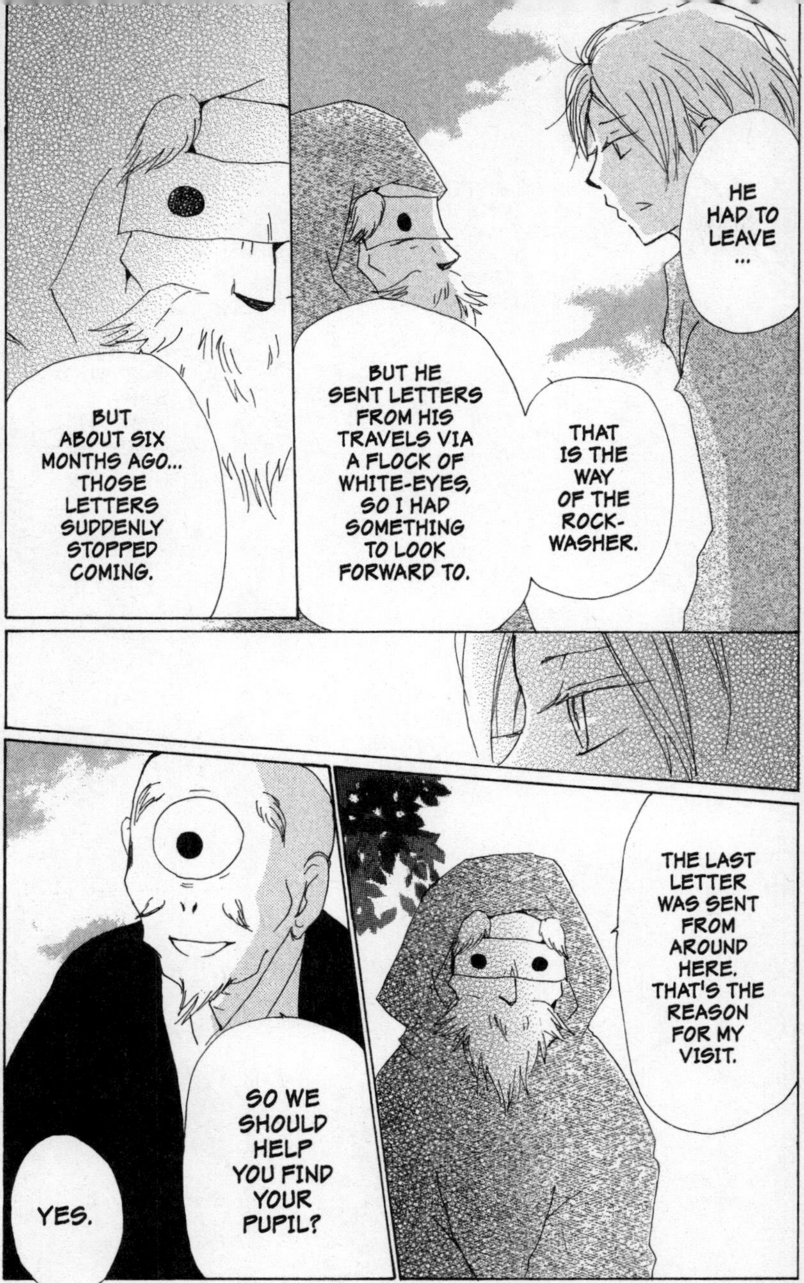
HE HAD TO LEAVE ...
THAT IS THE WAY OF THE ROCK-WASHER.
BUT HE SENT LETTERS FROM HIS TRAVELS VIA A FLOCK OF WHITE-EYES, SO I HAD SOMETHING TO LOOK FORWARD TO.
BUT ABOUT SIX MONTHS AGO... THOSE LETTERS SUDDENLY STOPPED COMING.
THE LAST LETTER WAS SENT FROM AROUND HERE. THAT'S THE REASON FOR MY VISIT.
SO WE SHOULD HELP YOU FIND YOUR PUPIL?
YES.

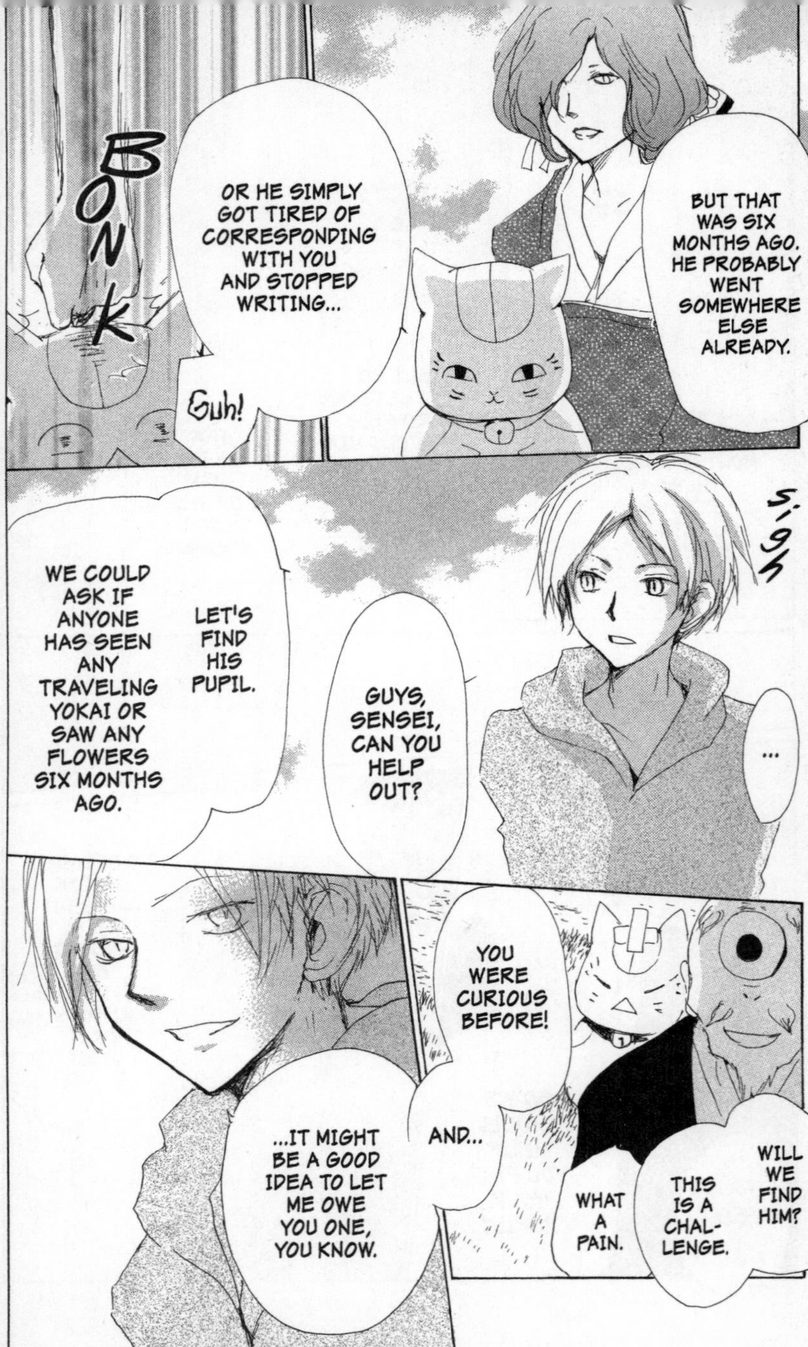
BUT THAT WAS SIX MONTHS AGO. HE PROBABLY WENT SOMEWHERE ELSE ALREADY.
OR HE SIMPLY GOT TIRED OF CORRESPONDING WITH YOU AND STOPPED WRITING...
Guh!
BONK
SIGH
...
GUYS, SENSEI, CAN YOU HELP OUT?
LET'S FIND HIS PUPIL.
WE COULD ASK IF ANYONE HAS SEEN ANY TRAVELING YOKAI OR SAW ANY FLOWERS SIX MONTHS AGO.
YOU WERE CURIOUS BEFORE!
WILL WE FIND HIM?
THIS IS A CHAL-LENGE.
WHAT A PAIN.
AND...
...IT MIGHT BE A GOOD IDEA TO LET ME OWE YOU ONE, YOU KNOW.

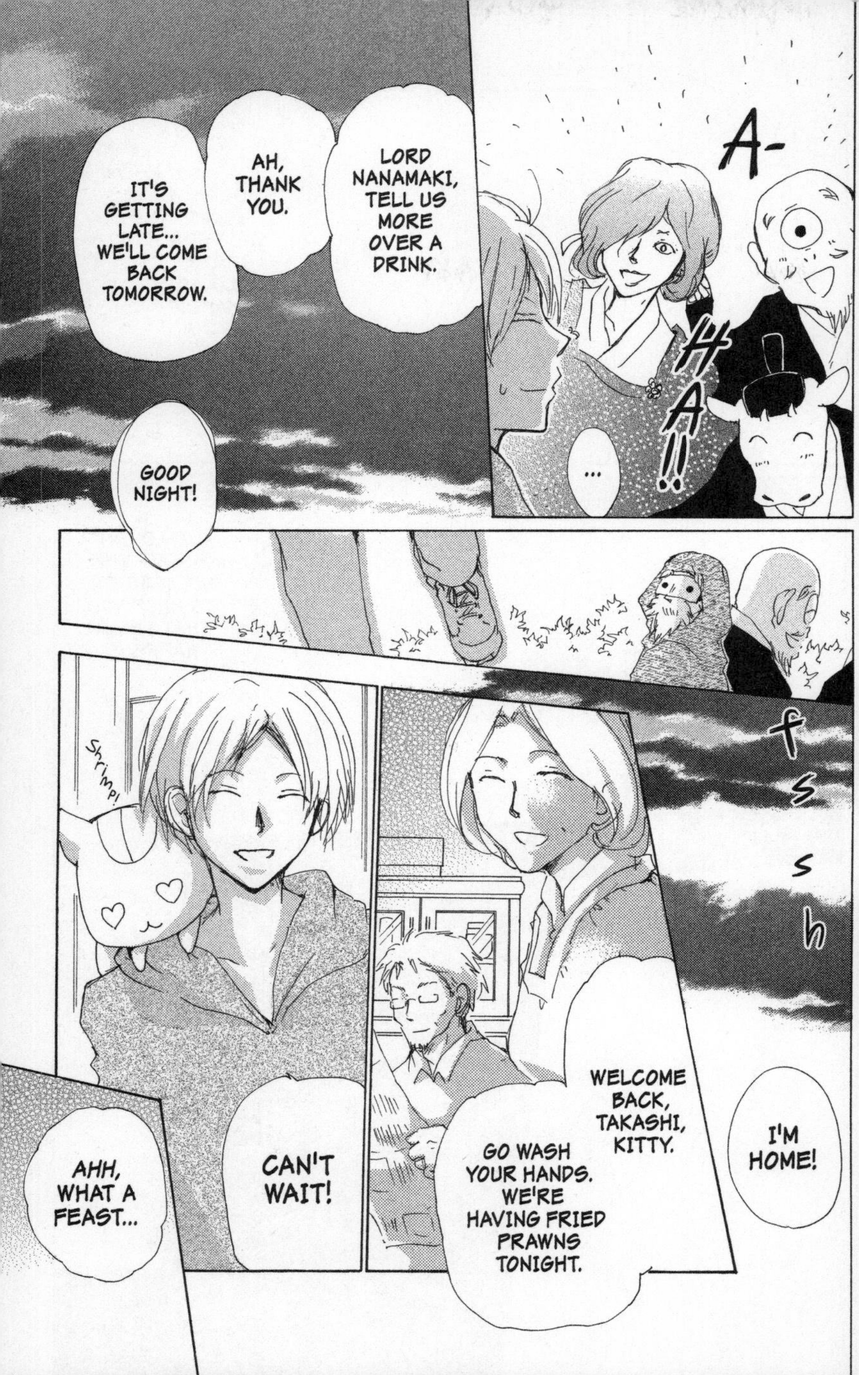
A-HA!!
...
LORD NANAMAKI, TELL US MORE OVER A DRINK.
AH, THANK YOU.
IT'S GETTING LATE... WE'LL COME BACK TOMORROW.
GOOD NIGHT!
fssh
I'M HOME!
WELCOME BACK, TAKASHI, KITTY.
GO WASH YOUR HANDS. WE'RE HAVING FRIED PRAWNS TONIGHT.
Shrimp!
CAN'T WAIT!
AHH, WHAT A FEAST...

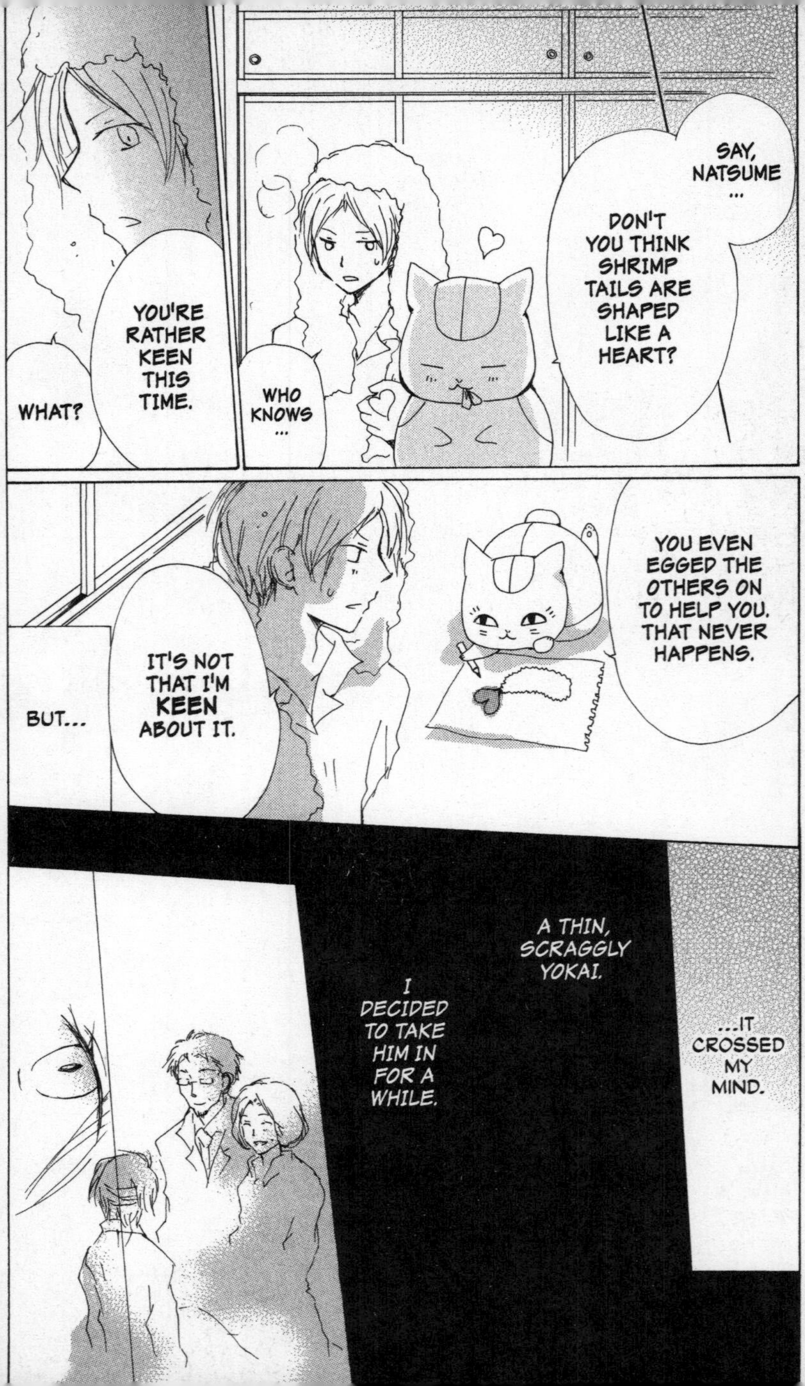
SAY, NATSUME...
DON'T YOU THINK SHRIMP TAILS ARE SHAPED LIKE A HEART?
WHO KNOWS...
YOU'RE RATHER KEEN THIS TIME.
WHAT?
YOU EVEN EGGED THE OTHERS ON TO HELP YOU. THAT NEVER HAPPENS.
IT'S NOT THAT I'M KEEN ABOUT IT.
BUT...
...IT CROSSED MY MIND.
A THIN, SCRAGGLY YOKAI.
I DECIDED TO TAKE HIM IN FOR A WHILE.

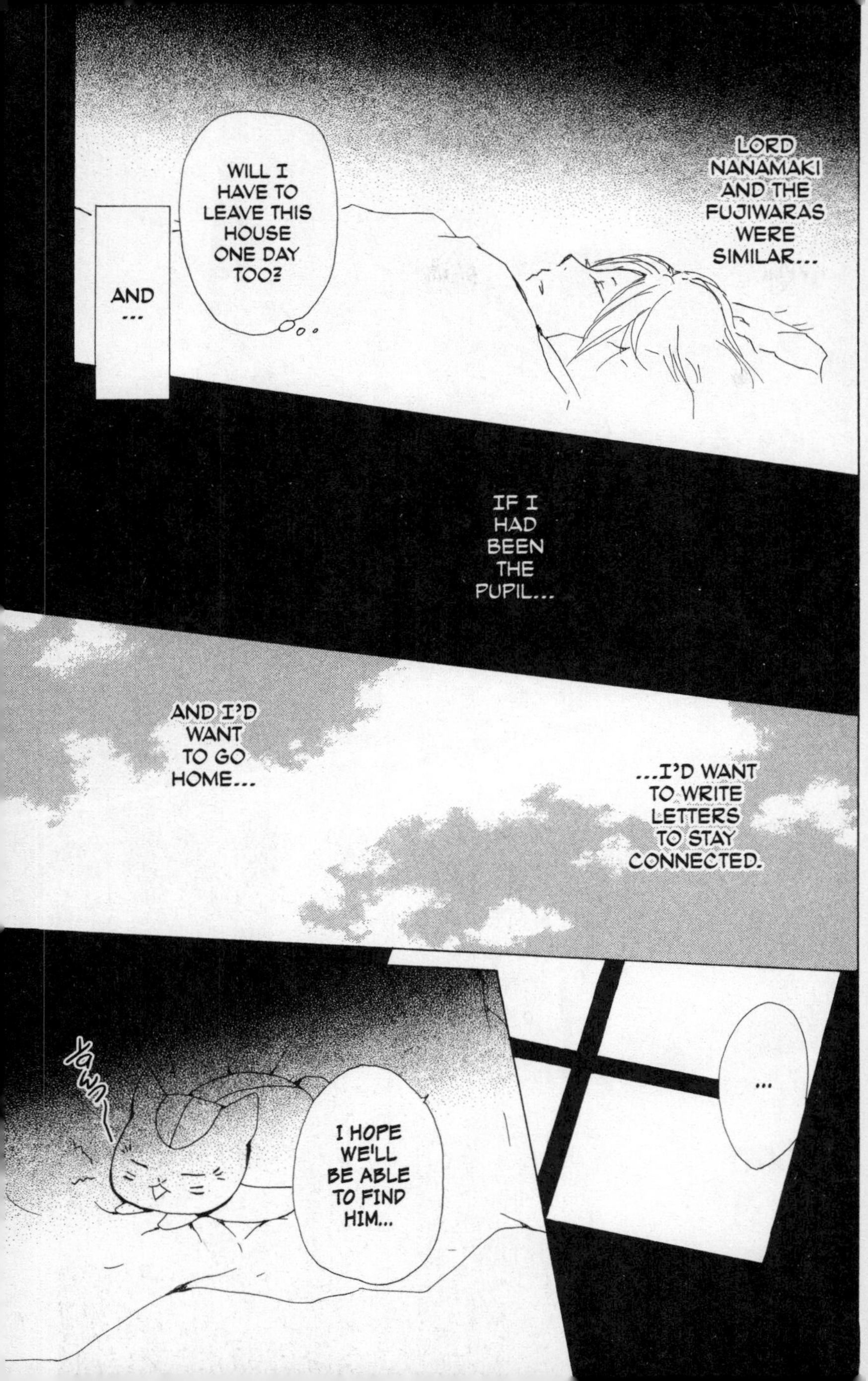
LORD NANAMAKI AND THE FUJIWARAS WERE SIMILAR...
WILL I HAVE TO LEAVE THIS HOUSE ONE DAY TOO?
AND ...
IF I HAD BEEN THE PUPIL...
...I'D WANT TO WRITE LETTERS TO STAY CONNECTED.
AND I'D WANT TO GO HOME...
...
I HOPE WE'LL BE ABLE TO FIND HIM...
Yawn~

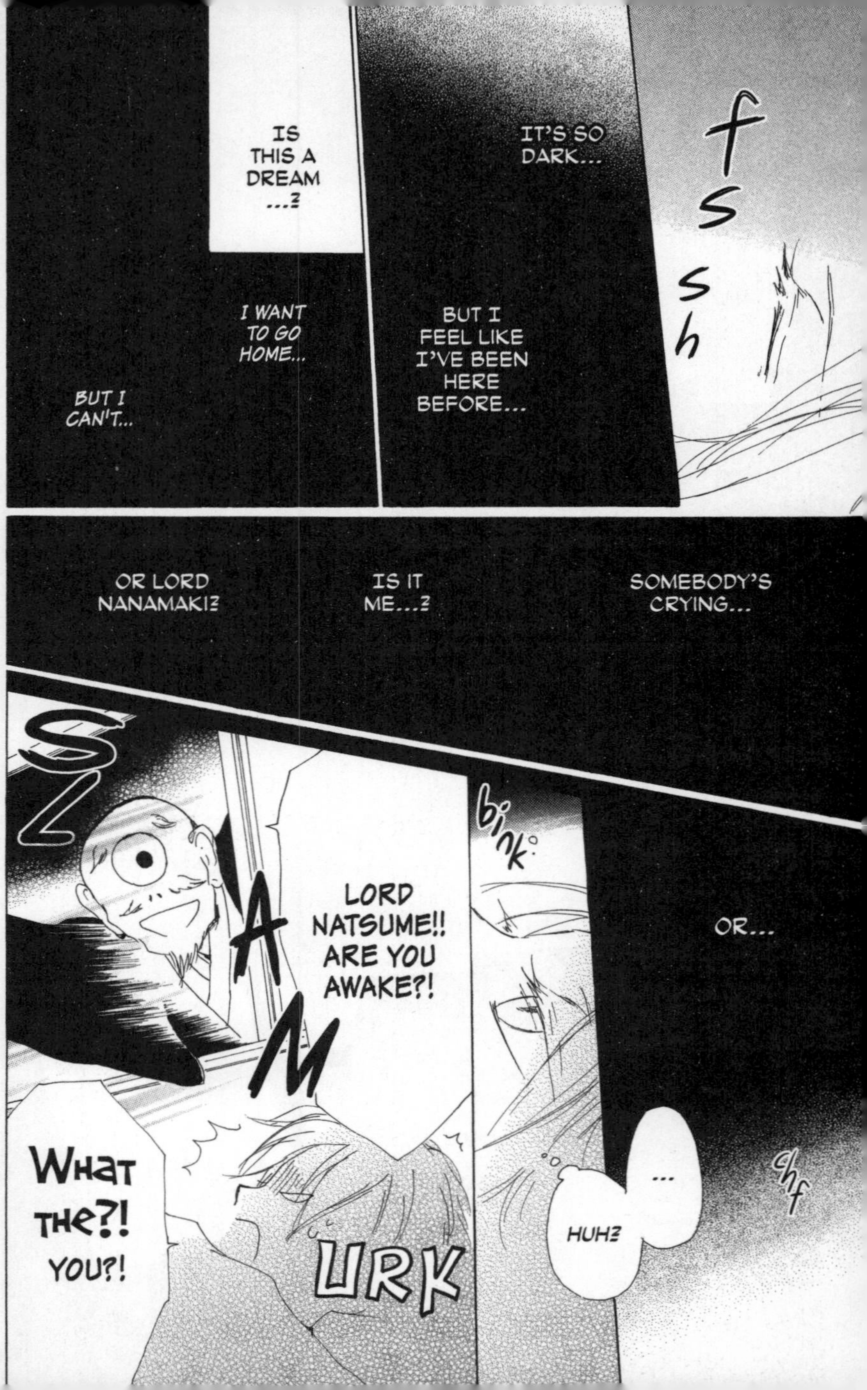
fssh
IT'S SO DARK...
BUT I FEEL LIKE I'VE BEEN HERE BEFORE...
IS THIS A DREAM...?
I WANT TO GO HOME...
BUT I CAN'T...
SOMEBODY'S CRYING...
IS IT ME...?
OR LORD NANAMAKI?
OR...
chf
blink
...
HUH?
SLAM
LORD NATSUME!! ARE YOU AWAKE?!
URK
WHAT THE?! YOU?!

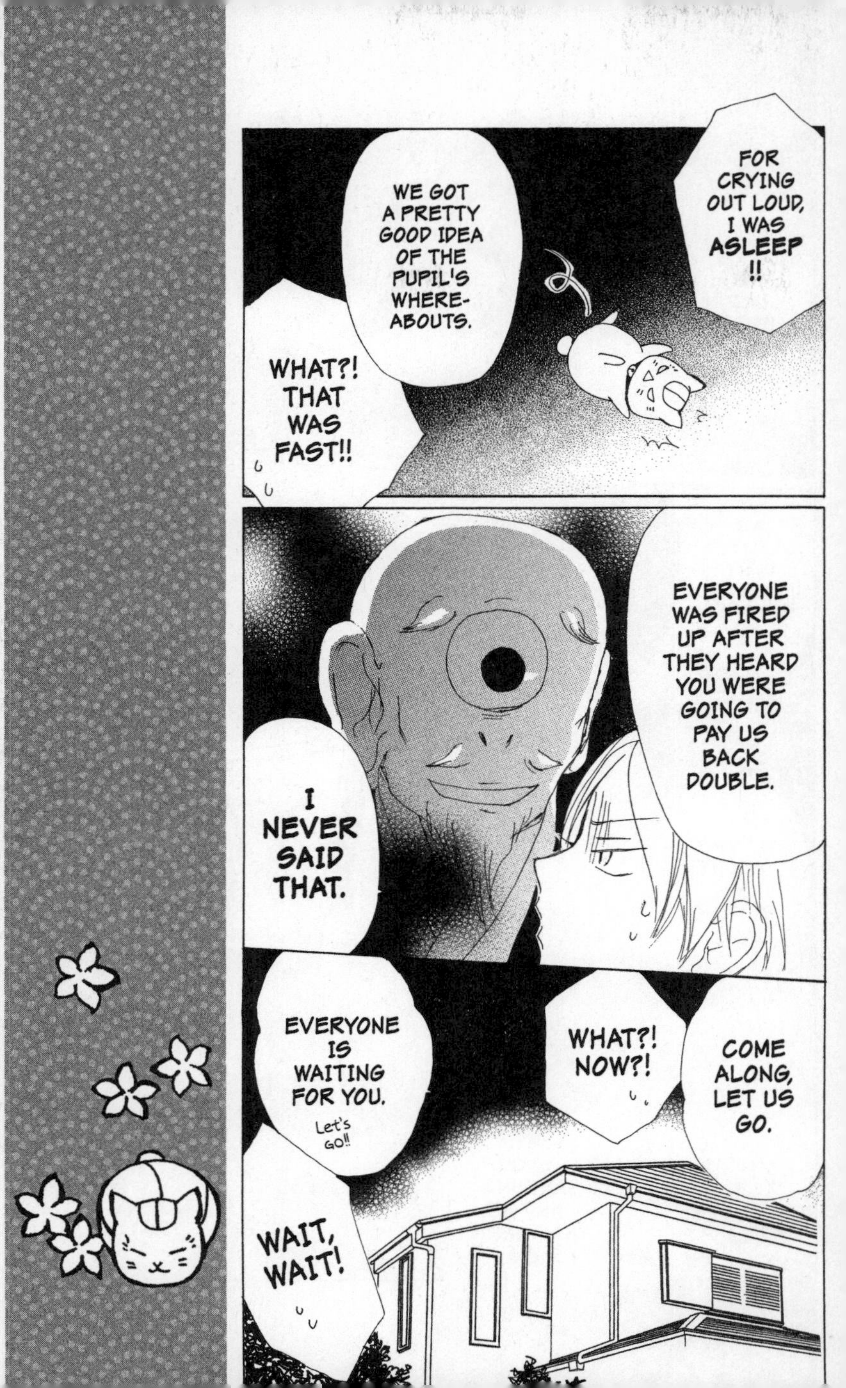
FOR CRYING OUT LOUD, I WAS ASLEEP!!
WE GOT A PRETTY GOOD IDEA OF THE PUPIL'S WHERE-ABOUTS.
WHAT?! THAT WAS FAST!!
EVERYONE WAS FIRED UP AFTER THEY HEARD YOU WERE GOING TO PAY US BACK DOUBLE.
I NEVER SAID THAT.
COME ALONG, LET US GO.
WHAT?! NOW?!
EVERYONE IS WAITING FOR YOU.
Let's GO!!
WAIT, WAIT!

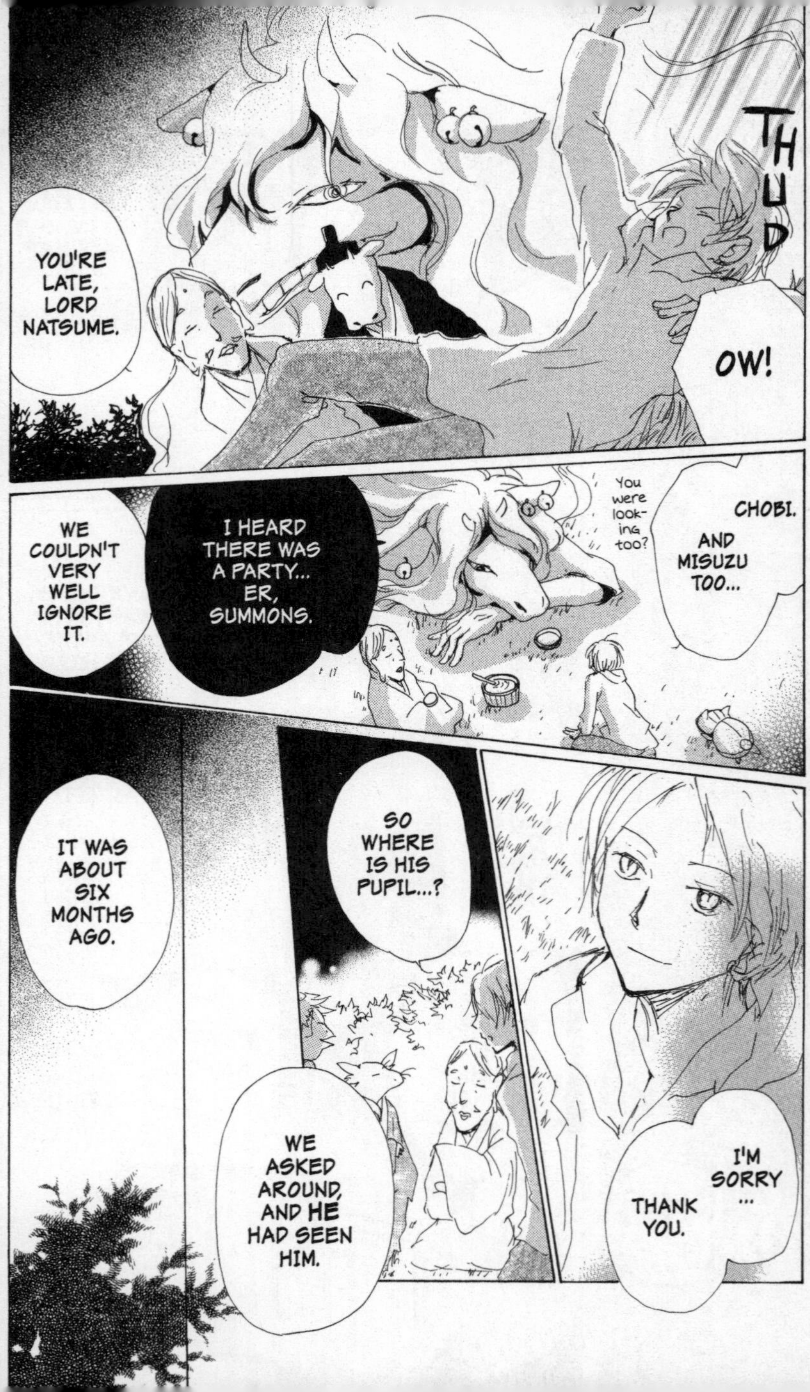
THUD
OW!
YOU'RE LATE, LORD NATSUME.
CHOBI.
AND MISUZU TOO...
You were looking too?
I HEARD THERE WAS A PARTY... ER, SUMMONS.
WE COULDN'T VERY WELL IGNORE IT.
I'M SORRY...
THANK YOU.
SO WHERE IS HIS PUPIL...?
WE ASKED AROUND, AND HE HAD SEEN HIM.
IT WAS ABOUT SIX MONTHS AGO.

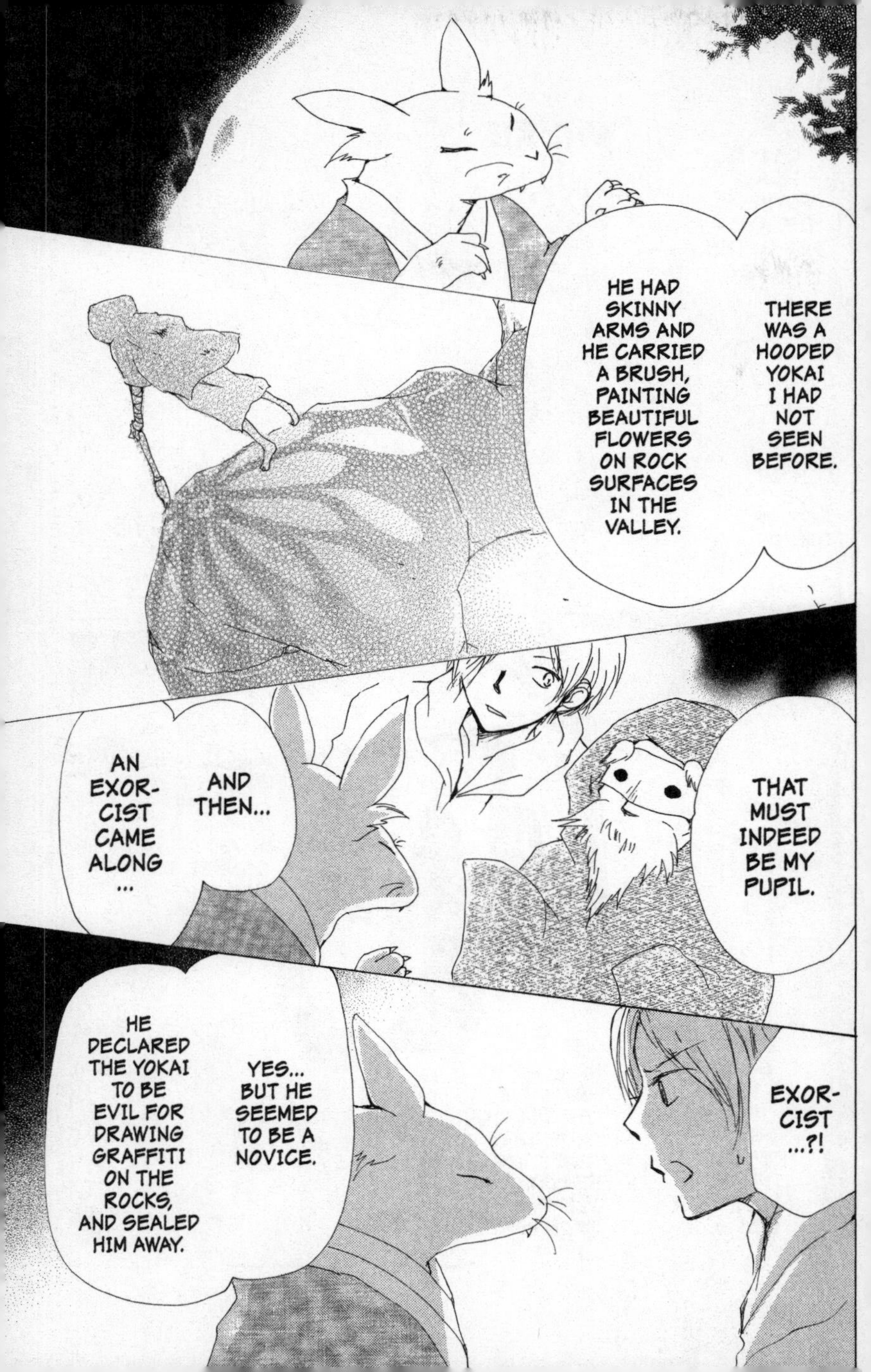
THERE WAS A HOODED YOKAI I HAD NOT SEEN BEFORE.
HE HAD SKINNY ARMS AND HE CARRIED A BRUSH, PAINTING BEAUTIFUL FLOWERS ON ROCK SURFACES IN THE VALLEY.
THAT MUST INDEED BE MY PUPIL.
AND THEN...
AN EXOR-CIST CAME ALONG...
EXOR-CIST...?!
YES... BUT HE SEEMED TO BE A NOVICE.
HE DECLARED THE YOKAI TO BE EVIL FOR DRAWING GRAFFITI ON THE ROCKS, AND SEALED HIM AWAY.

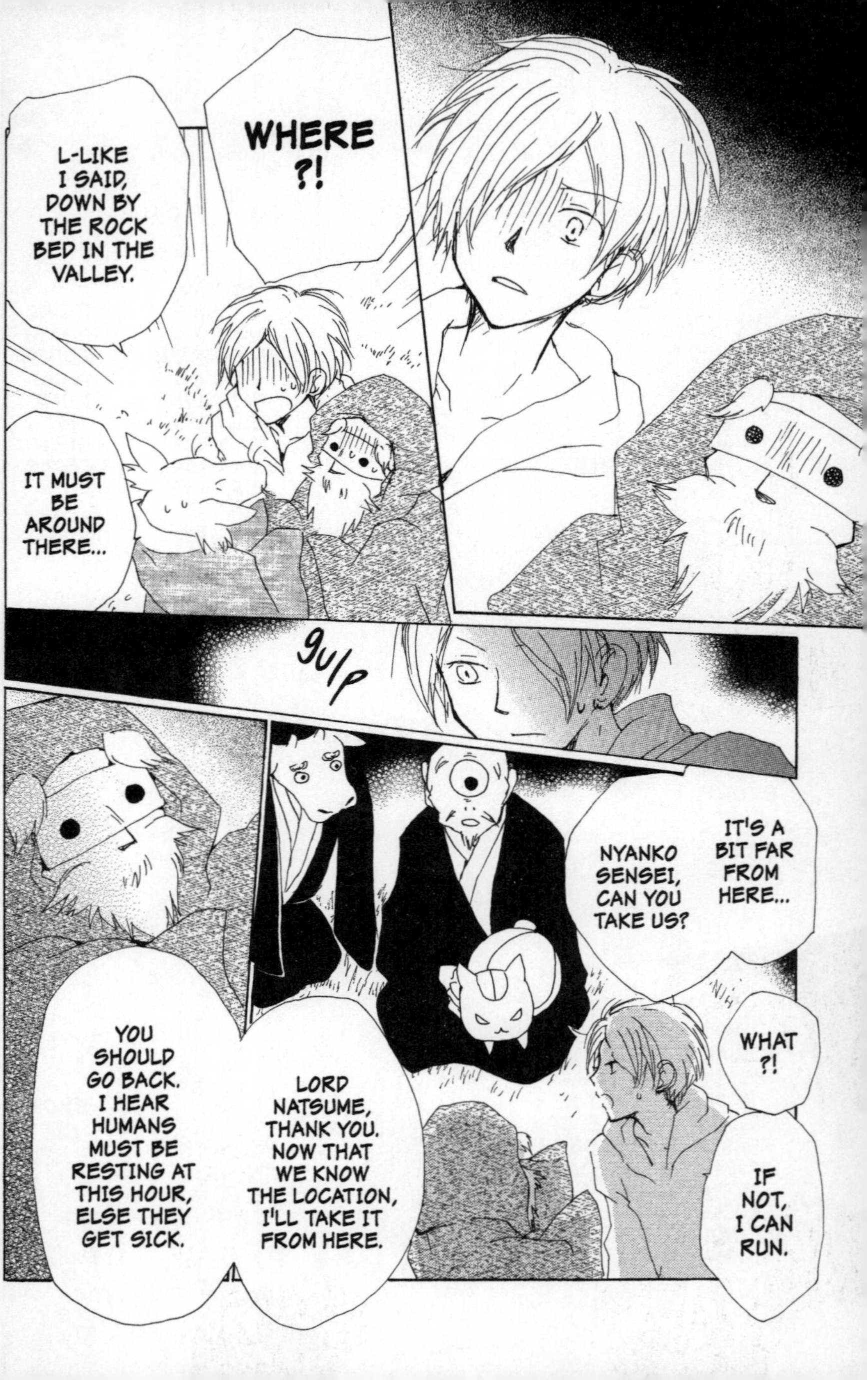
WHERE ?!
L-LIKE I SAID, DOWN BY THE ROCK BED IN THE VALLEY.
IT MUST BE AROUND THERE...
gulp
IT'S A BIT FAR FROM HERE...
NYANKO SENSEI, CAN YOU TAKE US?
WHAT ?!
IF NOT, I CAN RUN.
LORD NATSUME, THANK YOU. NOW THAT WE KNOW THE LOCATION, I'LL TAKE IT FROM HERE.
YOU SHOULD GO BACK. I HEAR HUMANS MUST BE RESTING AT THIS HOUR, ELSE THEY GET SICK.

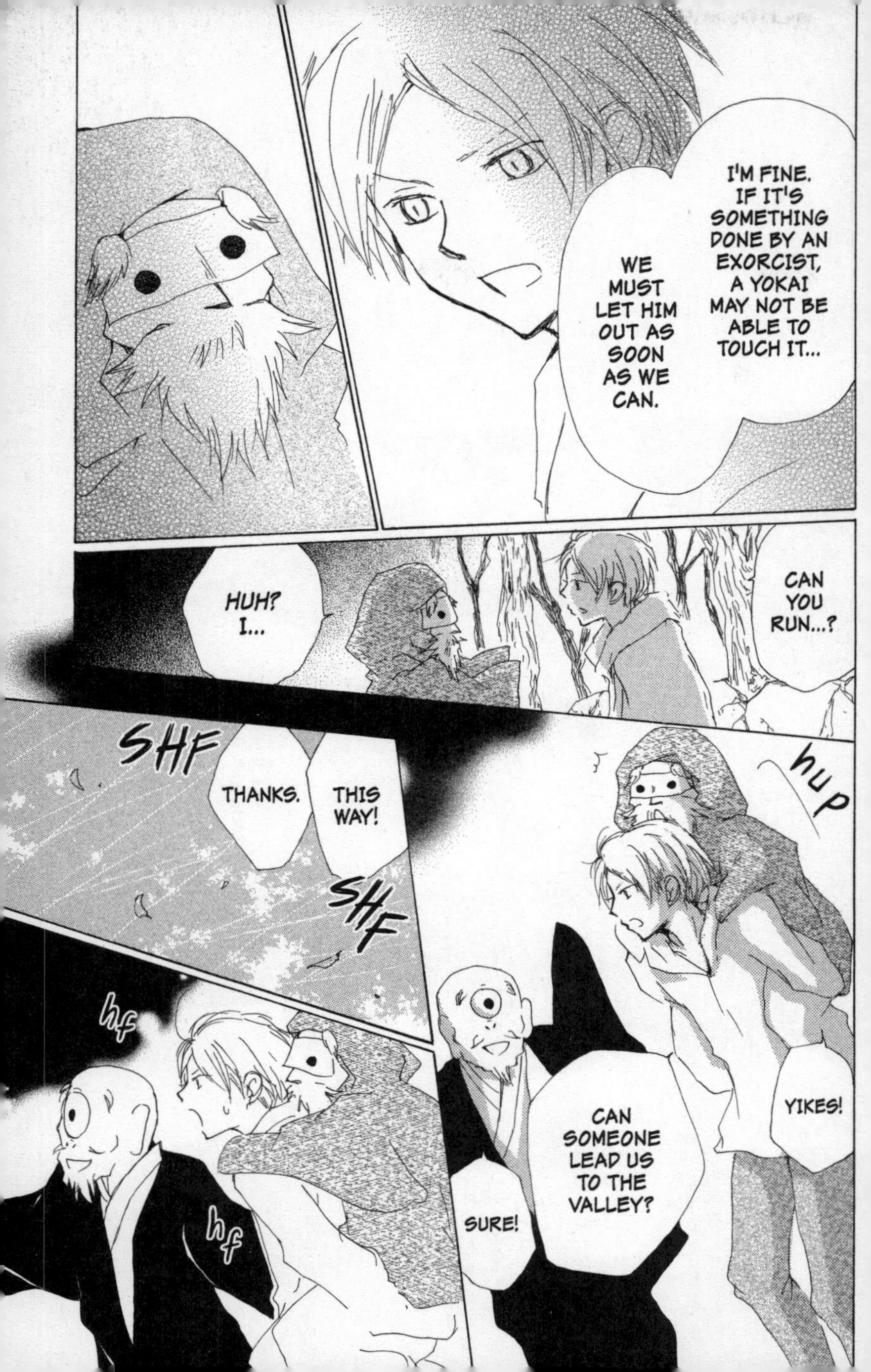
I'M FINE. IF IT'S SOMETHING DONE BY AN EXORCIST, A YOKAI MAY NOT BE ABLE TO TOUCH IT...
WE MUST LET HIM OUT AS SOON AS WE CAN.
CAN YOU RUN...?
HUH? I...
hup
YIKES!
CAN SOMEONE LEAD US TO THE VALLEY?
SURE!
THIS WAY!
THANKS.
SHF
SHF
hf
hf

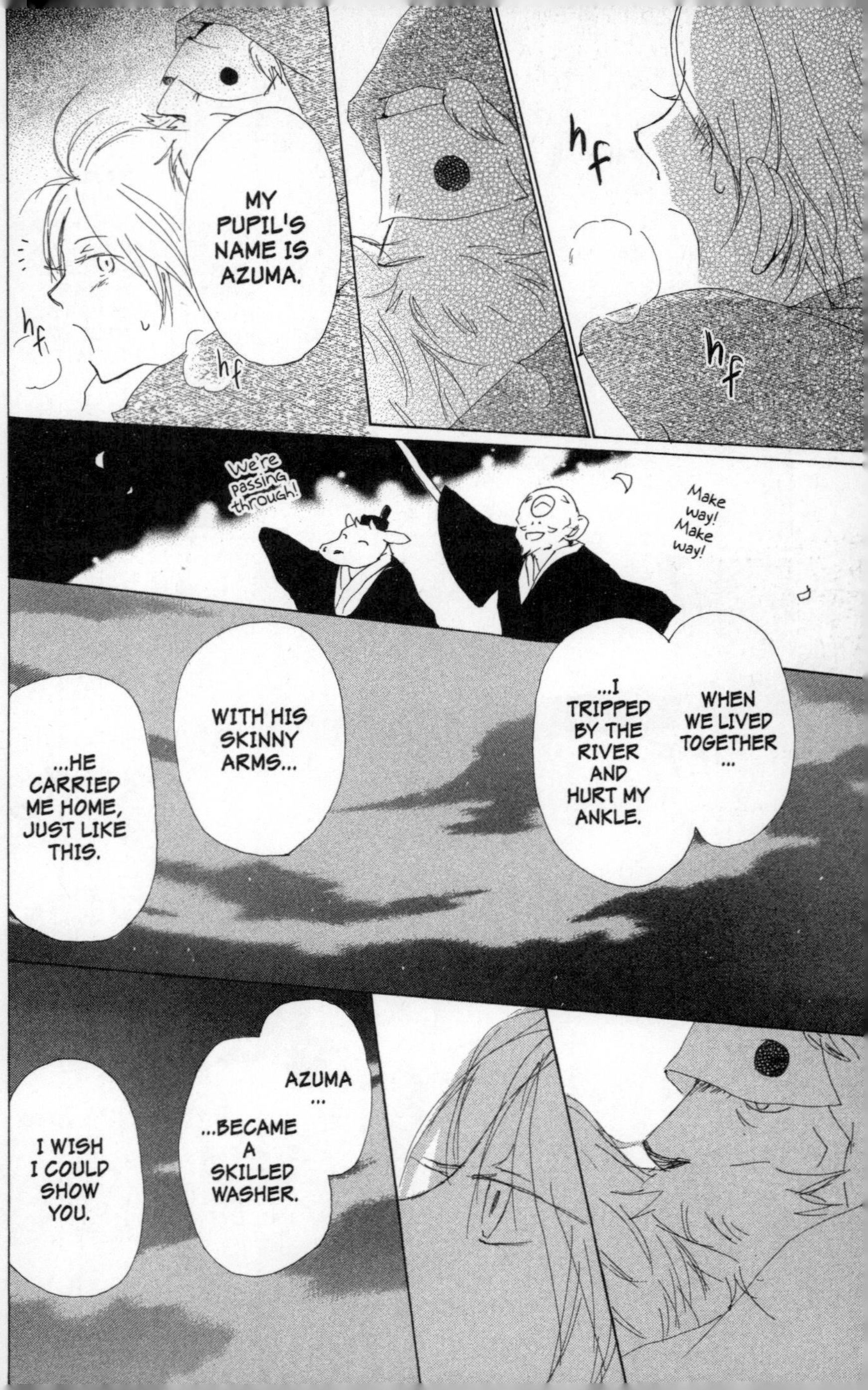
hf
hf
MY PUPIL'S NAME IS AZUMA.
hf
hf
Make way! Make way!
We're passing through!
WHEN WE LIVED TOGETHER...
...I TRIPPED BY THE RIVER AND HURT MY ANKLE.
WITH HIS SKINNY ARMS...
...HE CARRIED ME HOME, JUST LIKE THIS.
AZUMA...
...BECAME A SKILLED WASHER.
I WISH I COULD SHOW YOU.

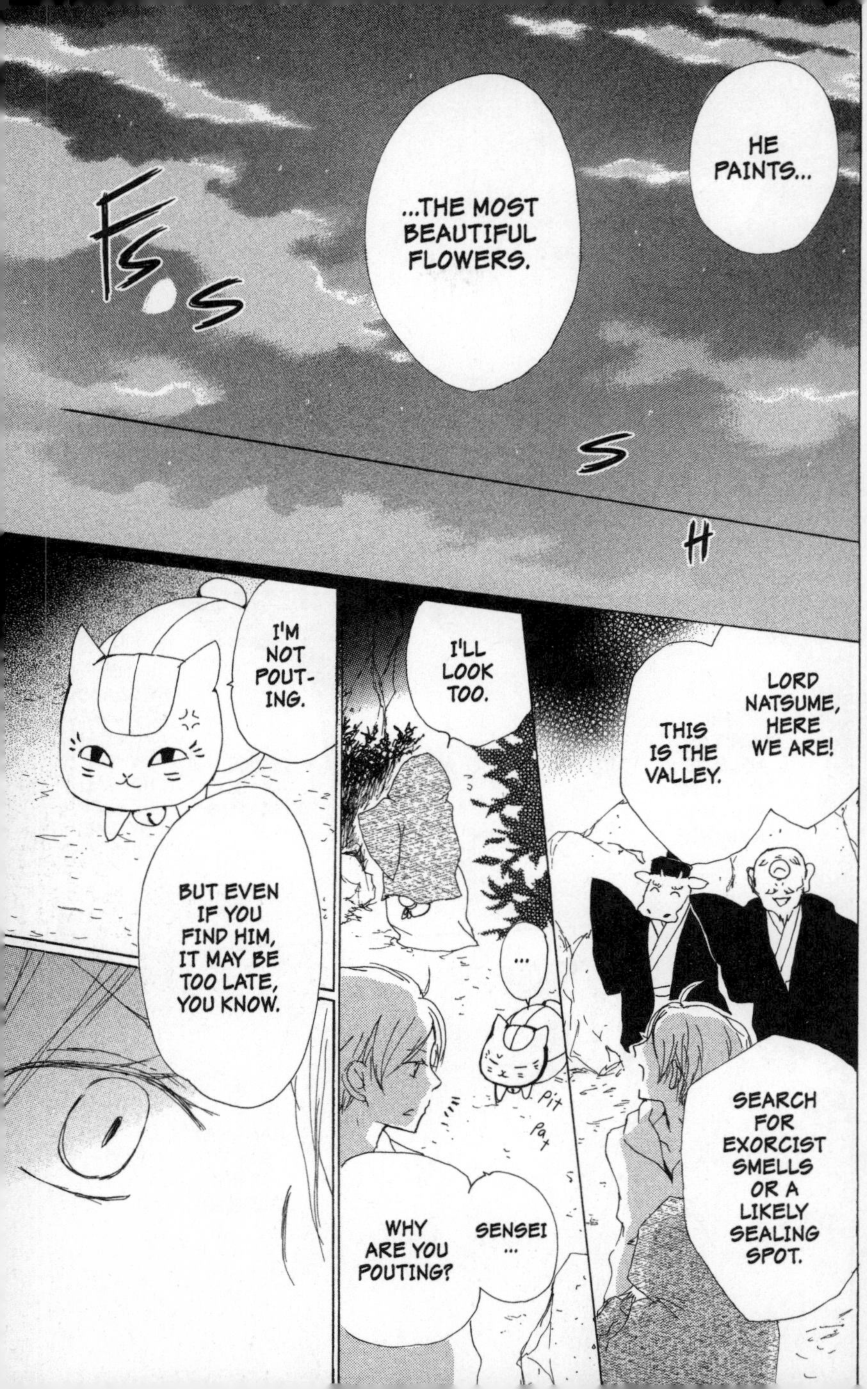
HE PAINTS...
...THE MOST BEAUTIFUL FLOWERS.
Fs S S H
LORD NATSUME, HERE WE ARE!
THIS IS THE VALLEY.
SEARCH FOR EXORCIST SMELLS OR A LIKELY SEALING SPOT.
I'LL LOOK TOO.
...
Pit Pat
SENSEI...
WHY ARE YOU POUTING?
I'M NOT POUT-ING.
BUT EVEN IF YOU FIND HIM, IT MAY BE TOO LATE, YOU KNOW.

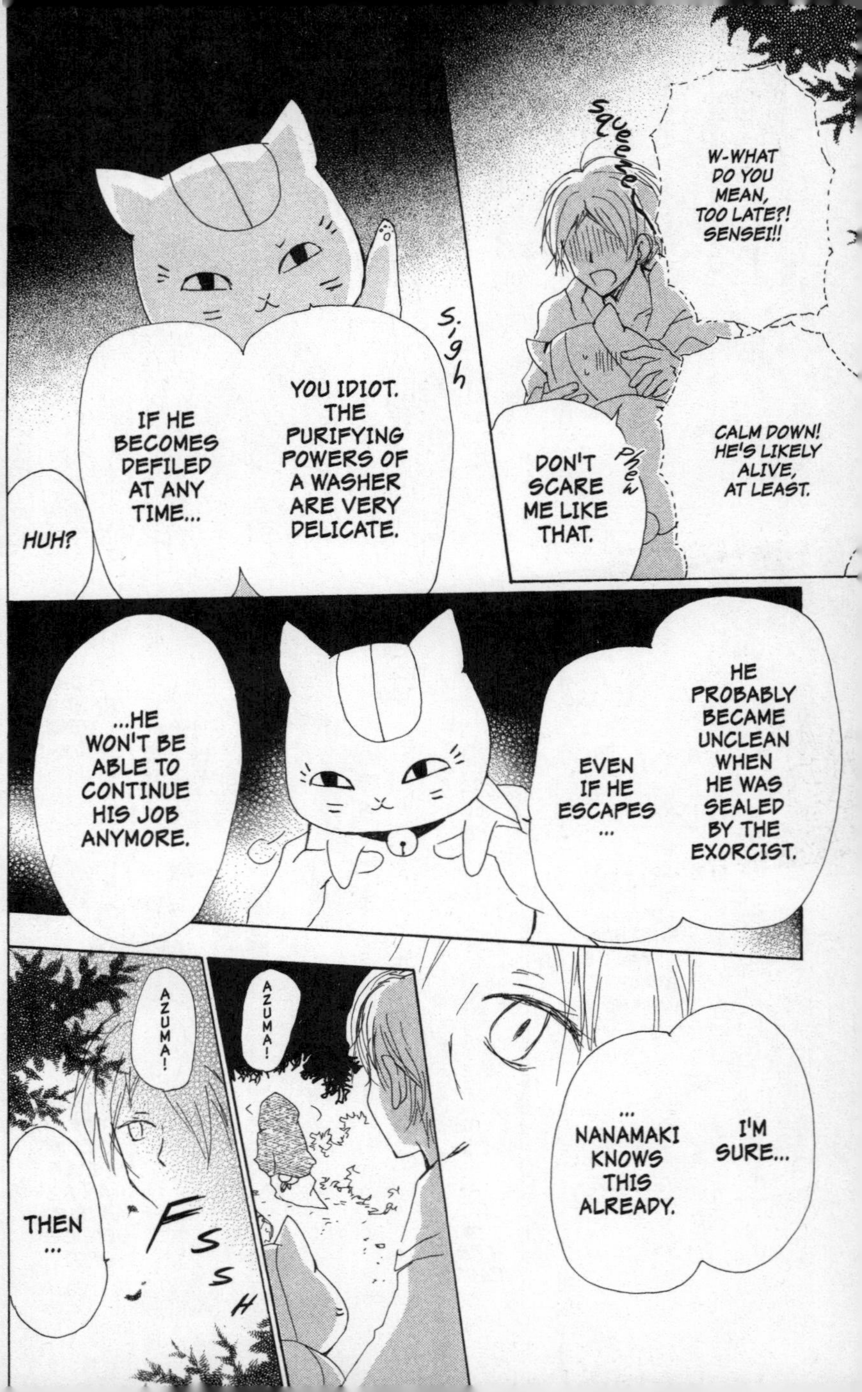
Squeeze
W-WHAT DO YOU MEAN, TOO LATE?! SENSEI!!
CALM DOWN! HE'S LIKELY ALIVE, AT LEAST.
DON'T SCARE ME LIKE THAT.
Phew
Sigh
YOU IDIOT. THE PURIFYING POWERS OF A WASHER ARE VERY DELICATE.
IF HE BECOMES DEFILED AT ANY TIME...
HUH?
HE PROBABLY BECAME UNCLEAN WHEN HE WAS SEALED BY THE EXORCIST.
EVEN IF HE ESCAPES ...
...HE WON'T BE ABLE TO CONTINUE HIS JOB ANYMORE.
I'M SURE...
... NANAMAKI KNOWS THIS ALREADY.
AZUMA!
AZUMA!
THEN ...
FSSH

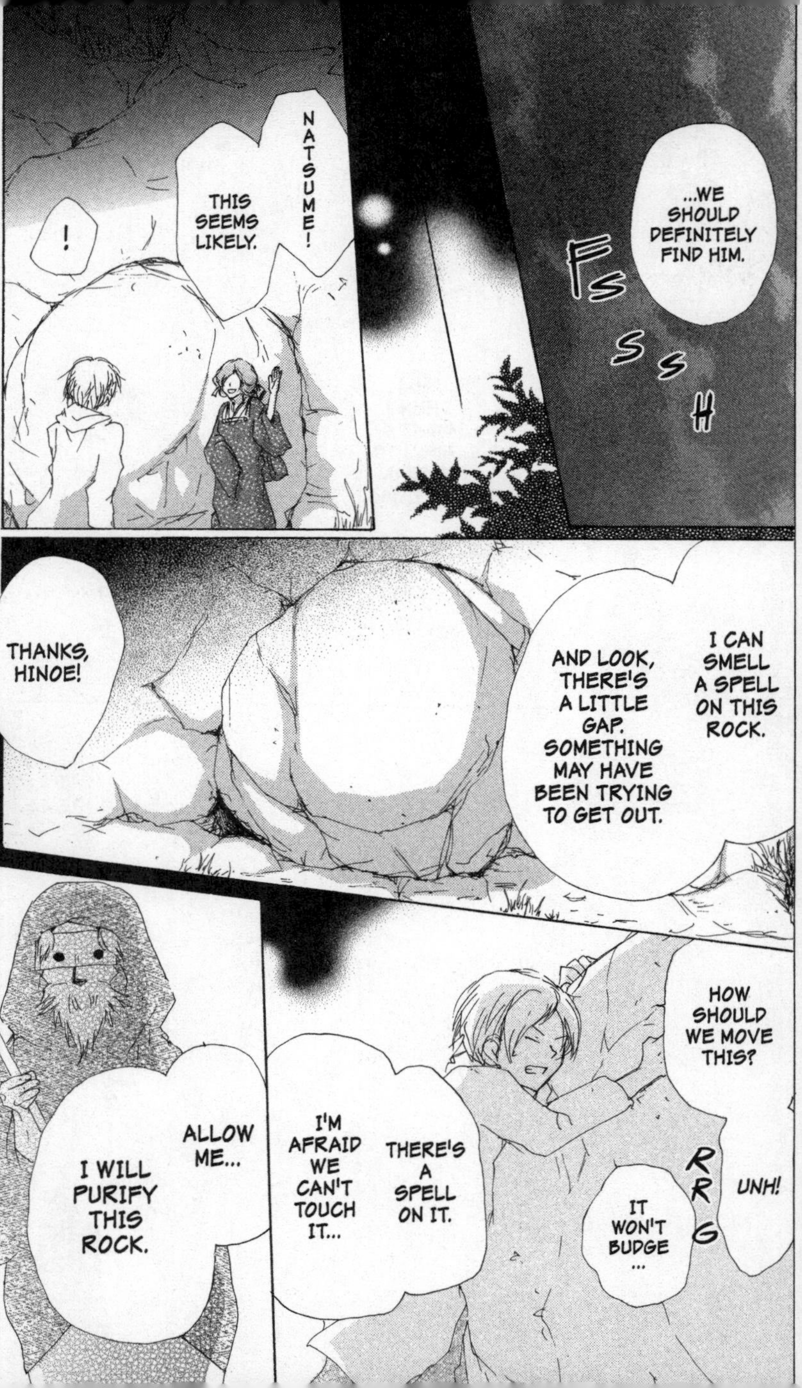
...WE SHOULD DEFINITELY FIND HIM.
FSSSH
NATSUME!
THIS SEEMS LIKELY.
!
I CAN SMELL A SPELL ON THIS ROCK.
AND LOOK, THERE'S A LITTLE GAP. SOMETHING MAY HAVE BEEN TRYING TO GET OUT.
THANKS, HINOE!
HOW SHOULD WE MOVE THIS?
UNH!
RRG
IT WON'T BUDGE...
THERE'S A SPELL ON IT.
I'M AFRAID WE CAN'T TOUCH IT...
ALLOW ME...
I WILL PURIFY THIS ROCK.

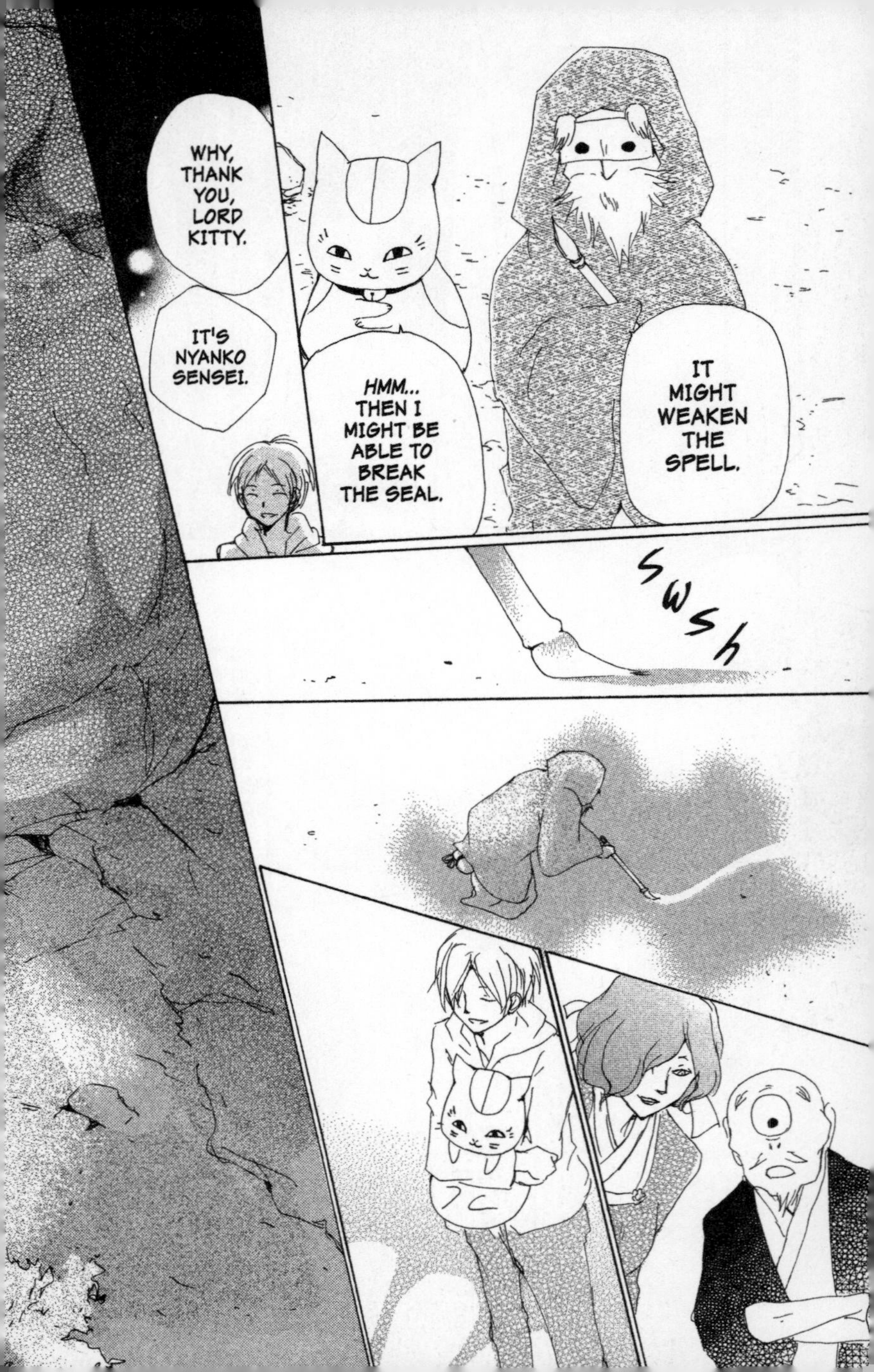
IT MIGHT WEAKEN THE SPELL.
HMM... THEN I MIGHT BE ABLE TO BREAK THE SEAL.
WHY, THANK YOU, LORD KITTY.
IT'S NYANKO SENSEI.
SWSH

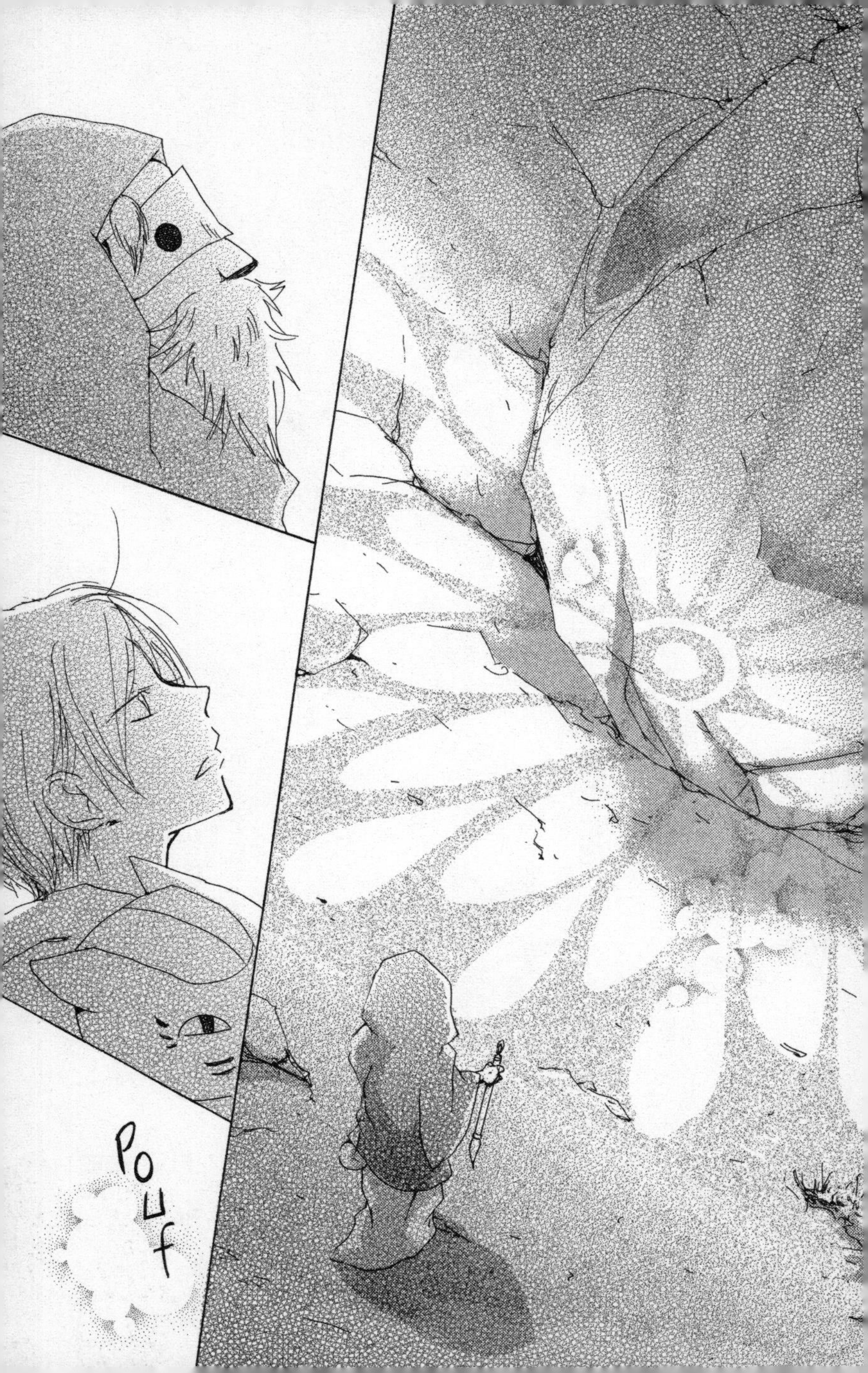
POUF

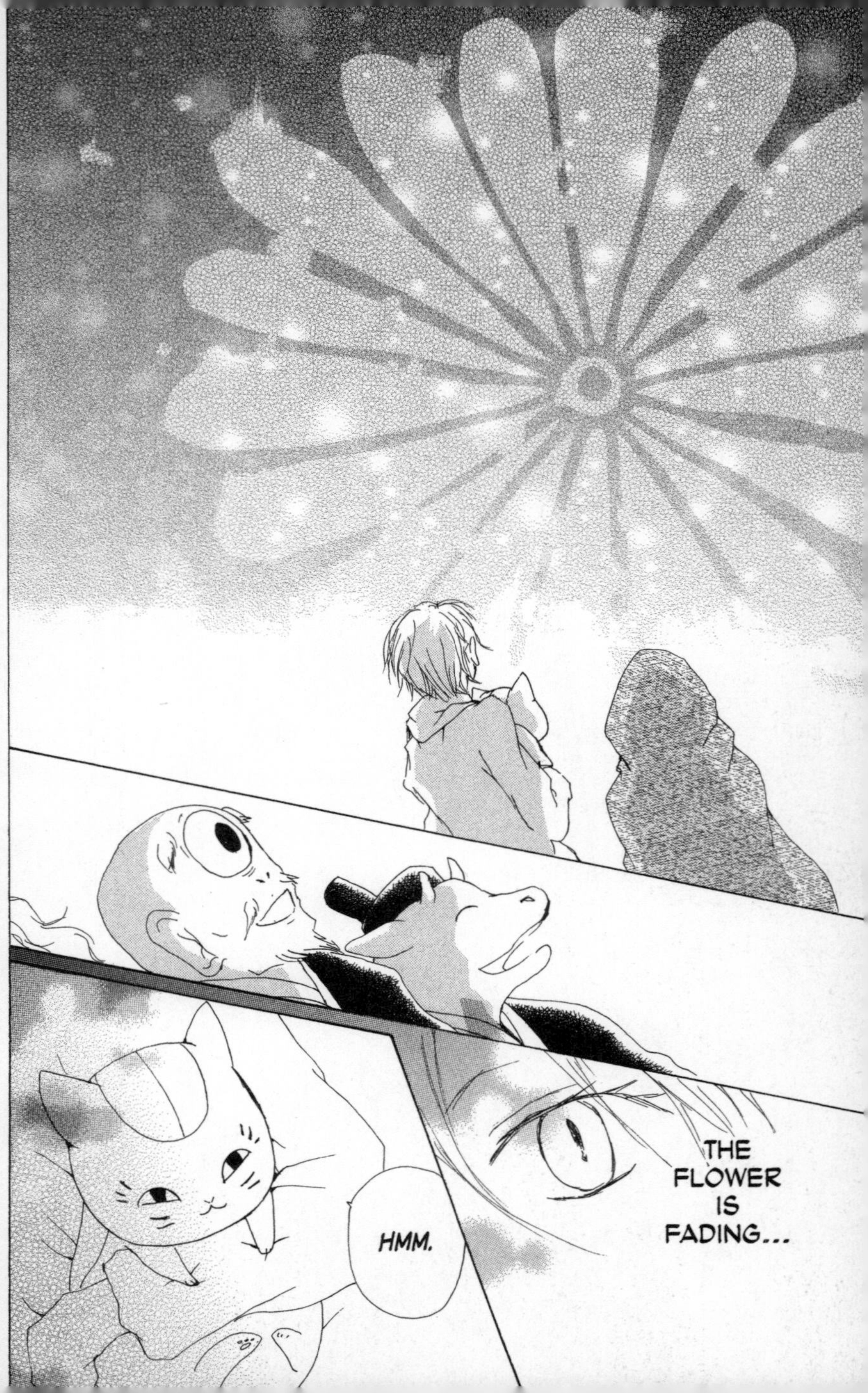
THE FLOWER IS FADING...
HMM.

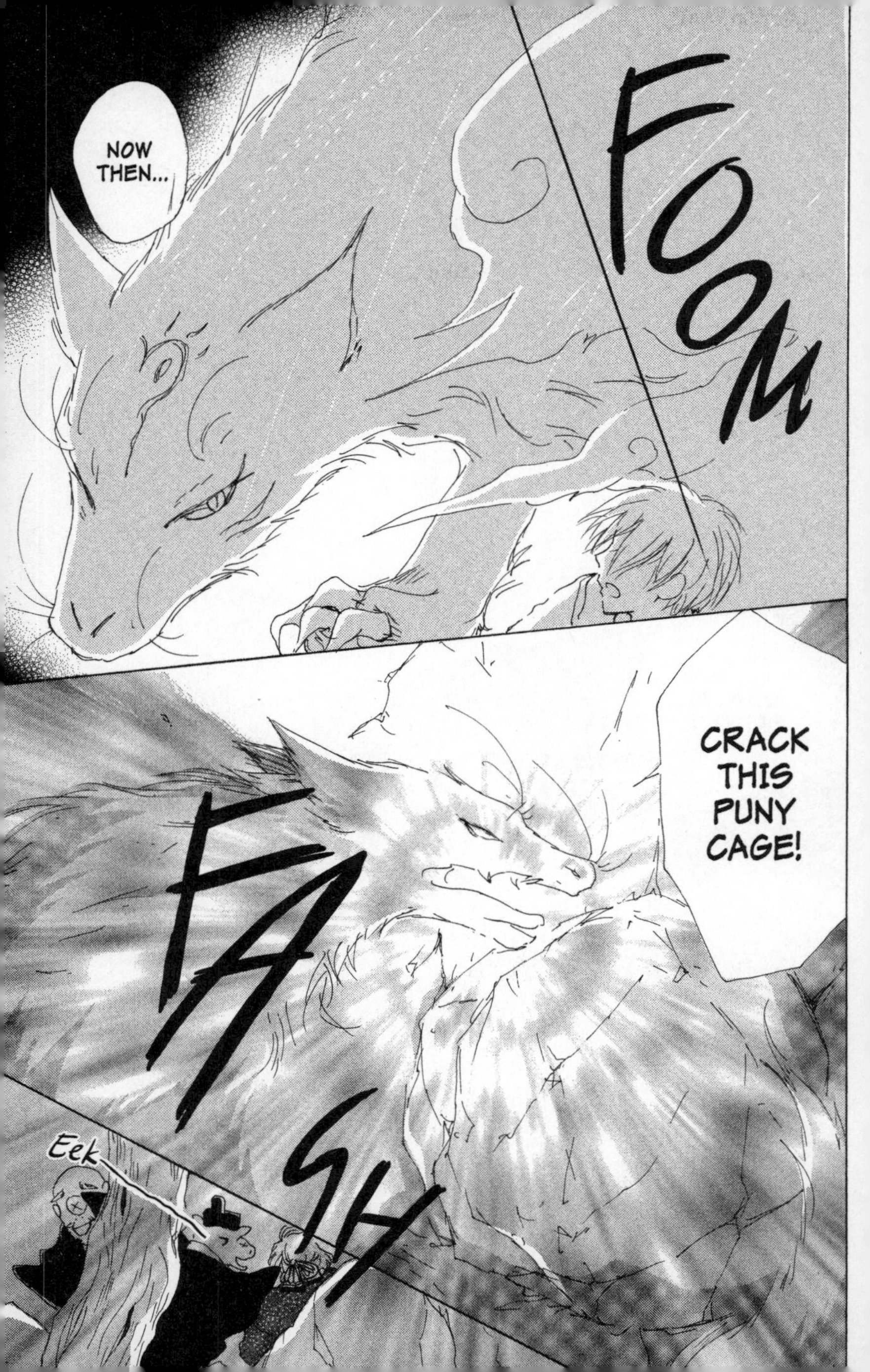
FOOM
NOW THEN...
CRACK THIS PUNY CAGE!
FASH
Eek

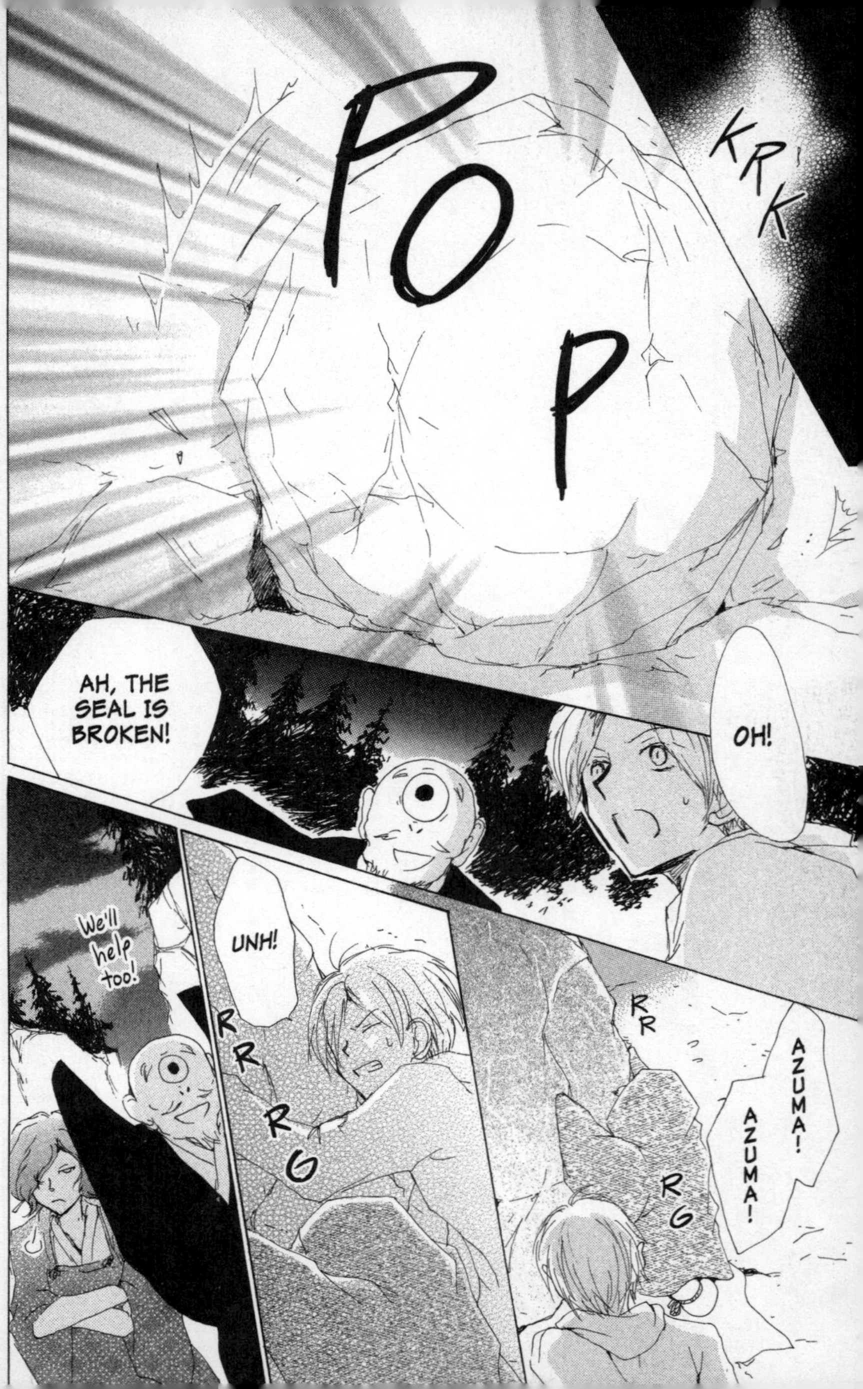
KRK
POP
OH!
AH, THE SEAL IS BROKEN!
AZUMA!
AZUMA!
RR
RG
UNH!
RRRG
We'll help too!

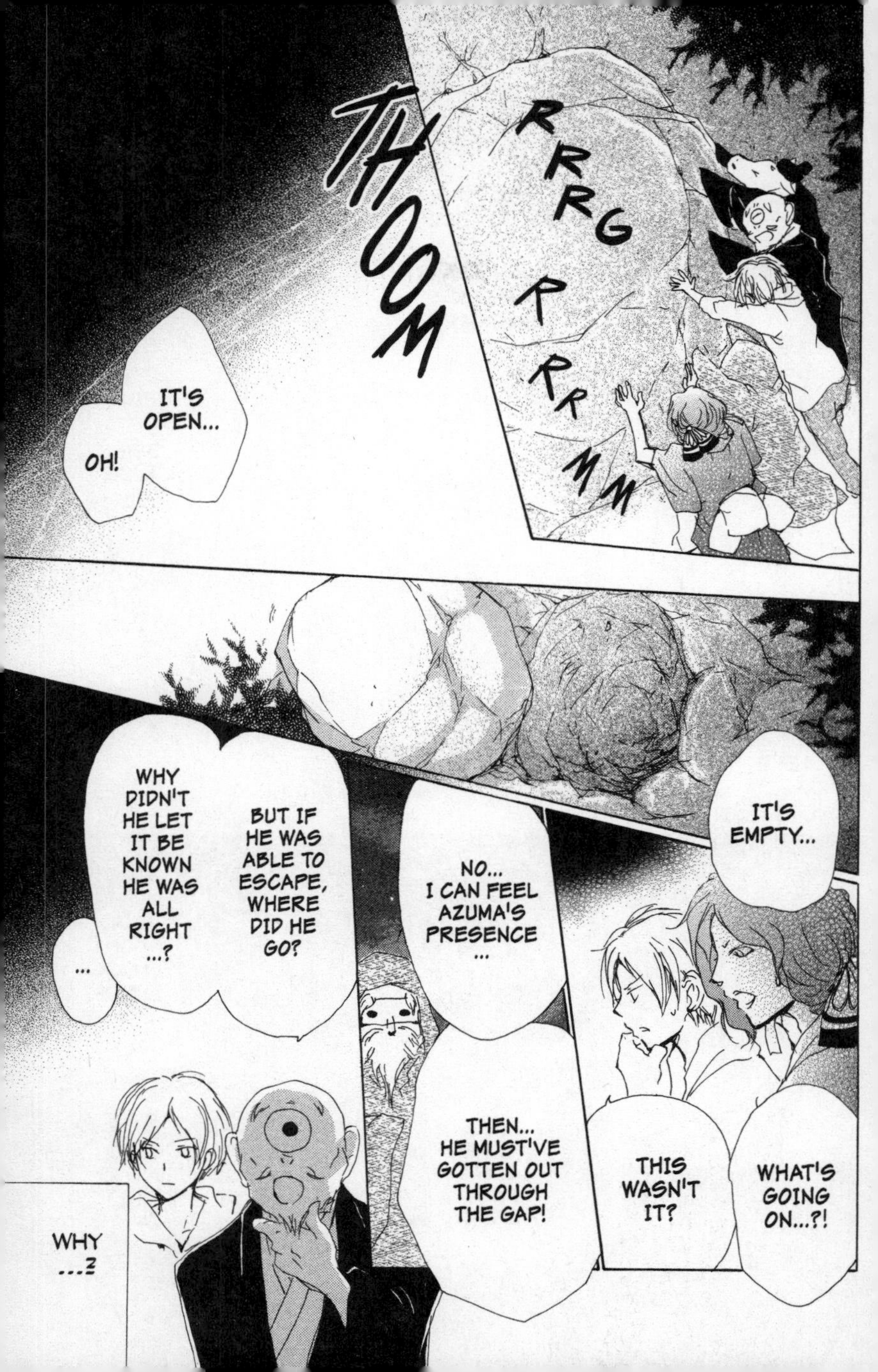
RRRG RRRMM
THOOOM
IT'S OPEN...
OH!
IT'S EMPTY...
NO... I CAN FEEL AZUMA'S PRESENCE...
WHAT'S GOING ON...?!
THIS WASN'T IT?
THEN... HE MUST'VE GOTTEN OUT THROUGH THE GAP!
BUT IF HE WAS ABLE TO ESCAPE, WHERE DID HE GO?
WHY DIDN'T HE LET IT BE KNOWN HE WAS ALL RIGHT...?
...
WHY...?

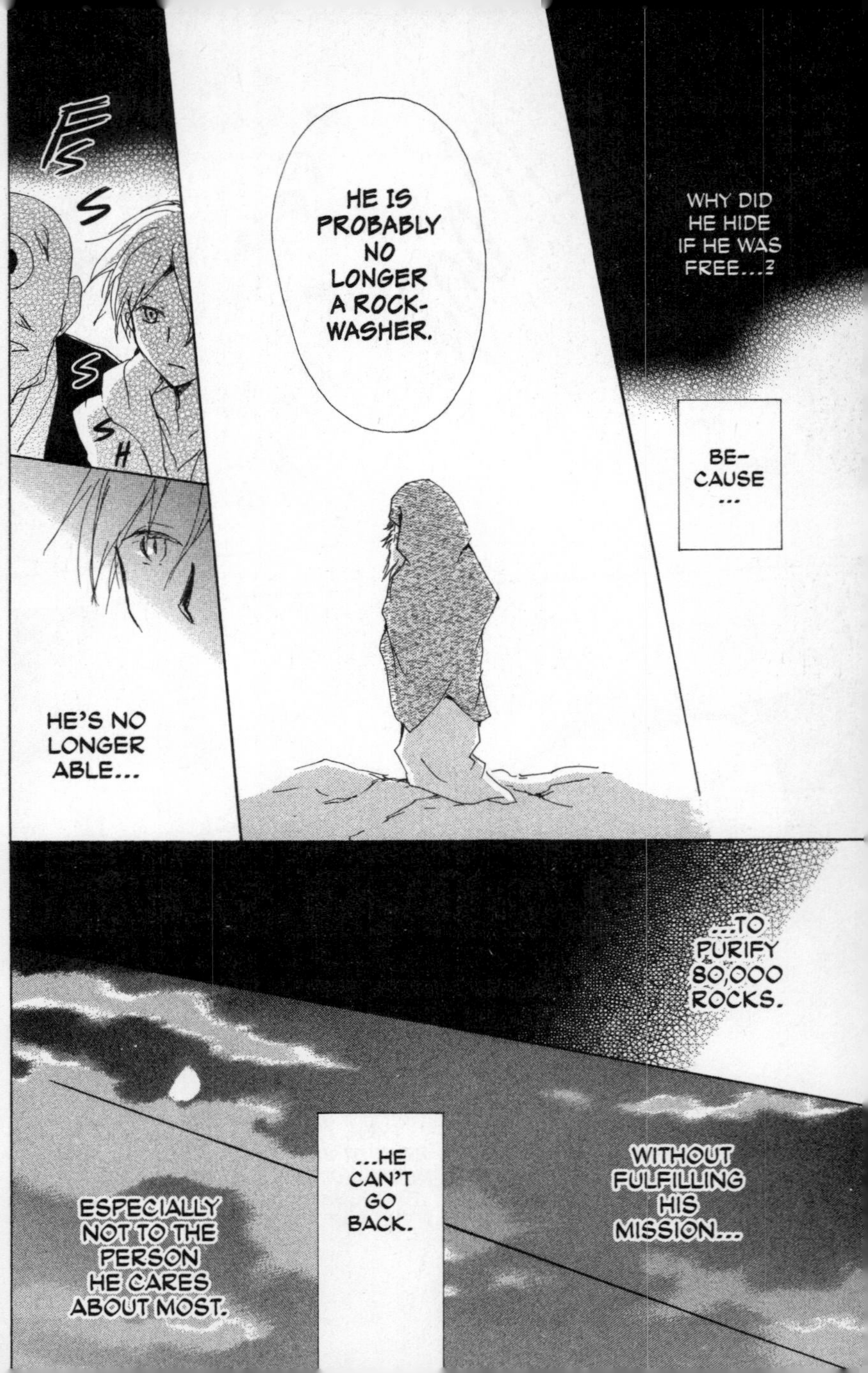
WHY DID HE HIDE IF HE WAS FREE...?
BE-CAUSE...
HE IS PROBABLY NO LONGER A ROCK-WASHER.
FSSSSH
HE'S NO LONGER ABLE...
...TO PURIFY 80,000 ROCKS.
WITHOUT FULFILLING HIS MISSION...
...HE CAN'T GO BACK.
ESPECIALLY NOT TO THE PERSON HE CARES ABOUT MOST.

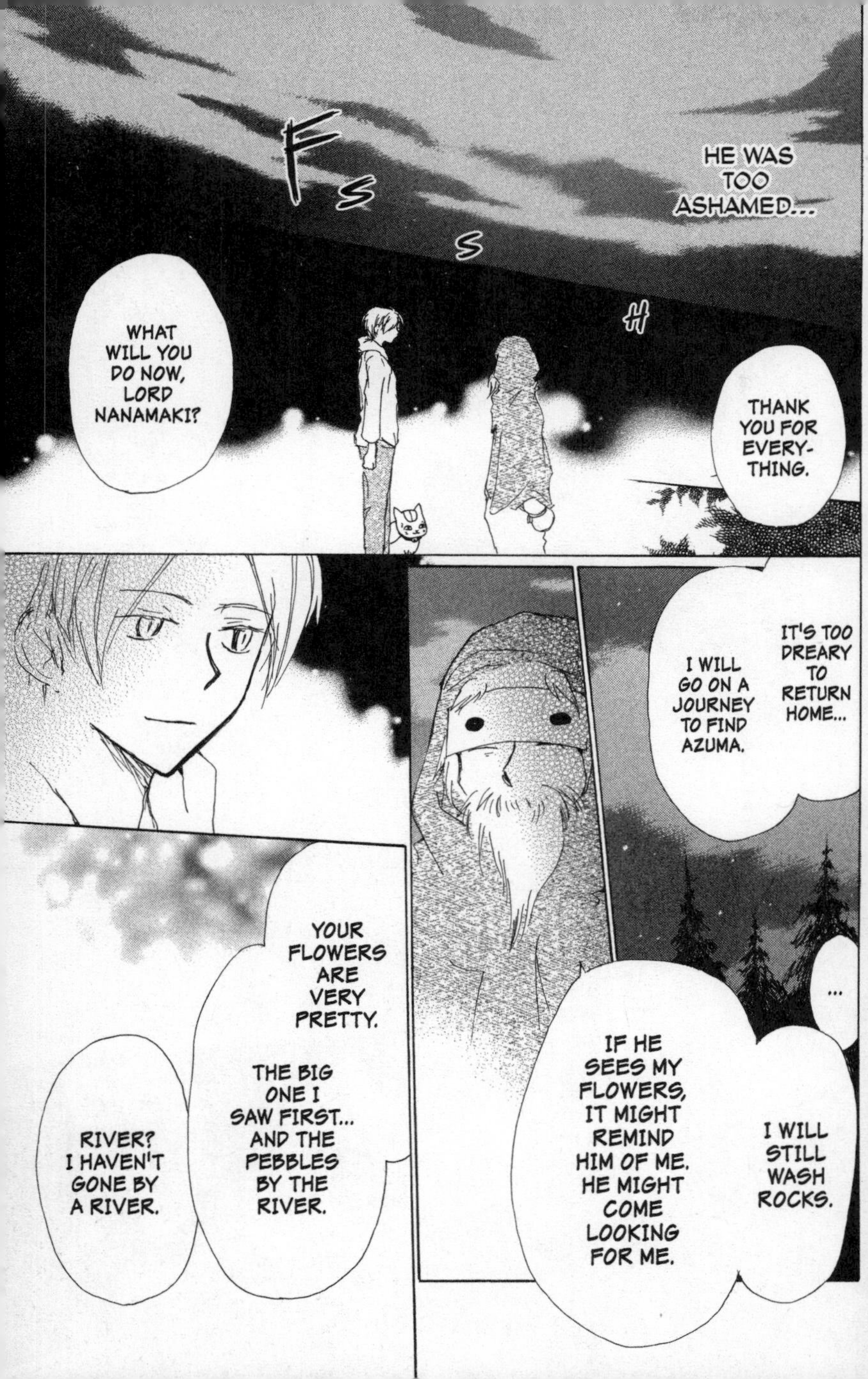
HE WAS TOO ASHAMED...
FSSH
THANK YOU FOR EVERYTHING.
WHAT WILL YOU DO NOW, LORD NANAMAKI?
IT'S TOO DREARY TO RETURN HOME...
I WILL GO ON A JOURNEY TO FIND AZUMA.
...
I WILL STILL WASH ROCKS.
IF HE SEES MY FLOWERS, IT MIGHT REMIND HIM OF ME. HE MIGHT COME LOOKING FOR ME.
YOUR FLOWERS ARE VERY PRETTY.
THE BIG ONE I SAW FIRST... AND THE PEBBLES BY THE RIVER.
RIVER? I HAVEN'T GONE BY A RIVER.

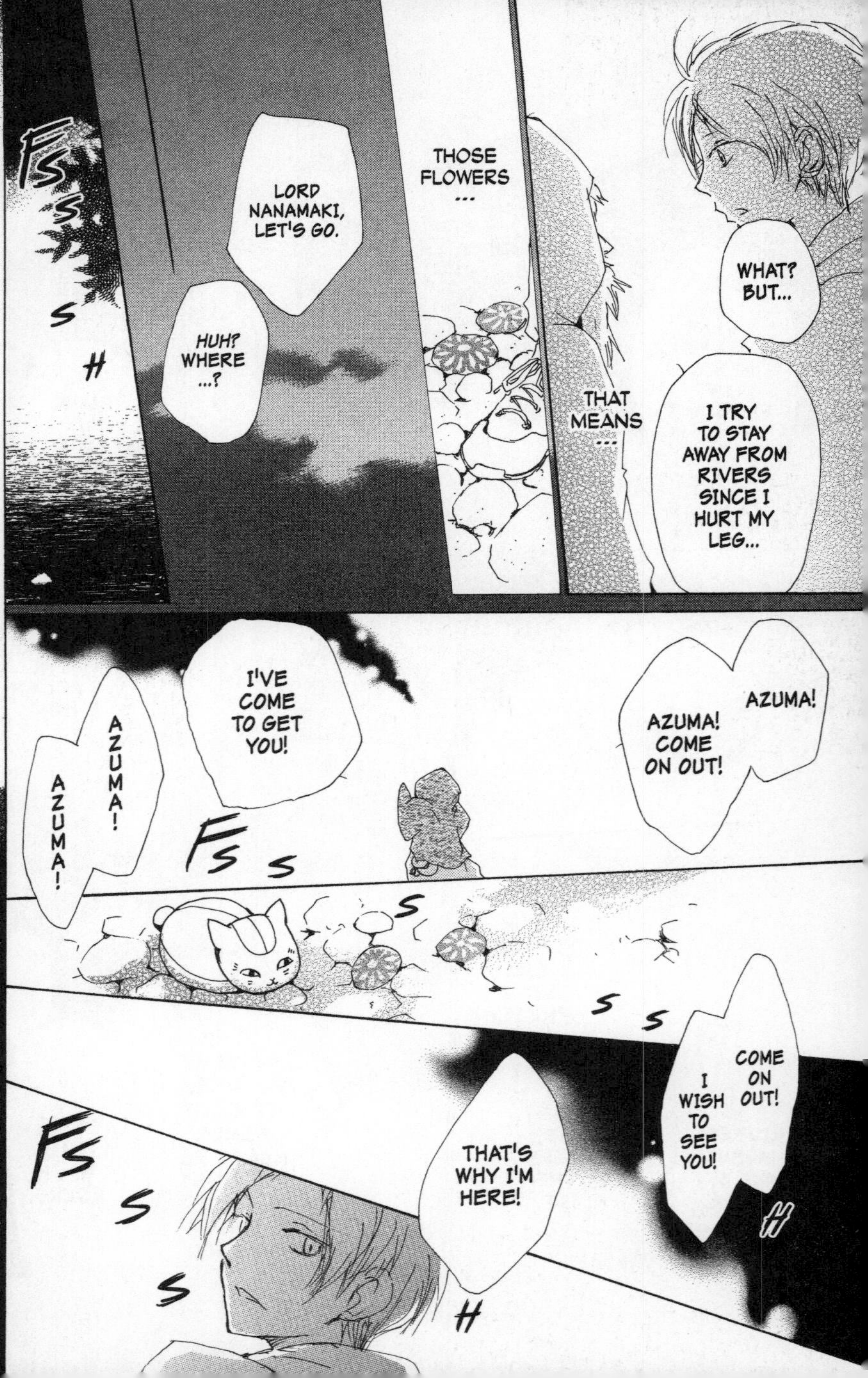
WHAT? BUT...
I TRY TO STAY AWAY FROM RIVERS SINCE I HURT MY LEG...
THAT MEANS...
THOSE FLOWERS...
LORD NANAMAKI, LET'S GO.
HUH? WHERE ...?
FSSSSH
AZUMA!
AZUMA! COME ON OUT!
I'VE COME TO GET YOU!
AZUMA!
AZUMA!
FSS
S
SS
COME ON OUT!
I WISH TO SEE YOU!
H
THAT'S WHY I'M HERE!
FSSSH

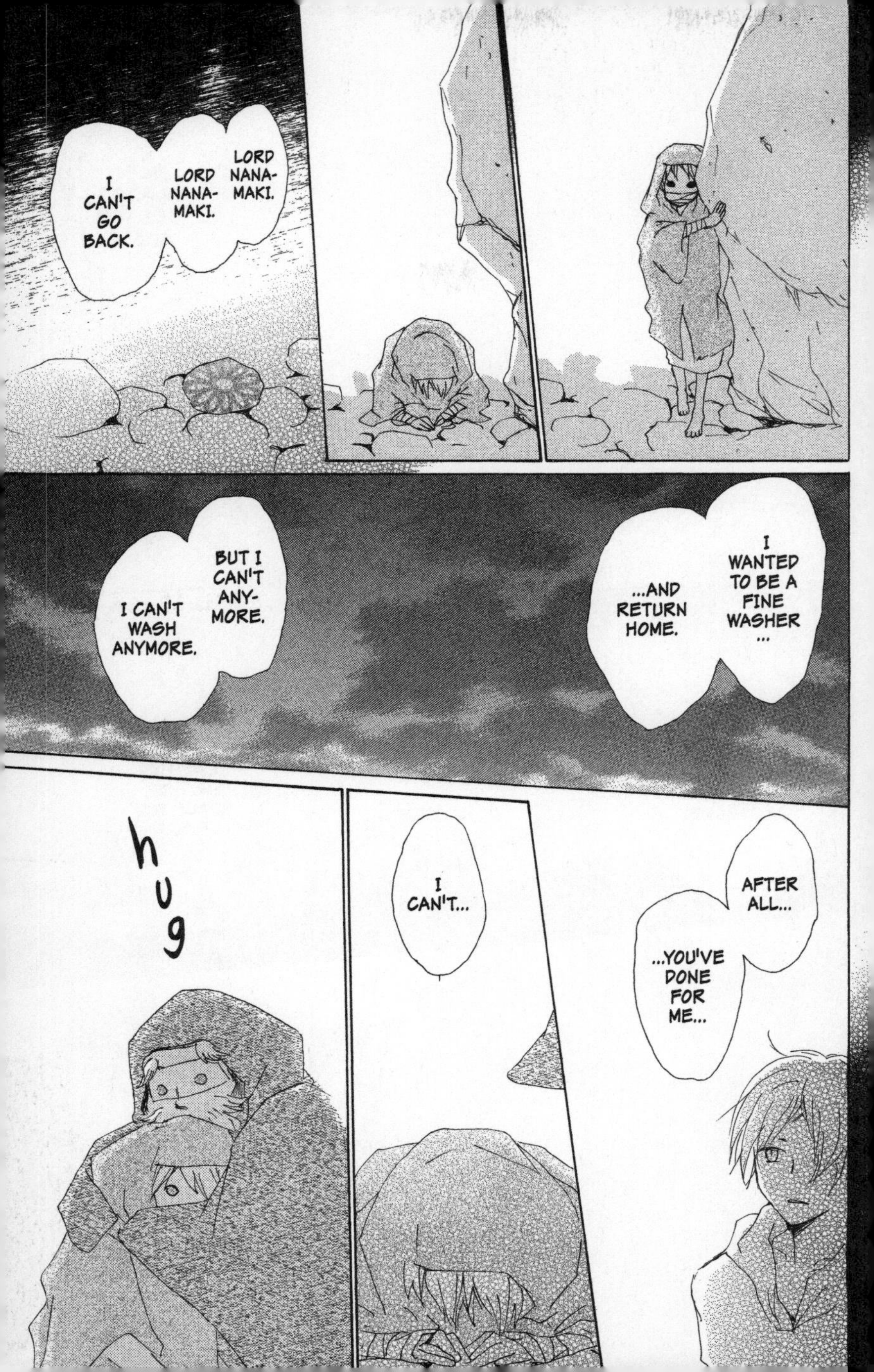

LORD NANA-MAKI.
LORD NANA-MAKI.
I CAN'T GO BACK.
I WANTED TO BE A FINE WASHER...
...AND RETURN HOME.
BUT I CAN'T ANYMORE.
I CAN'T WASH ANYMORE.
AFTER ALL...
...YOU'VE DONE FOR ME...
I CAN'T...
hug

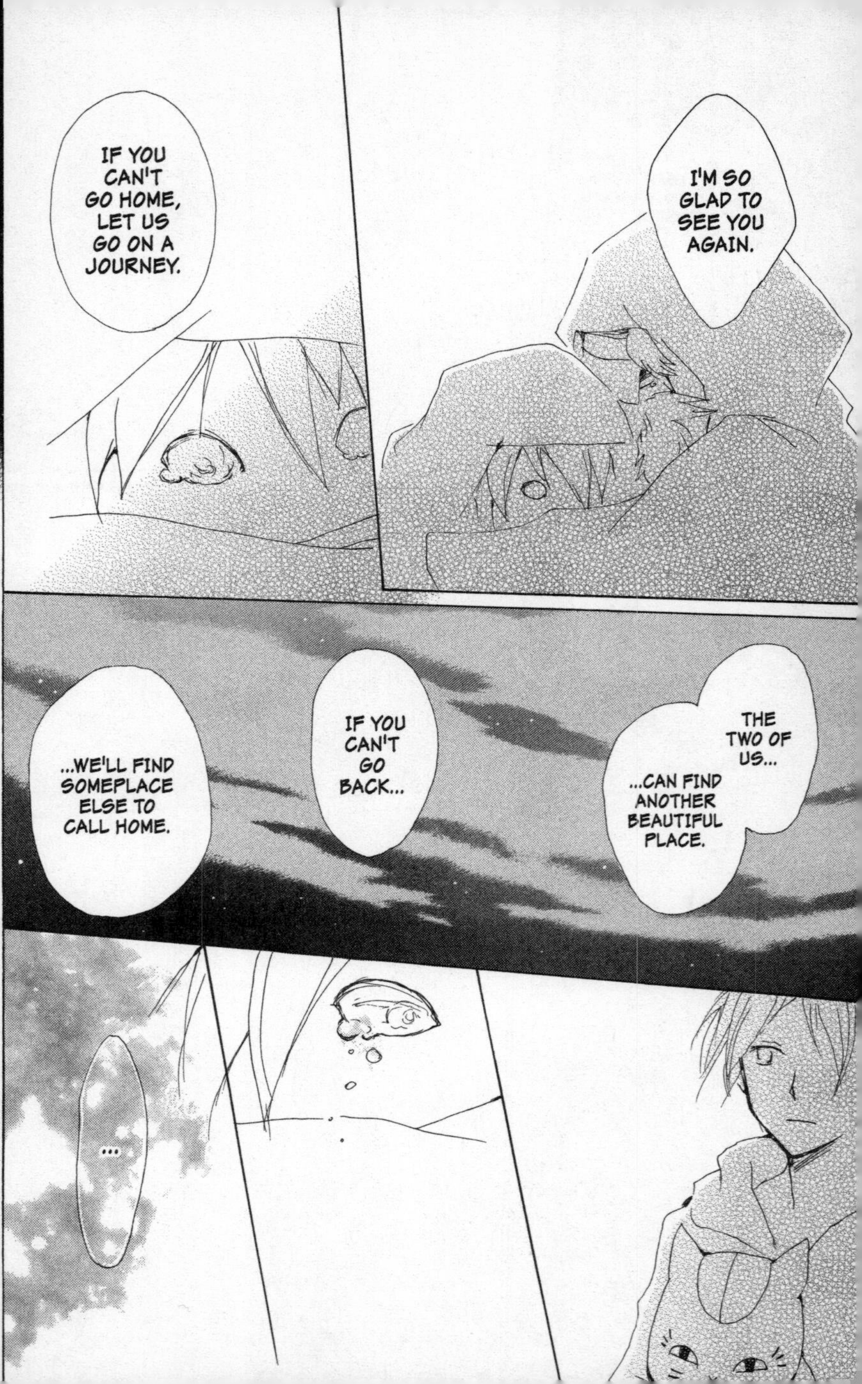
I'M SO GLAD TO SEE YOU AGAIN.
IF YOU CAN'T GO HOME, LET US GO ON A JOURNEY.
THE TWO OF US...
...CAN FIND ANOTHER BEAUTIFUL PLACE.
IF YOU CAN'T GO BACK...
...WE'LL FIND SOMEPLACE ELSE TO CALL HOME.
...

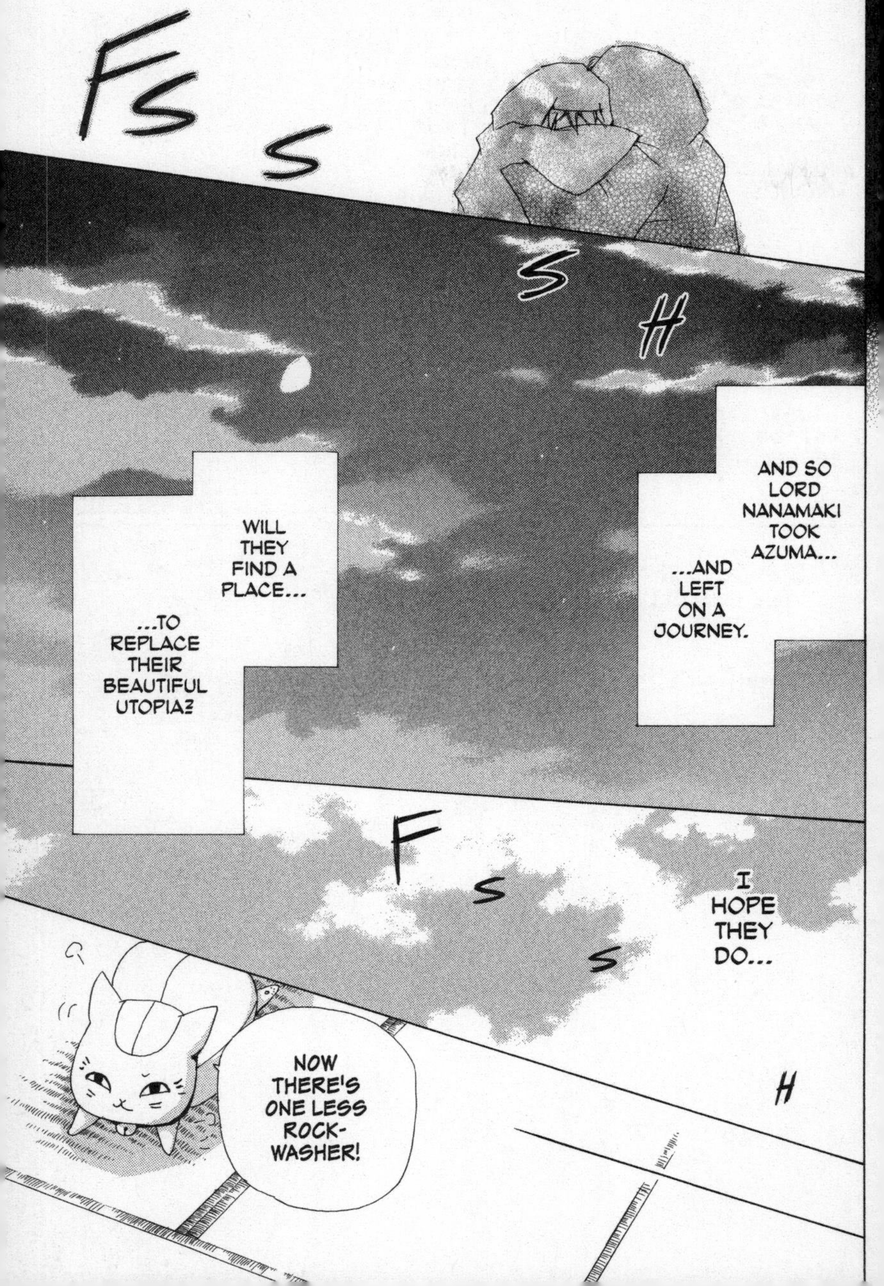
FSSSH
AND SO LORD NANAMAKI TOOK AZUMA...
...AND LEFT ON A JOURNEY.
WILL THEY FIND A PLACE...
...TO REPLACE THEIR BEAUTIFUL UTOPIA?
FSSH
I HOPE THEY DO...
NOW THERE'S ONE LESS ROCK-WASHER!

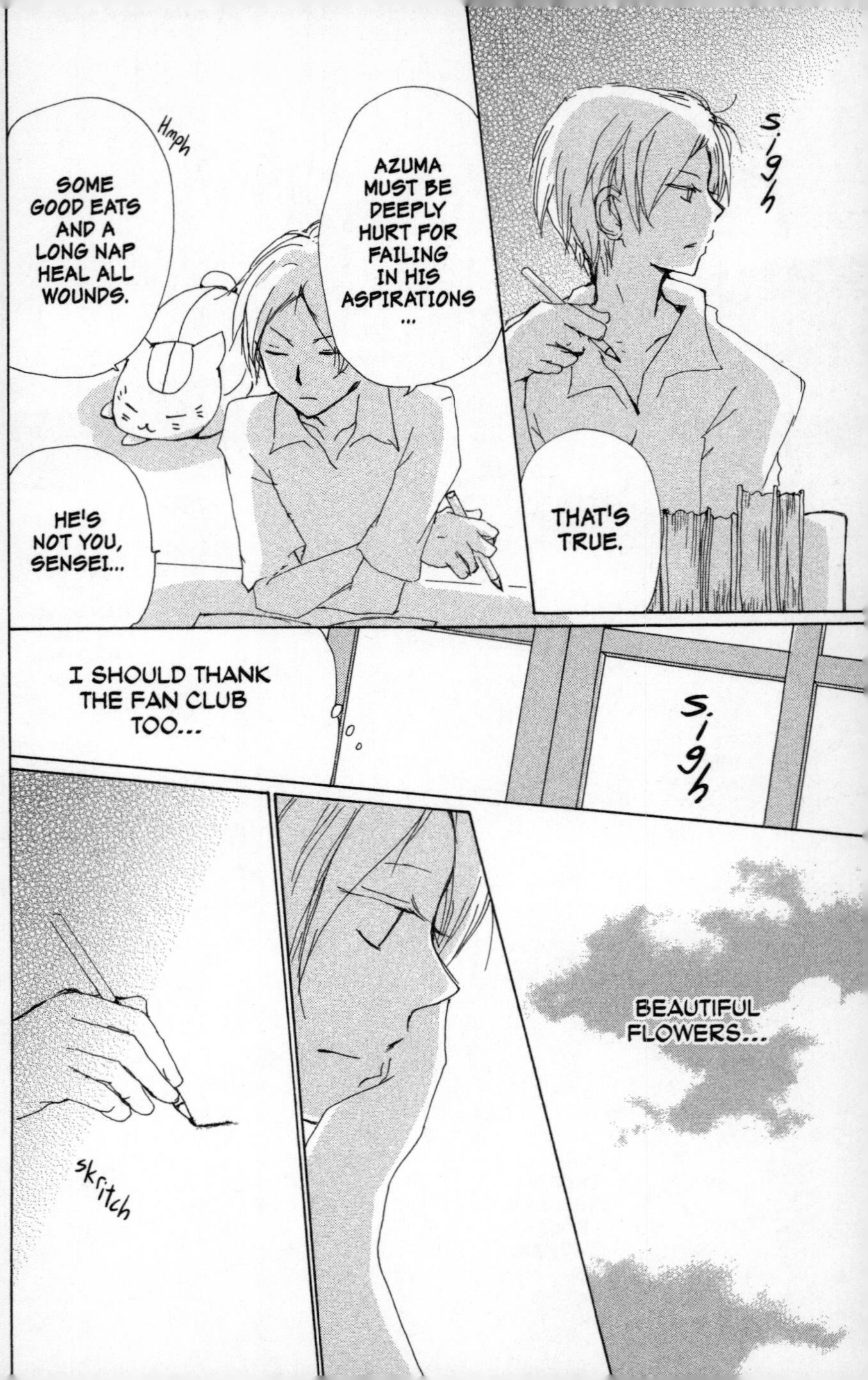
sigh
THAT'S TRUE.
AZUMA MUST BE DEEPLY HURT FOR FAILING IN HIS ASPIRATIONS ...
Hmph
SOME GOOD EATS AND A LONG NAP HEAL ALL WOUNDS.
HE'S NOT YOU, SENSEI...
sigh
I SHOULD THANK THE FAN CLUB TOO...
BEAUTIFUL FLOWERS...
skritch

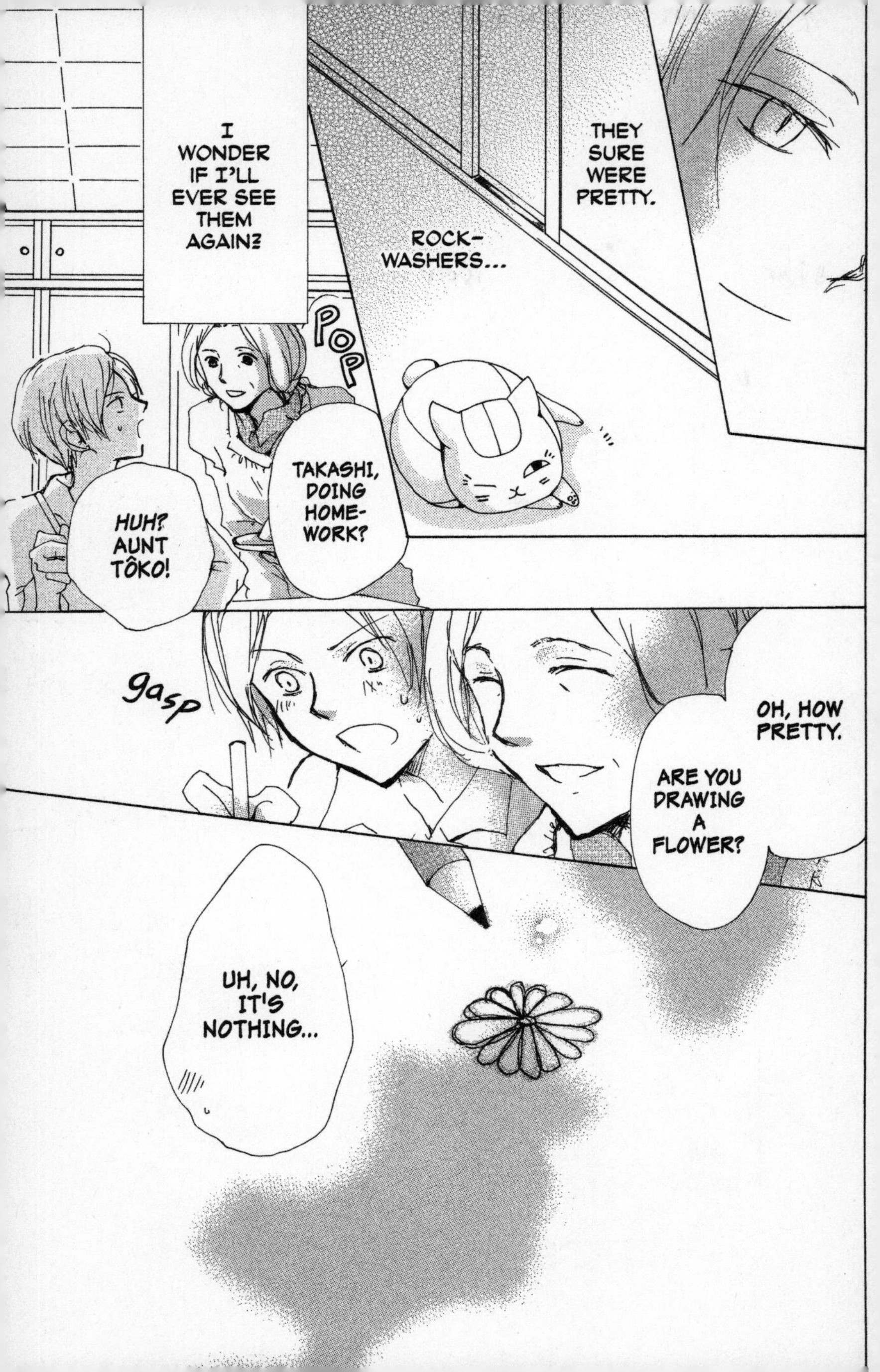
THEY SURE WERE PRETTY.
ROCK-WASHERS...
I WONDER IF I'LL EVER SEE THEM AGAIN?
POP
TAKASHI, DOING HOMEWORK?
HUH? AUNT TÔKO!
OH, HOW PRETTY.
ARE YOU DRAWING A FLOWER?
gasp
UH, NO, IT'S NOTHING...

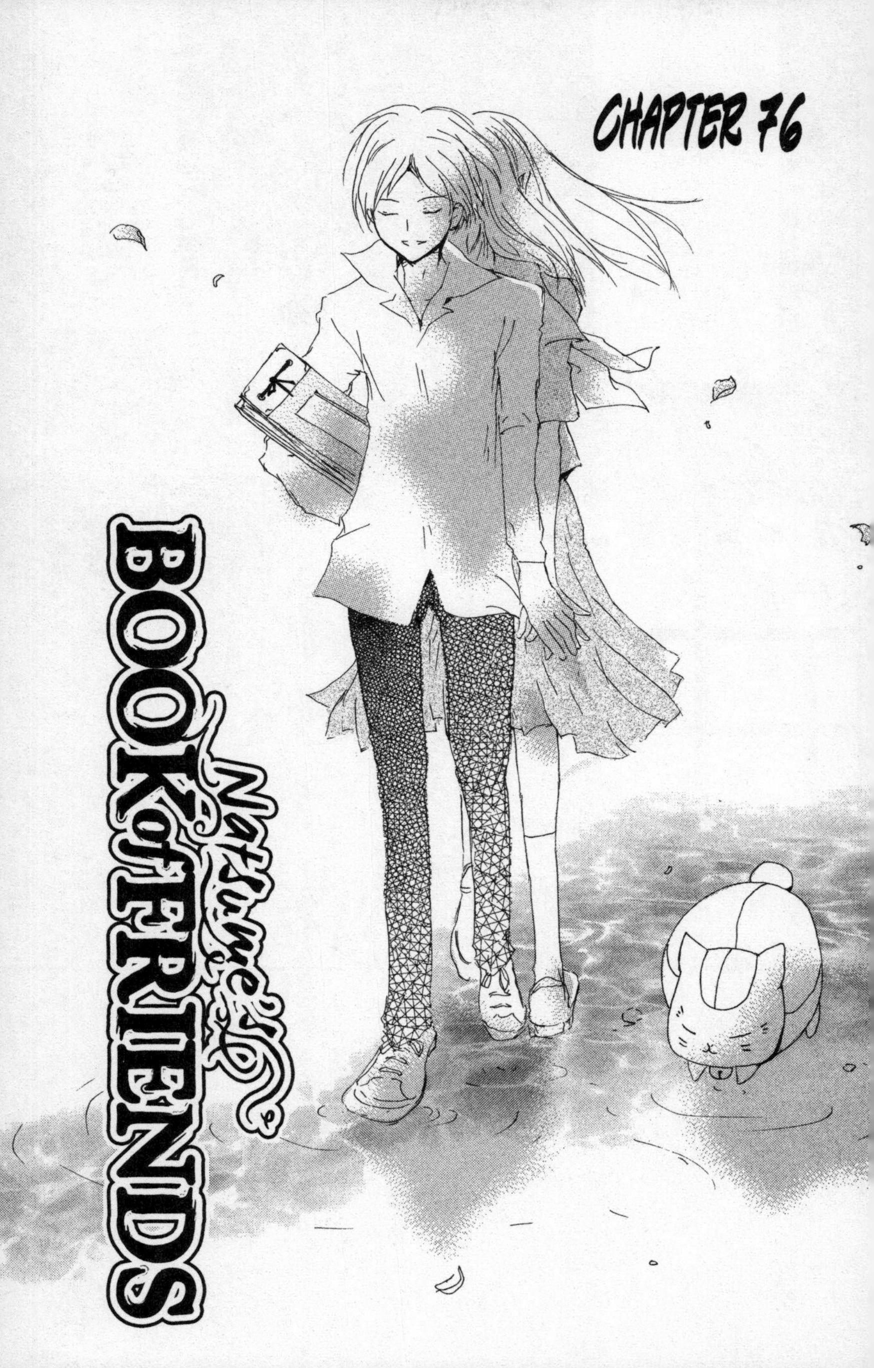
CHAPTER 76
Natsume's BOOK of FRIENDS

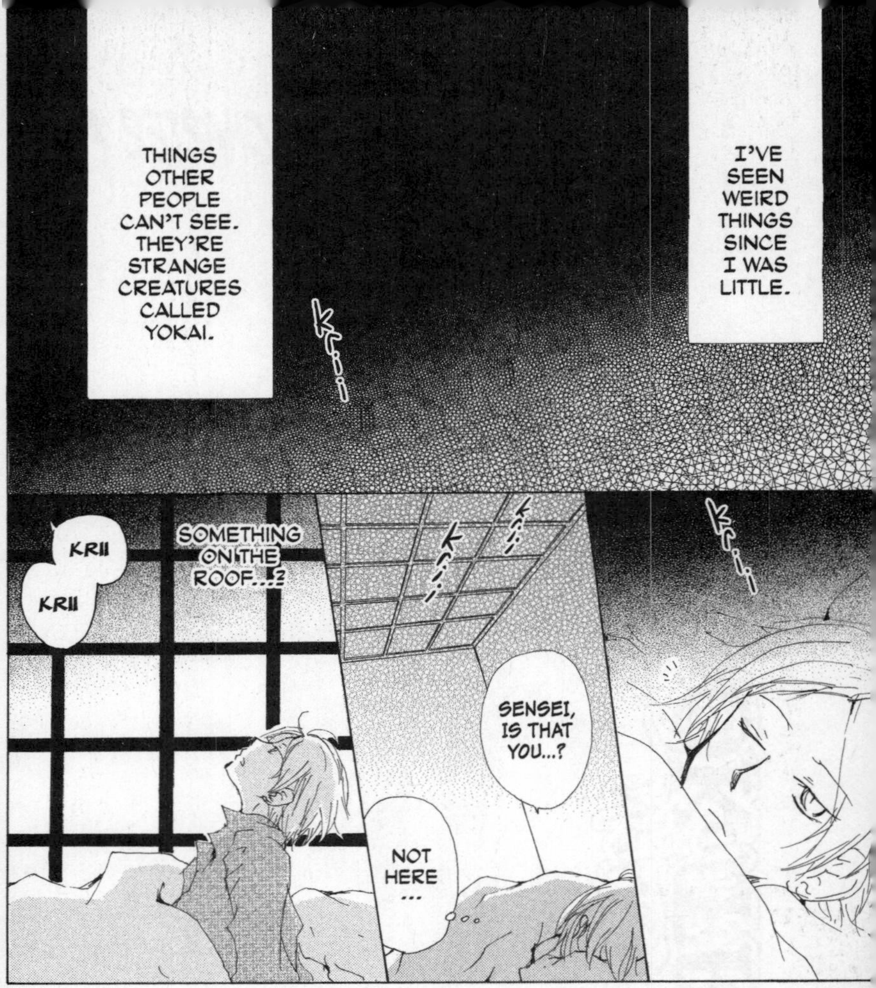
I'VE SEEN WEIRD THINGS SINCE I WAS LITTLE.
THINGS OTHER PEOPLE CAN'T SEE. THEY'RE STRANGE CREATURES CALLED YOKAI.
SENSEI, IS THAT YOU...?
NOT HERE...
SOMETHING ON THE ROOF...?
KRII
KRII

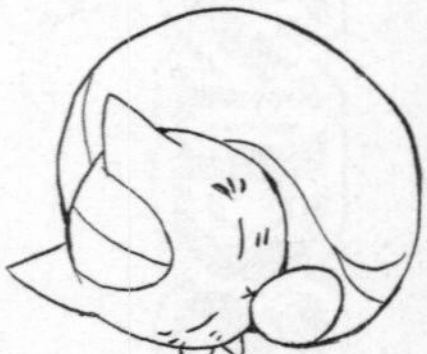

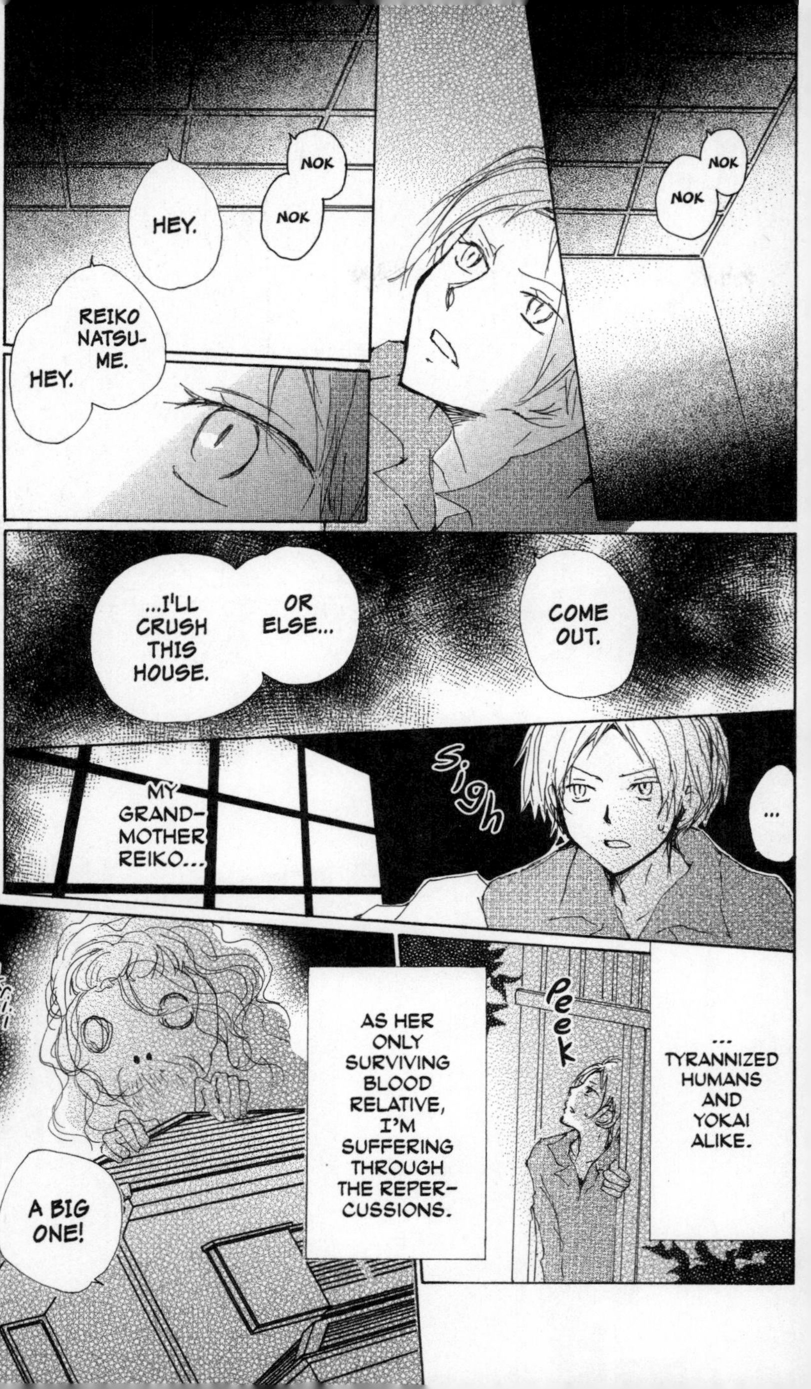
NOK NOK
NOK NOK
HEY.
REIKO NATSUME. HEY.
COME OUT.
OR ELSE...
...I'LL CRUSH THIS HOUSE.
...
Sigh
MY GRANDMOTHER REIKO...
...TYRANNIZED HUMANS AND YOKAI ALIKE.
Peek
AS HER ONLY SURVIVING BLOOD RELATIVE, I'M SUFFERING THROUGH THE REPERCUSSIONS.
A BIG ONE!

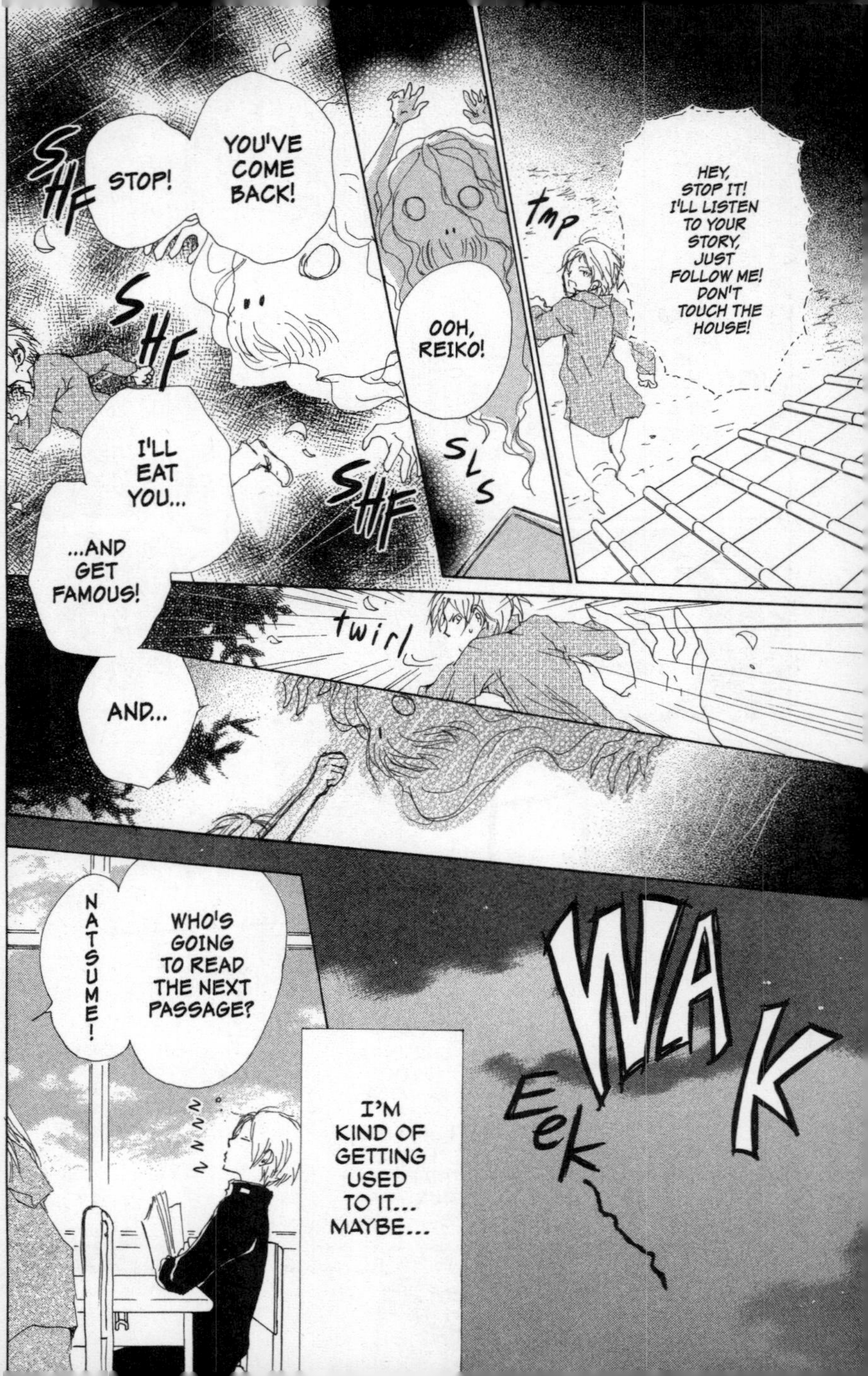
tmp
HEY, STOP IT! I'LL LISTEN TO YOUR STORY, JUST FOLLOW ME! DON'T TOUCH THE HOUSE!
OOH, REIKO!
SLS
YOU'VE COME BACK!
STOP!
SHF
SHF
I'LL EAT YOU...
...AND GET FAMOUS!
SHF
twirl
AND...
WAK
Eek
NATSUME!
WHO'S GOING TO READ THE NEXT PASSAGE?
I'M KIND OF GETTING USED TO IT... MAYBE...

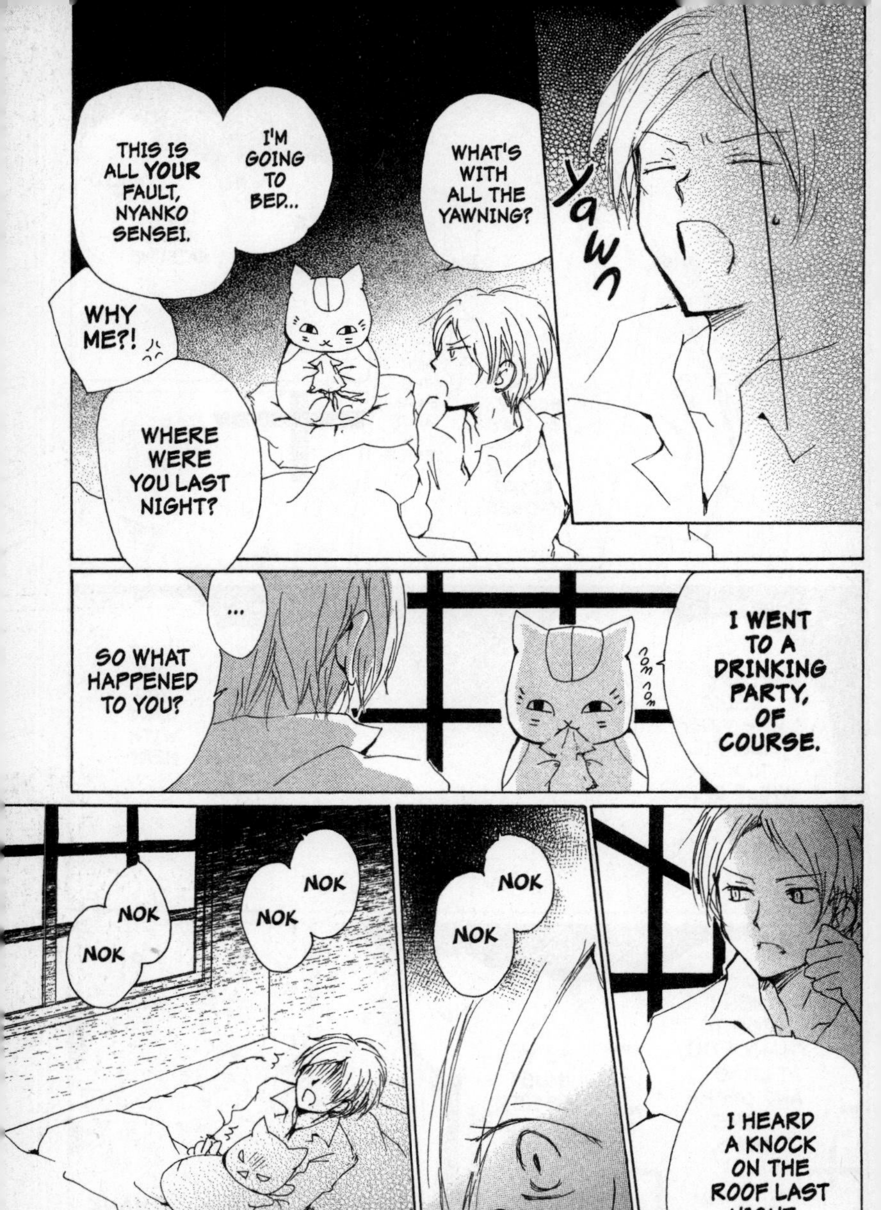

yawn
WHAT'S WITH ALL THE YAWNING?
I'M GOING TO BED...
THIS IS ALL YOUR FAULT, NYANKO SENSEI.
WHY ME?!
WHERE WERE YOU LAST NIGHT?
I WENT TO A DRINKING PARTY, OF COURSE.
nom nom
...
SO WHAT HAPPENED TO YOU?
I HEARD A KNOCK ON THE ROOF LAST NIGHT...
NOK NOK
gasp
NOK NOK
NOK NOK

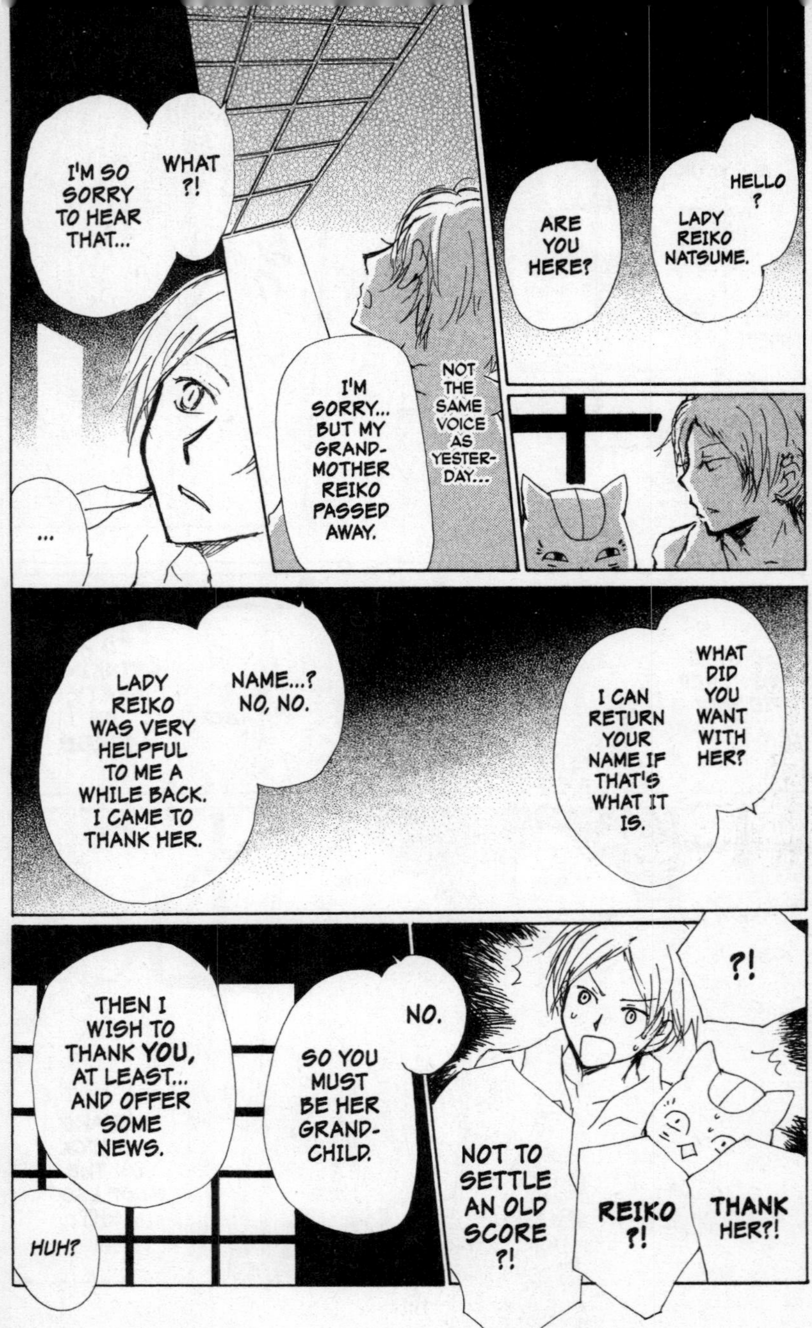
HELLO? LADY REIKO NATSUME.
ARE YOU HERE?
NOT THE SAME VOICE AS YESTERDAY...
I'M SORRY... BUT MY GRANDMOTHER REIKO PASSED AWAY.
WHAT?!
I'M SO SORRY TO HEAR THAT...
...
WHAT DID YOU WANT WITH HER?
I CAN RETURN YOUR NAME IF THAT'S WHAT IT IS.
NAME...? NO, NO.
LADY REIKO WAS VERY HELPFUL TO ME A WHILE BACK. I CAME TO THANK HER.
?!
THANK HER?!
REIKO?!
NOT TO SETTLE AN OLD SCORE?!
NO.
SO YOU MUST BE HER GRANDCHILD.
THEN I WISH TO THANK YOU, AT LEAST... AND OFFER SOME NEWS.
HUH?

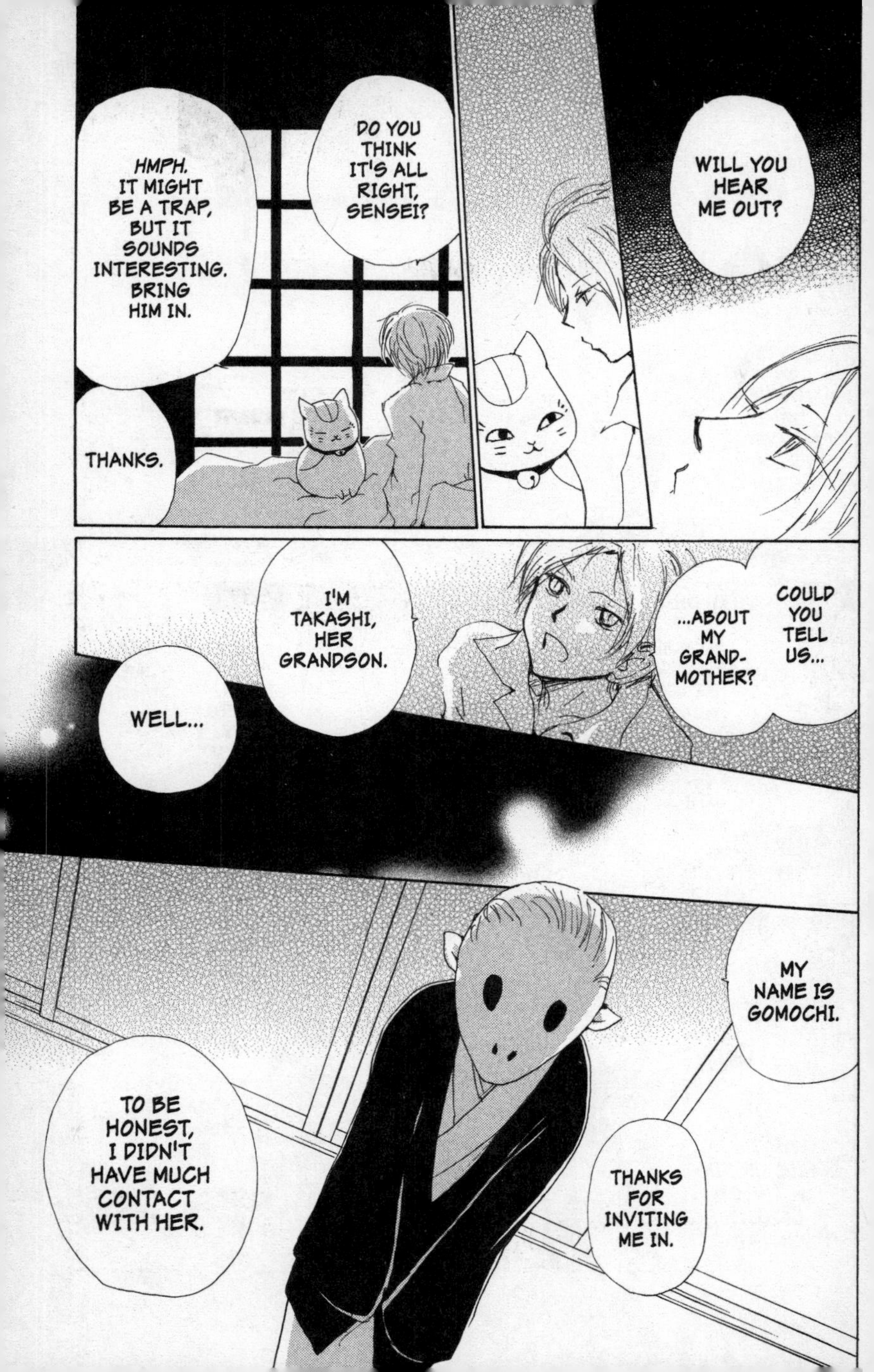
WILL YOU HEAR ME OUT?
DO YOU THINK IT'S ALL RIGHT, SENSEI?
HMPH. IT MIGHT BE A TRAP, BUT IT SOUNDS INTERESTING. BRING HIM IN.
THANKS.
COULD YOU TELL US...
...ABOUT MY GRAND-MOTHER?
I'M TAKASHI, HER GRANDSON.
WELL...
MY NAME IS GOMOCHI.
THANKS FOR INVITING ME IN.
TO BE HONEST, I DIDN'T HAVE MUCH CONTACT WITH HER.

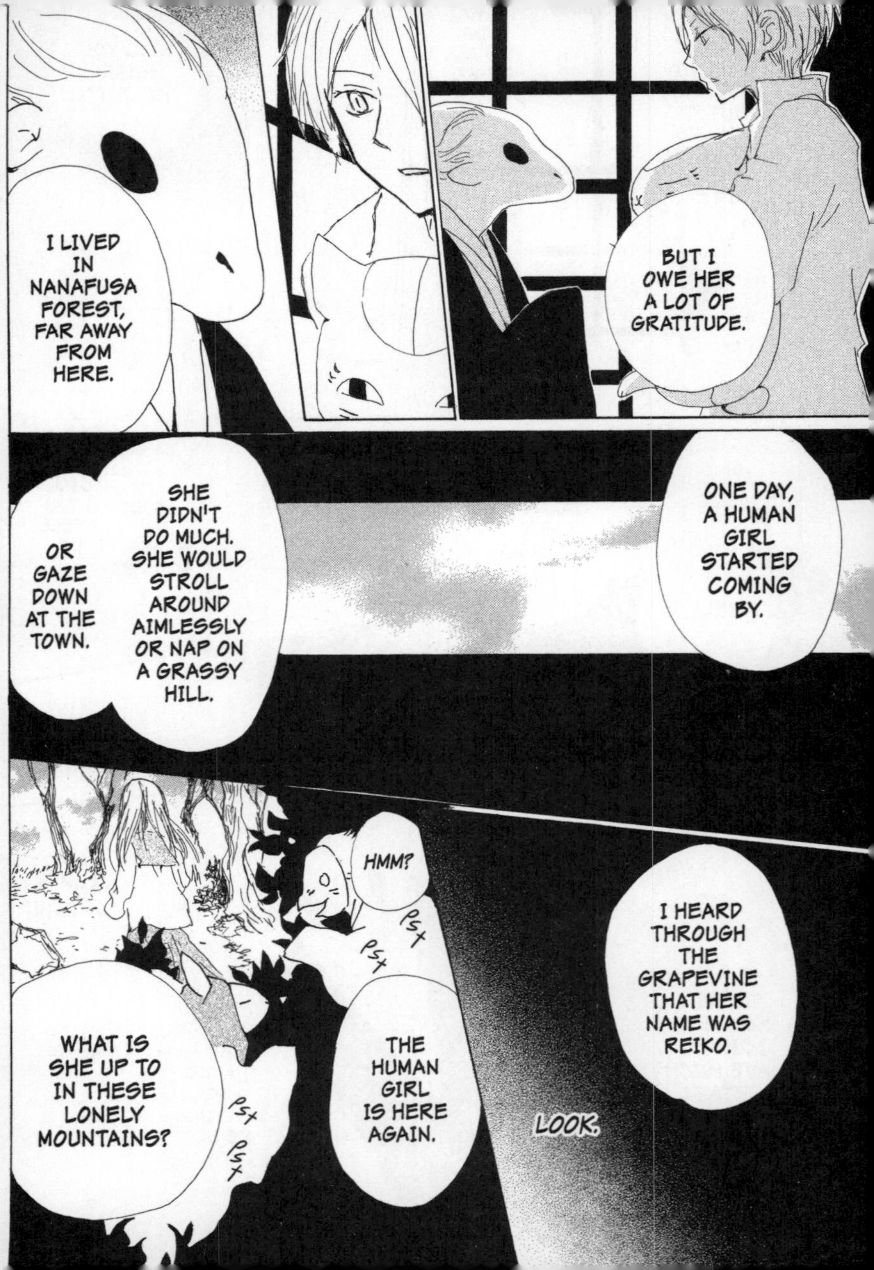
BUT I OWE HER A LOT OF GRATITUDE.
I LIVED IN NANAFUSA FOREST, FAR AWAY FROM HERE.
ONE DAY, A HUMAN GIRL STARTED COMING BY.
SHE DIDN'T DO MUCH. SHE WOULD STROLL AROUND AIMLESSLY OR NAP ON A GRASSY HILL.
OR GAZE DOWN AT THE TOWN.
I HEARD THROUGH THE GRAPEVINE THAT HER NAME WAS REIKO.
LOOK.
HMM?
PST
PST
THE HUMAN GIRL IS HERE AGAIN.
WHAT IS SHE UP TO IN THESE LONELY MOUNTAINS?
PST
PST

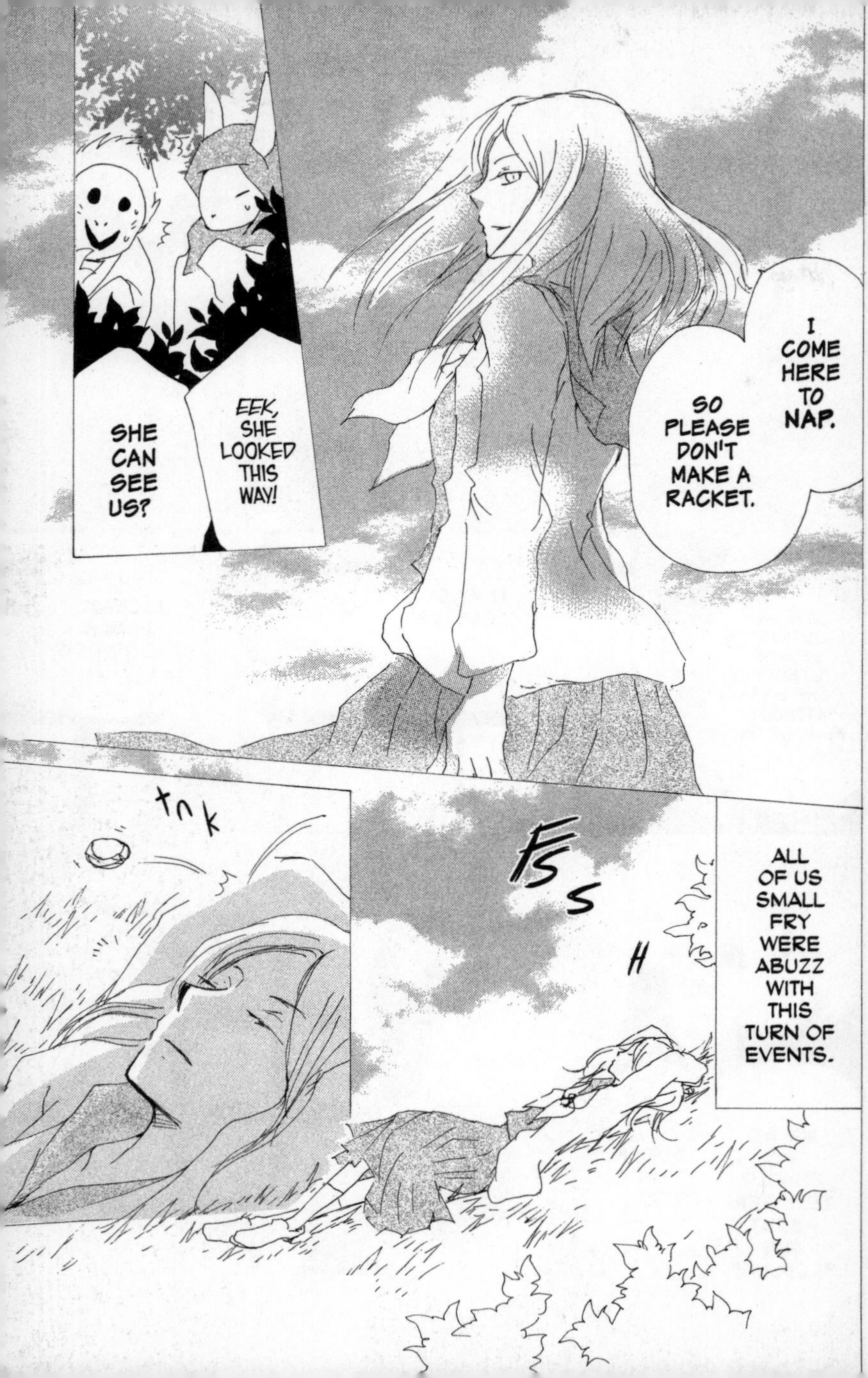
I COME HERE TO NAP.
SO PLEASE DON'T MAKE A RACKET.
EEK, SHE LOOKED THIS WAY!
SHE CAN SEE US?
ALL OF US SMALL FRY WERE ABUZZ WITH THIS TURN OF EVENTS.
FSSH
tnk

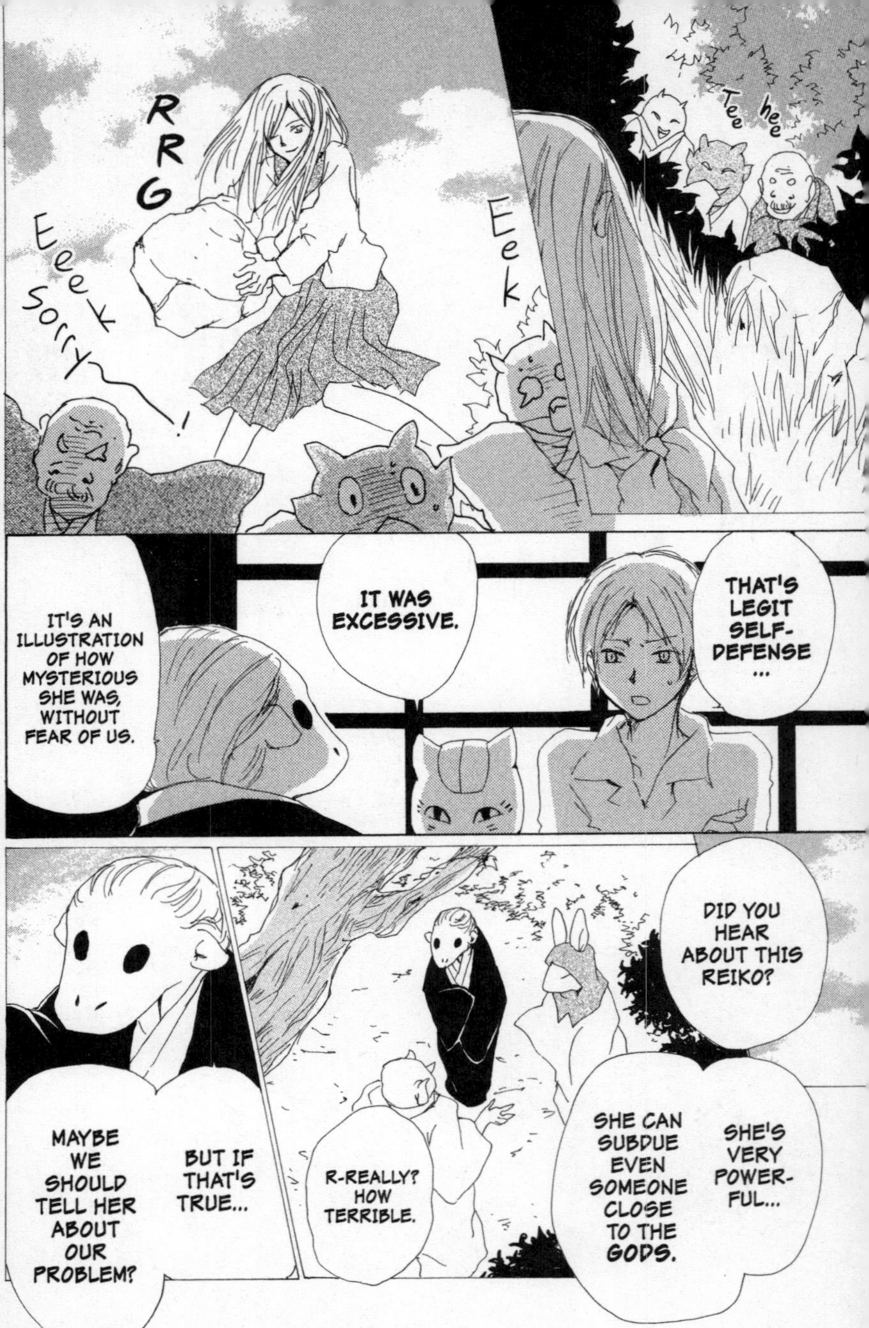
Tee hee
Eek
RRG
Eeeek Sorry~!
THAT'S LEGIT SELF-DEFENSE...
IT WAS EXCESSIVE.
IT'S AN ILLUSTRATION OF HOW MYSTERIOUS SHE WAS, WITHOUT FEAR OF US.
DID YOU HEAR ABOUT THIS REIKO?
SHE'S VERY POWER-FUL...
SHE CAN SUBDUE EVEN SOMEONE CLOSE TO THE GODS.
R-REALLY? HOW TERRIBLE.
BUT IF THAT'S TRUE...
MAYBE WE SHOULD TELL HER ABOUT OUR PROBLEM?

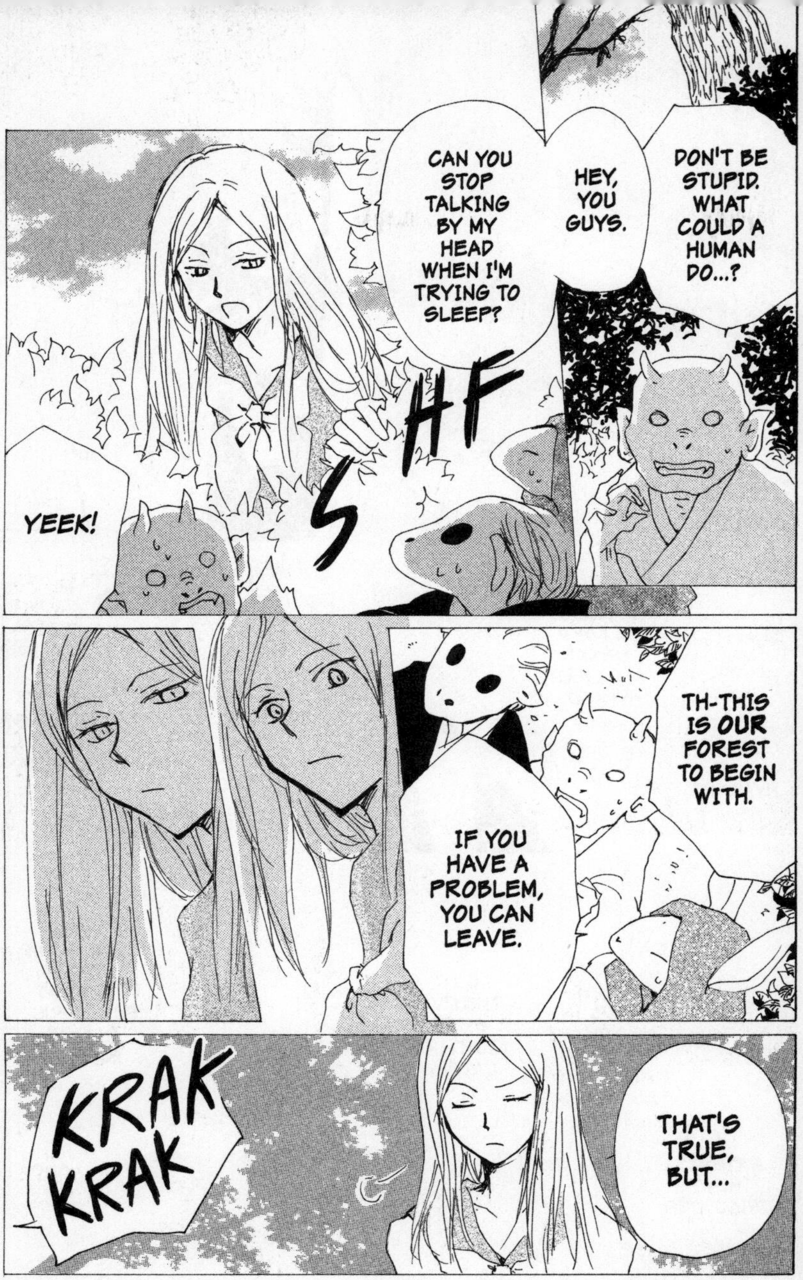
DON'T BE STUPID. WHAT COULD A HUMAN DO...?
HEY, YOU GUYS.
CAN YOU STOP TALKING BY MY HEAD WHEN I'M TRYING TO SLEEP?
SHF
YEEK!
TH-THIS IS OUR FOREST TO BEGIN WITH.
IF YOU HAVE A PROBLEM, YOU CAN LEAVE.
THAT'S TRUE, BUT...
KRAK KRAK

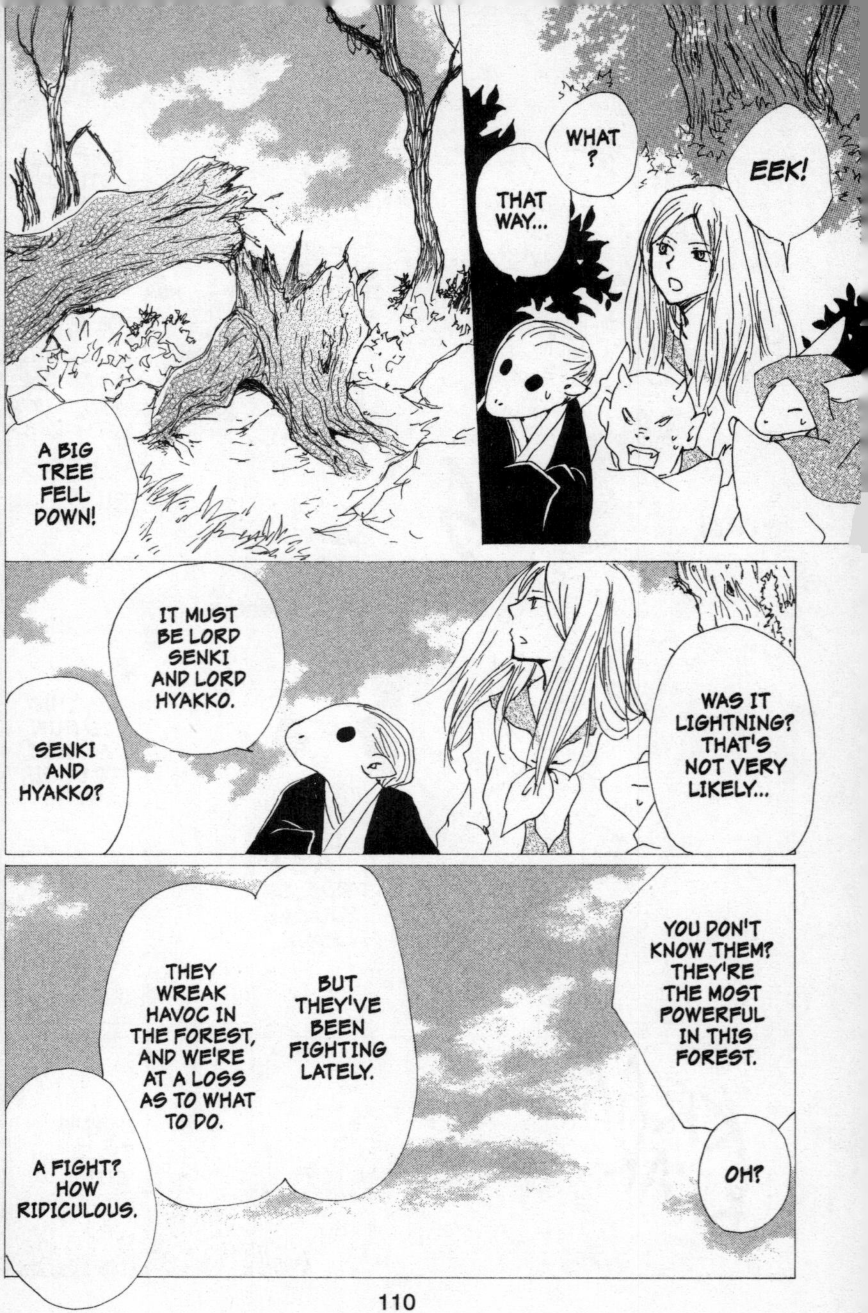
EEK!
WHAT?
THAT WAY...
A BIG TREE FELL DOWN!
WAS IT LIGHTNING? THAT'S NOT VERY LIKELY...
IT MUST BE LORD SENKI AND LORD HYAKKO.
SENKI AND HYAKKO?
YOU DON'T KNOW THEM? THEY'RE THE MOST POWERFUL IN THIS FOREST.
OH?
BUT THEY'VE BEEN FIGHTING LATELY.
THEY WREAK HAVOC IN THE FOREST, AND WE'RE AT A LOSS AS TO WHAT TO DO.
A FIGHT? HOW RIDICULOUS.

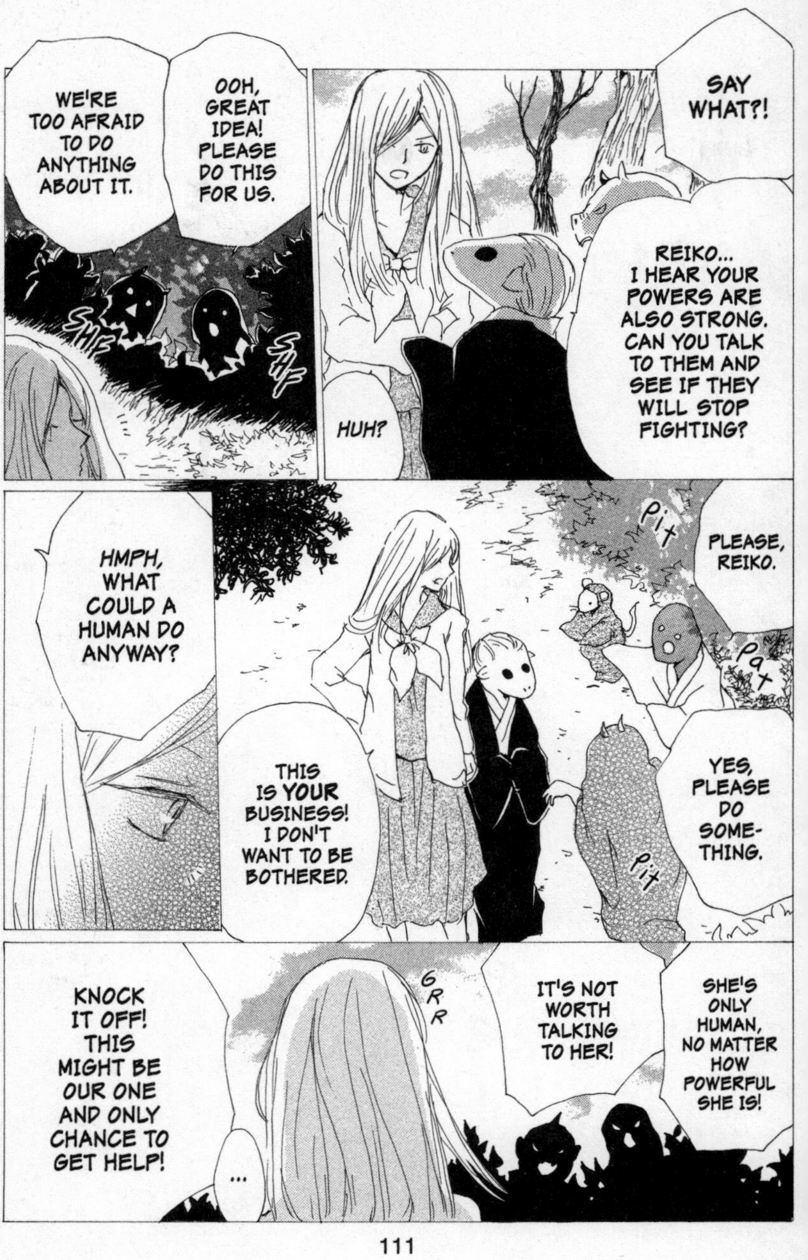
SAY WHAT?!
REIKO... I HEAR YOUR POWERS ARE ALSO STRONG. CAN YOU TALK TO THEM AND SEE IF THEY WILL STOP FIGHTING?
HUH?
OOH, GREAT IDEA! PLEASE DO THIS FOR US.
WE'RE TOO AFRAID TO DO ANYTHING ABOUT IT.
SHF
SHF
PLEASE, REIKO.
PIT
YES, PLEASE DO SOME-THING.
PAT
PIT
THIS IS YOUR BUSINESS! I DON'T WANT TO BE BOTHERED.
HMPH, WHAT COULD A HUMAN DO ANYWAY?
SHE'S ONLY HUMAN, NO MATTER HOW POWERFUL SHE IS!
IT'S NOT WORTH TALKING TO HER!
GRR
KNOCK IT OFF! THIS MIGHT BE OUR ONE AND ONLY CHANCE TO GET HELP!
...

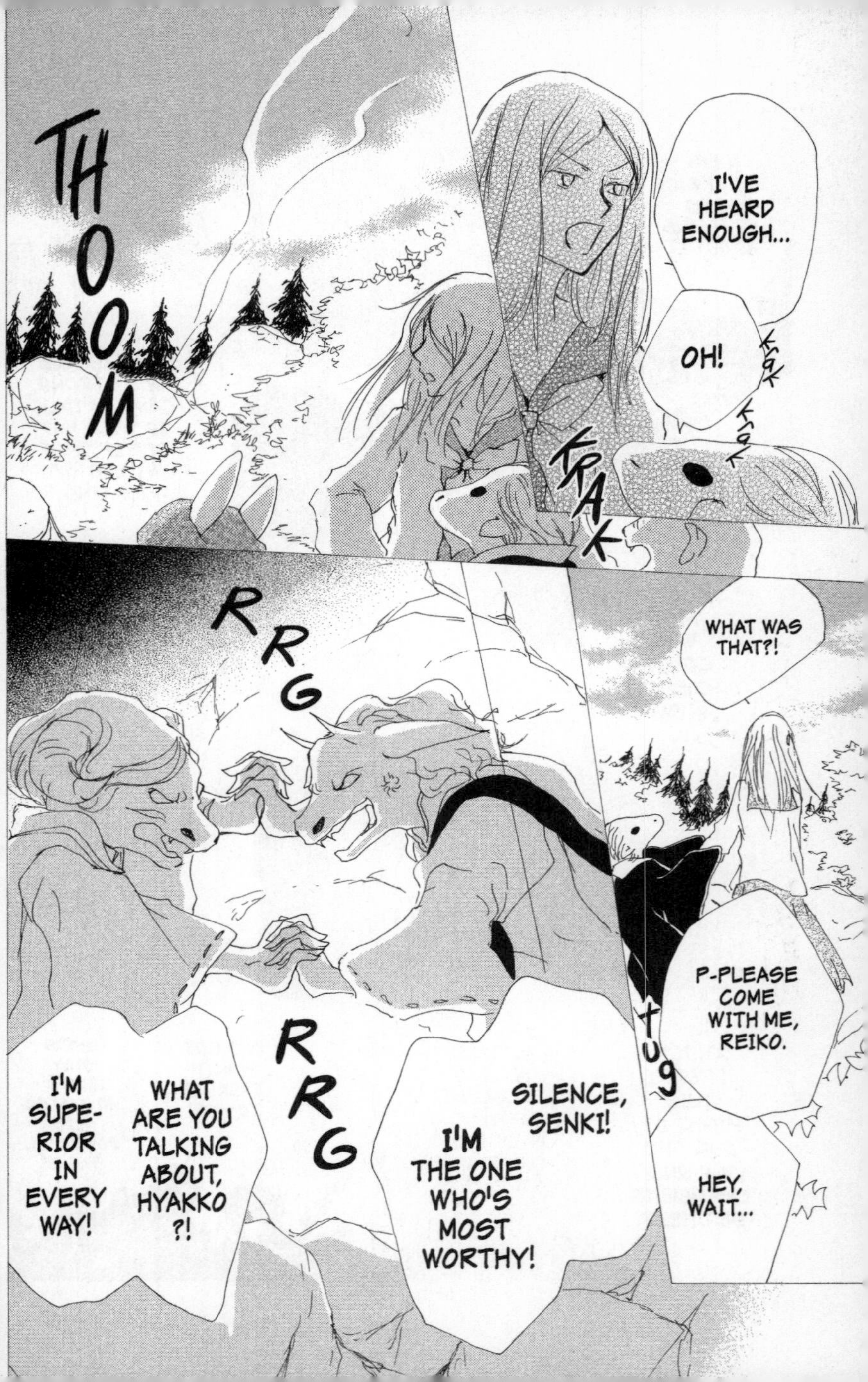
I'VE HEARD ENOUGH...
OH!
krak
krak
KRAK
THOOM
WHAT WAS THAT?!
P-PLEASE COME WITH ME, REIKO.
tug
HEY, WAIT...
RRG
SILENCE, SENKI!
I'M THE ONE WHO'S MOST WORTHY!
RRG
WHAT ARE YOU TALKING ABOUT, HYAKKO?!
I'M SUPERIOR IN EVERY WAY!

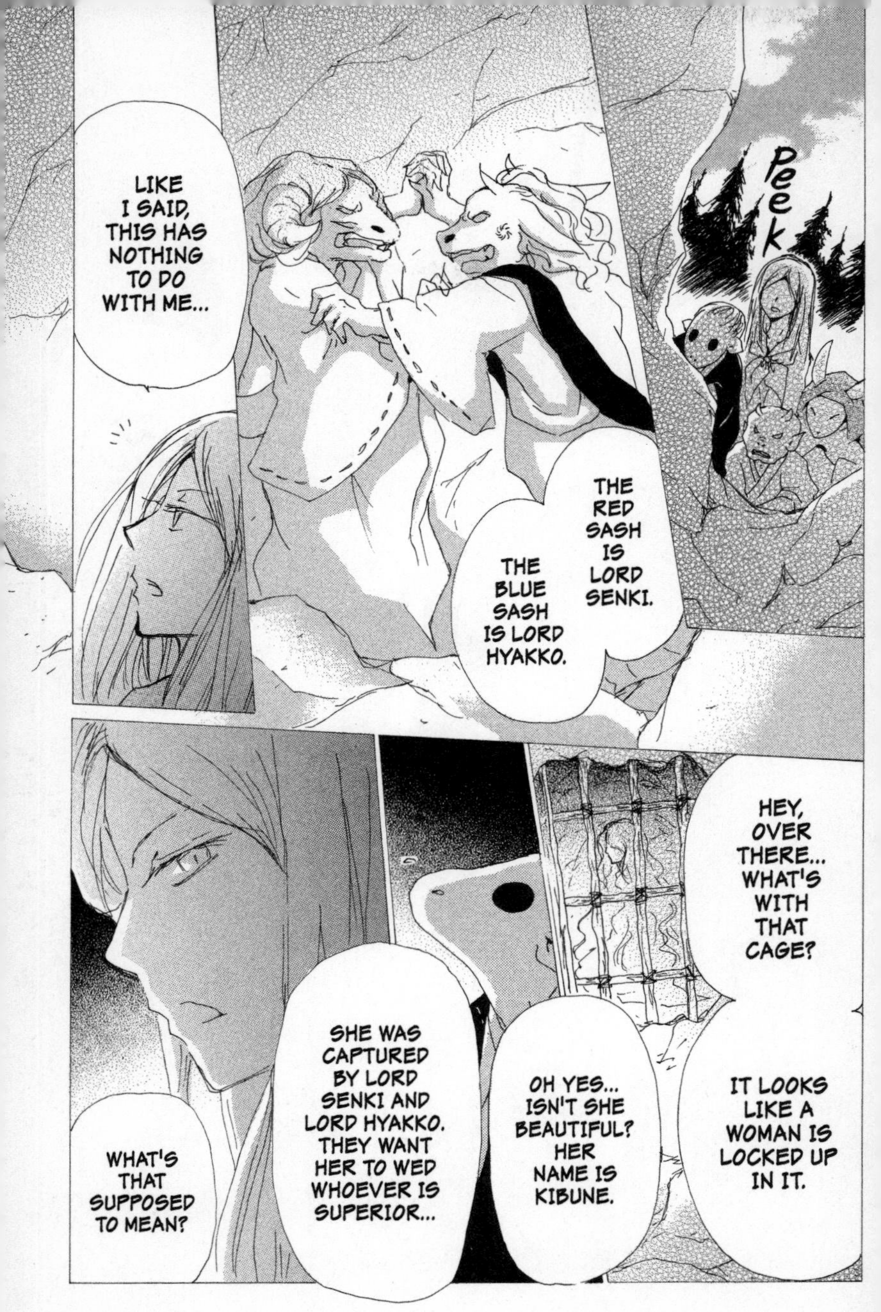
Peek
THE RED SASH IS LORD SENKI.
THE BLUE SASH IS LORD HYAKKO.
LIKE I SAID, THIS HAS NOTHING TO DO WITH ME...
HEY, OVER THERE... WHAT'S WITH THAT CAGE?
IT LOOKS LIKE A WOMAN IS LOCKED UP IN IT.
OH YES... ISN'T SHE BEAUTIFUL? HER NAME IS KIBUNE.
SHE WAS CAPTURED BY LORD SENKI AND LORD HYAKKO. THEY WANT HER TO WED WHOEVER IS SUPERIOR...
WHAT'S THAT SUPPOSED TO MEAN?

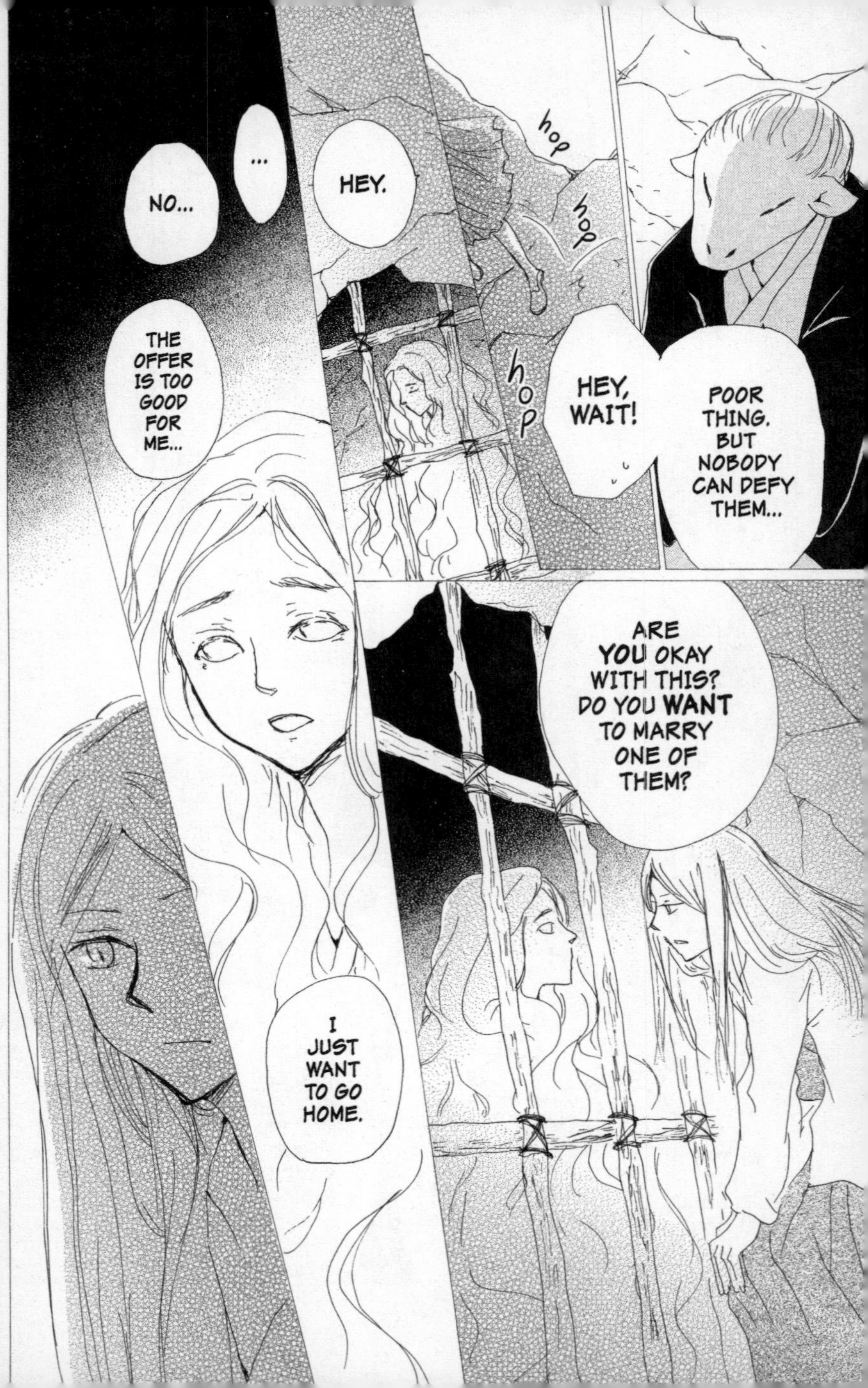

POOR THING. BUT NOBODY CAN DEFY THEM...
hop
hop
hop
HEY, WAIT!
HEY.
ARE YOU OKAY WITH THIS? DO YOU WANT TO MARRY ONE OF THEM?
...
NO...
THE OFFER IS TOO GOOD FOR ME...
I JUST WANT TO GO HOME.

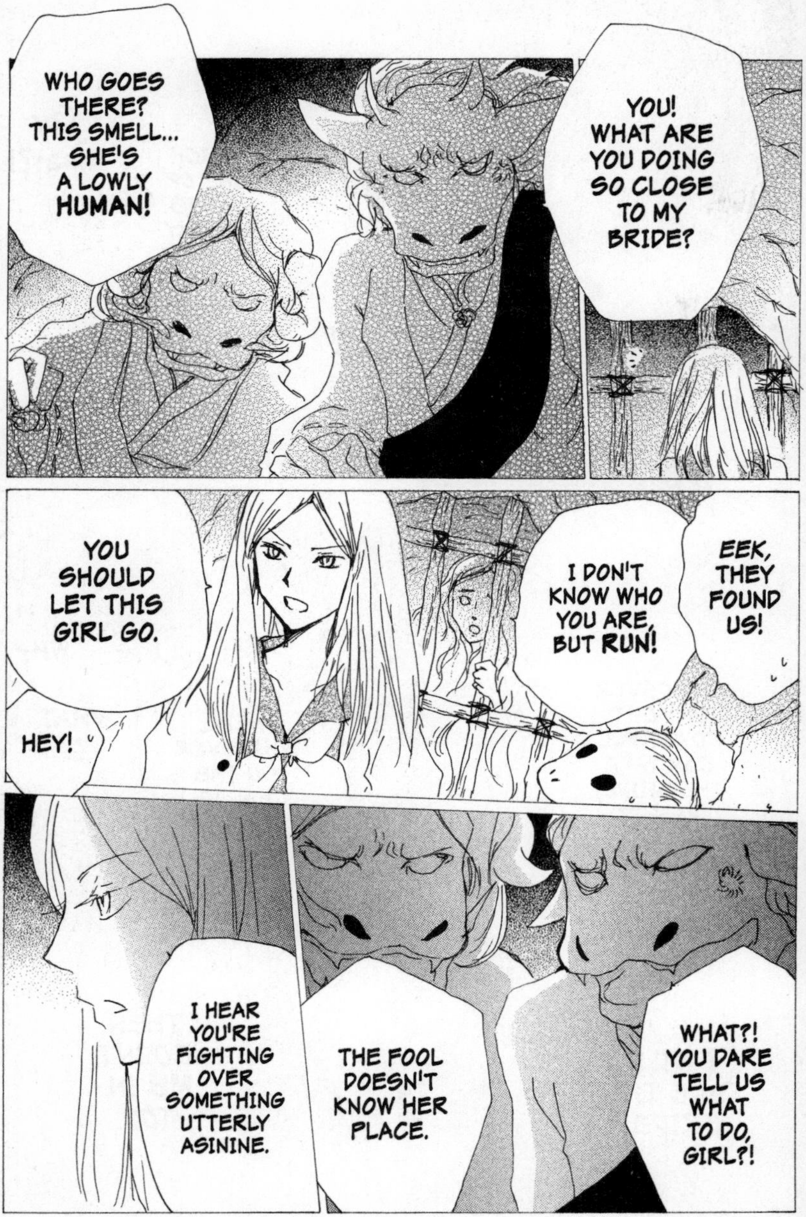
YOU! WHAT ARE YOU DOING SO CLOSE TO MY BRIDE?
WHO GOES THERE? THIS SMELL... SHE'S A LOWLY HUMAN!
EEK, THEY FOUND US!
I DON'T KNOW WHO YOU ARE, BUT RUN!
YOU SHOULD LET THIS GIRL GO.
HEY!
WHAT?! YOU DARE TELL US WHAT TO DO, GIRL?!
THE FOOL DOESN'T KNOW HER PLACE.
I HEAR YOU'RE FIGHTING OVER SOMETHING UTTERLY ASININE.

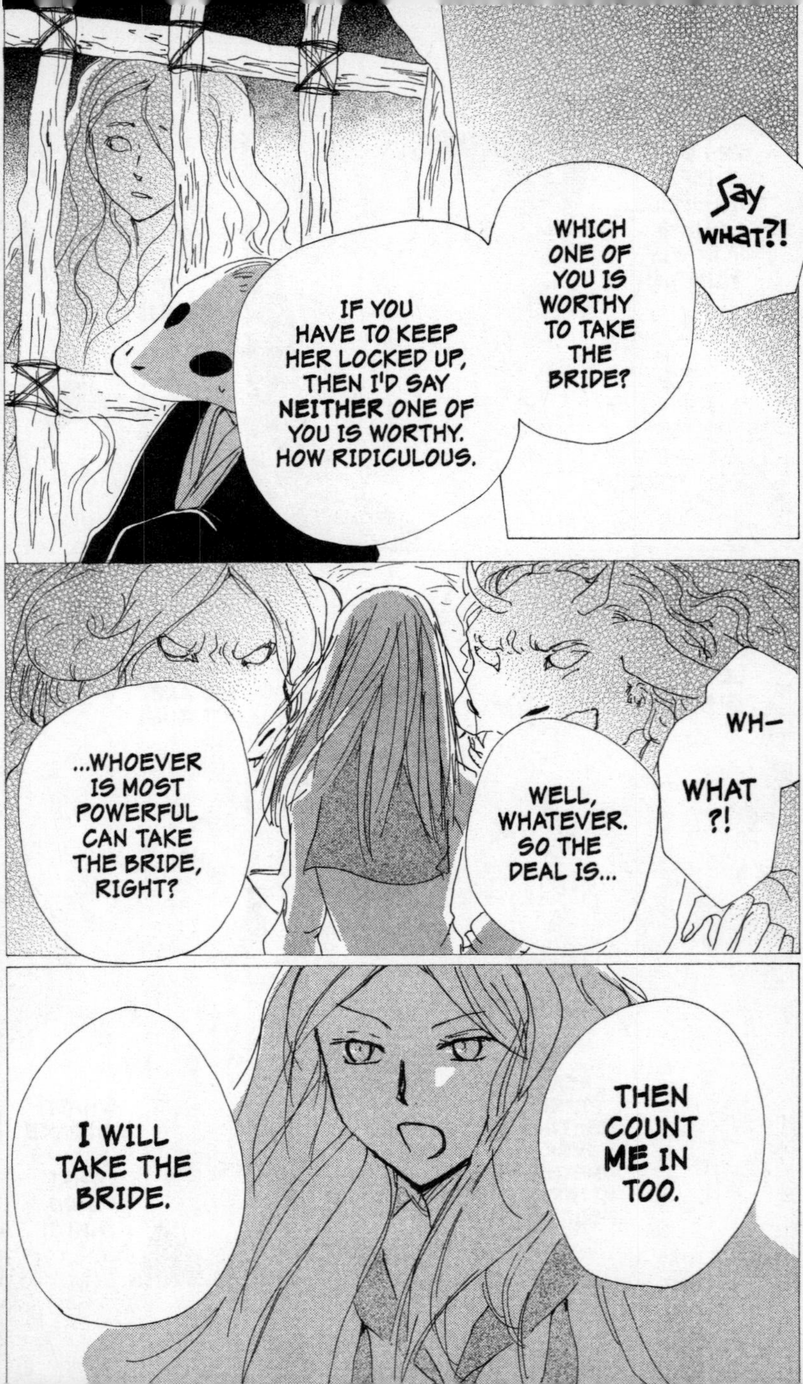
Say what?!
WHICH ONE OF YOU IS WORTHY TO TAKE THE BRIDE?
IF YOU HAVE TO KEEP HER LOCKED UP, THEN I'D SAY NEITHER ONE OF YOU IS WORTHY. HOW RIDICULOUS.
WH- WHAT?!
WELL, WHATEVER. SO THE DEAL IS...
...WHOEVER IS MOST POWERFUL CAN TAKE THE BRIDE, RIGHT?
THEN COUNT ME IN TOO.
I WILL TAKE THE BRIDE.

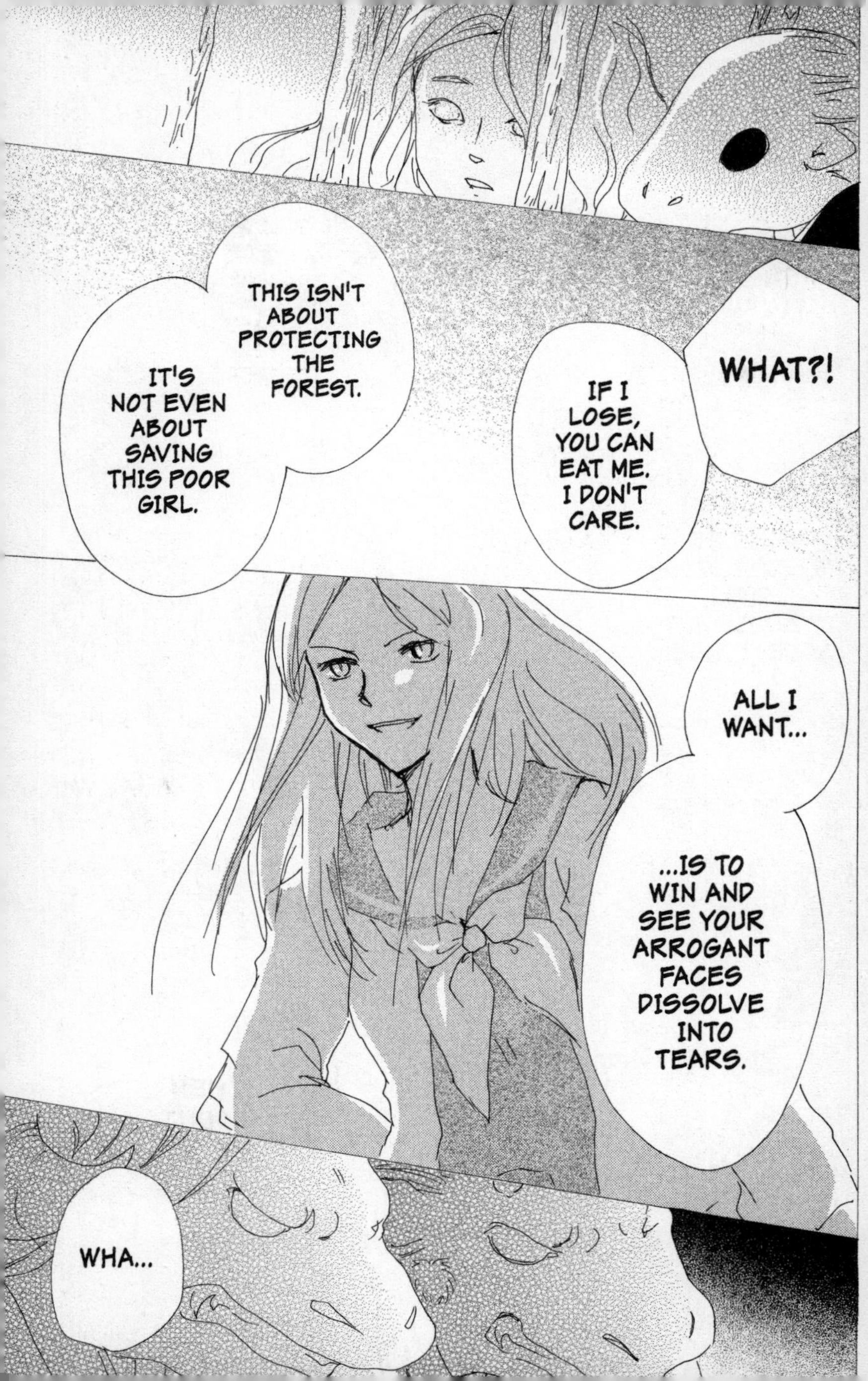
WHAT?!
IF I LOSE, YOU CAN EAT ME. I DON'T CARE.
THIS ISN'T ABOUT PROTECTING THE FOREST.
IT'S NOT EVEN ABOUT SAVING THIS POOR GIRL.
ALL I WANT...
...IS TO WIN AND SEE YOUR ARROGANT FACES DISSOLVE INTO TEARS.
WHA...

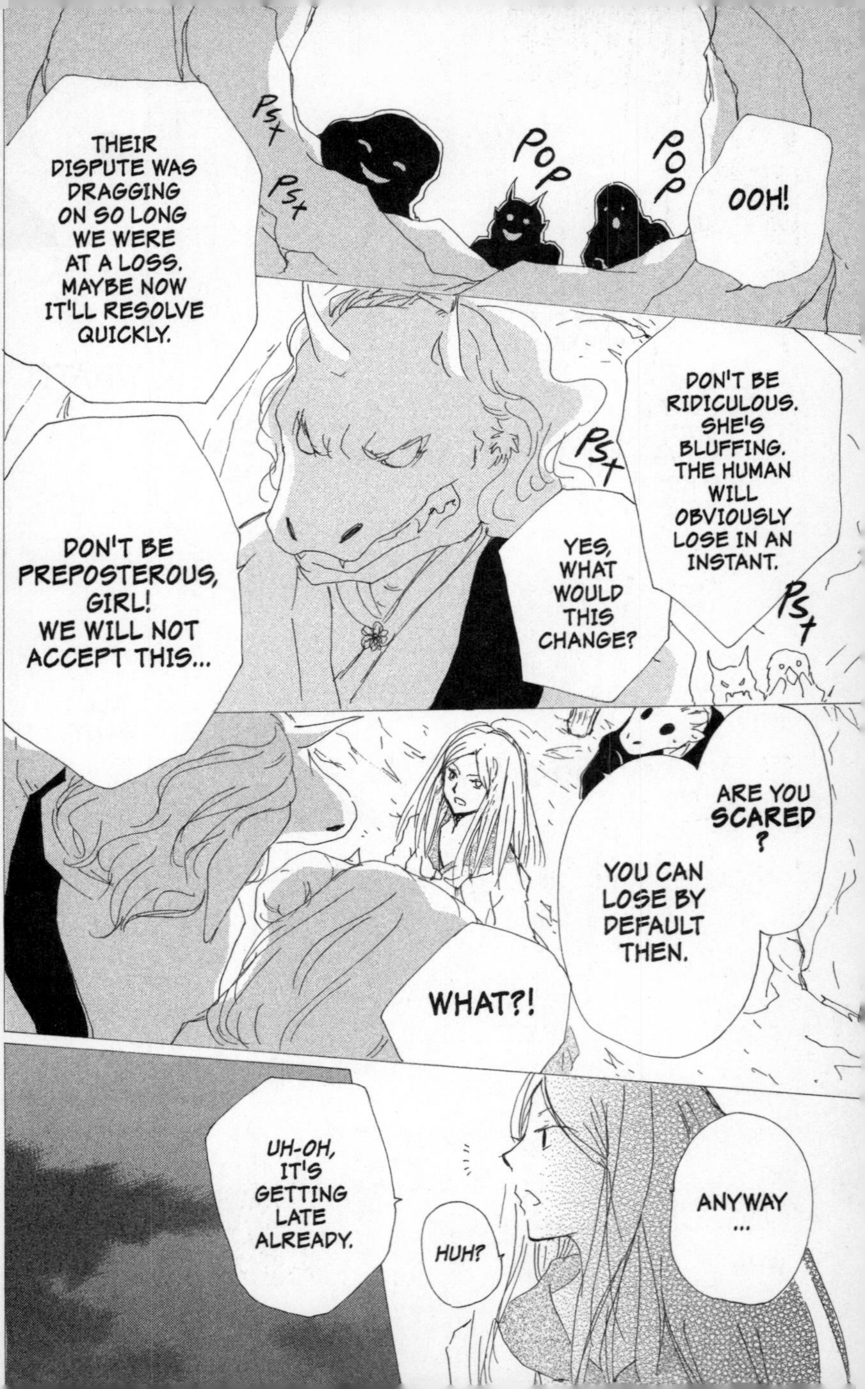
OOH!
POP
POP
PST
PST
THEIR DISPUTE WAS DRAGGING ON SO LONG WE WERE AT A LOSS. MAYBE NOW IT'LL RESOLVE QUICKLY.
DON'T BE RIDICULOUS. SHE'S BLUFFING. THE HUMAN WILL OBVIOUSLY LOSE IN AN INSTANT.
PST
PST
YES, WHAT WOULD THIS CHANGE?
DON'T BE PREPOSTEROUS, GIRL! WE WILL NOT ACCEPT THIS...
ARE YOU SCARED?
YOU CAN LOSE BY DEFAULT THEN.
WHAT?!
ANYWAY...
HUH?
UH-OH, IT'S GETTING LATE ALREADY.

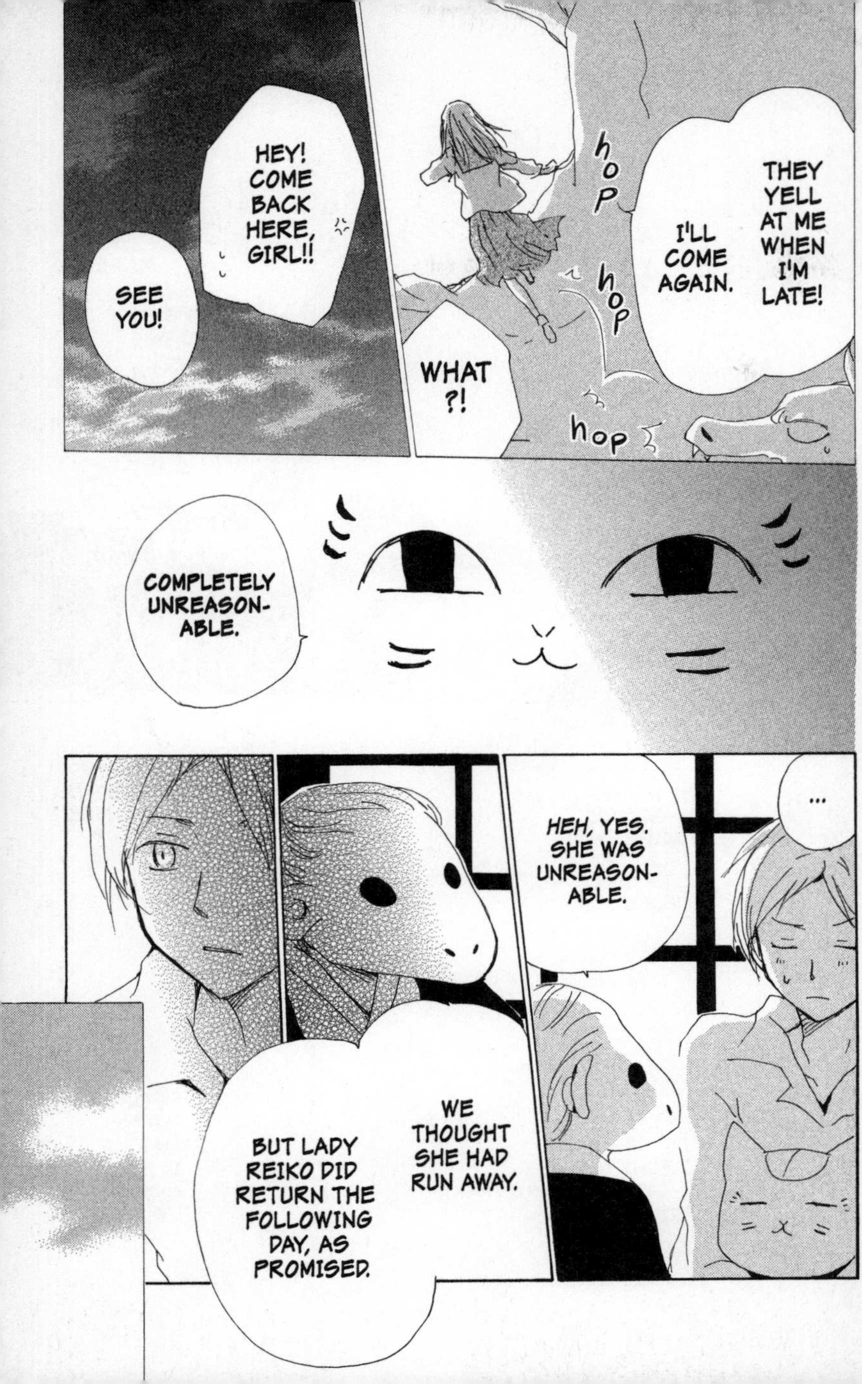
THEY YELL AT ME WHEN I'M LATE!
I'LL COME AGAIN.
hop
hop
hop
WHAT ?!
HEY! COME BACK HERE, GIRL!!
SEE YOU!
COMPLETELY UNREASON-ABLE.
...
HEH, YES. SHE WAS UNREASON-ABLE.
WE THOUGHT SHE HAD RUN AWAY.
BUT LADY REIKO DID RETURN THE FOLLOWING DAY, AS PROMISED.

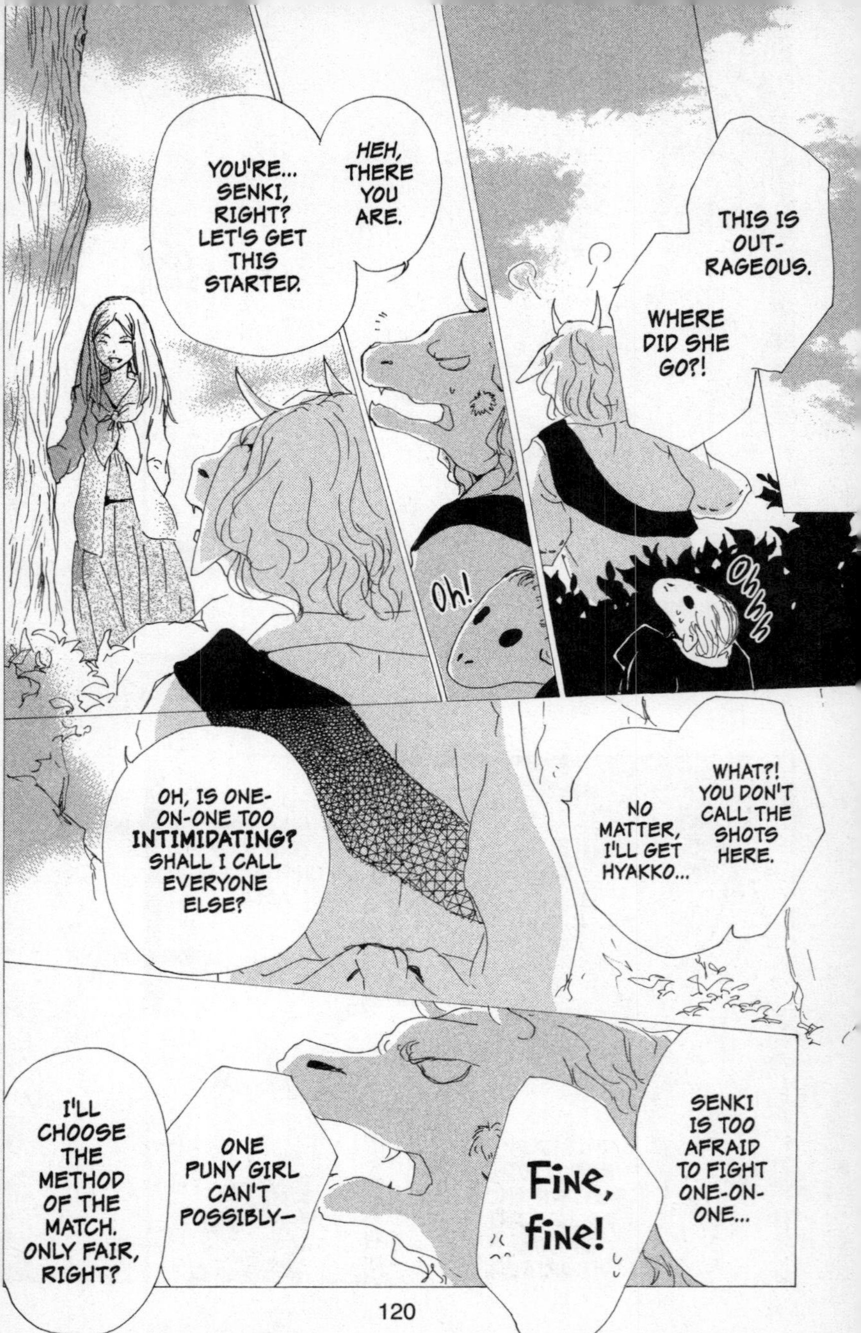
THIS IS OUT-RAGEOUS.
WHERE DID SHE GO?!
Ohhh
HEH, THERE YOU ARE.
Oh!
YOU'RE... SENKI, RIGHT? LET'S GET THIS STARTED.
WHAT?! YOU DON'T CALL THE SHOTS HERE.
NO MATTER, I'LL GET HYAKKO...
OH, IS ONE-ON-ONE TOO **INTIMIDATING?** SHALL I CALL EVERYONE ELSE?
SENKI IS TOO AFRAID TO FIGHT ONE-ON-ONE...
Fine, fine!
ONE PUNY GIRL CAN'T POSSIBLY—
I'LL CHOOSE THE METHOD OF THE MATCH. ONLY FAIR, RIGHT?

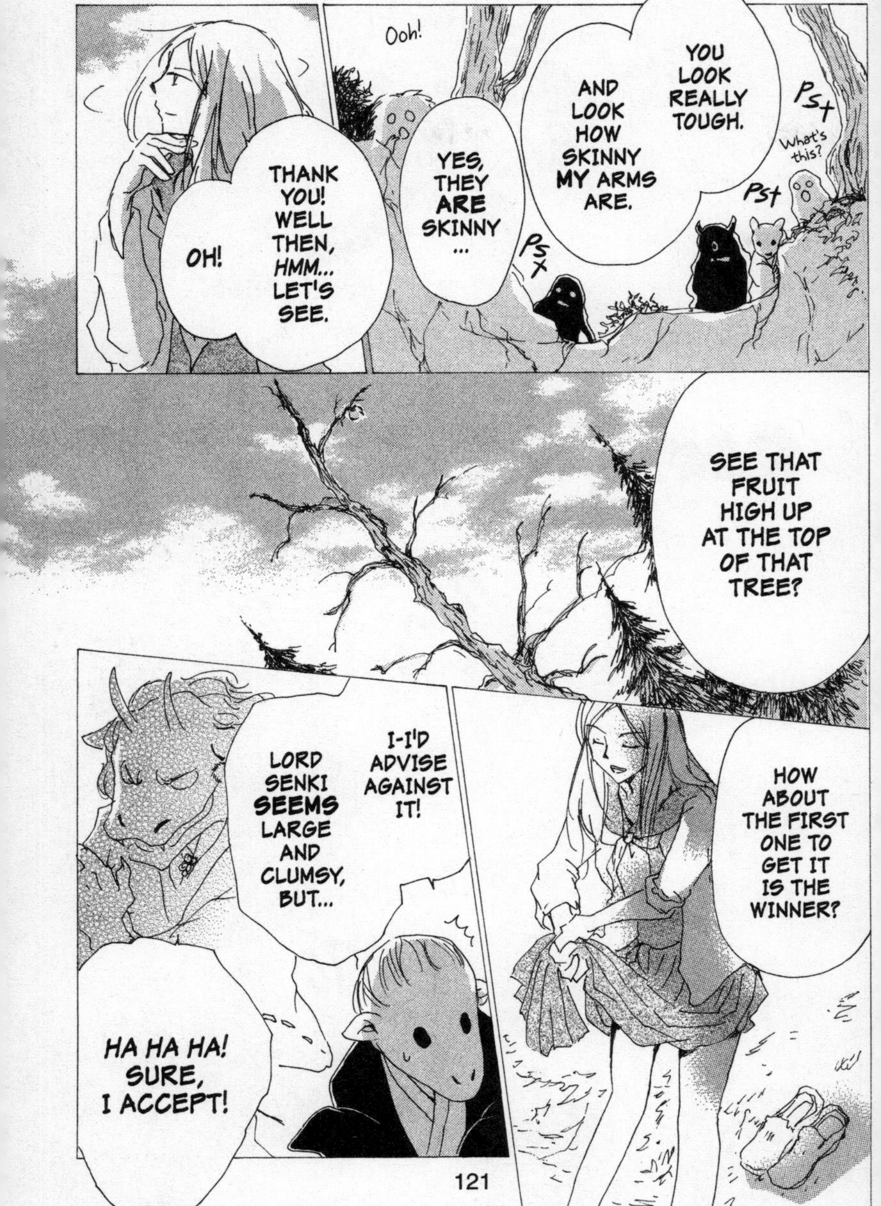
YOU LOOK REALLY TOUGH.
AND LOOK HOW SKINNY MY ARMS ARE.
Pst
What's this?
Pst
Ooh!
YES, THEY ARE SKINNY...
Pst
THANK YOU! WELL THEN, HMM... LET'S SEE.
OH!
SEE THAT FRUIT HIGH UP AT THE TOP OF THAT TREE?
HOW ABOUT THE FIRST ONE TO GET IT IS THE WINNER?
I-I'D ADVISE AGAINST IT!
LORD SENKI SEEMS LARGE AND CLUMSY, BUT...
HA HA HA! SURE, I ACCEPT!

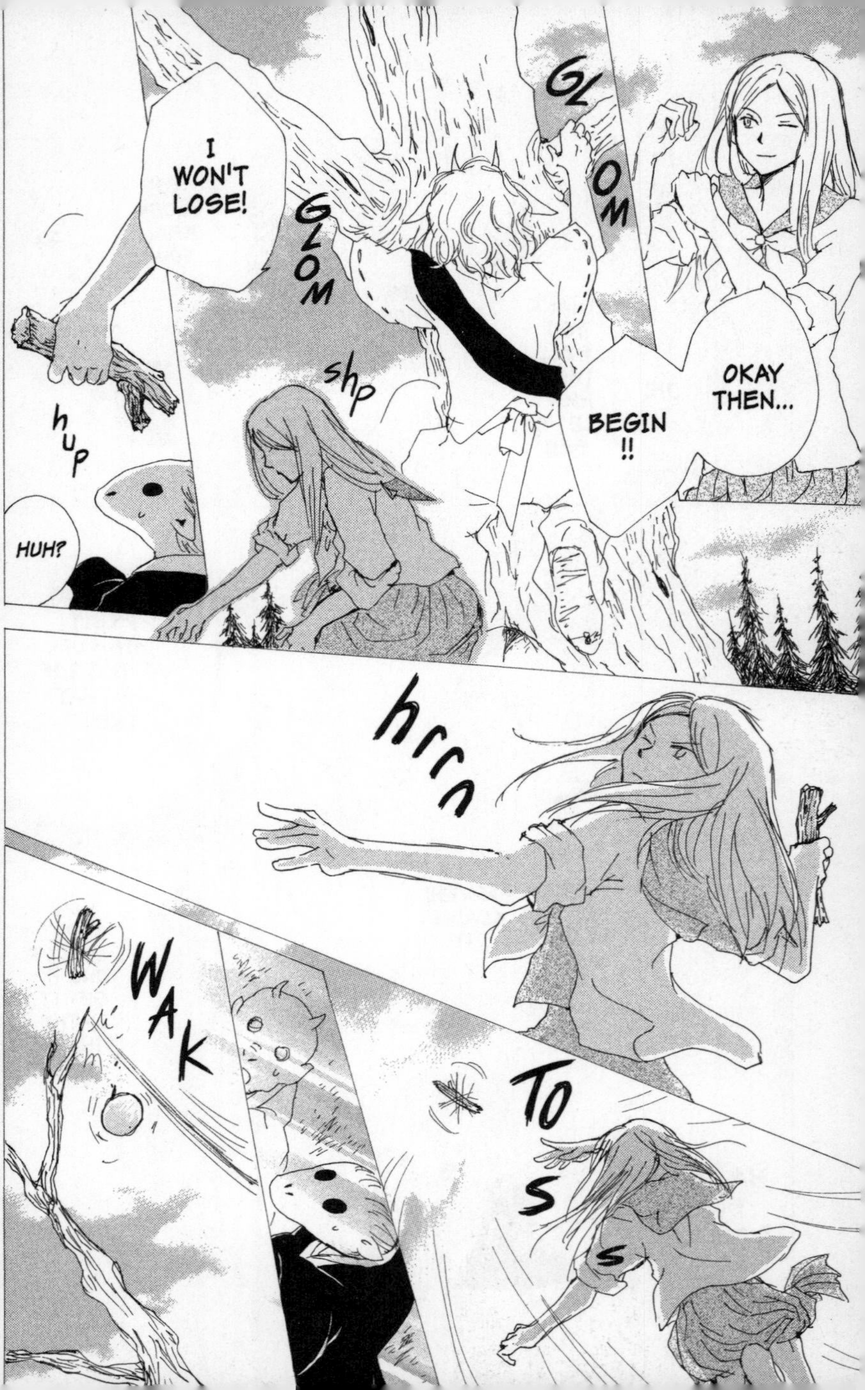
OKAY THEN...
BEGIN!!
GLOM
GLOM
I WON'T LOSE!
shp
hup
HUH?
hrrn
TOSS
WAK

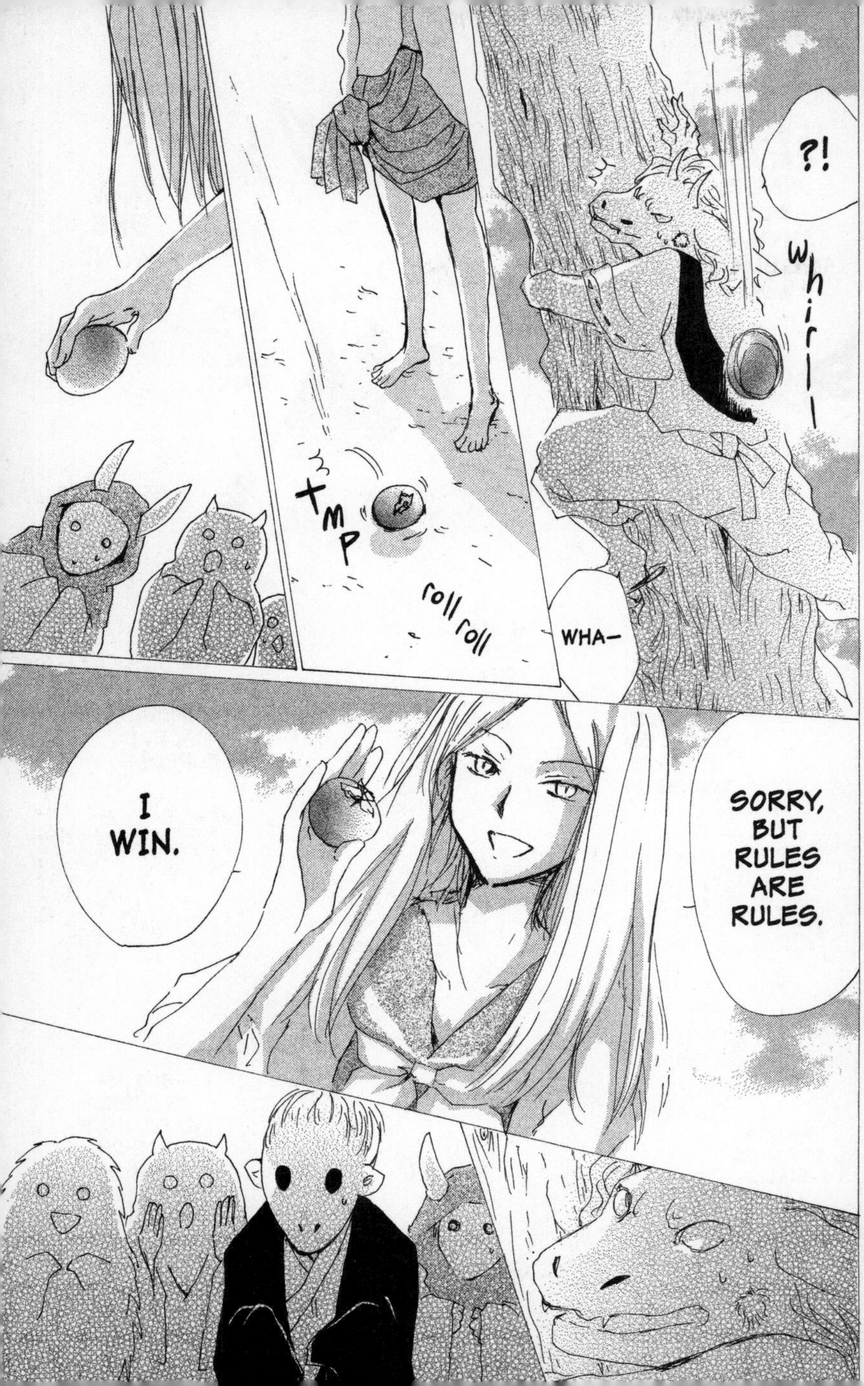
?!
whirl
WHA-
tmp
roll roll
SORRY, BUT RULES ARE RULES.
I WIN.

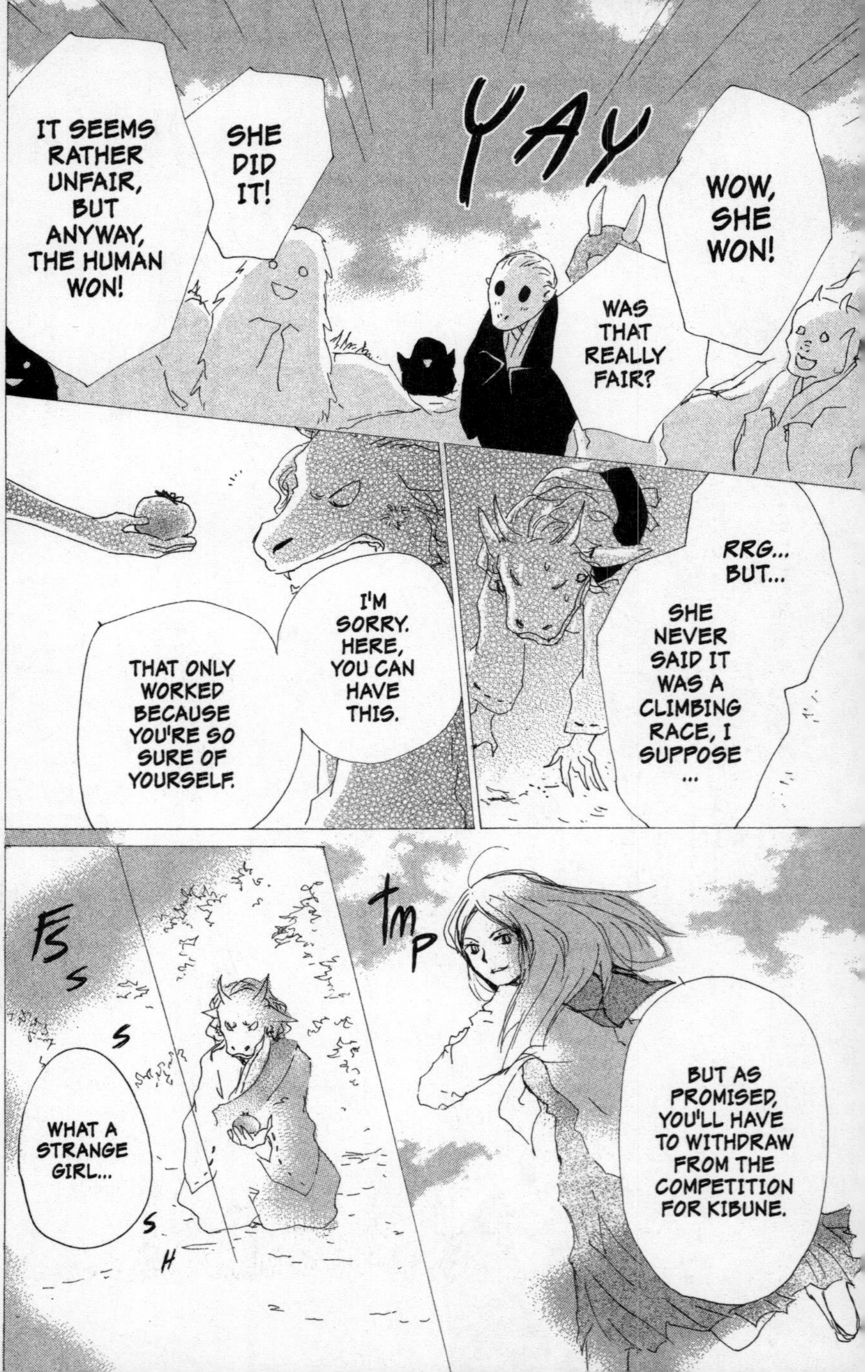
YAY
WOW, SHE WON!
WAS THAT REALLY FAIR?
SHE DID IT!
IT SEEMS RATHER UNFAIR, BUT ANYWAY, THE HUMAN WON!
RRG... BUT...
SHE NEVER SAID IT WAS A CLIMBING RACE, I SUPPOSE...
I'M SORRY. HERE, YOU CAN HAVE THIS.
THAT ONLY WORKED BECAUSE YOU'RE SO SURE OF YOURSELF.
TMP
BUT AS PROMISED, YOU'LL HAVE TO WITHDRAW FROM THE COMPETITION FOR KIBUNE.
FSSSH
WHAT A STRANGE GIRL...

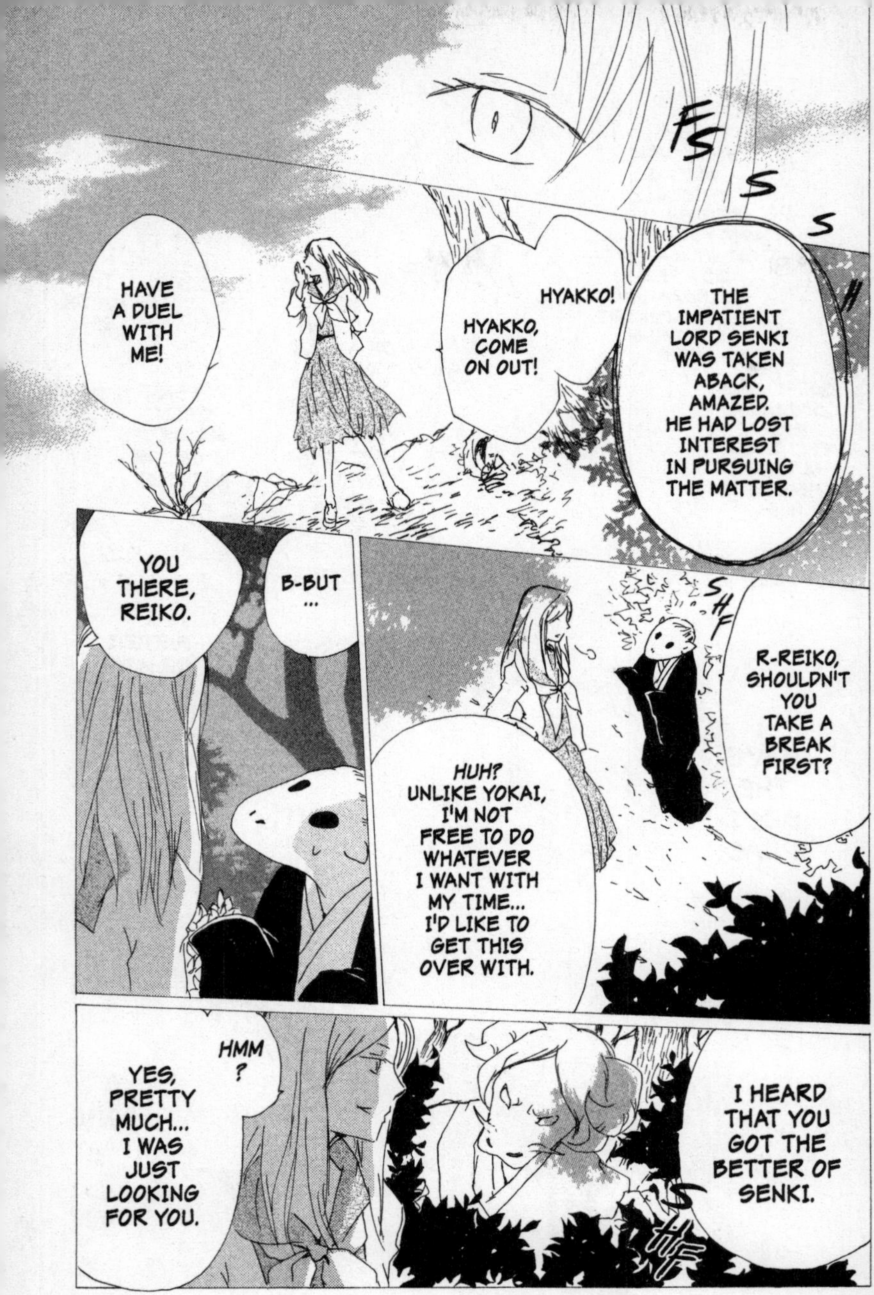
FSSS
THE IMPATIENT LORD SENKI WAS TAKEN ABACK, AMAZED. HE HAD LOST INTEREST IN PURSUING THE MATTER.
HYAKKO!
HYAKKO, COME ON OUT!
HAVE A DUEL WITH ME!
R-REIKO, SHOULDN'T YOU TAKE A BREAK FIRST?
SHF
HUH? UNLIKE YOKAI, I'M NOT FREE TO DO WHATEVER I WANT WITH MY TIME... I'D LIKE TO GET THIS OVER WITH.
B-BUT ...
YOU THERE, REIKO.
I HEARD THAT YOU GOT THE BETTER OF SENKI.
HMM ?
YES, PRETTY MUCH... I WAS JUST LOOKING FOR YOU.

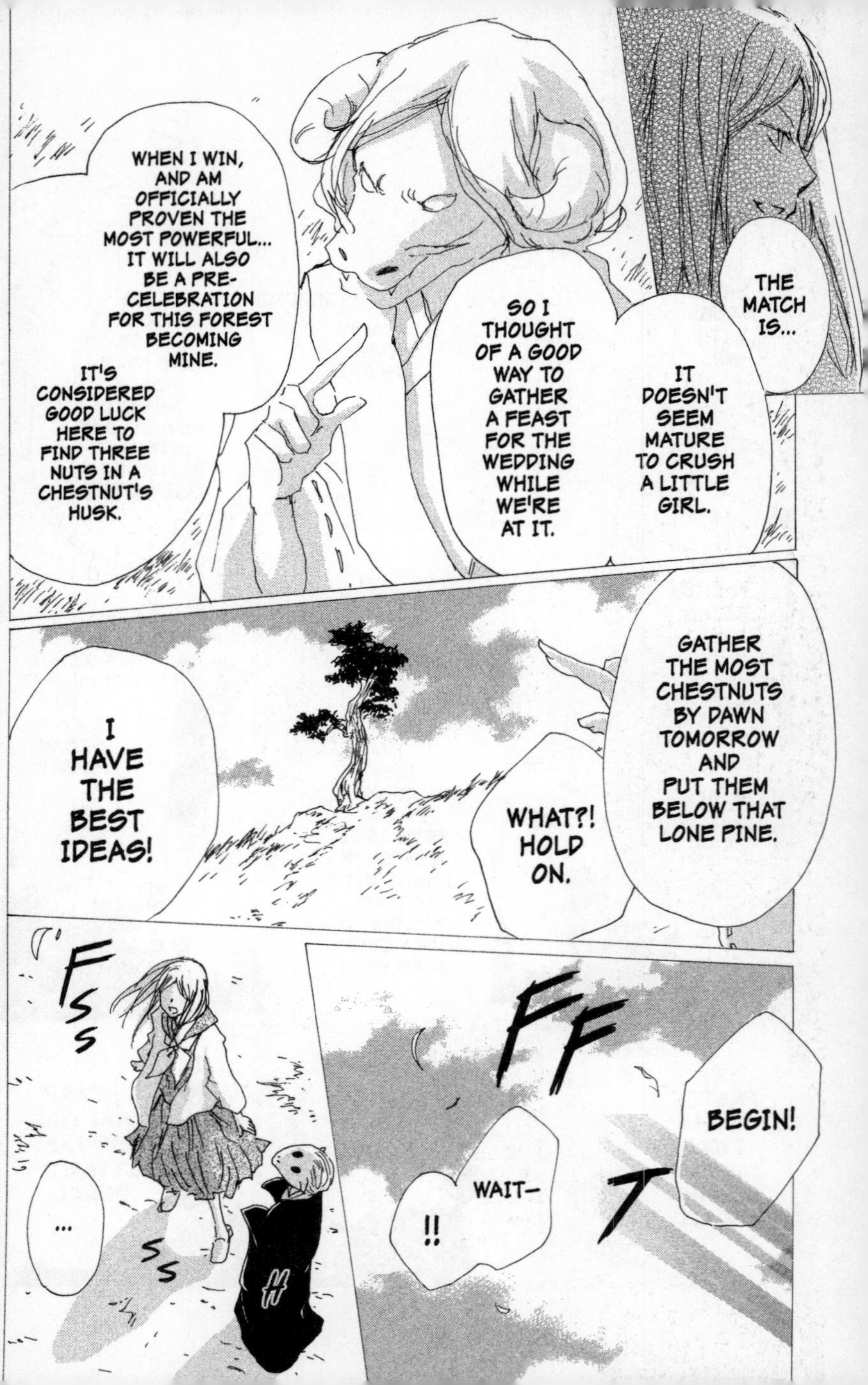
THE MATCH IS...
IT DOESN'T SEEM MATURE TO CRUSH A LITTLE GIRL.
SO I THOUGHT OF A GOOD WAY TO GATHER A FEAST FOR THE WEDDING WHILE WE'RE AT IT.
WHEN I WIN, AND AM OFFICIALLY PROVEN THE MOST POWERFUL... IT WILL ALSO BE A PRE-CELEBRATION FOR THIS FOREST BECOMING MINE.
IT'S CONSIDERED GOOD LUCK HERE TO FIND THREE NUTS IN A CHESTNUT'S HUSK.
GATHER THE MOST CHESTNUTS BY DAWN TOMORROW AND PUT THEM BELOW THAT LONE PINE.
WHAT?! HOLD ON.
I HAVE THE BEST IDEAS!
BEGIN!
FFT
WAIT–
!!
FSS
SS
...

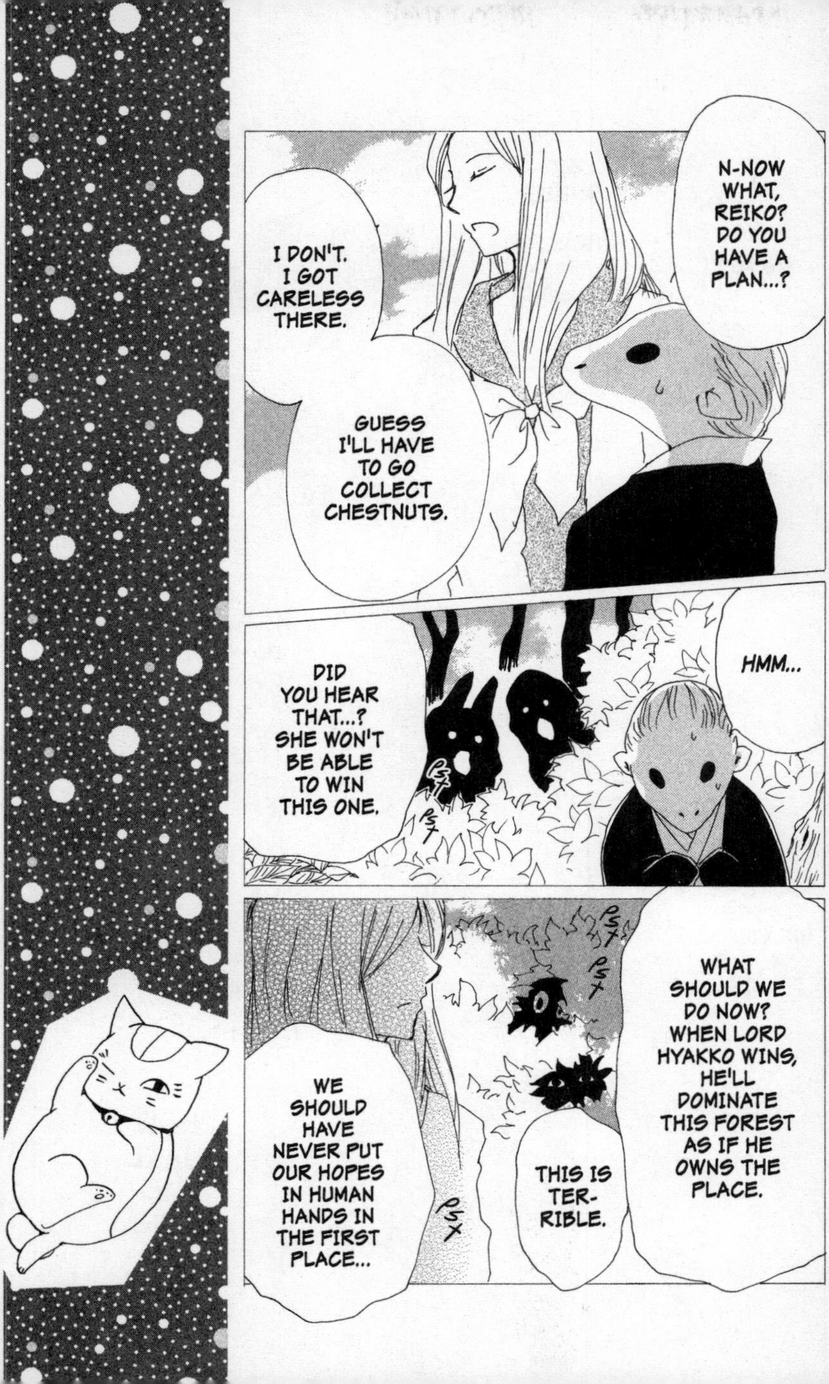
N-NOW WHAT, REIKO? DO YOU HAVE A PLAN...?
I DON'T. I GOT CARELESS THERE.
GUESS I'LL HAVE TO GO COLLECT CHESTNUTS.
HMM...
DID YOU HEAR THAT...? SHE WON'T BE ABLE TO WIN THIS ONE.
PST
PST
WHAT SHOULD WE DO NOW? WHEN LORD HYAKKO WINS, HE'LL DOMINATE THIS FOREST AS IF HE OWNS THE PLACE.
PST
PST
THIS IS TER-RIBLE.
WE SHOULD HAVE NEVER PUT OUR HOPES IN HUMAN HANDS IN THE FIRST PLACE...
PST

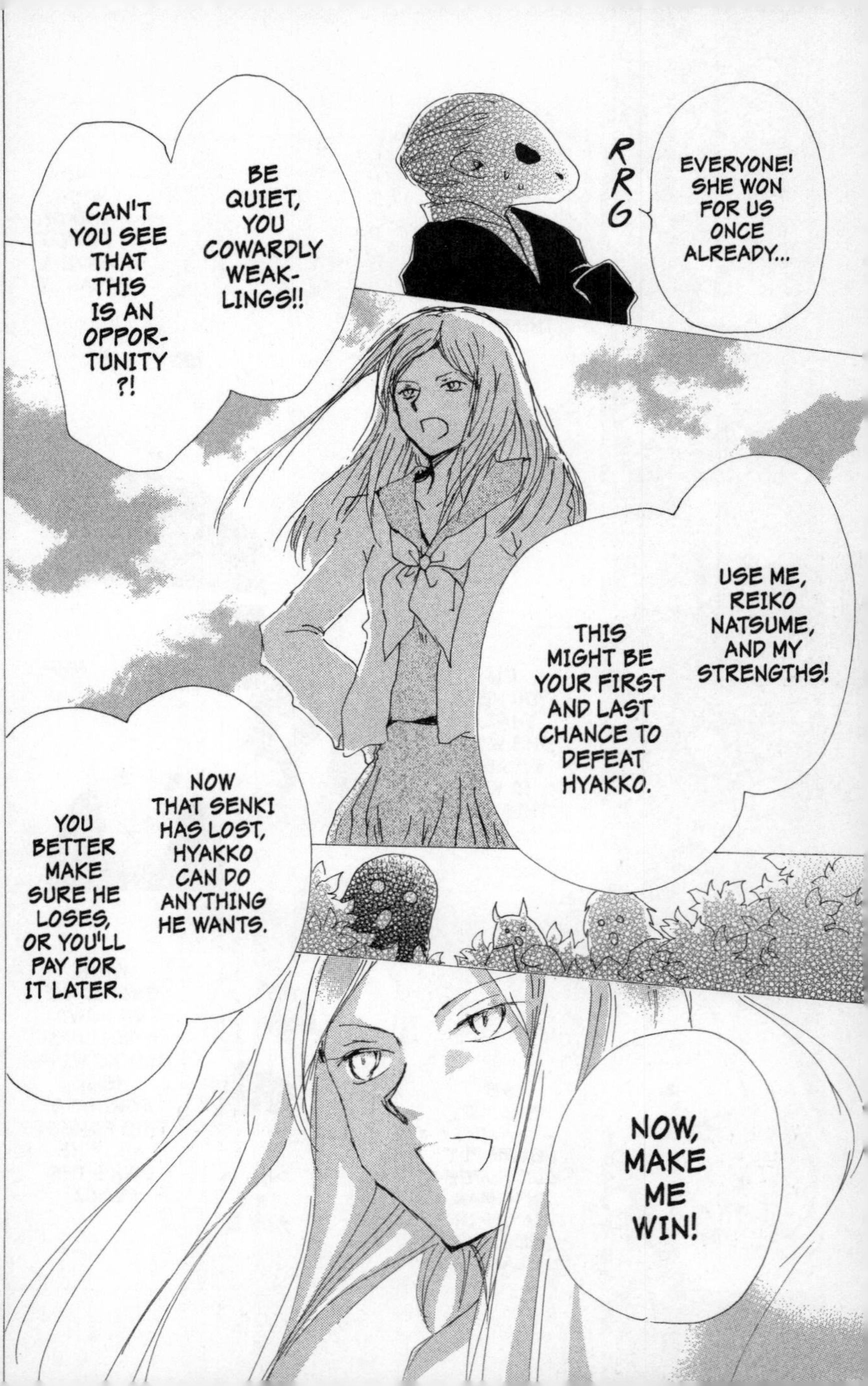
EVERYONE! SHE WON FOR US ONCE ALREADY...
RRG
BE QUIET, YOU COWARDLY WEAK-LINGS!!
CAN'T YOU SEE THAT THIS IS AN OPPOR-TUNITY?!
USE ME, REIKO NATSUME, AND MY STRENGTHS!
THIS MIGHT BE YOUR FIRST AND LAST CHANCE TO DEFEAT HYAKKO.
NOW THAT SENKI HAS LOST, HYAKKO CAN DO ANYTHING HE WANTS.
YOU BETTER MAKE SURE HE LOSES, OR YOU'LL PAY FOR IT LATER.
NOW, MAKE ME WIN!

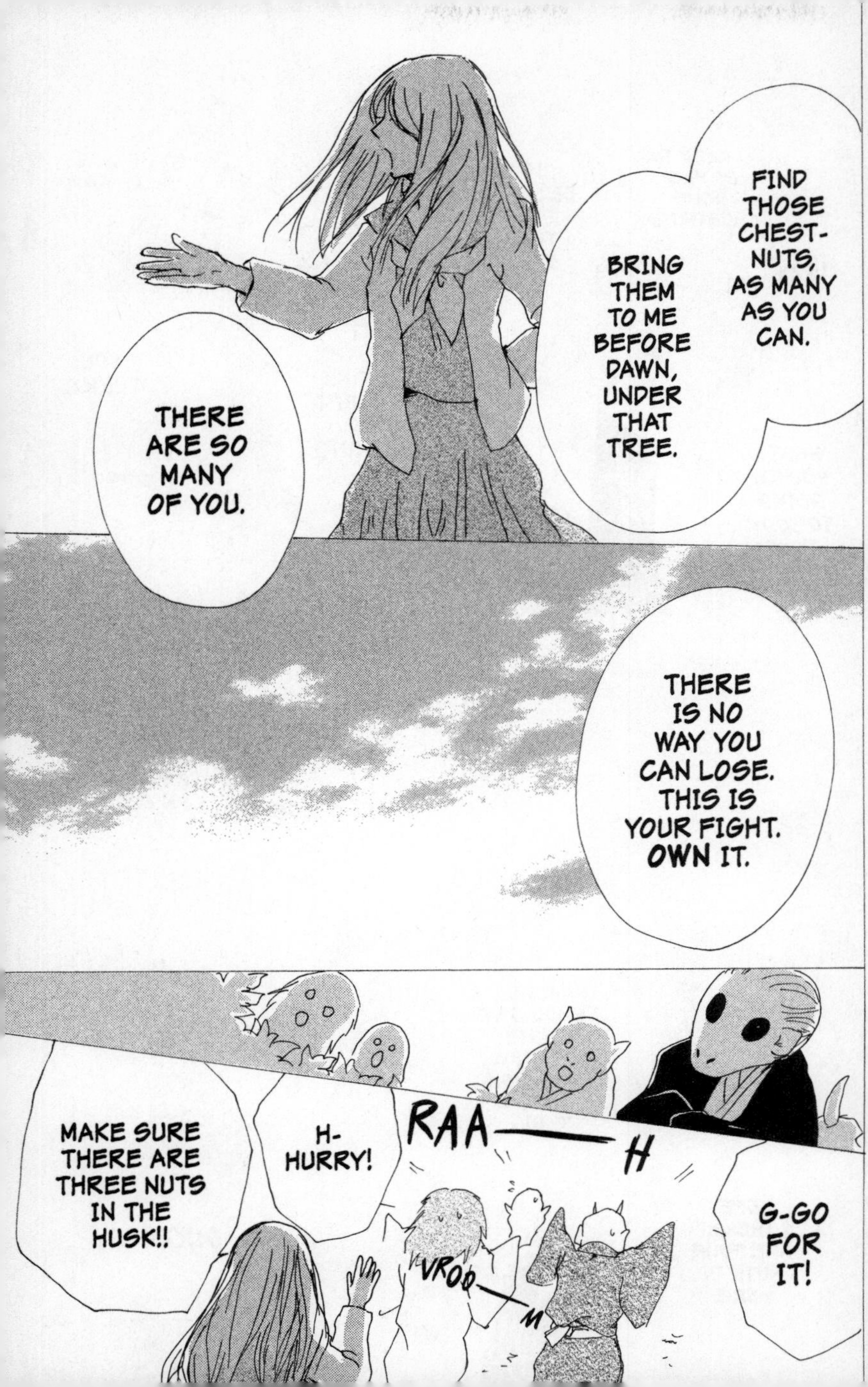
FIND THOSE CHEST-NUTS, AS MANY AS YOU CAN.
BRING THEM TO ME BEFORE DAWN, UNDER THAT TREE.
THERE ARE SO MANY OF YOU.
THERE IS NO WAY YOU CAN LOSE. THIS IS YOUR FIGHT. **OWN** IT.
G-GO FOR IT!
RAA—H
H-HURRY!
VROO—M
MAKE SURE THERE ARE THREE NUTS IN THE HUSK!!

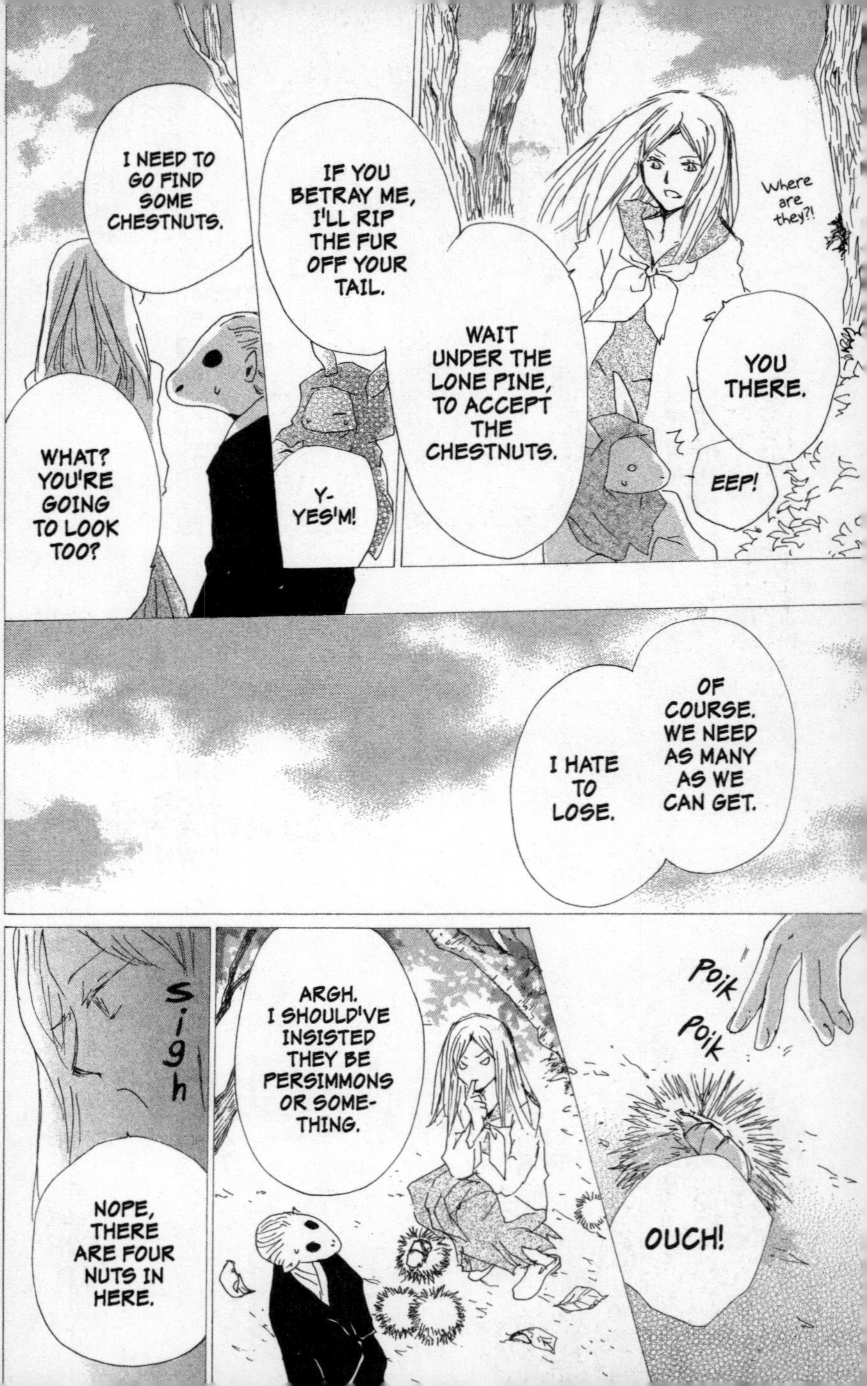
Where are they?!
YOU THERE.
EEP!
WAIT UNDER THE LONE PINE, TO ACCEPT THE CHESTNUTS.
IF YOU BETRAY ME, I'LL RIP THE FUR OFF YOUR TAIL.
Y- YES'M!
I NEED TO GO FIND SOME CHESTNUTS.
WHAT? YOU'RE GOING TO LOOK TOO?
OF COURSE. WE NEED AS MANY AS WE CAN GET.
I HATE TO LOSE.
Poik
Poik
OUCH!
ARGH. I SHOULD'VE INSISTED THEY BE PERSIMMONS OR SOME-THING.
Sigh
NOPE, THERE ARE FOUR NUTS IN HERE.

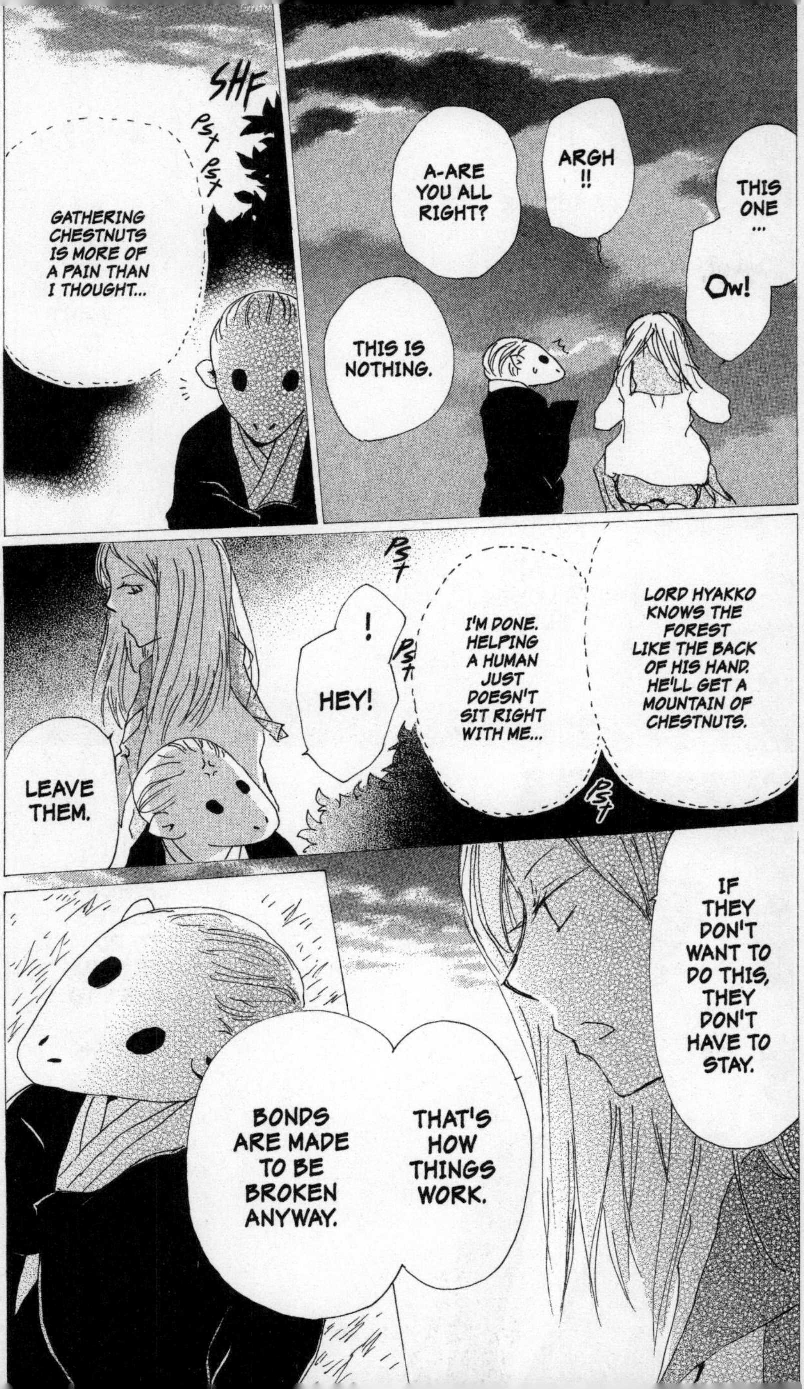
THIS ONE ...
Ow!
ARGH !!
A-ARE YOU ALL RIGHT?
THIS IS NOTHING.
SHF
Pst Pst
GATHERING CHESTNUTS IS MORE OF A PAIN THAN I THOUGHT...
LORD HYAKKO KNOWS THE FOREST LIKE THE BACK OF HIS HAND. HE'LL GET A MOUNTAIN OF CHESTNUTS.
Pst
I'M DONE. HELPING A HUMAN JUST DOESN'T SIT RIGHT WITH ME...
Pst
Pst
!
HEY!
LEAVE THEM.
IF THEY DON'T WANT TO DO THIS, THEY DON'T HAVE TO STAY.
THAT'S HOW THINGS WORK.
BONDS ARE MADE TO BE BROKEN ANYWAY.

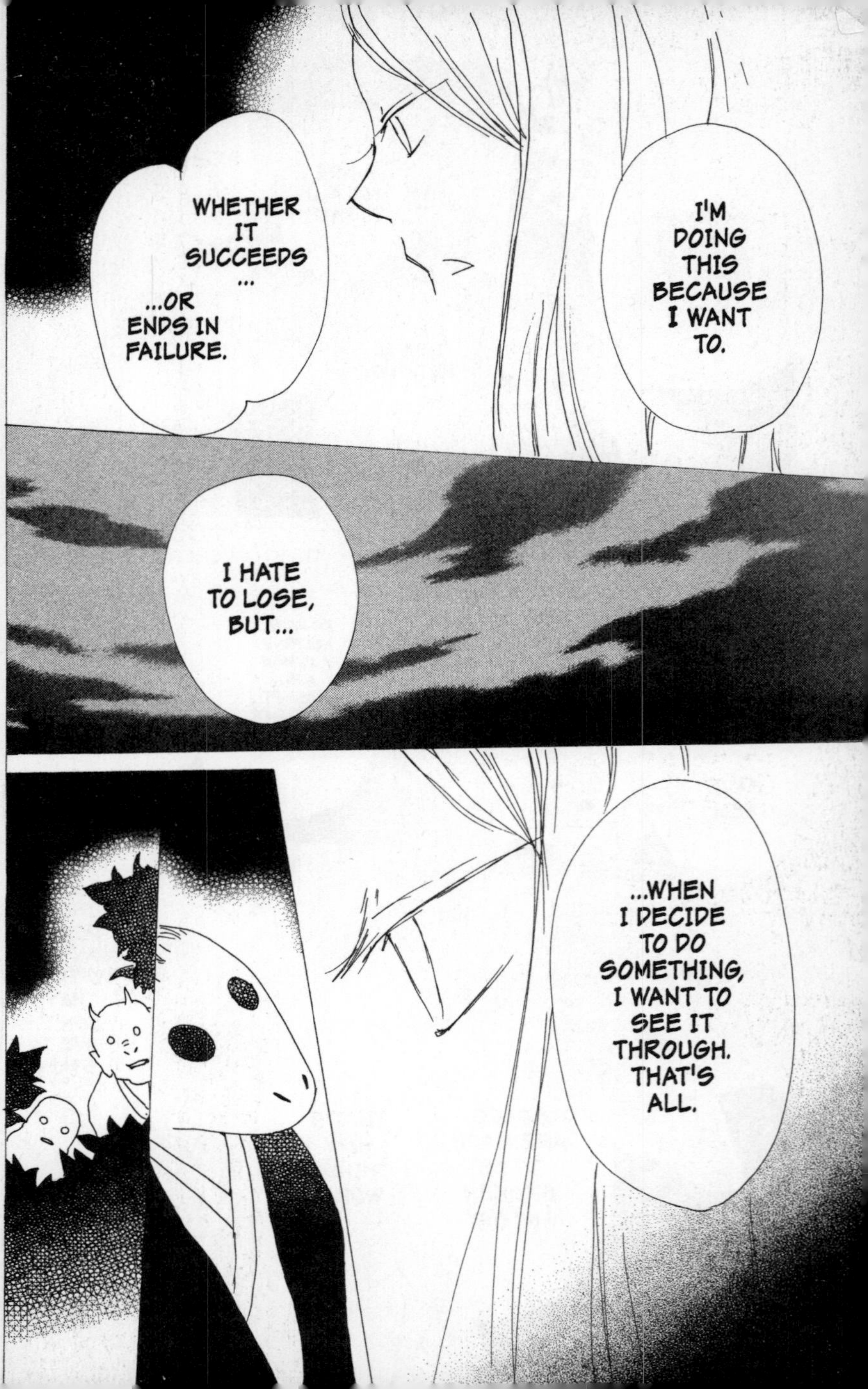
I'M DOING THIS BECAUSE I WANT TO.
WHETHER IT SUCCEEDS...
...OR ENDS IN FAILURE.
I HATE TO LOSE, BUT...
...WHEN I DECIDE TO DO SOMETHING, I WANT TO SEE IT THROUGH. THAT'S ALL.

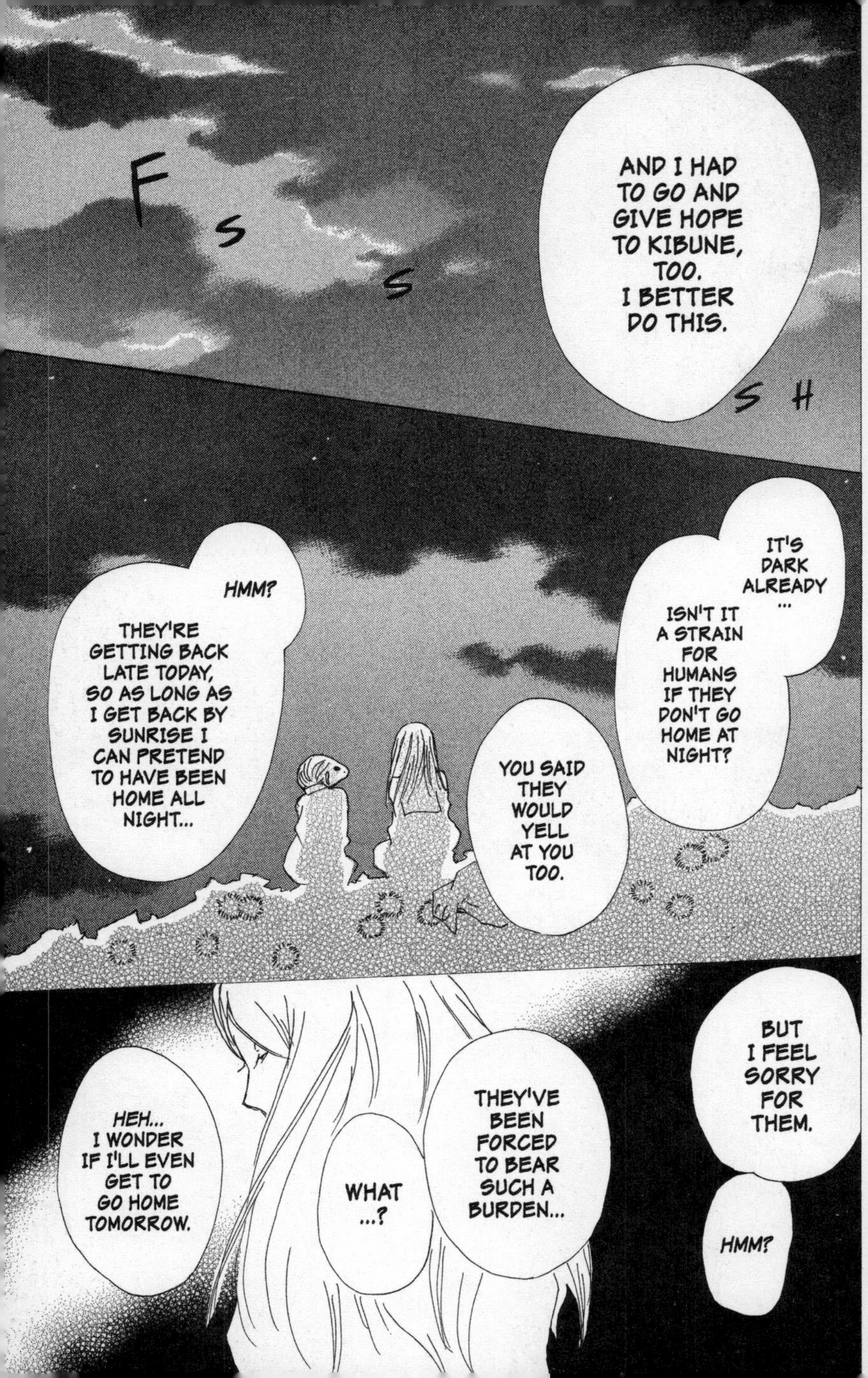
AND I HAD TO GO AND GIVE HOPE TO KIBUNE, TOO. I BETTER DO THIS.
F S S S H
IT'S DARK ALREADY...
ISN'T IT A STRAIN FOR HUMANS IF THEY DON'T GO HOME AT NIGHT?
YOU SAID THEY WOULD YELL AT YOU TOO.
HMM?
THEY'RE GETTING BACK LATE TODAY, SO AS LONG AS I GET BACK BY SUNRISE I CAN PRETEND TO HAVE BEEN HOME ALL NIGHT...
BUT I FEEL SORRY FOR THEM.
HMM?
THEY'VE BEEN FORCED TO BEAR SUCH A BURDEN...
WHAT...?
HEH... I WONDER IF I'LL EVEN GET TO GO HOME TOMORROW.

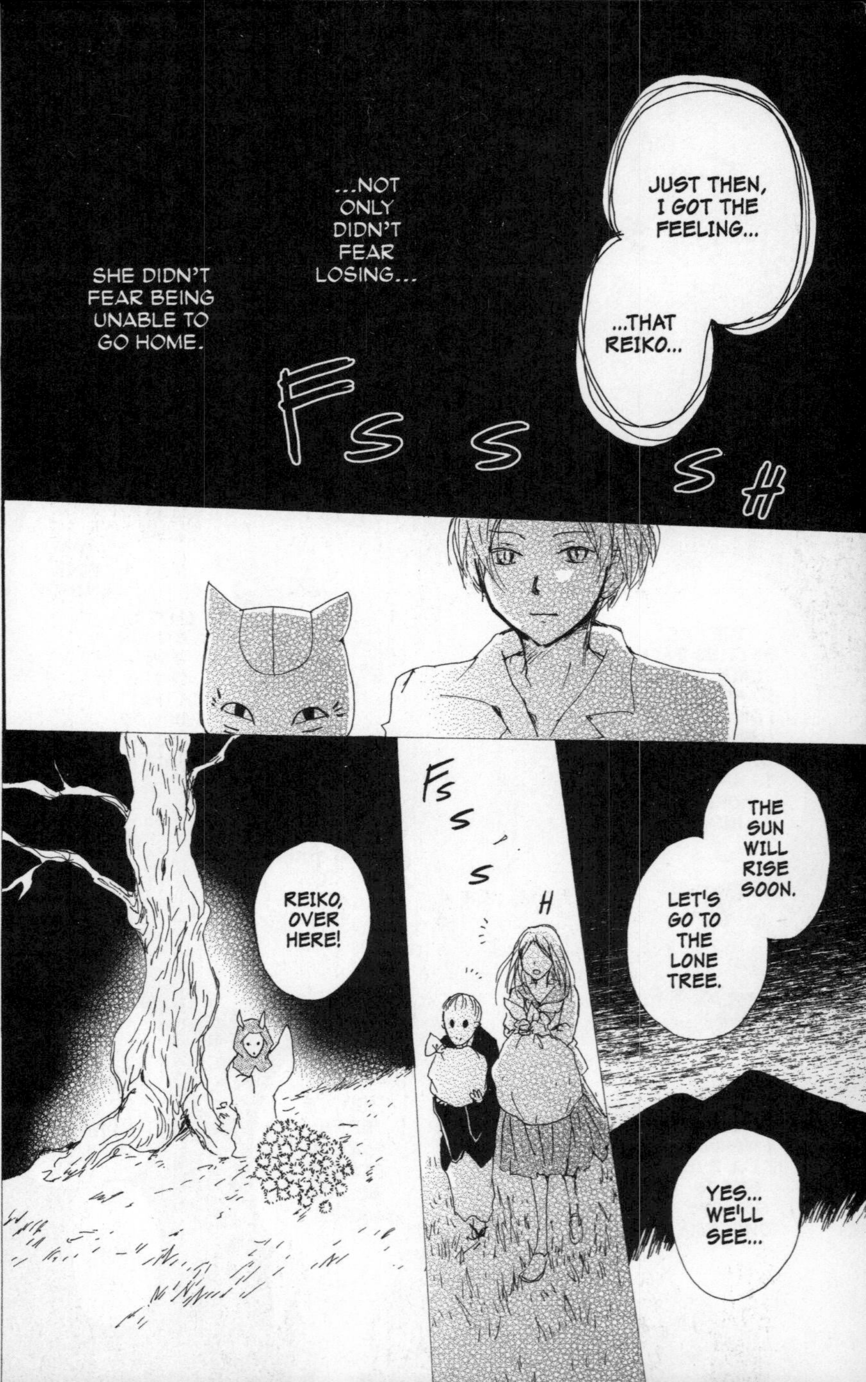
JUST THEN, I GOT THE FEELING...
...THAT REIKO...
...NOT ONLY DIDN'T FEAR LOSING...
SHE DIDN'T FEAR BEING UNABLE TO GO HOME.
FSSSH
THE SUN WILL RISE SOON.
LET'S GO TO THE LONE TREE.
YES... WE'LL SEE...
FSSSH
REIKO, OVER HERE!

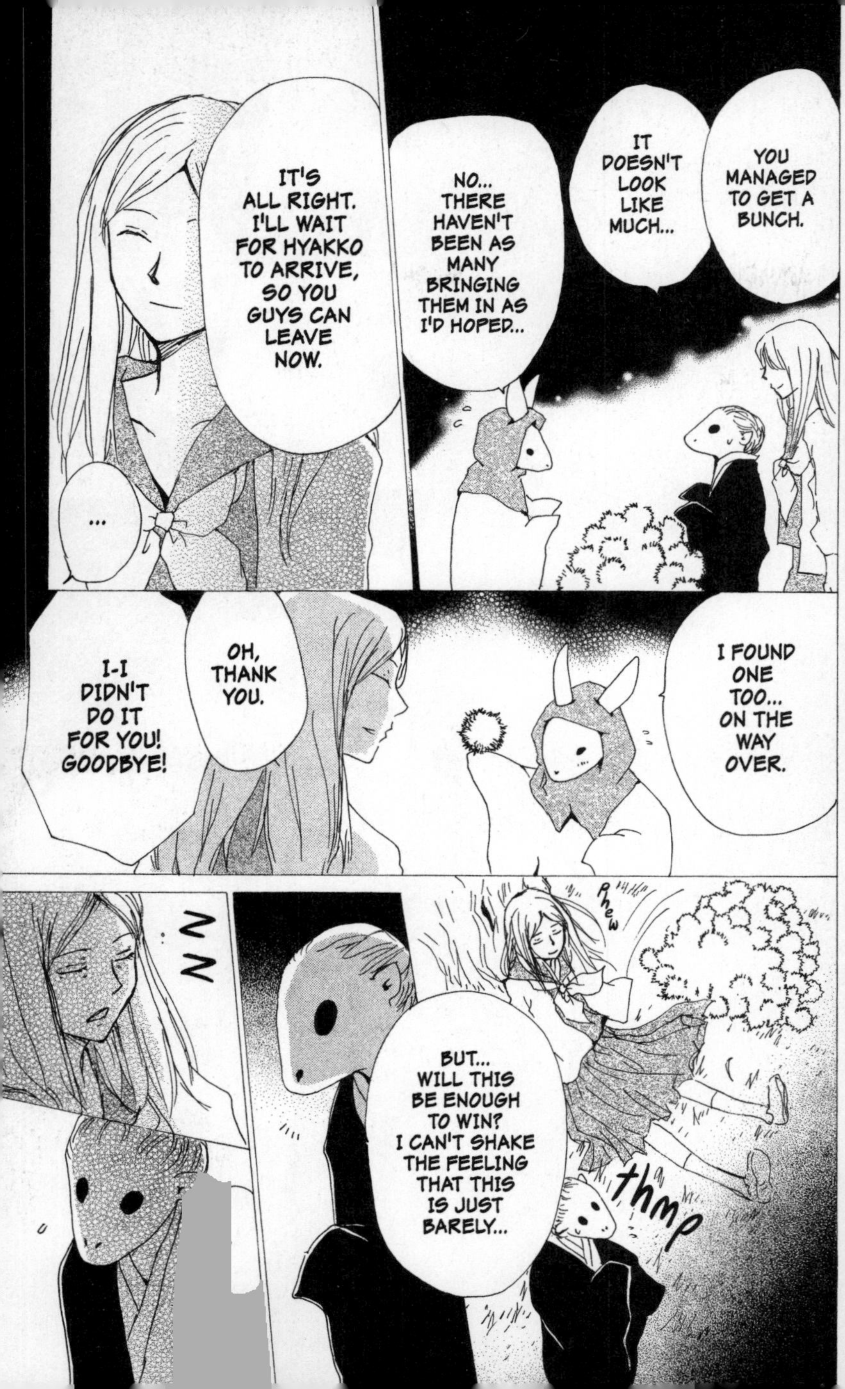
YOU MANAGED TO GET A BUNCH.
IT DOESN'T LOOK LIKE MUCH...
NO... THERE HAVEN'T BEEN AS MANY BRINGING THEM IN AS I'D HOPED...
IT'S ALL RIGHT. I'LL WAIT FOR HYAKKO TO ARRIVE, SO YOU GUYS CAN LEAVE NOW.
...
I FOUND ONE TOO... ON THE WAY OVER.
OH, THANK YOU.
I-I DIDN'T DO IT FOR YOU! GOODBYE!
Phew
thmp
BUT... WILL THIS BE ENOUGH TO WIN? I CAN'T SHAKE THE FEELING THAT THIS IS JUST BARELY...

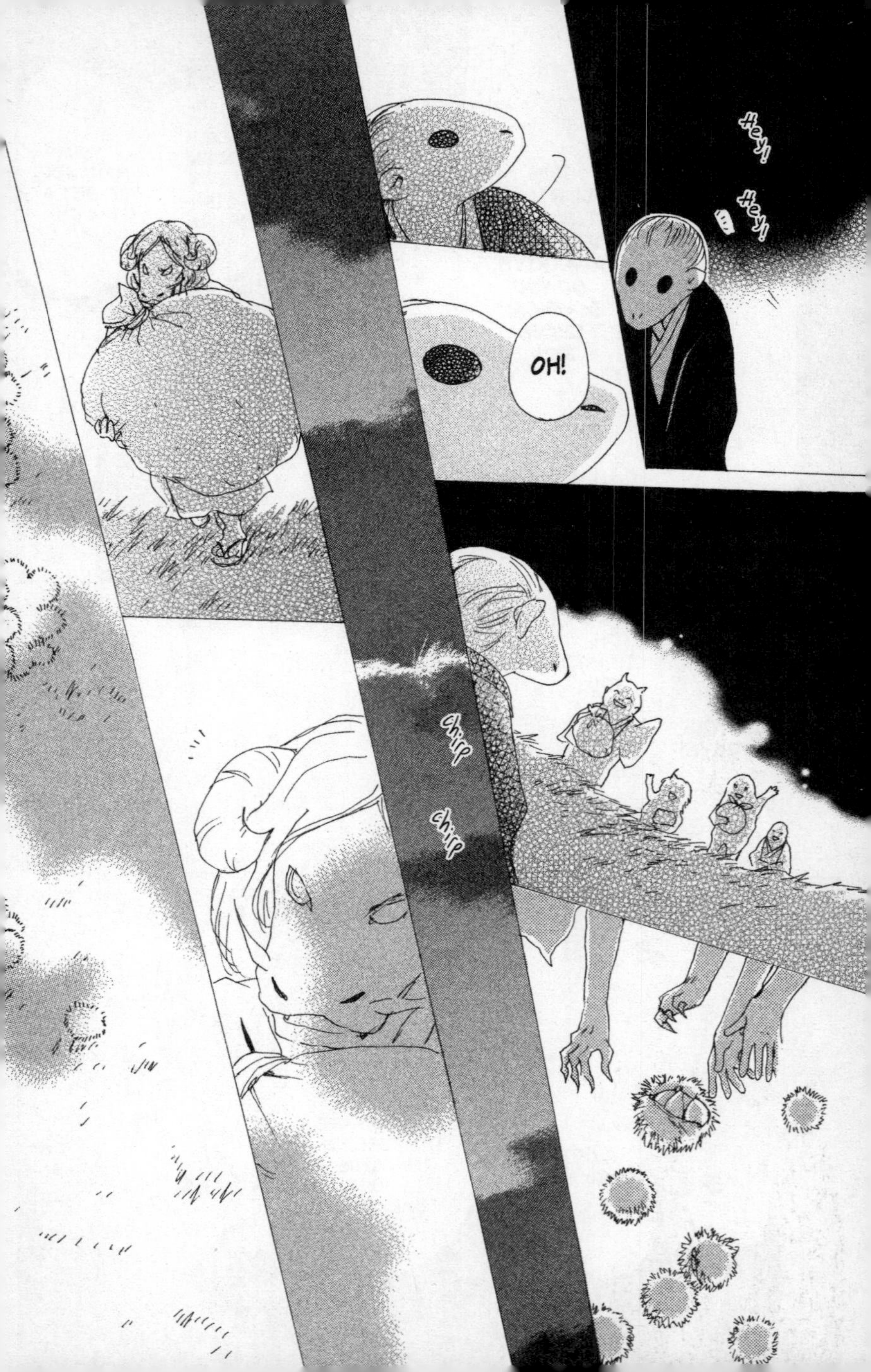
Hey!
Hey!
...
OH!
chirp
chirp

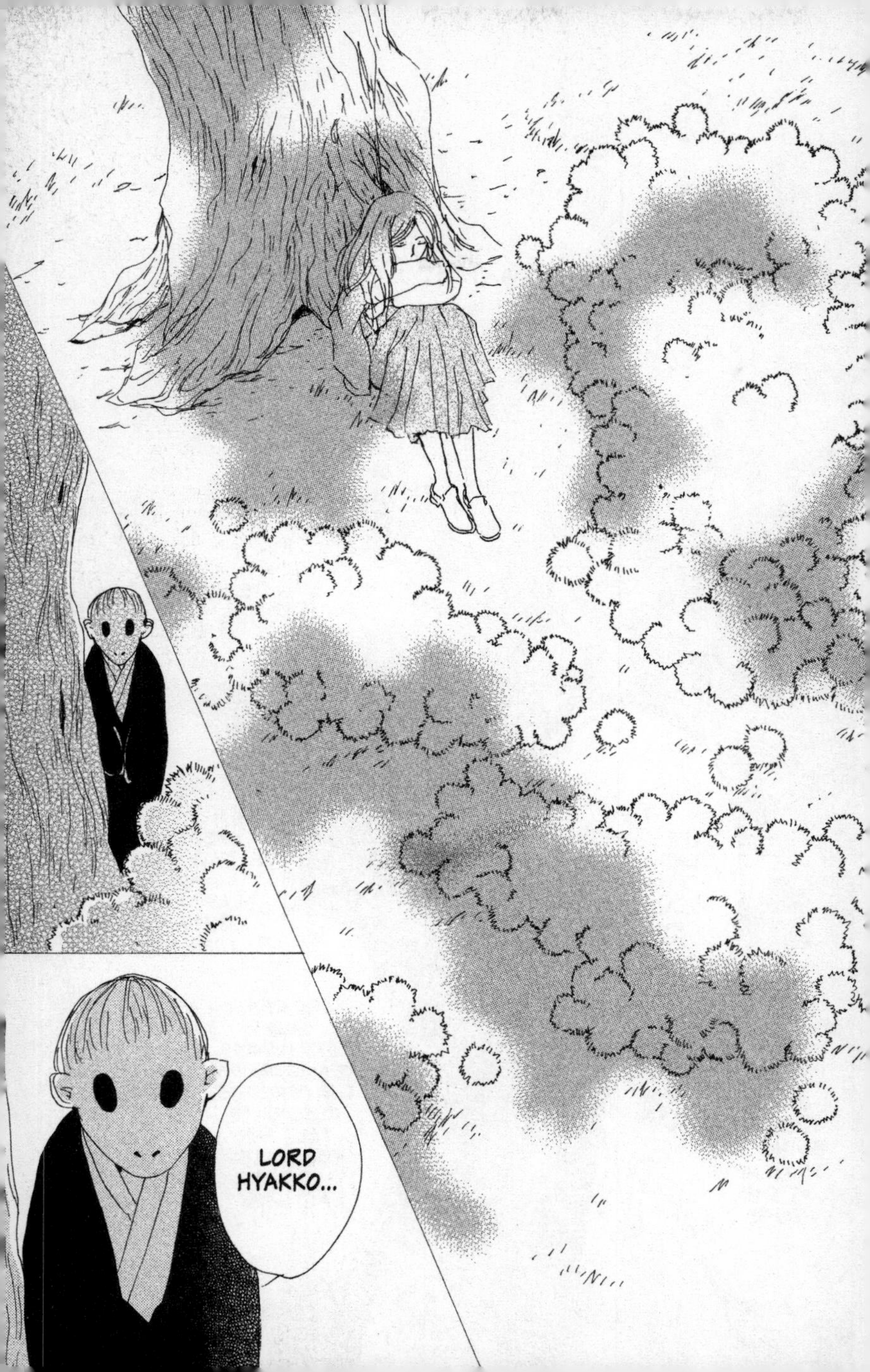
LORD HYAKKO...

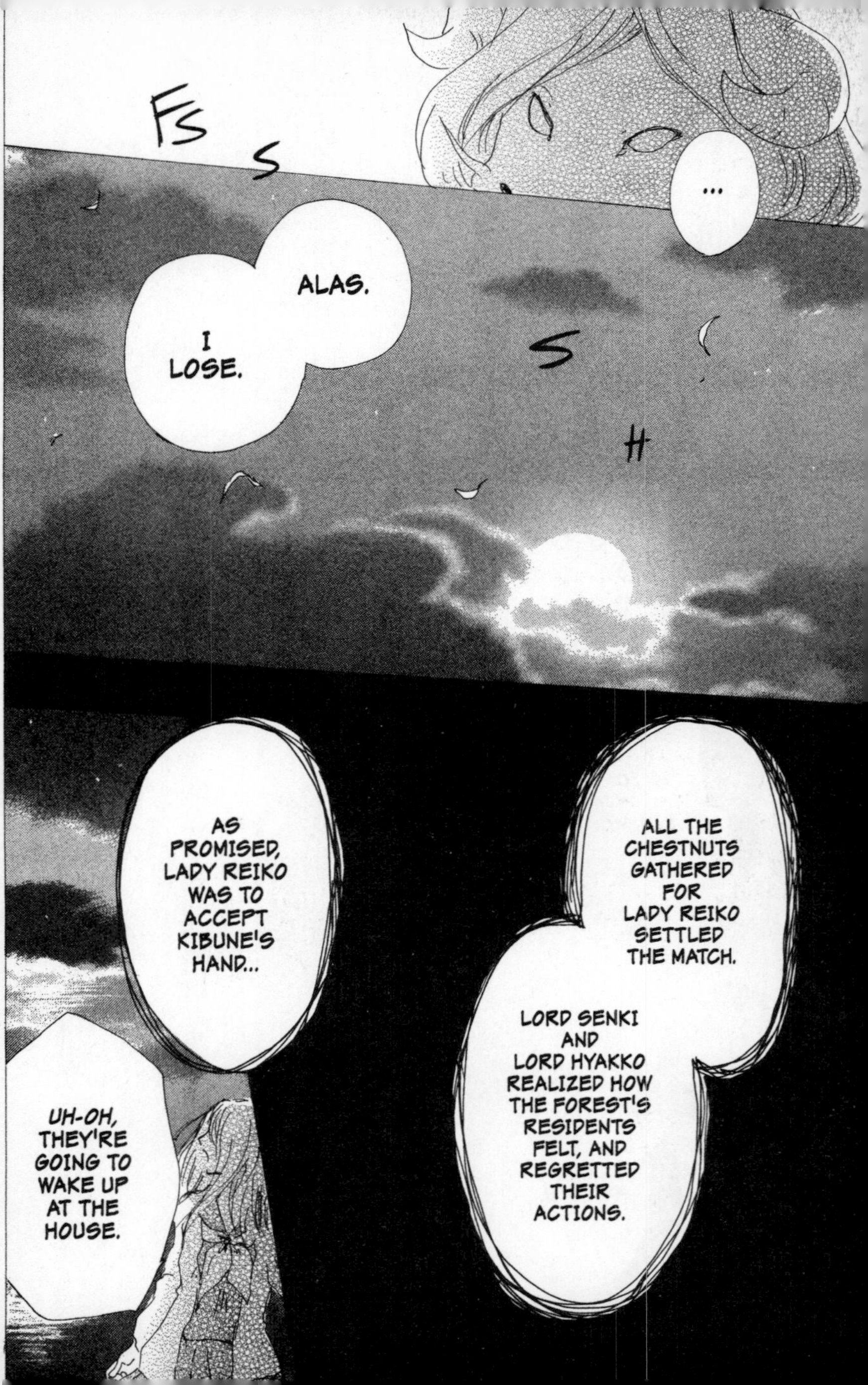
FS
S
...
ALAS.
I LOSE.
S
H
ALL THE CHESTNUTS GATHERED FOR LADY REIKO SETTLED THE MATCH.
LORD SENKI AND LORD HYAKKO REALIZED HOW THE FOREST'S RESIDENTS FELT, AND REGRETTED THEIR ACTIONS.
AS PROMISED, LADY REIKO WAS TO ACCEPT KIBUNE'S HAND...
UH-OH, THEY'RE GOING TO WAKE UP AT THE HOUSE.

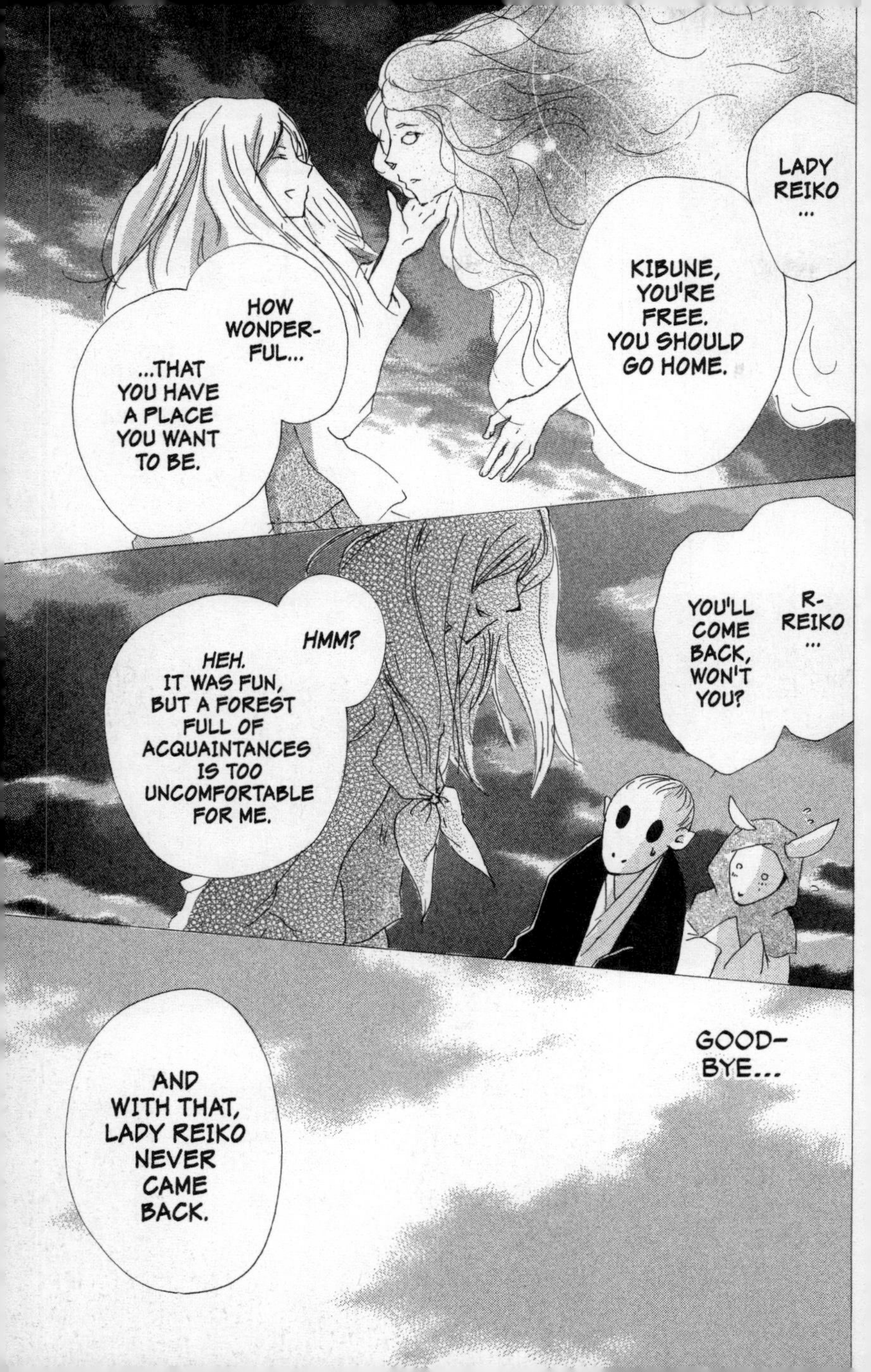
LADY REIKO ...
KIBUNE, YOU'RE FREE. YOU SHOULD GO HOME.
HOW WONDER-FUL...
...THAT YOU HAVE A PLACE YOU WANT TO BE.
R-REIKO ...
YOU'LL COME BACK, WON'T YOU?
HMM?
HEH. IT WAS FUN, BUT A FOREST FULL OF ACQUAINTANCES IS TOO UNCOMFORTABLE FOR ME.
GOOD-BYE...
AND WITH THAT, LADY REIKO NEVER CAME BACK.

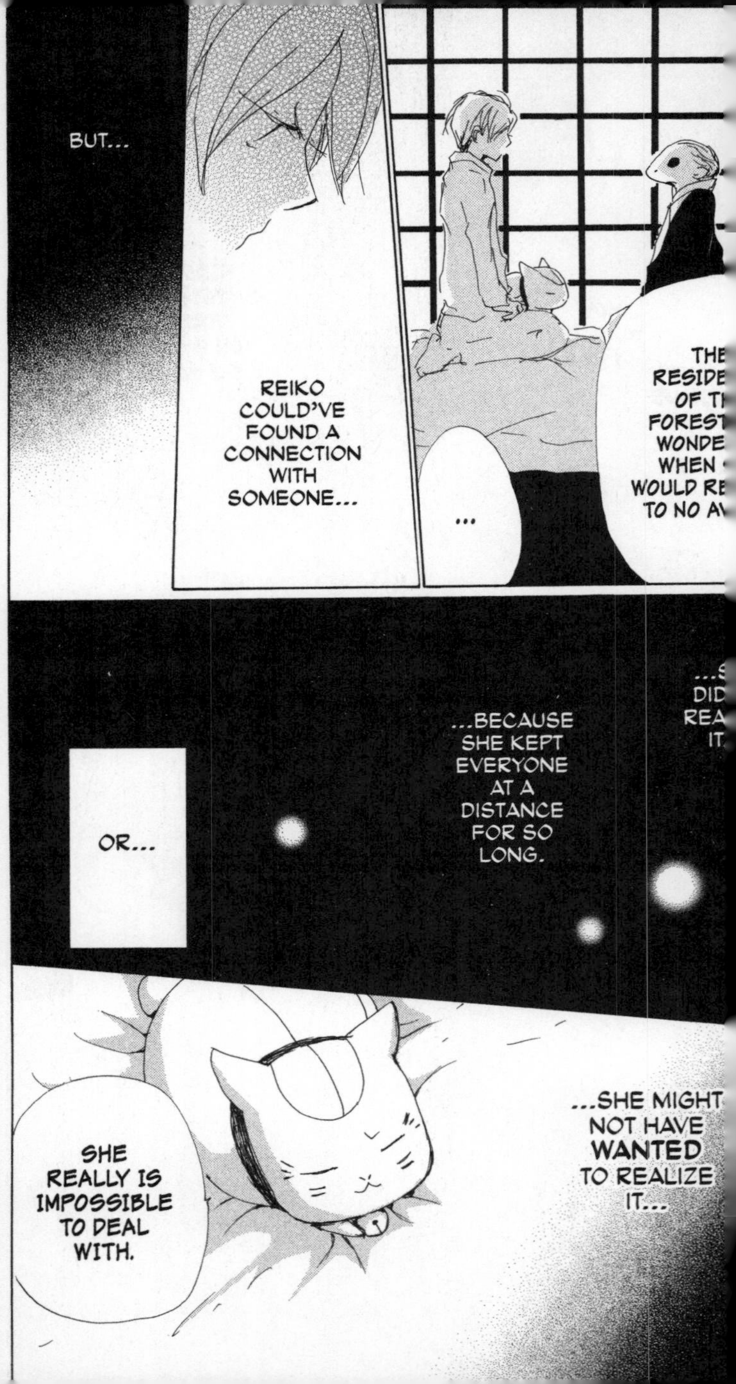
THE RESIDE OF TH FOREST WONDE WHEN WOULD RE TO NO AV
...
REIKO COULD'VE FOUND A CONNECTION WITH SOMEONE...
BUT...
...S DID REA IT
...BECAUSE SHE KEPT EVERYONE AT A DISTANCE FOR SO LONG.
OR...
...SHE MIGHT NOT HAVE **WANTED** TO REALIZE IT...
SHE REALLY IS IMPOSSIBLE TO DEAL WITH.

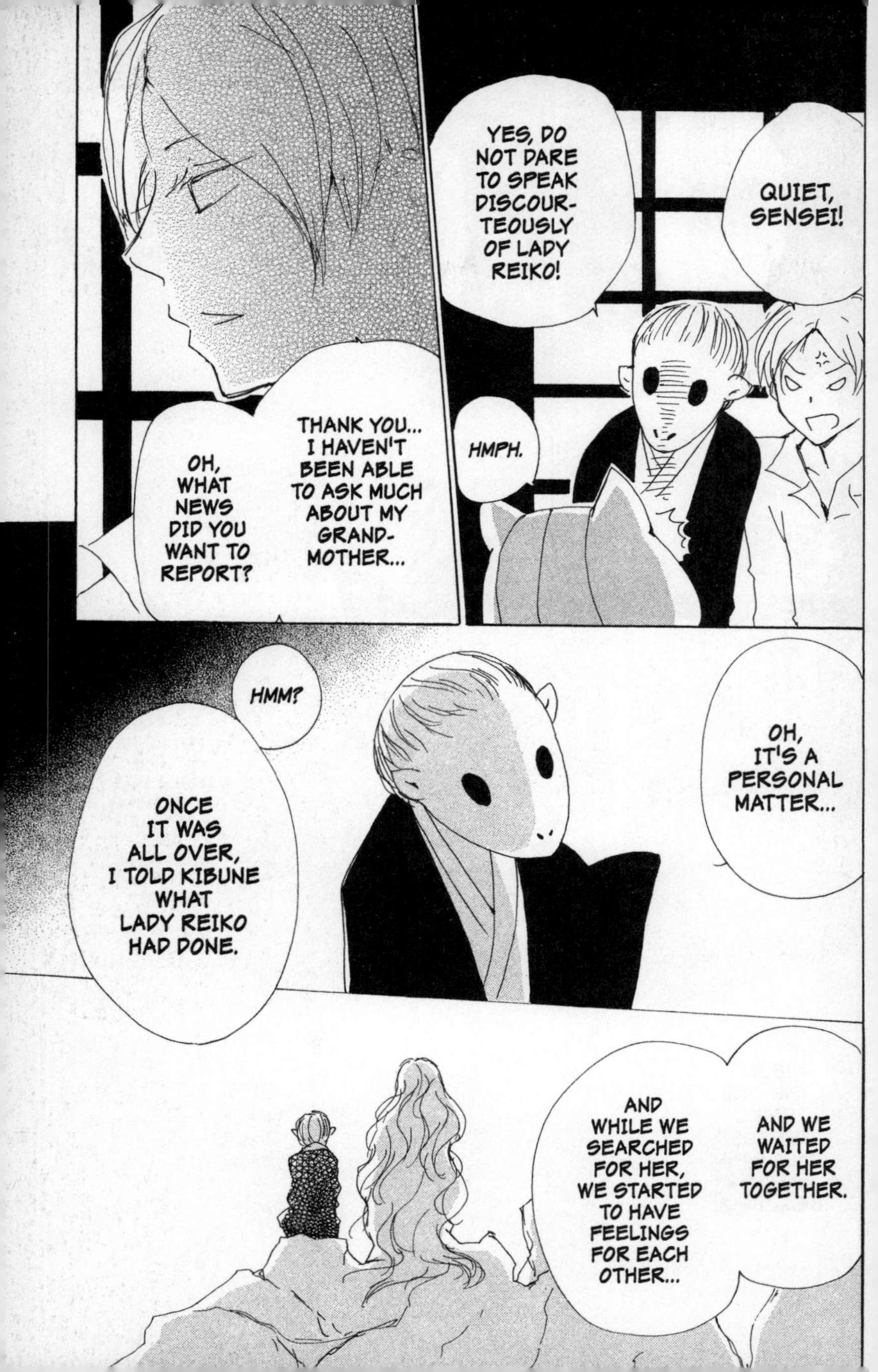
QUIET, SENSEI!
YES, DO NOT DARE TO SPEAK DISCOURTEOUSLY OF LADY REIKO!
HMPH.
THANK YOU... I HAVEN'T BEEN ABLE TO ASK MUCH ABOUT MY GRANDMOTHER...
OH, WHAT NEWS DID YOU WANT TO REPORT?
OH, IT'S A PERSONAL MATTER...
HMM?
ONCE IT WAS ALL OVER, I TOLD KIBUNE WHAT LADY REIKO HAD DONE.
AND WE WAITED FOR HER TOGETHER.
AND WHILE WE SEARCHED FOR HER, WE STARTED TO HAVE FEELINGS FOR EACH OTHER...

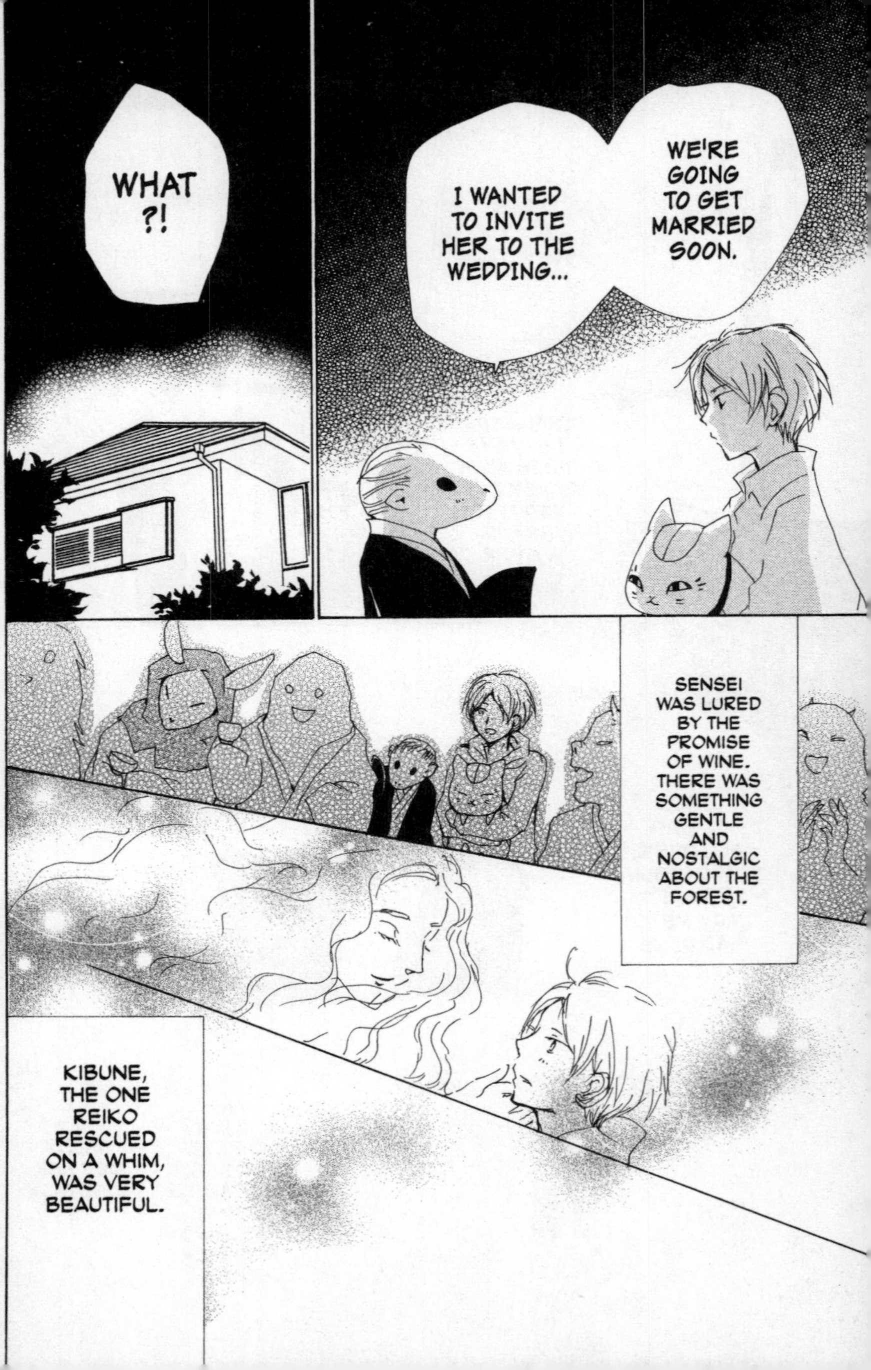
WE'RE GOING TO GET MARRIED SOON.
I WANTED TO INVITE HER TO THE WEDDING...
WHAT?!
SENSEI WAS LURED BY THE PROMISE OF WINE. THERE WAS SOMETHING GENTLE AND NOSTALGIC ABOUT THE FOREST.
KIBUNE, THE ONE REIKO RESCUED ON A WHIM, WAS VERY BEAUTIFUL.

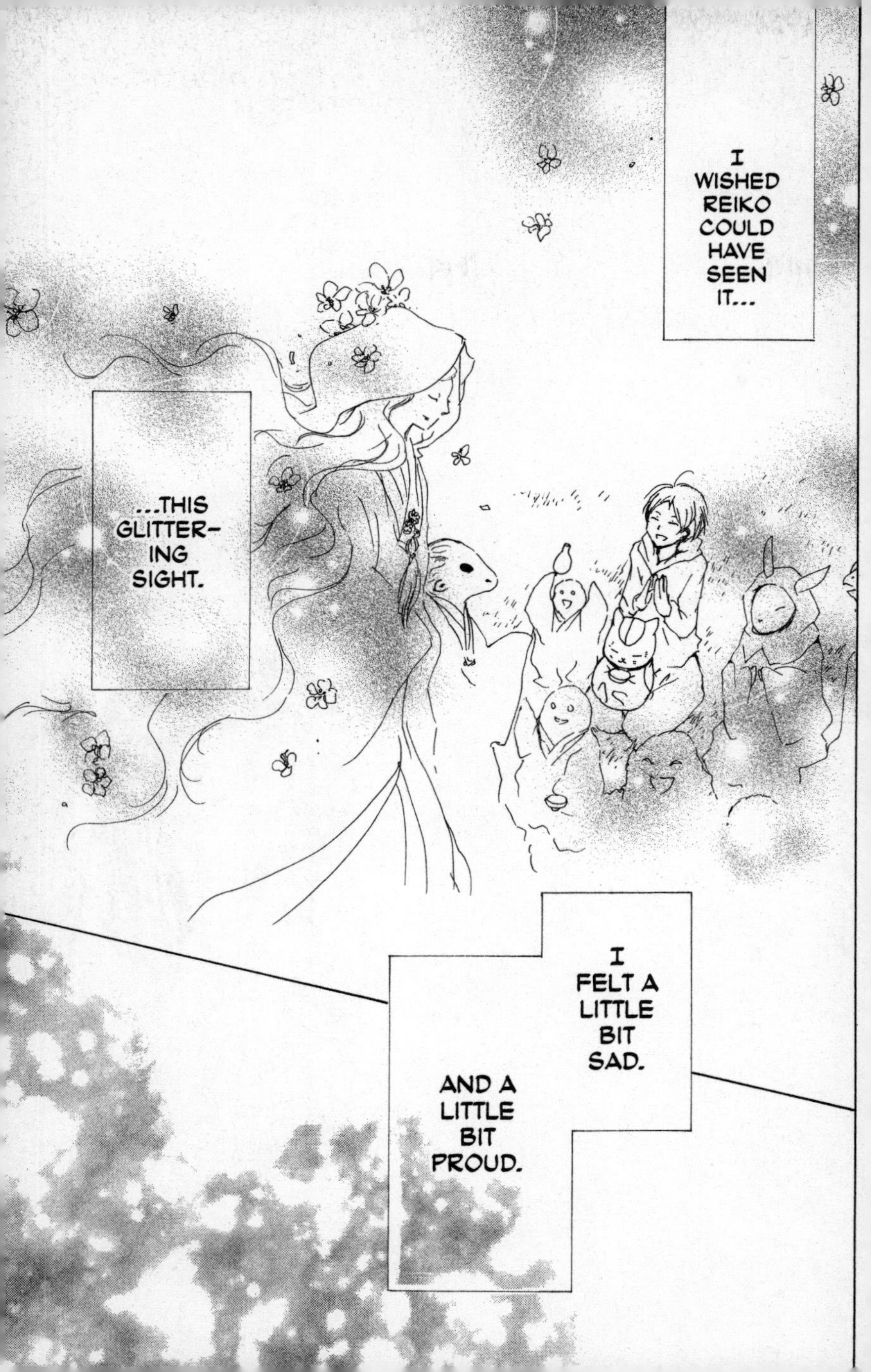
I WISHED REIKO COULD HAVE SEEN IT...
...THIS GLITTER-ING SIGHT.
I FELT A LITTLE BIT SAD.
AND A LITTLE BIT PROUD.

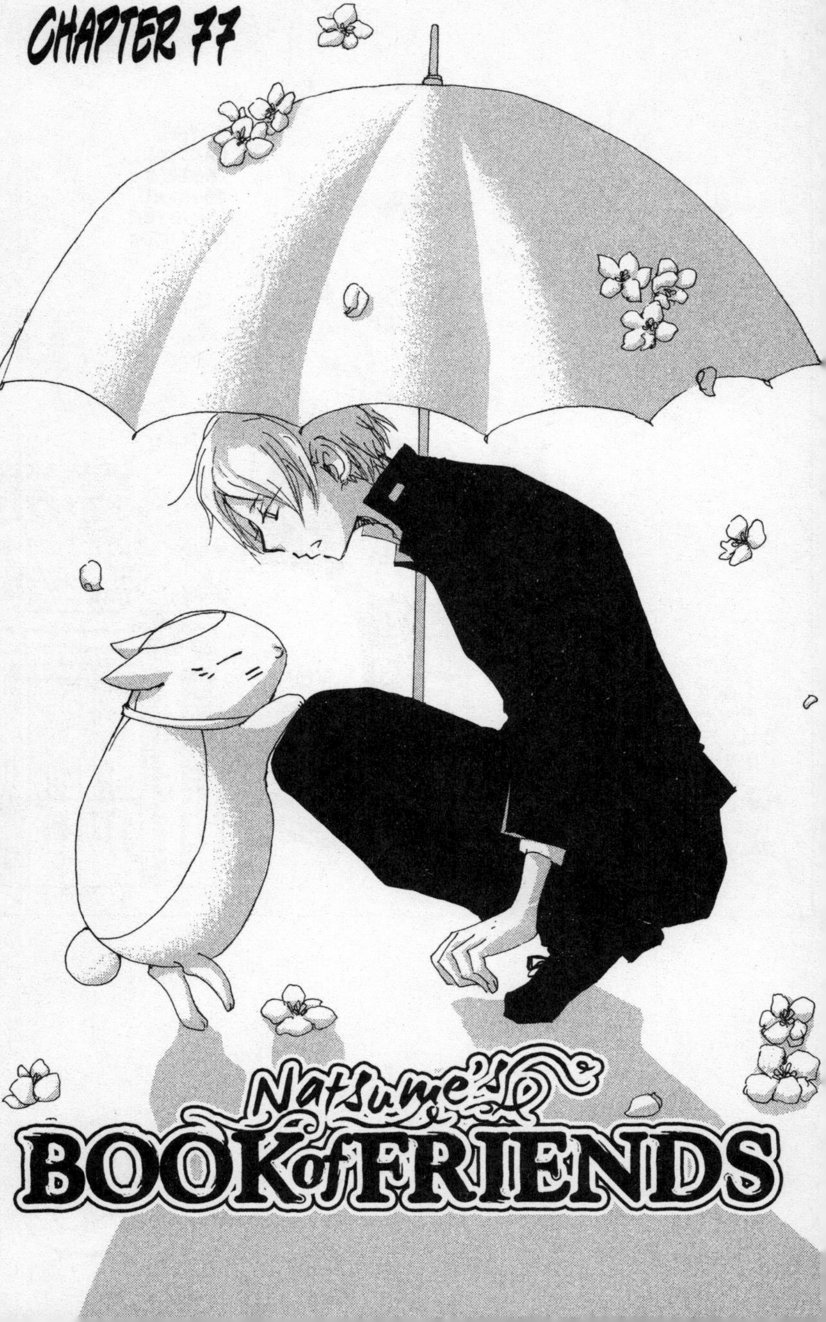
CHAPTER 77
Natsume's
BOOK of FRIENDS

THE HAKOZAKI ESTATE IS HUGE, NO MATTER HOW I LOOK AT IT.

YEAH...

I GOT A PHONE CALL FROM BENIKO, MR. HAKOZAKI'S GRAND-DAUGHTER.

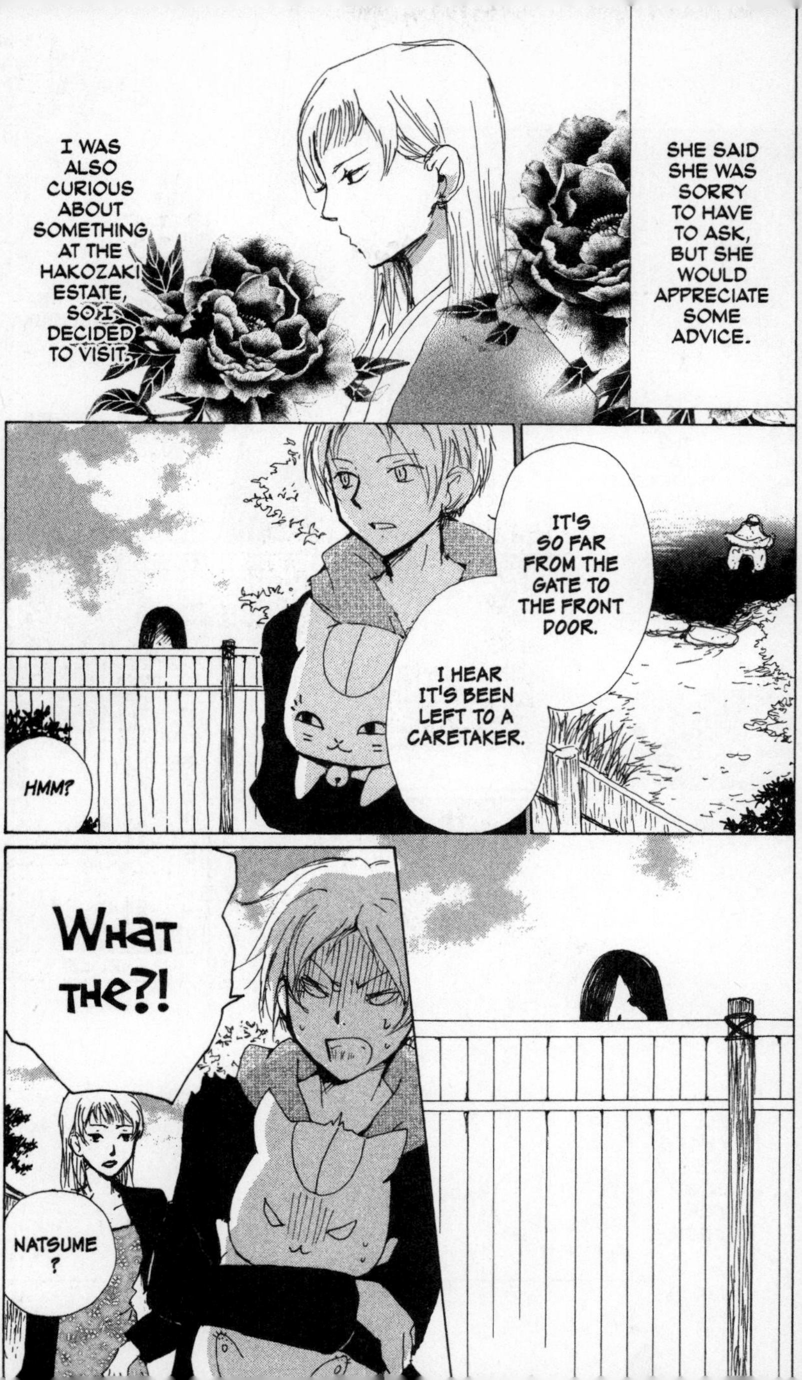
SHE SAID SHE WAS SORRY TO HAVE TO ASK, BUT SHE WOULD APPRECIATE SOME ADVICE.
I WAS ALSO CURIOUS ABOUT SOMETHING AT THE HAKOZAKI ESTATE, SO I DECIDED TO VISIT.
IT'S SO FAR FROM THE GATE TO THE FRONT DOOR.
I HEAR IT'S BEEN LEFT TO A CARETAKER.
HMM?
WHAT THE?!
NATSUME ?

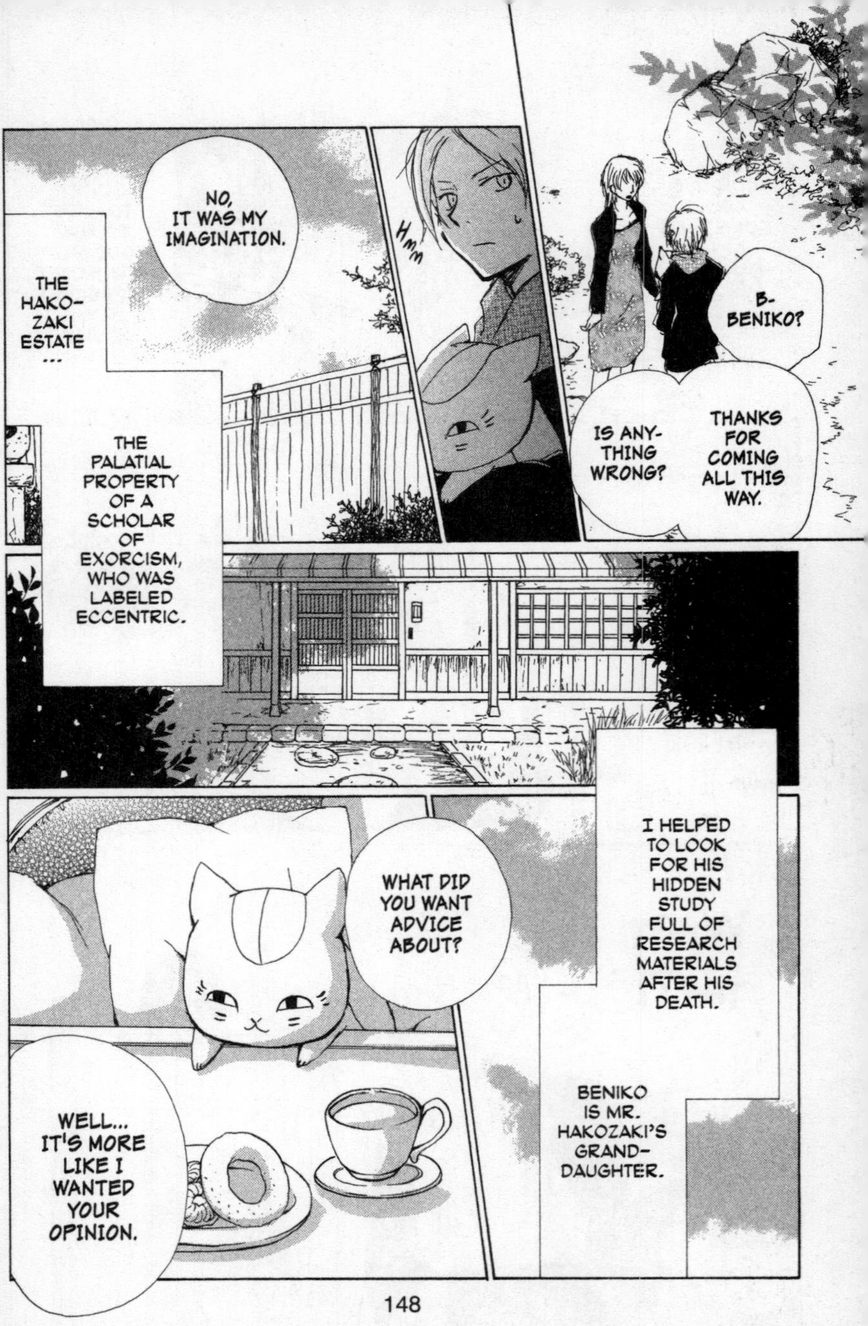
B- BENIKO?
THANKS FOR COMING ALL THIS WAY.
IS ANYTHING WRONG?
Hmm
NO, IT WAS MY IMAGINATION.
THE HAKOZAKI ESTATE...
THE PALATIAL PROPERTY OF A SCHOLAR OF EXORCISM, WHO WAS LABELED ECCENTRIC.
I HELPED TO LOOK FOR HIS HIDDEN STUDY FULL OF RESEARCH MATERIALS AFTER HIS DEATH.
BENIKO IS MR. HAKOZAKI'S GRANDDAUGHTER.
WHAT DID YOU WANT ADVICE ABOUT?
WELL... IT'S MORE LIKE I WANTED YOUR OPINION.

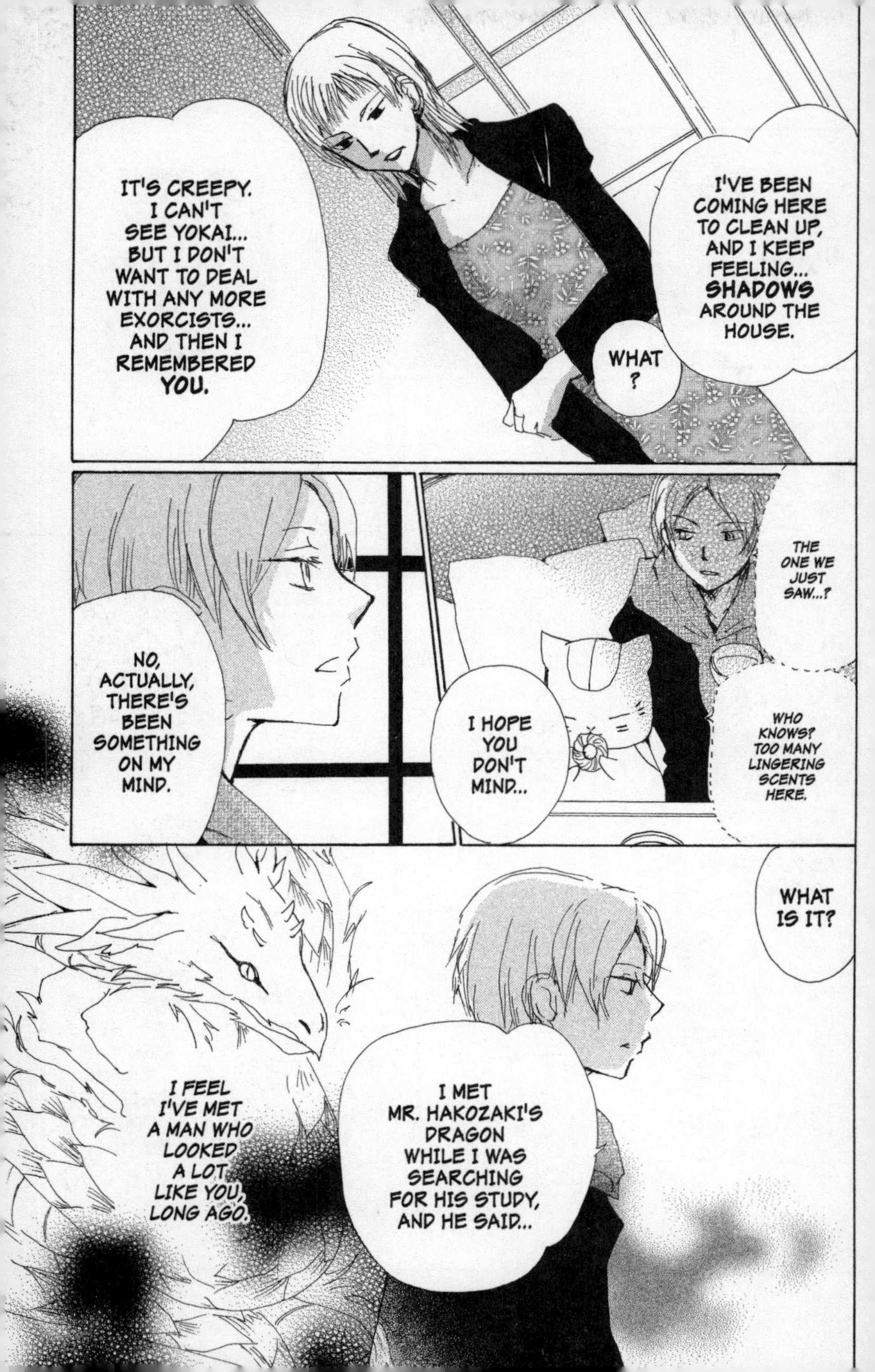

I'VE BEEN COMING HERE TO CLEAN UP, AND I KEEP FEELING... SHADOWS AROUND THE HOUSE.
WHAT?
IT'S CREEPY. I CAN'T SEE YOKAI... BUT I DON'T WANT TO DEAL WITH ANY MORE EXORCISTS... AND THEN I REMEMBERED YOU.
THE ONE WE JUST SAW...?
WHO KNOWS? TOO MANY LINGERING SCENTS HERE.
I HOPE YOU DON'T MIND...
NO, ACTUALLY, THERE'S BEEN SOMETHING ON MY MIND.
WHAT IS IT?
I MET MR. HAKOZAKI'S DRAGON WHILE I WAS SEARCHING FOR HIS STUDY, AND HE SAID...
I FEEL I'VE MET A MAN WHO LOOKED A LOT LIKE YOU, LONG AGO.

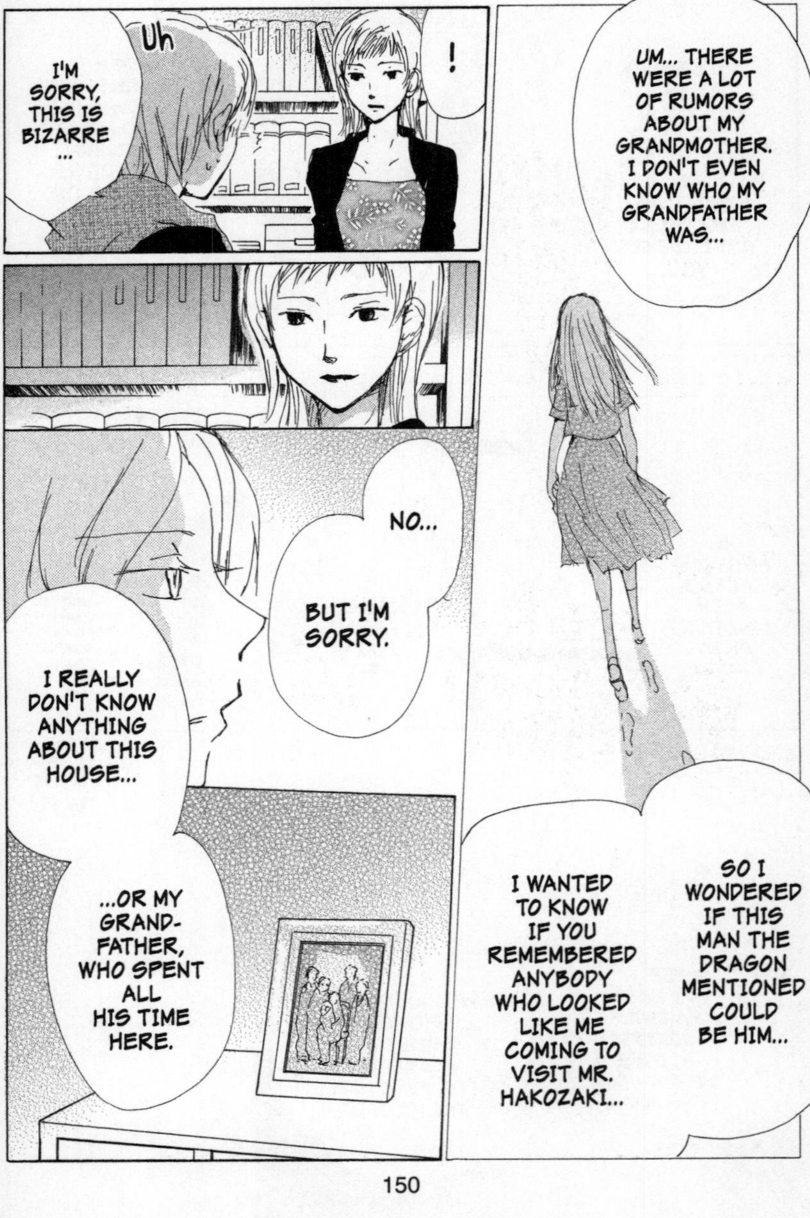
UM... THERE WERE A LOT OF RUMORS ABOUT MY GRANDMOTHER. I DON'T EVEN KNOW WHO MY GRANDFATHER WAS...
SO I WONDERED IF THIS MAN THE DRAGON MENTIONED COULD BE HIM...
I WANTED TO KNOW IF YOU REMEMBERED ANYBODY WHO LOOKED LIKE ME COMING TO VISIT MR. HAKOZAKI...
!
Uh
I'M SORRY, THIS IS BIZARRE...
NO...
BUT I'M SORRY.
I REALLY DON'T KNOW ANYTHING ABOUT THIS HOUSE...
...OR MY GRAND-FATHER, WHO SPENT ALL HIS TIME HERE.

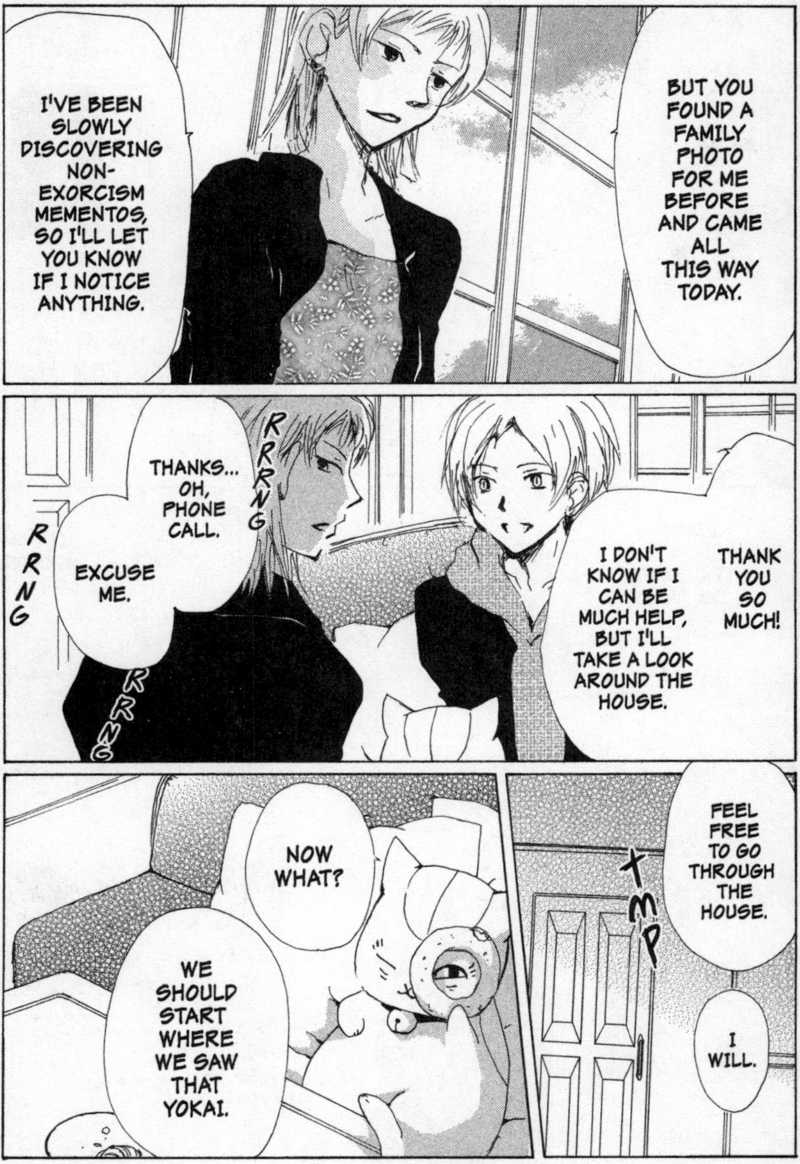
BUT YOU FOUND A FAMILY PHOTO FOR ME BEFORE AND CAME ALL THIS WAY TODAY.
I'VE BEEN SLOWLY DISCOVERING NON-EXORCISM MEMENTOS, SO I'LL LET YOU KNOW IF I NOTICE ANYTHING.
THANK YOU SO MUCH!
I DON'T KNOW IF I CAN BE MUCH HELP, BUT I'LL TAKE A LOOK AROUND THE HOUSE.
RRRNG
THANKS... OH, PHONE CALL.
EXCUSE ME.
RRNG
RRRNG
FEEL FREE TO GO THROUGH THE HOUSE.
TMP
I WILL.
NOW WHAT?
WE SHOULD START WHERE WE SAW THAT YOKAI.

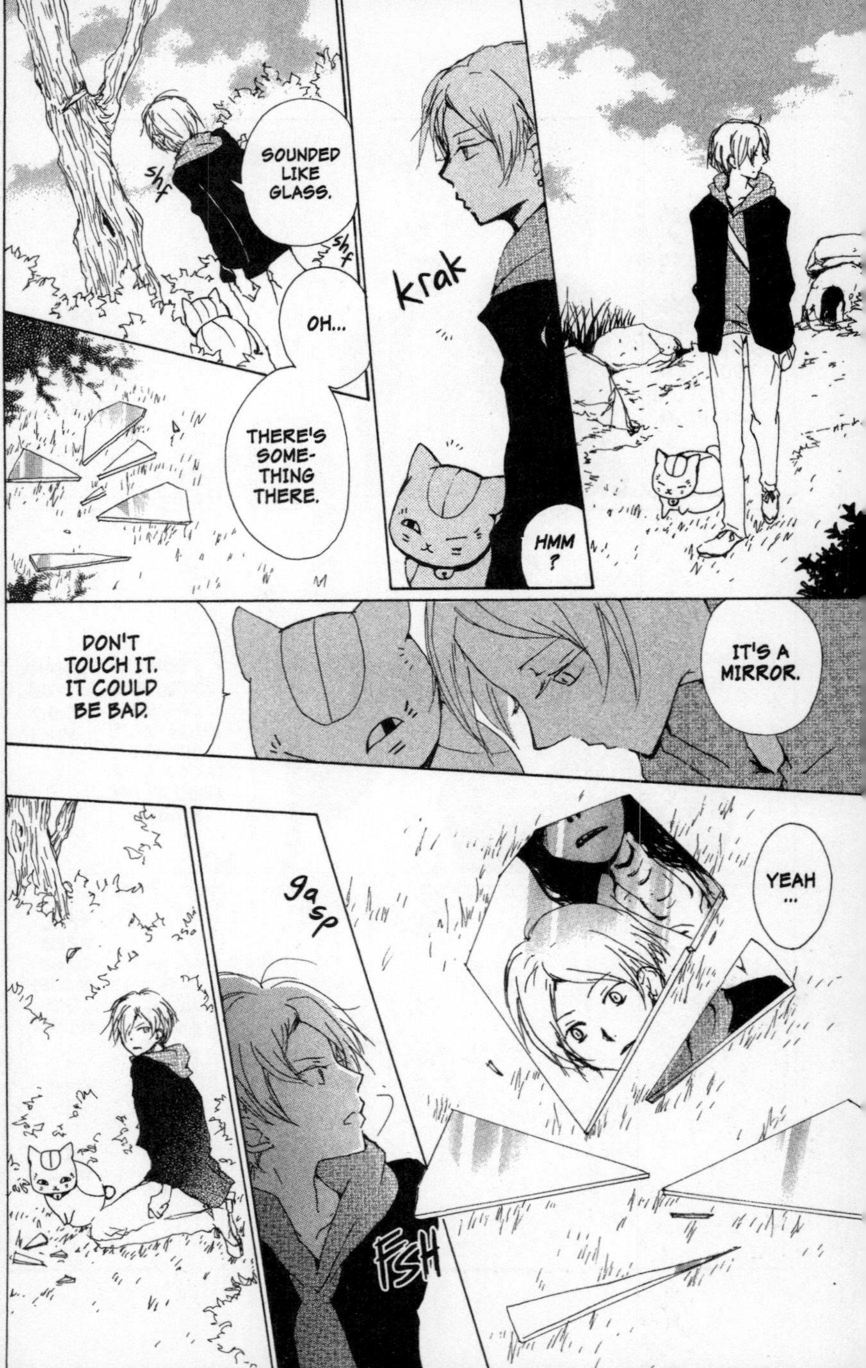
krak
HMM ?
SOUNDED LIKE GLASS.
shf
shf
OH...
THERE'S SOME-THING THERE.
IT'S A MIRROR.
DON'T TOUCH IT. IT COULD BE BAD.
YEAH ...
gasp
FSH

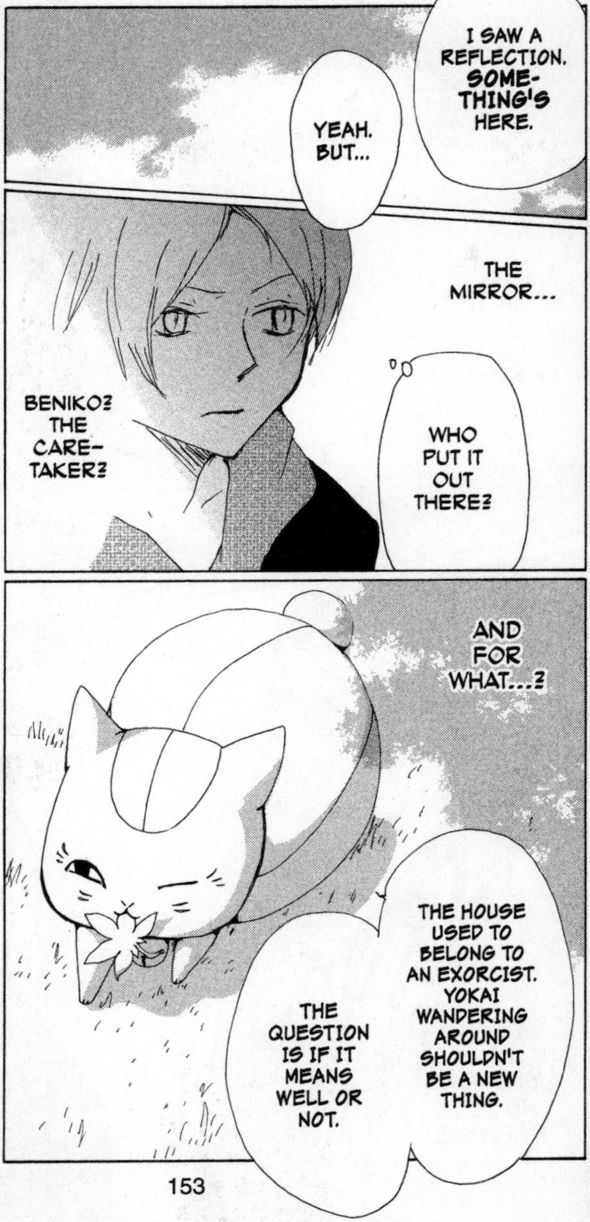
I SAW A REFLECTION. SOME-THING'S HERE.
YEAH. BUT...
THE MIRROR...
WHO PUT IT OUT THERE?
BENIKO? THE CARE-TAKER?
AND FOR WHAT...?
THE HOUSE USED TO BELONG TO AN EXORCIST. YOKAI WANDERING AROUND SHOULDN'T BE A NEW THING.
THE QUESTION IS IF IT MEANS WELL OR NOT.

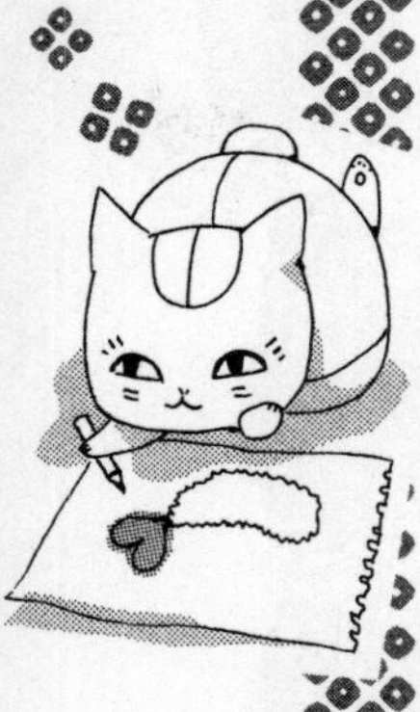

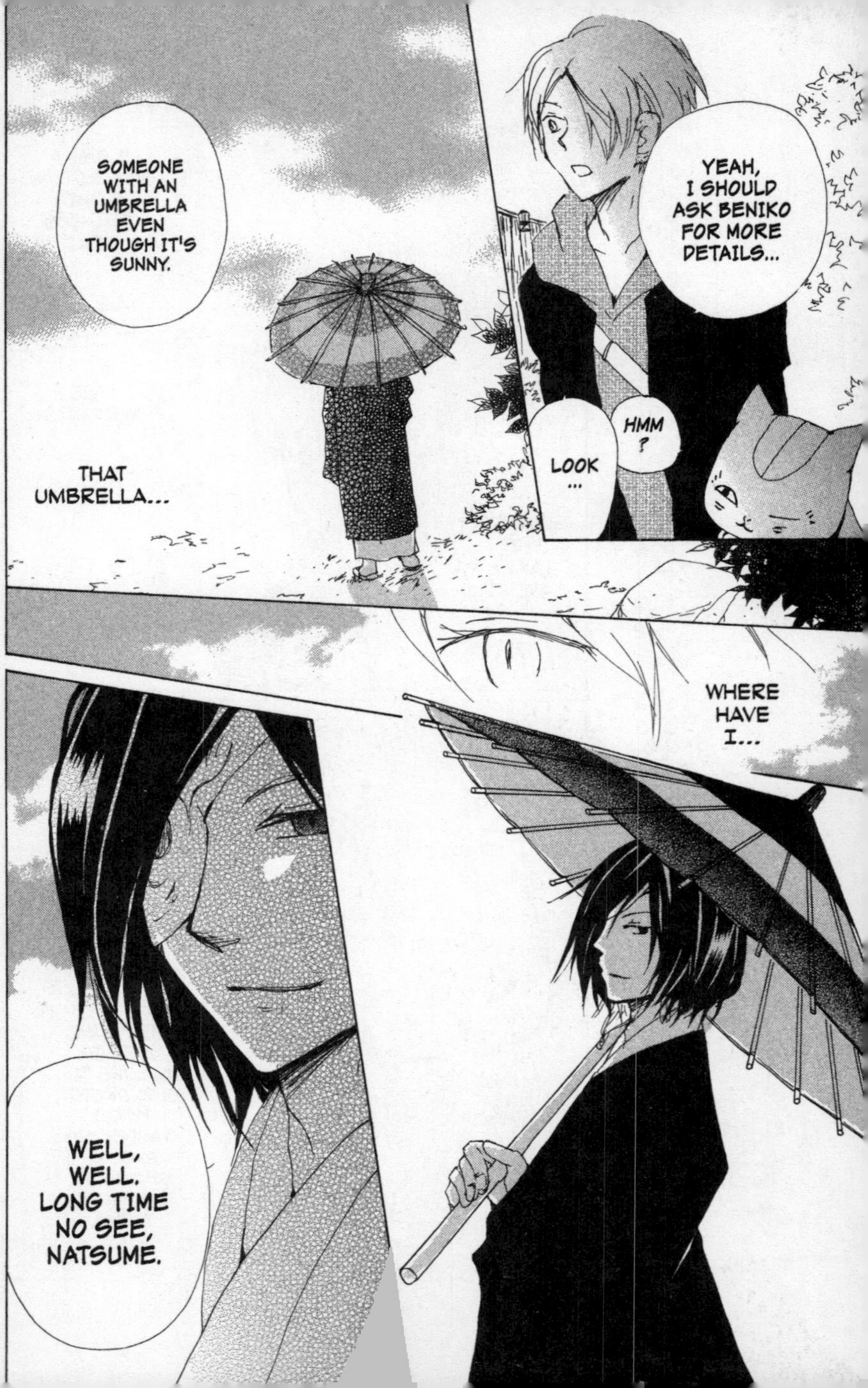
YEAH, I SHOULD ASK BENIKO FOR MORE DETAILS...
HMM ?
LOOK ...
SOMEONE WITH AN UMBRELLA EVEN THOUGH IT'S SUNNY.
THAT UMBRELLA...
WHERE HAVE I...
WELL, WELL. LONG TIME NO SEE, NATSUME.

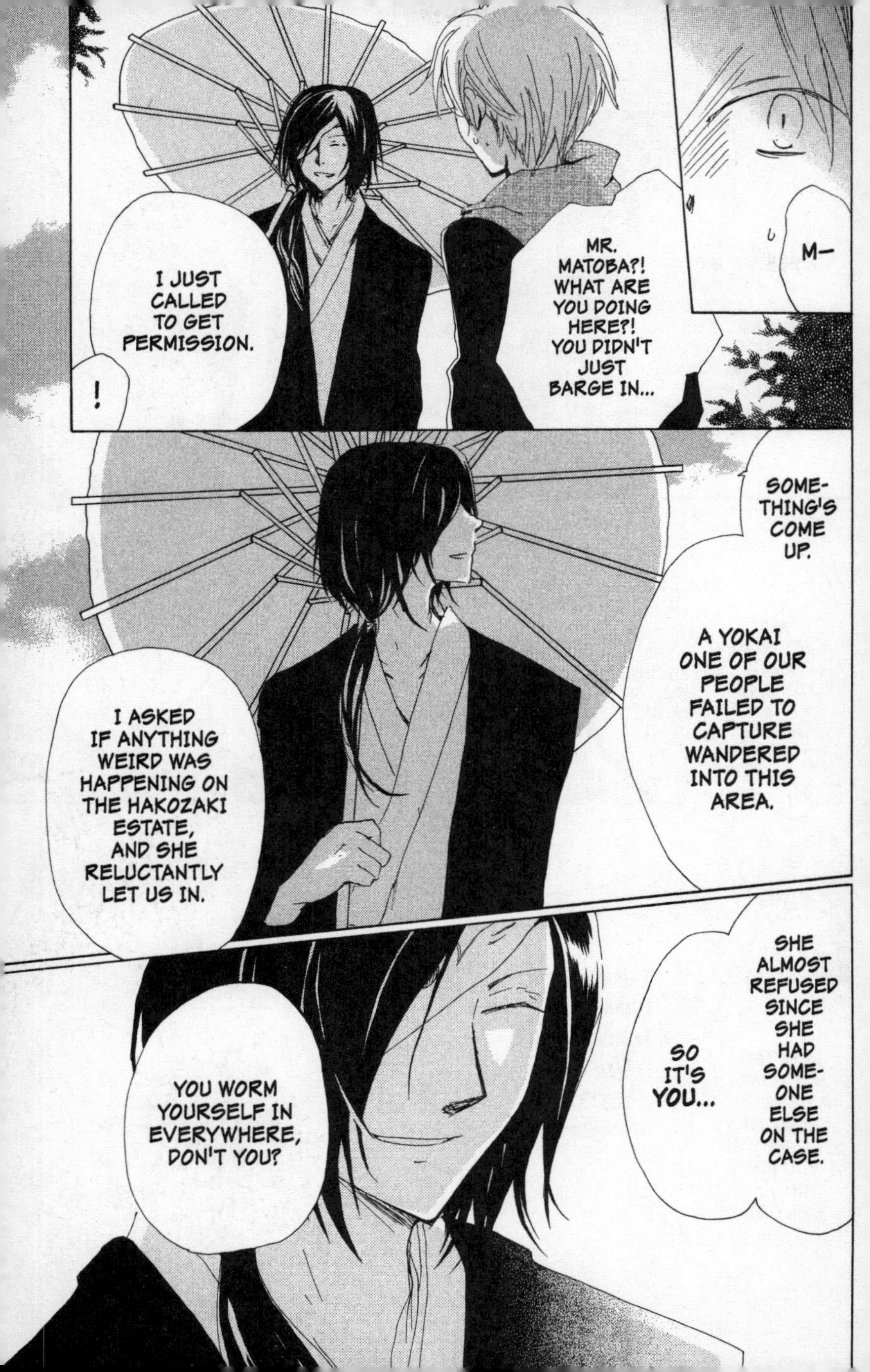
M—
MR. MATOBA?! WHAT ARE YOU DOING HERE?! YOU DIDN'T JUST BARGE IN...
I JUST CALLED TO GET PERMISSION.
!
SOME-THING'S COME UP.
A YOKAI ONE OF OUR PEOPLE FAILED TO CAPTURE WANDERED INTO THIS AREA.
I ASKED IF ANYTHING WEIRD WAS HAPPENING ON THE HAKOZAKI ESTATE, AND SHE RELUCTANTLY LET US IN.
SHE ALMOST REFUSED SINCE SHE HAD SOME-ONE ELSE ON THE CASE.
SO IT'S YOU...
YOU WORM YOURSELF IN EVERYWHERE, DON'T YOU?

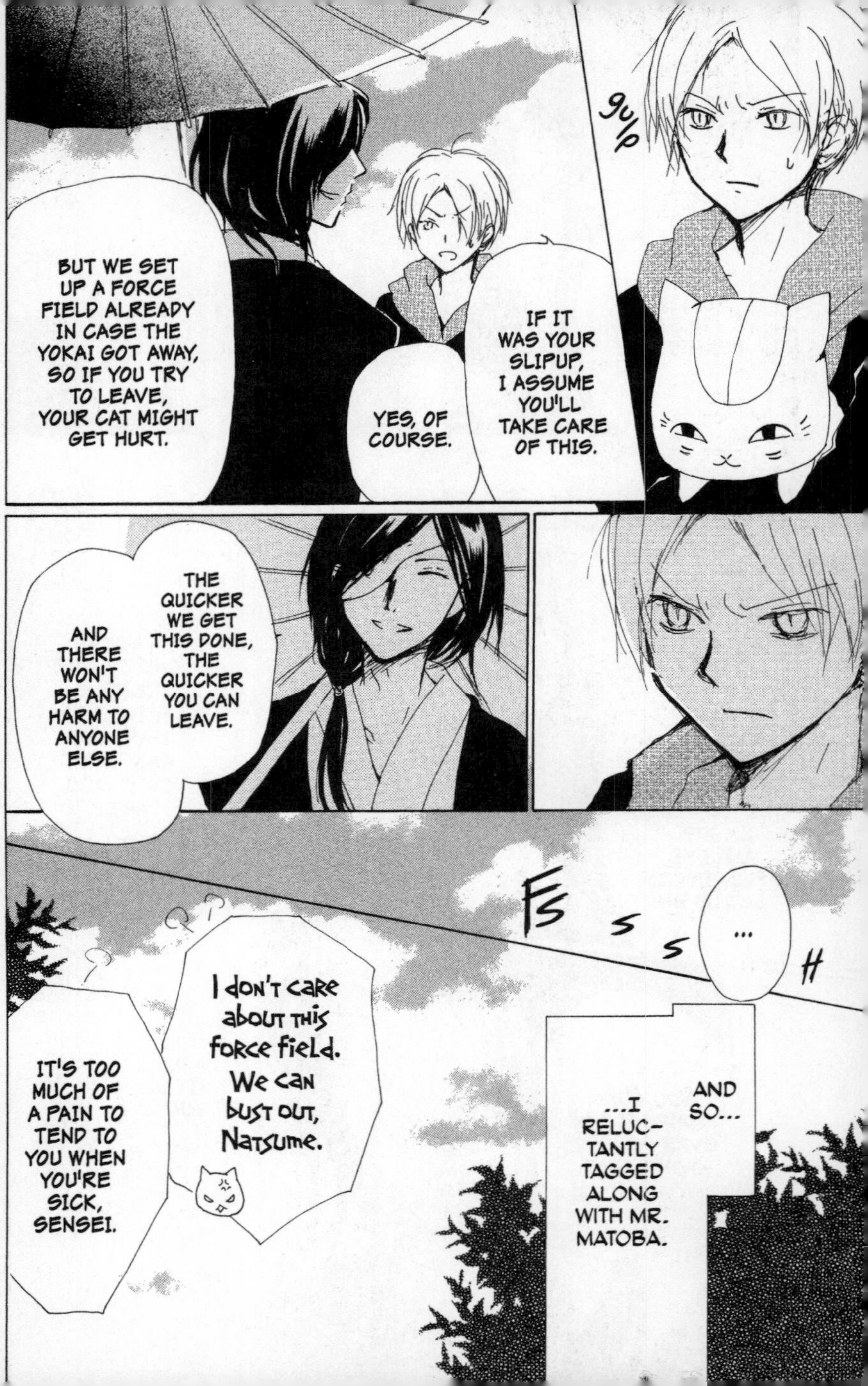
gulp
IF IT WAS YOUR SLIPUP, I ASSUME YOU'LL TAKE CARE OF THIS.
YES, OF COURSE.
BUT WE SET UP A FORCE FIELD ALREADY IN CASE THE YOKAI GOT AWAY, SO IF YOU TRY TO LEAVE, YOUR CAT MIGHT GET HURT.
THE QUICKER WE GET THIS DONE, THE QUICKER YOU CAN LEAVE.
AND THERE WON'T BE ANY HARM TO ANYONE ELSE.
FSSSH
...
AND SO...
...I RELUCTANTLY TAGGED ALONG WITH MR. MATOBA.
I don't care about this force field. We can bust out, Natsume.
IT'S TOO MUCH OF A PAIN TO TEND TO YOU WHEN YOU'RE SICK, SENSEI.

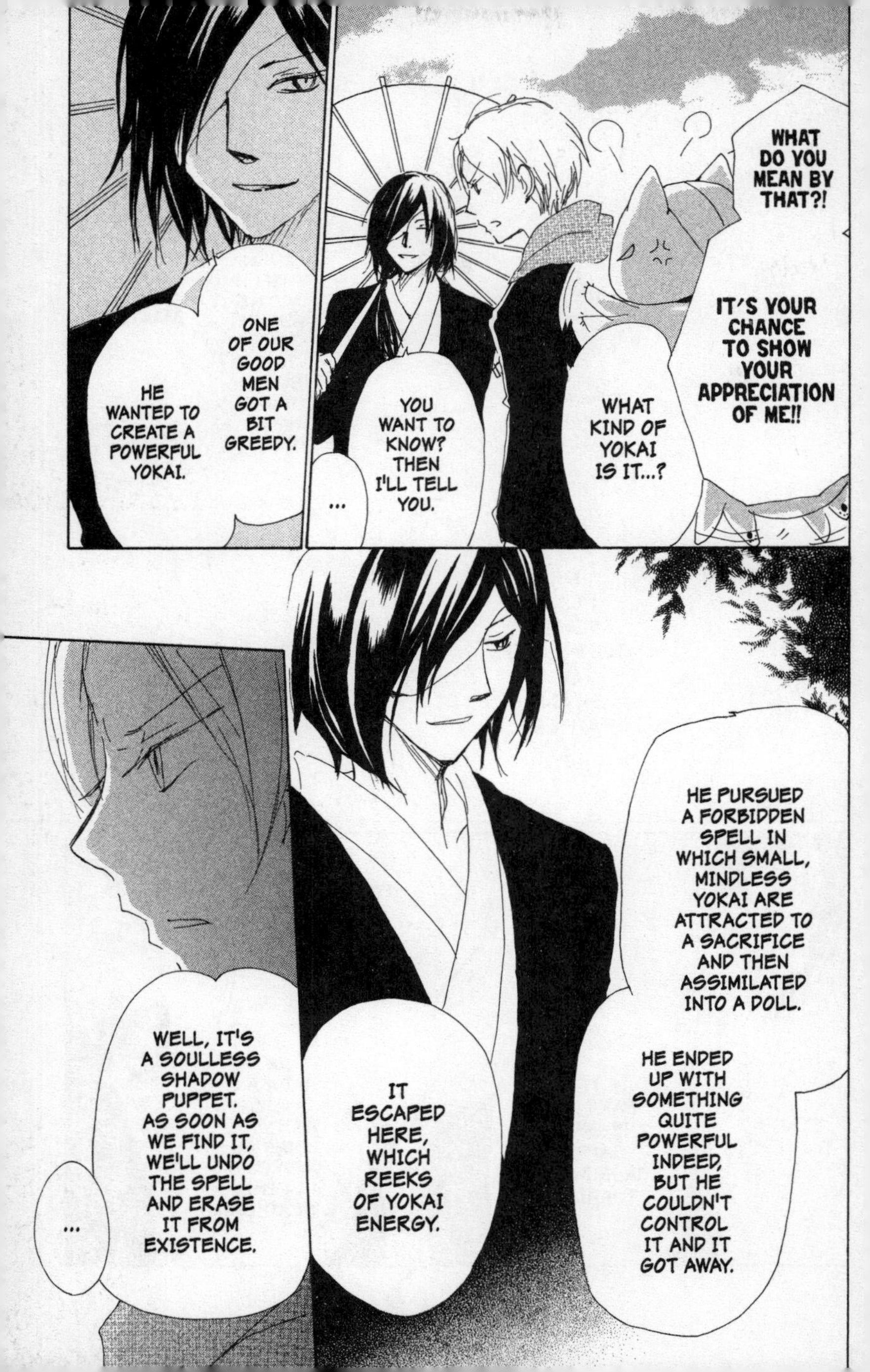
WHAT DO YOU MEAN BY THAT?!
IT'S YOUR CHANCE TO SHOW YOUR APPRECIATION OF ME!!
WHAT KIND OF YOKAI IS IT...?
YOU WANT TO KNOW? THEN I'LL TELL YOU.
...
ONE OF OUR GOOD MEN GOT A BIT GREEDY.
HE WANTED TO CREATE A POWERFUL YOKAI.
HE PURSUED A FORBIDDEN SPELL IN WHICH SMALL, MINDLESS YOKAI ARE ATTRACTED TO A SACRIFICE AND THEN ASSIMILATED INTO A DOLL.
HE ENDED UP WITH SOMETHING QUITE POWERFUL INDEED, BUT HE COULDN'T CONTROL IT AND IT GOT AWAY.
IT ESCAPED HERE, WHICH REEKS OF YOKAI ENERGY.
WELL, IT'S A SOULLESS SHADOW PUPPET. AS SOON AS WE FIND IT, WE'LL UNDO THE SPELL AND ERASE IT FROM EXISTENCE.
...

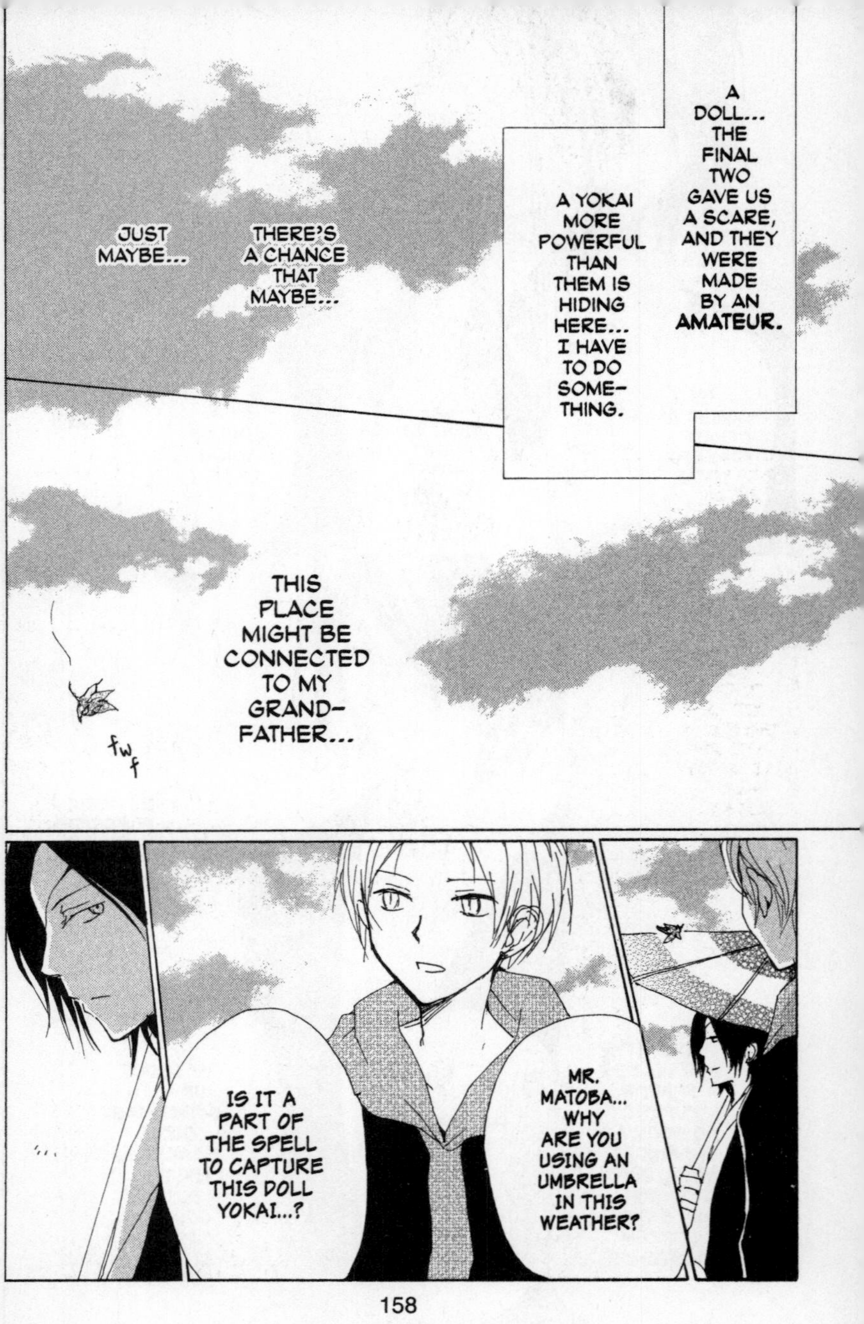
A DOLL... THE FINAL TWO GAVE US A SCARE, AND THEY WERE MADE BY AN **AMATEUR.**
A YOKAI MORE POWERFUL THAN THEM IS HIDING HERE... I HAVE TO DO SOME-THING.
THERE'S A CHANCE THAT MAYBE...
JUST MAYBE...
THIS PLACE MIGHT BE CONNECTED TO MY GRAND-FATHER...
fwf
MR. MATOBA... WHY ARE YOU USING AN UMBRELLA IN THIS WEATHER?
IS IT A PART OF THE SPELL TO CAPTURE THIS DOLL YOKAI...?
...

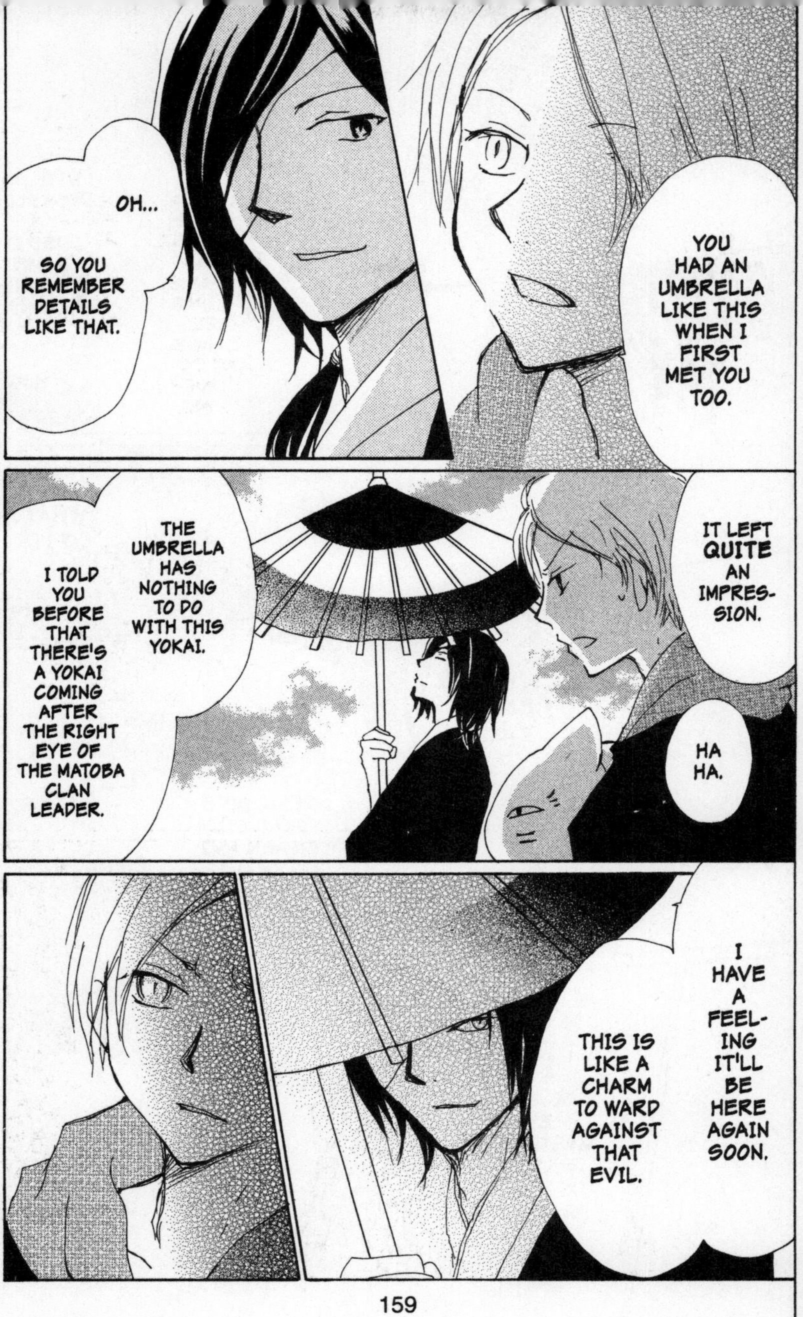
YOU HAD AN UMBRELLA LIKE THIS WHEN I FIRST MET YOU TOO.
OH...
SO YOU REMEMBER DETAILS LIKE THAT.
IT LEFT QUITE AN IMPRES-SION.
HA HA.
THE UMBRELLA HAS NOTHING TO DO WITH THIS YOKAI.
I TOLD YOU BEFORE THAT THERE'S A YOKAI COMING AFTER THE RIGHT EYE OF THE MATOBA CLAN LEADER.
I HAVE A FEEL-ING IT'LL BE HERE AGAIN SOON.
THIS IS LIKE A CHARM TO WARD AGAINST THAT EVIL.

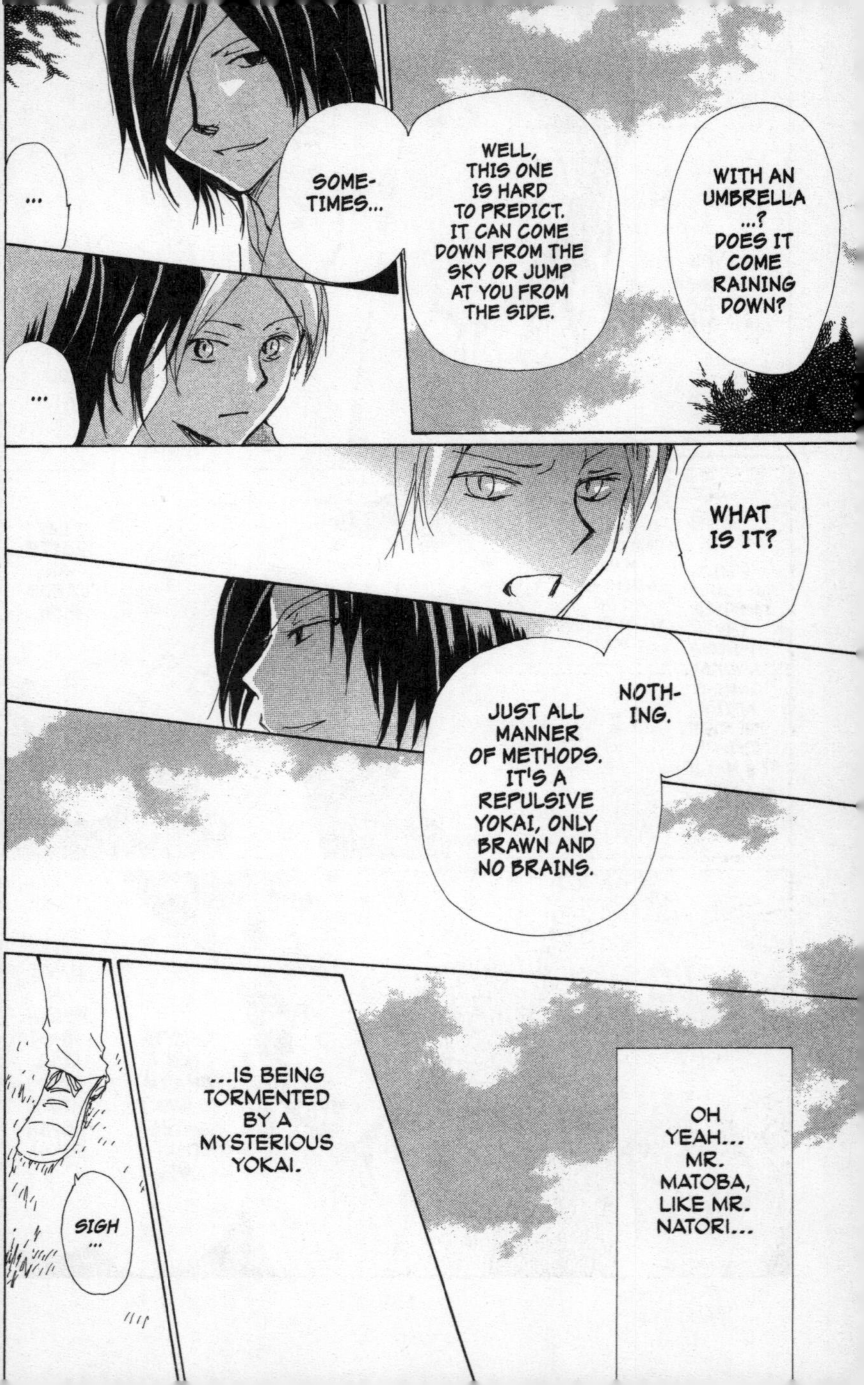
WITH AN UMBRELLA ...? DOES IT COME RAINING DOWN?
WELL, THIS ONE IS HARD TO PREDICT. IT CAN COME DOWN FROM THE SKY OR JUMP AT YOU FROM THE SIDE.
SOME-TIMES...
...
...
WHAT IS IT?
NOTH-ING.
JUST ALL MANNER OF METHODS. IT'S A REPULSIVE YOKAI, ONLY BRAWN AND NO BRAINS.
OH YEAH... MR. MATOBA, LIKE MR. NATORI...
...IS BEING TORMENTED BY A MYSTERIOUS YOKAI.
SIGH ...

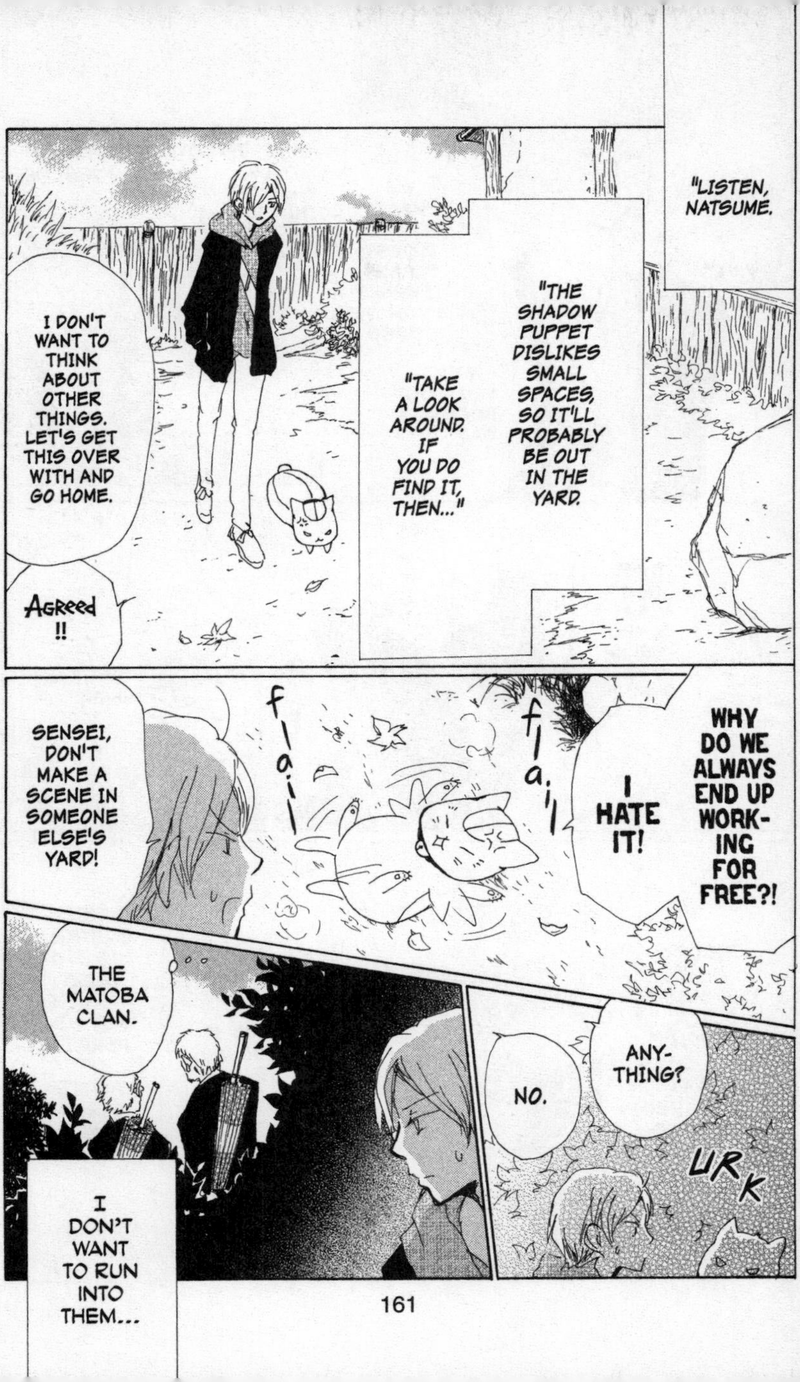
"LISTEN, NATSUME.
"THE SHADOW PUPPET DISLIKES SMALL SPACES, SO IT'LL PROBABLY BE OUT IN THE YARD.
"TAKE A LOOK AROUND. IF YOU DO FIND IT, THEN..."
I DON'T WANT TO THINK ABOUT OTHER THINGS. LET'S GET THIS OVER WITH AND GO HOME.
Agreed !!
WHY DO WE ALWAYS END UP WORKING FOR FREE?!
I HATE IT!
flail
flail
SENSEI, DON'T MAKE A SCENE IN SOMEONE ELSE'S YARD!
ANY-THING?
NO.
URK
THE MATOBA CLAN.
I DON'T WANT TO RUN INTO THEM...

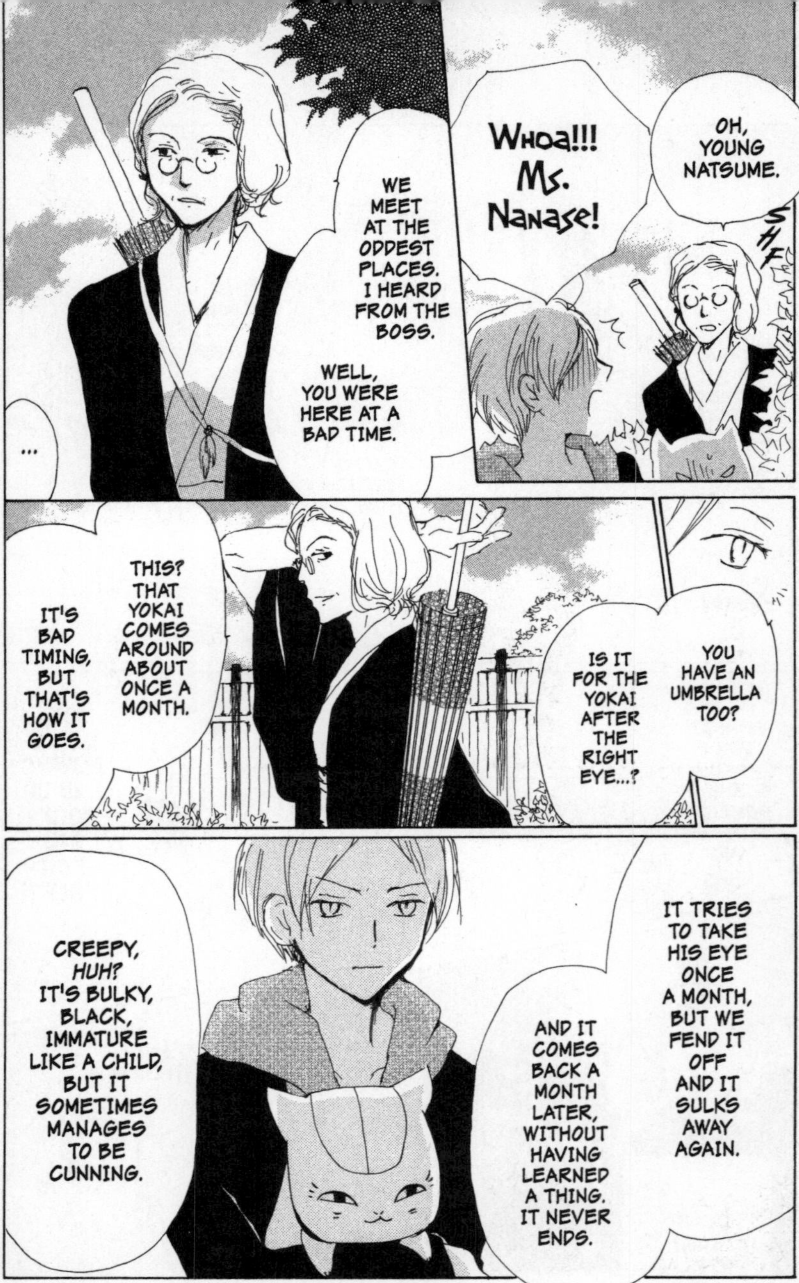
OH, YOUNG NATSUME.
SHF
Whoa!!! Ms. Nanase!
WE MEET AT THE ODDEST PLACES. I HEARD FROM THE BOSS.
WELL, YOU WERE HERE AT A BAD TIME.
...
YOU HAVE AN UMBRELLA TOO?
IS IT FOR THE YOKAI AFTER THE RIGHT EYE...?
THIS? THAT YOKAI COMES AROUND ABOUT ONCE A MONTH.
IT'S BAD TIMING, BUT THAT'S HOW IT GOES.
IT TRIES TO TAKE HIS EYE ONCE A MONTH, BUT WE FEND IT OFF AND IT SULKS AWAY AGAIN.
AND IT COMES BACK A MONTH LATER, WITHOUT HAVING LEARNED A THING. IT NEVER ENDS.
CREEPY, *HUH?* IT'S BULKY, BLACK, IMMATURE LIKE A CHILD, BUT IT SOMETIMES MANAGES TO BE CUNNING.

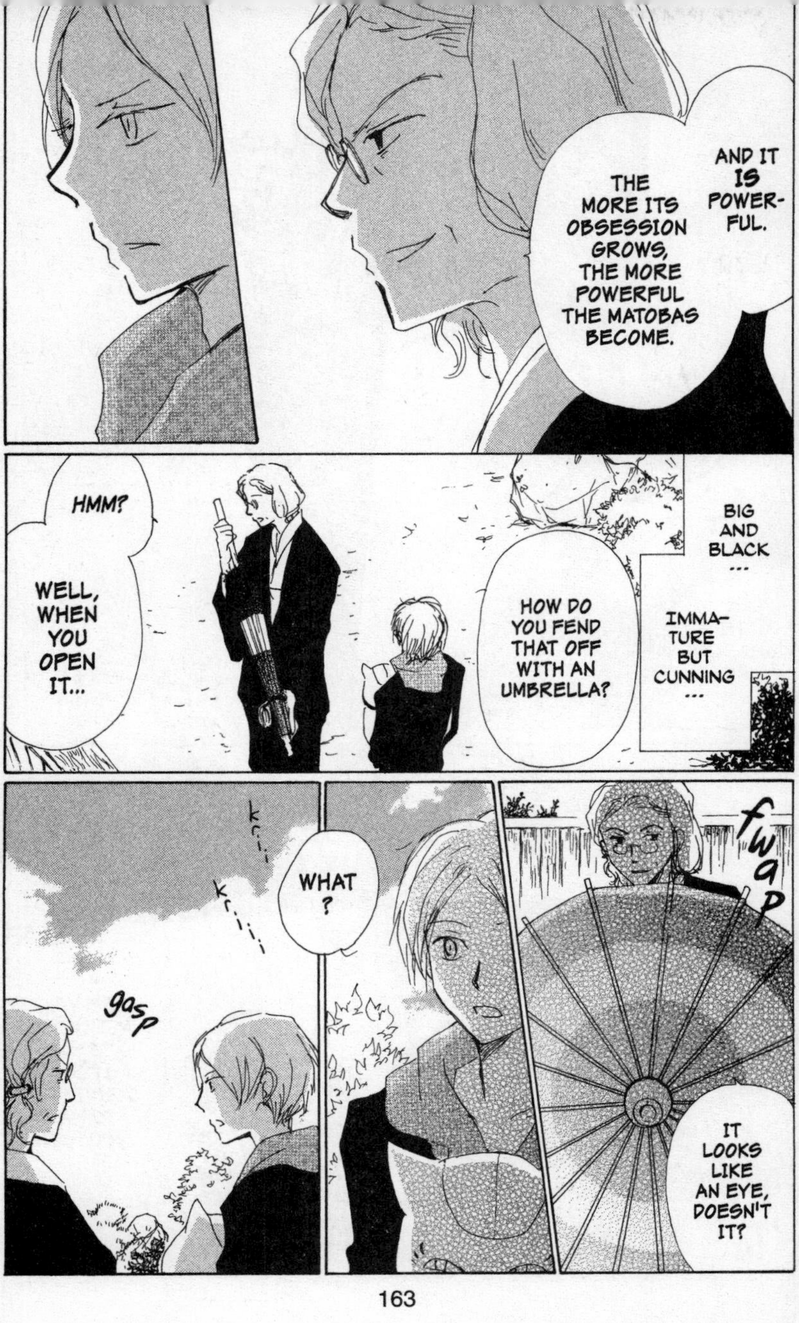
AND IT IS POWERFUL.
THE MORE ITS OBSESSION GROWS, THE MORE POWERFUL THE MATOBAS BECOME.
BIG AND BLACK...
IMMATURE BUT CUNNING...
HOW DO YOU FEND THAT OFF WITH AN UMBRELLA?
HMM?
WELL, WHEN YOU OPEN IT...
fwap
IT LOOKS LIKE AN EYE, DOESN'T IT?
WHAT?
gasp

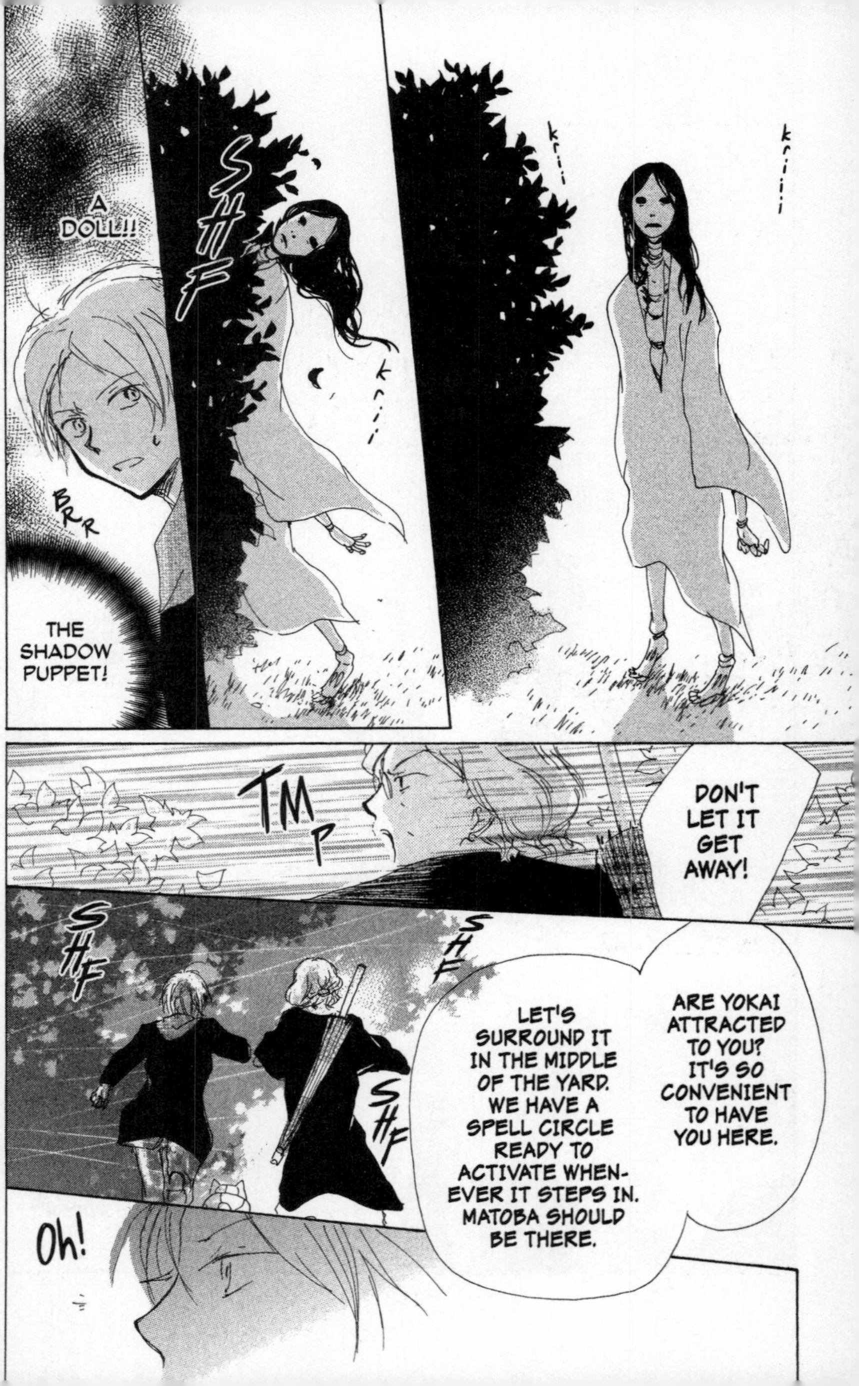
kriii
kriii
SHF
kriii
A DOLL!!
BRR
THE SHADOW PUPPET!
DON'T LET IT GET AWAY!
TMP
ARE YOKAI ATTRACTED TO YOU? IT'S SO CONVENIENT TO HAVE YOU HERE.
LET'S SURROUND IT IN THE MIDDLE OF THE YARD. WE HAVE A SPELL CIRCLE READY TO ACTIVATE WHEN-EVER IT STEPS IN. MATOBA SHOULD BE THERE.
SHF
SHF
SHF
Oh!

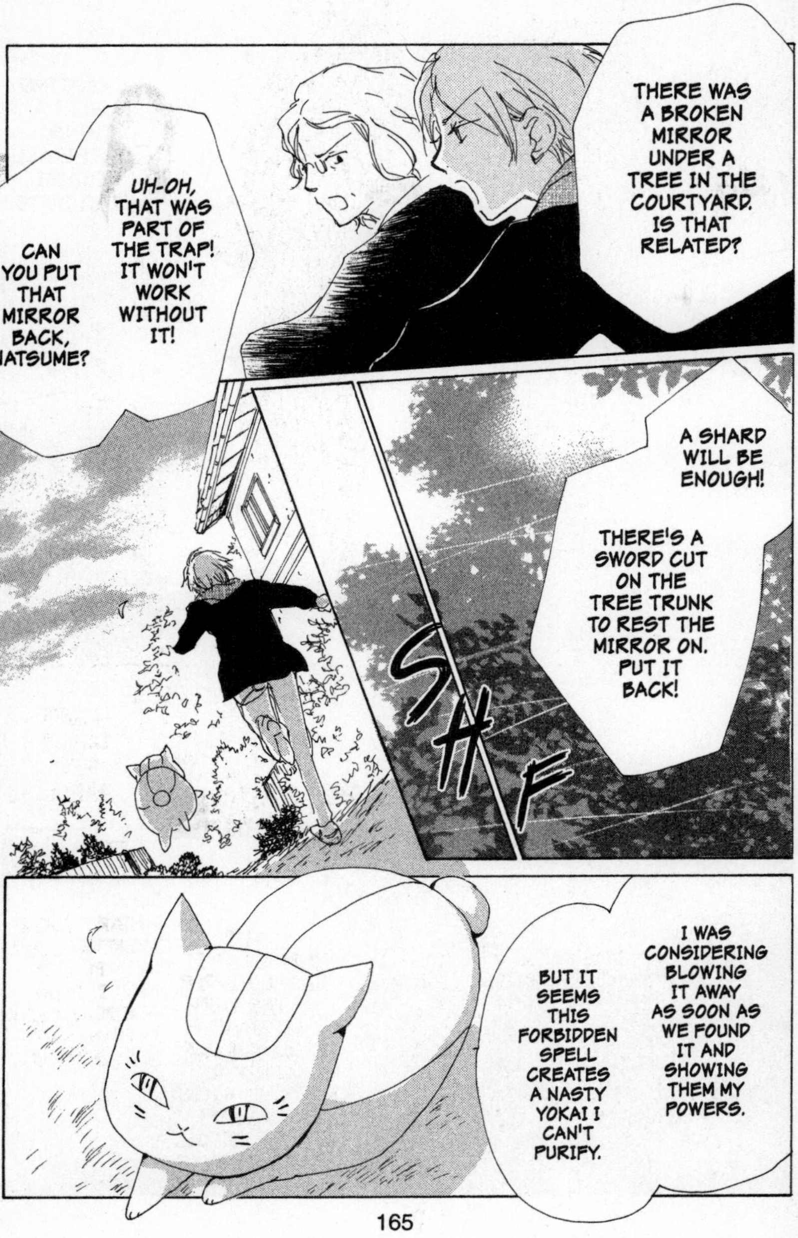
THERE WAS A BROKEN MIRROR UNDER A TREE IN THE COURTYARD. IS THAT RELATED?
UH-OH, THAT WAS PART OF THE TRAP! IT WON'T WORK WITHOUT IT!
CAN YOU PUT THAT MIRROR BACK, NATSUME?
A SHARD WILL BE ENOUGH!
THERE'S A SWORD CUT ON THE TREE TRUNK TO REST THE MIRROR ON. PUT IT BACK!
SHF
I WAS CONSIDERING BLOWING IT AWAY AS SOON AS WE FOUND IT AND SHOWING THEM MY POWERS.
BUT IT SEEMS THIS FORBIDDEN SPELL CREATES A NASTY YOKAI I CAN'T PURIFY.

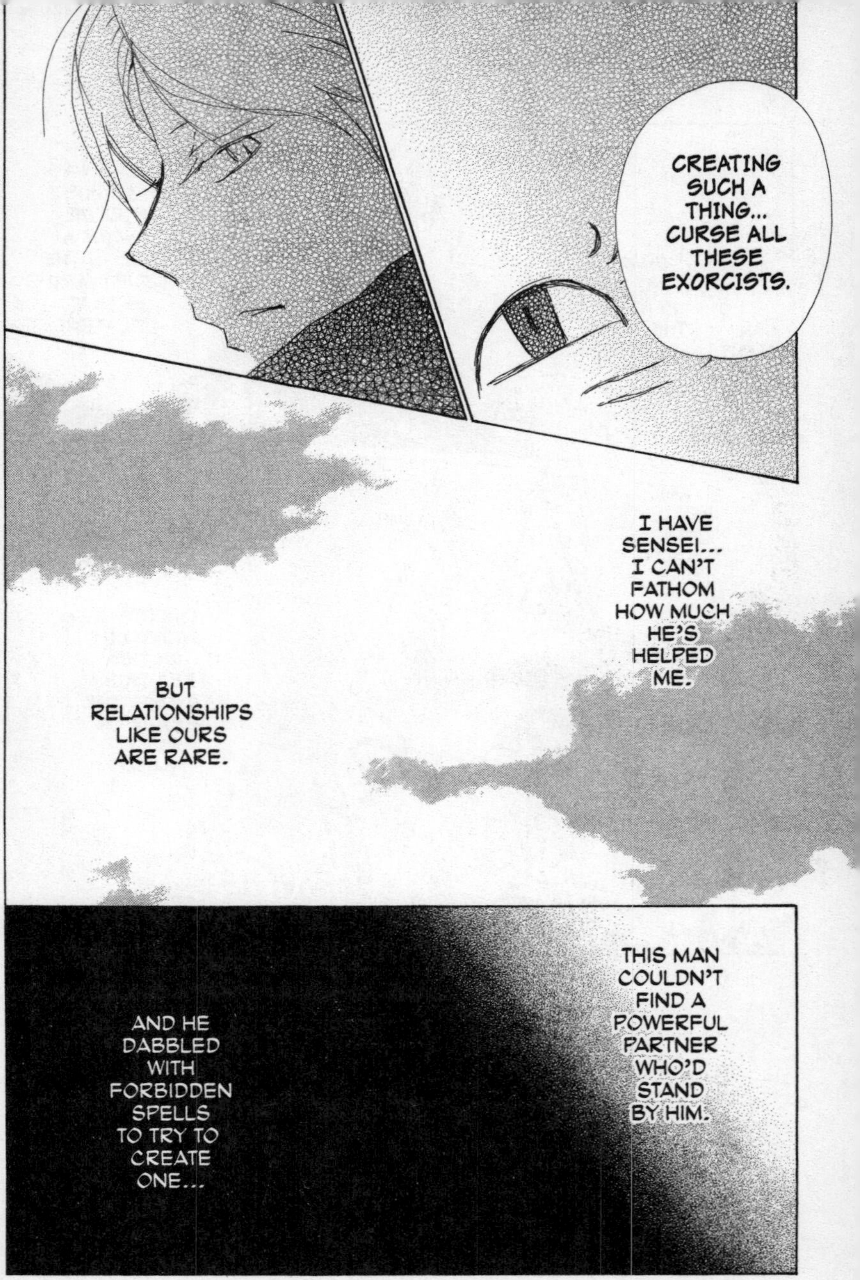
CREATING SUCH A THING... CURSE ALL THESE EXORCISTS.
I HAVE SENSEI... I CAN'T FATHOM HOW MUCH HE'S HELPED ME.
BUT RELATIONSHIPS LIKE OURS ARE RARE.
THIS MAN COULDN'T FIND A POWERFUL PARTNER WHO'D STAND BY HIM.
AND HE DABBLED WITH FORBIDDEN SPELLS TO TRY TO CREATE ONE...

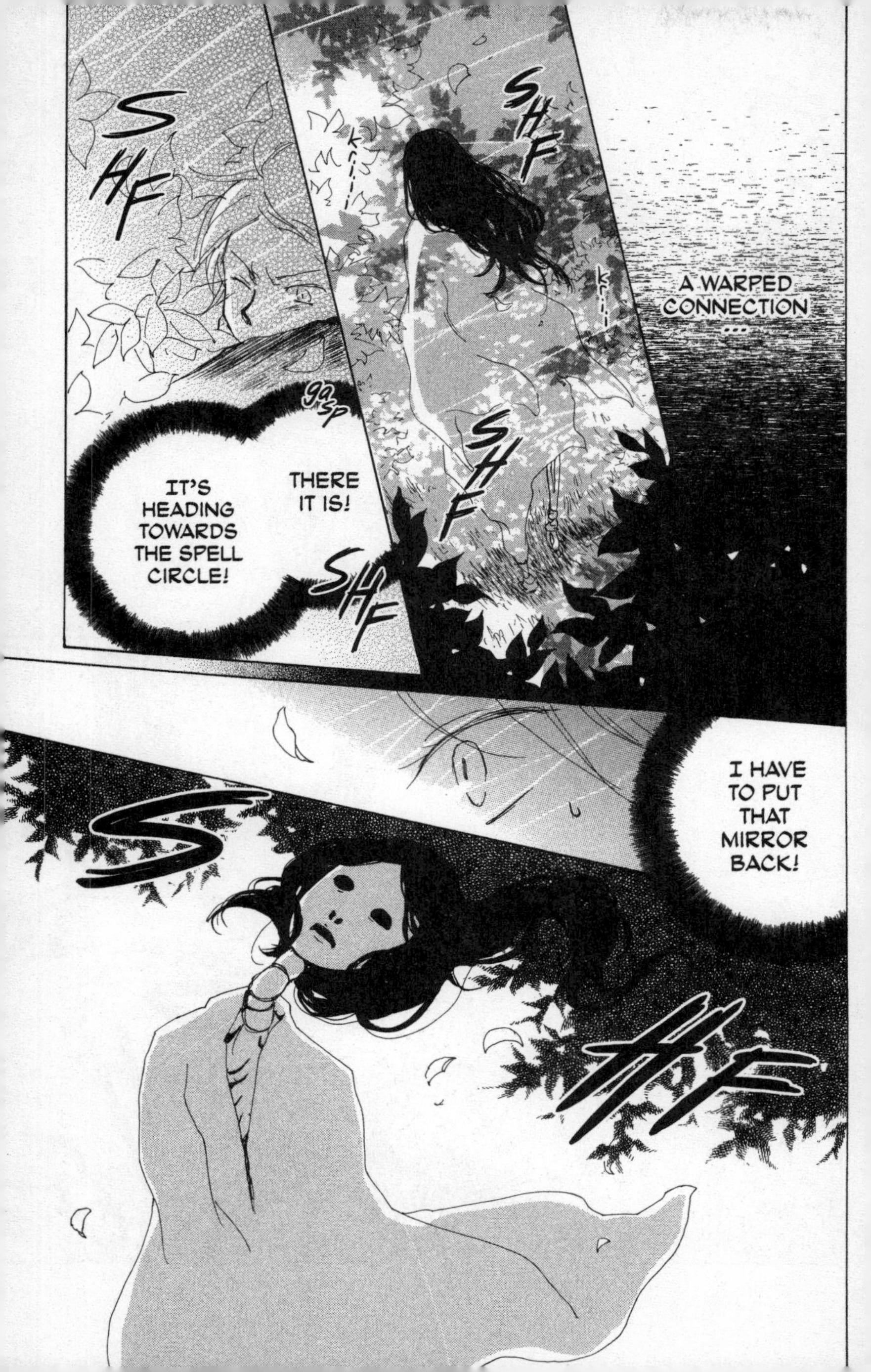
A WARPED CONNECTION ...
SHF
SHF
THERE IT IS!
SHF
gasp
IT'S HEADING TOWARDS THE SPELL CIRCLE!
SHF
I HAVE TO PUT THAT MIRROR BACK!
S
HF

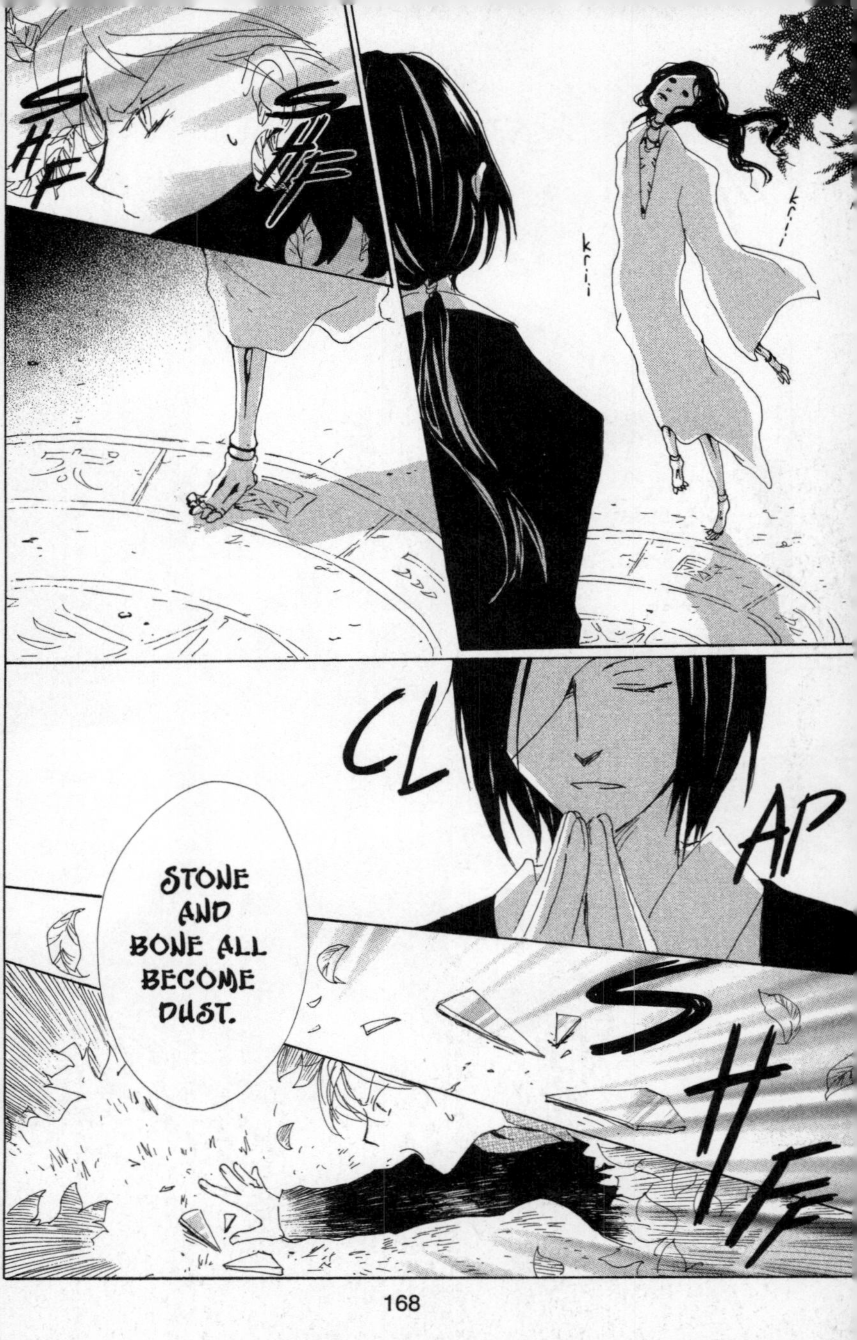
kri...
kri...
SHF
SHF
CLAP
STONE AND BONE ALL BECOME DUST.
SHF

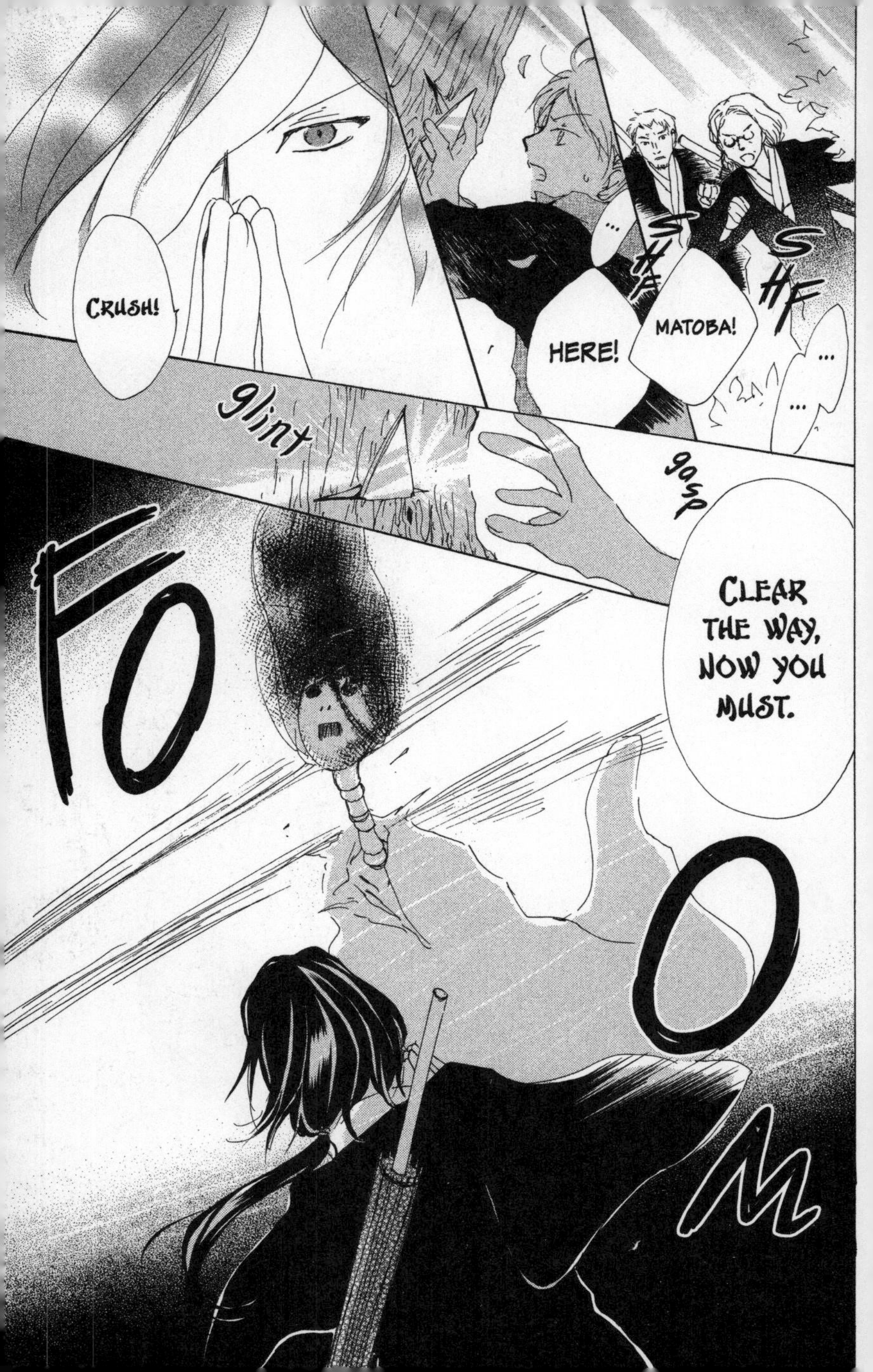
SHF
SHF
...
...
...
MATOBA!
HERE!
CRUSH!
glint
gasp
CLEAR THE WAY, NOW YOU MUST.
FOOOM

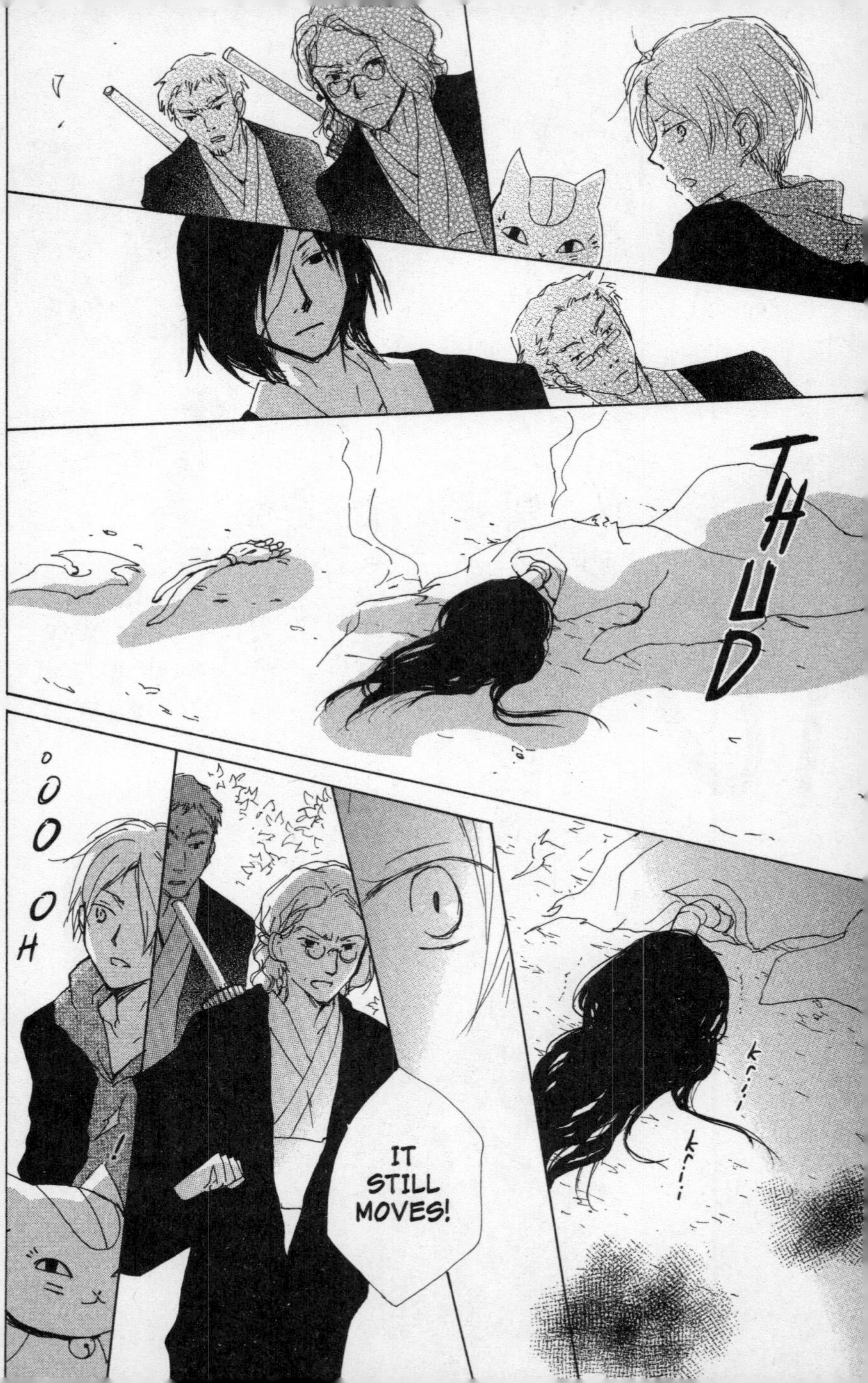
THUD
kr...
kr...
IT STILL MOVES!
OOOOH
!

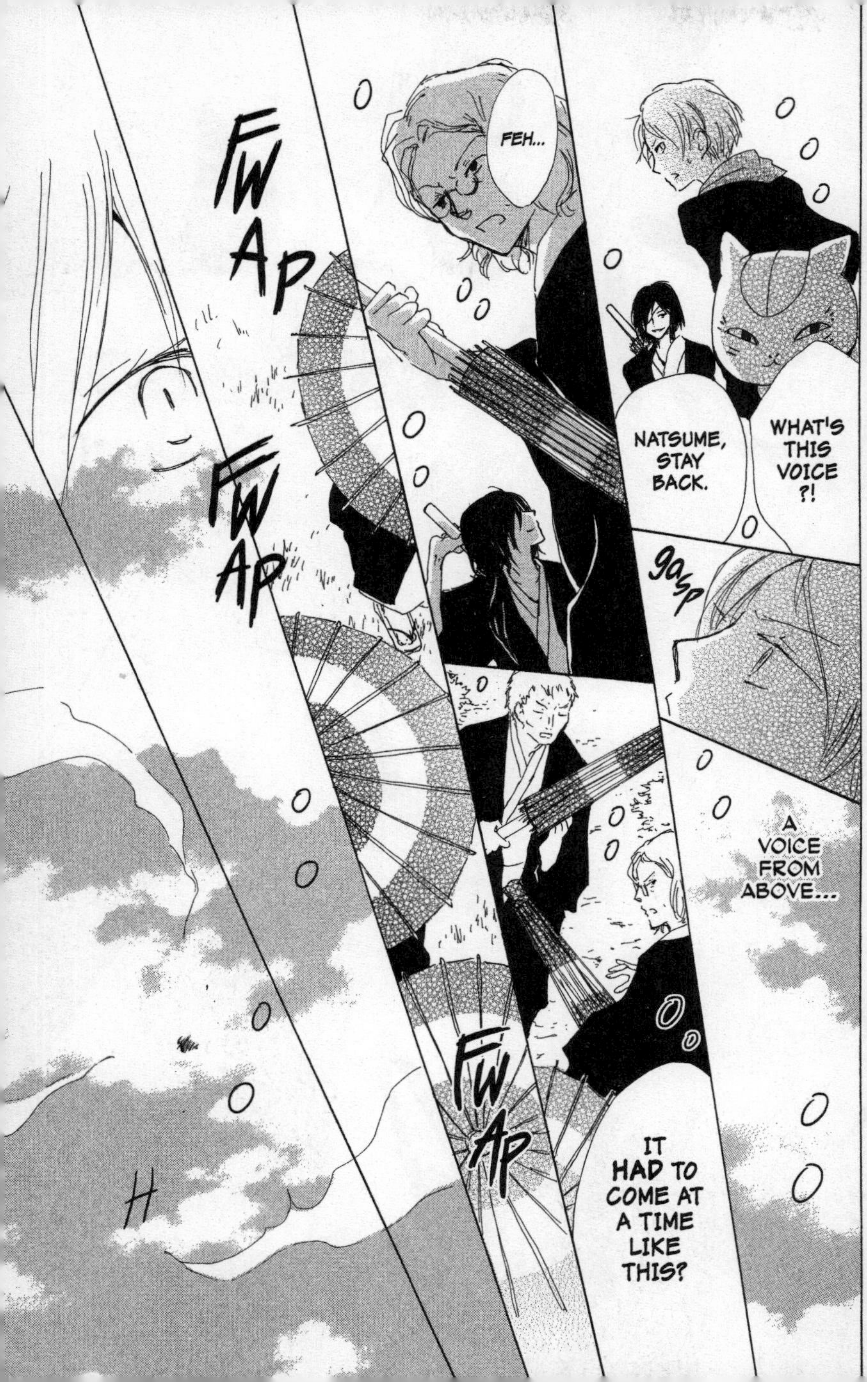

WHAT'S THIS VOICE ?!
NATSUME, STAY BACK.
gasp
A VOICE FROM ABOVE...
IT HAD TO COME AT A TIME LIKE THIS?
FEH...
FWAP
FWAP
FWAP

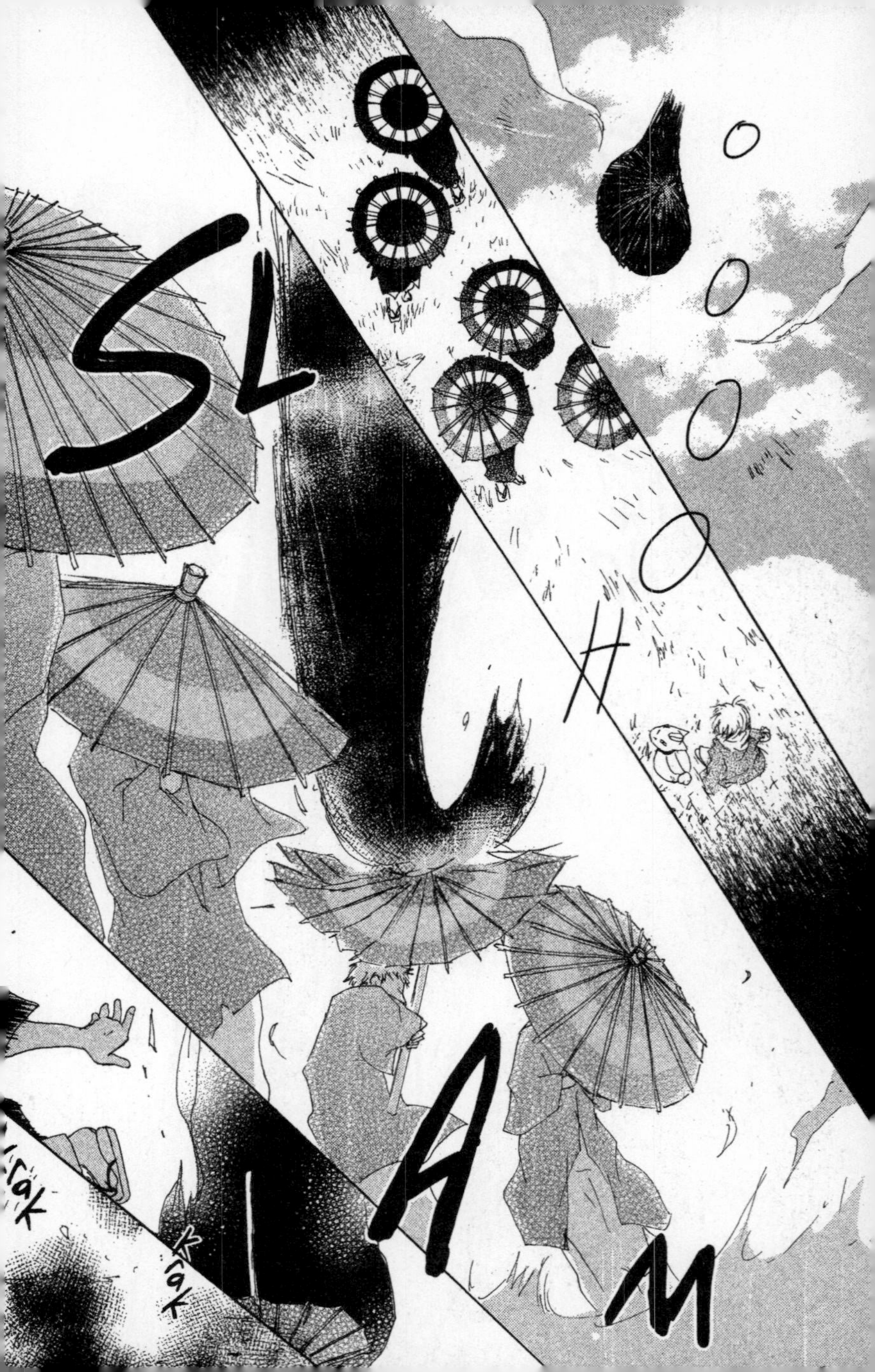
SLAM
krak krak

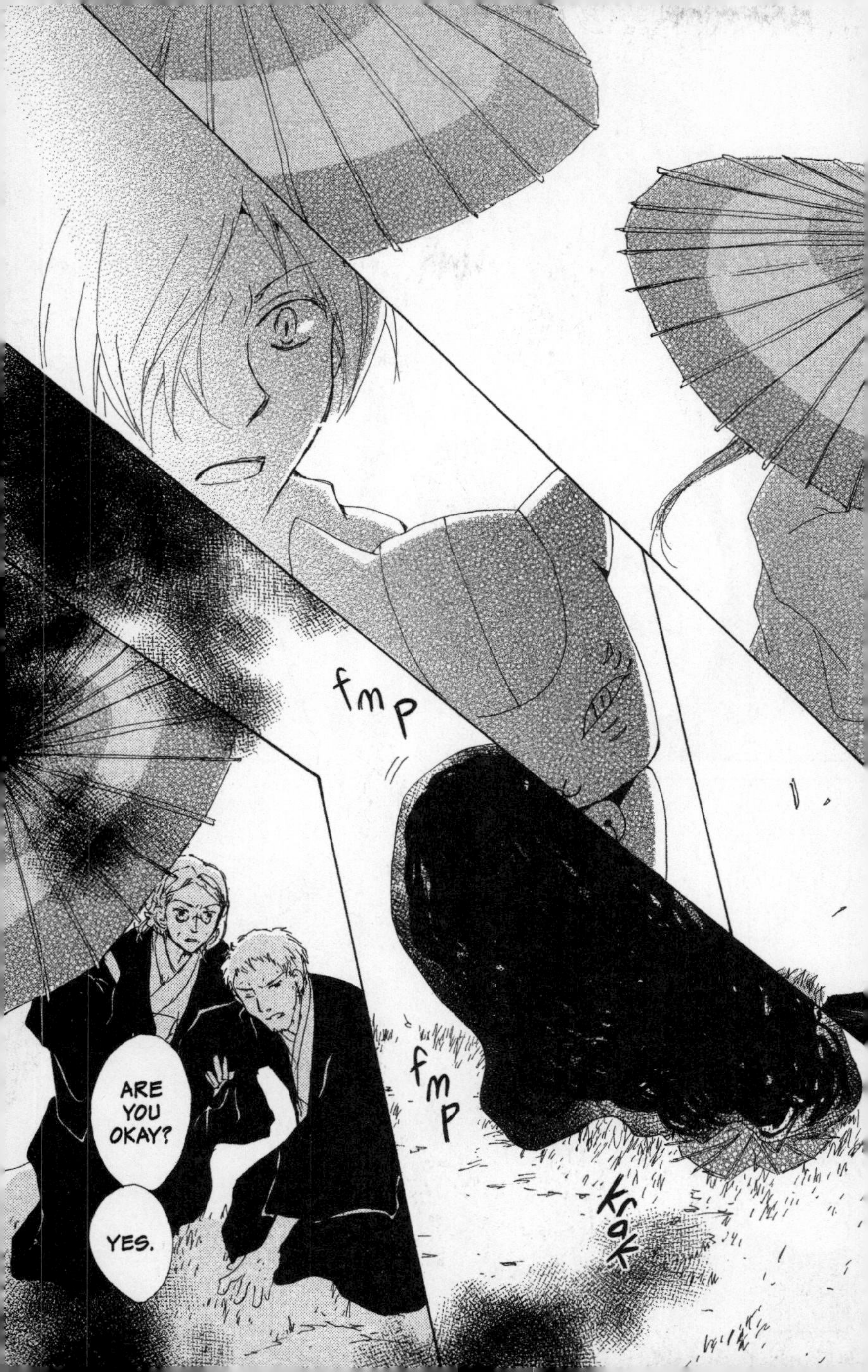
fmp
fmp
krak
ARE YOU OKAY?
YES.

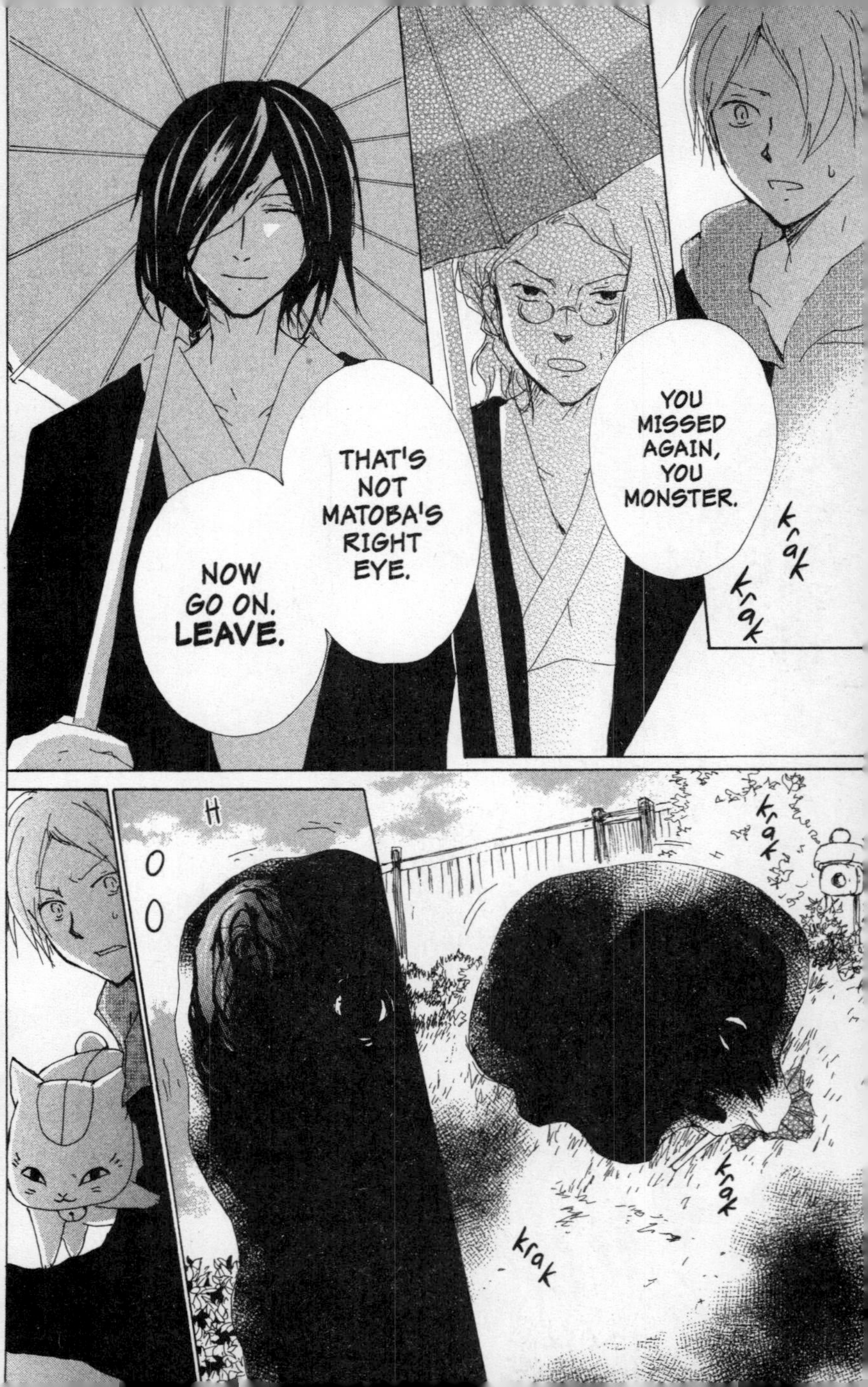
krak
krak
YOU MISSED AGAIN, YOU MONSTER.
THAT'S NOT MATOBA'S RIGHT EYE.
NOW GO ON. LEAVE.
krak
krak
krak
krak
HOO

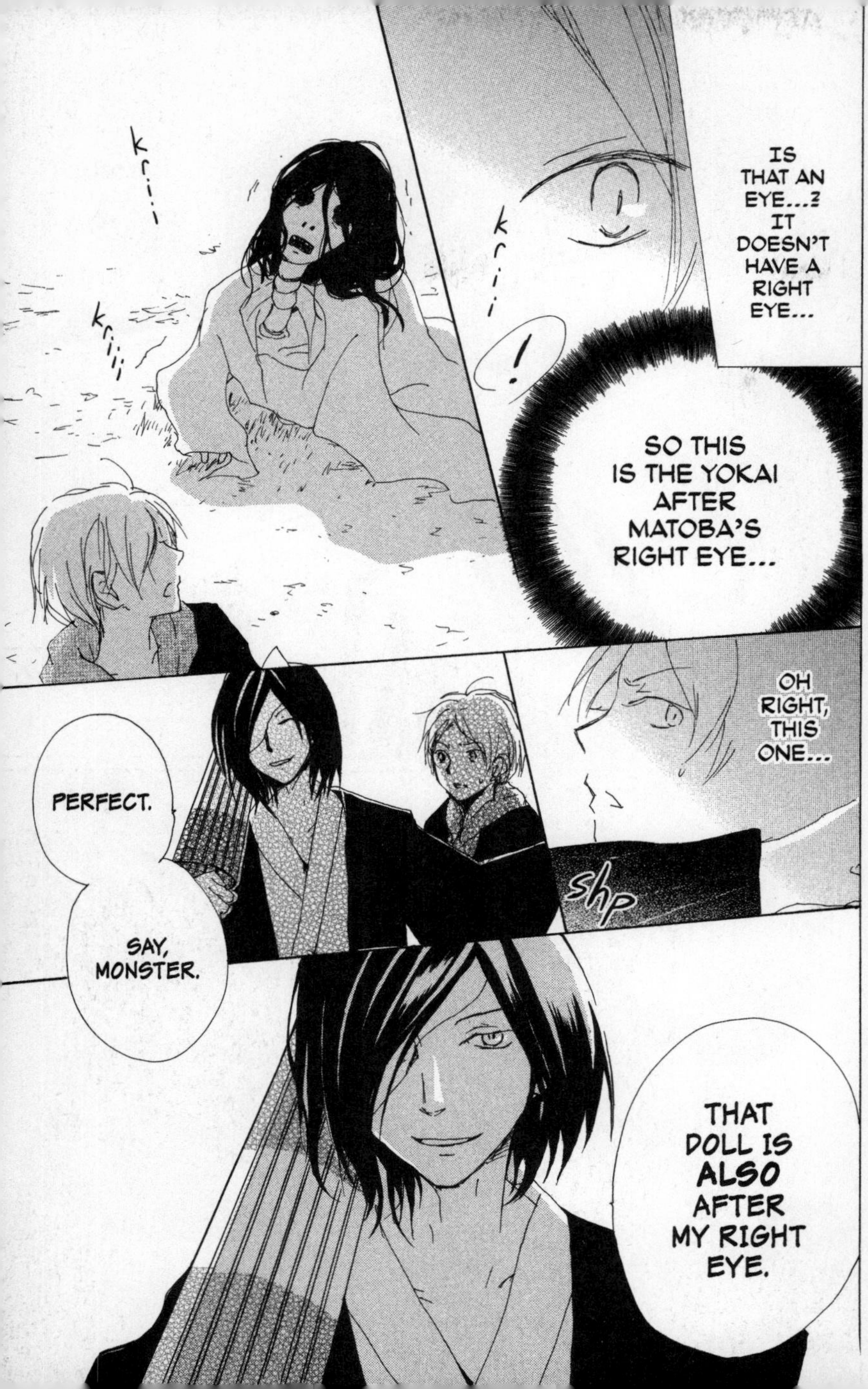
IS THAT AN EYE...? IT DOESN'T HAVE A RIGHT EYE...
kri...
!
SO THIS IS THE YOKAI AFTER MATOBA'S RIGHT EYE...
kri...
kriii
OH RIGHT, THIS ONE...
shp
PERFECT.
SAY, MONSTER.
THAT DOLL IS **ALSO** AFTER MY RIGHT EYE.

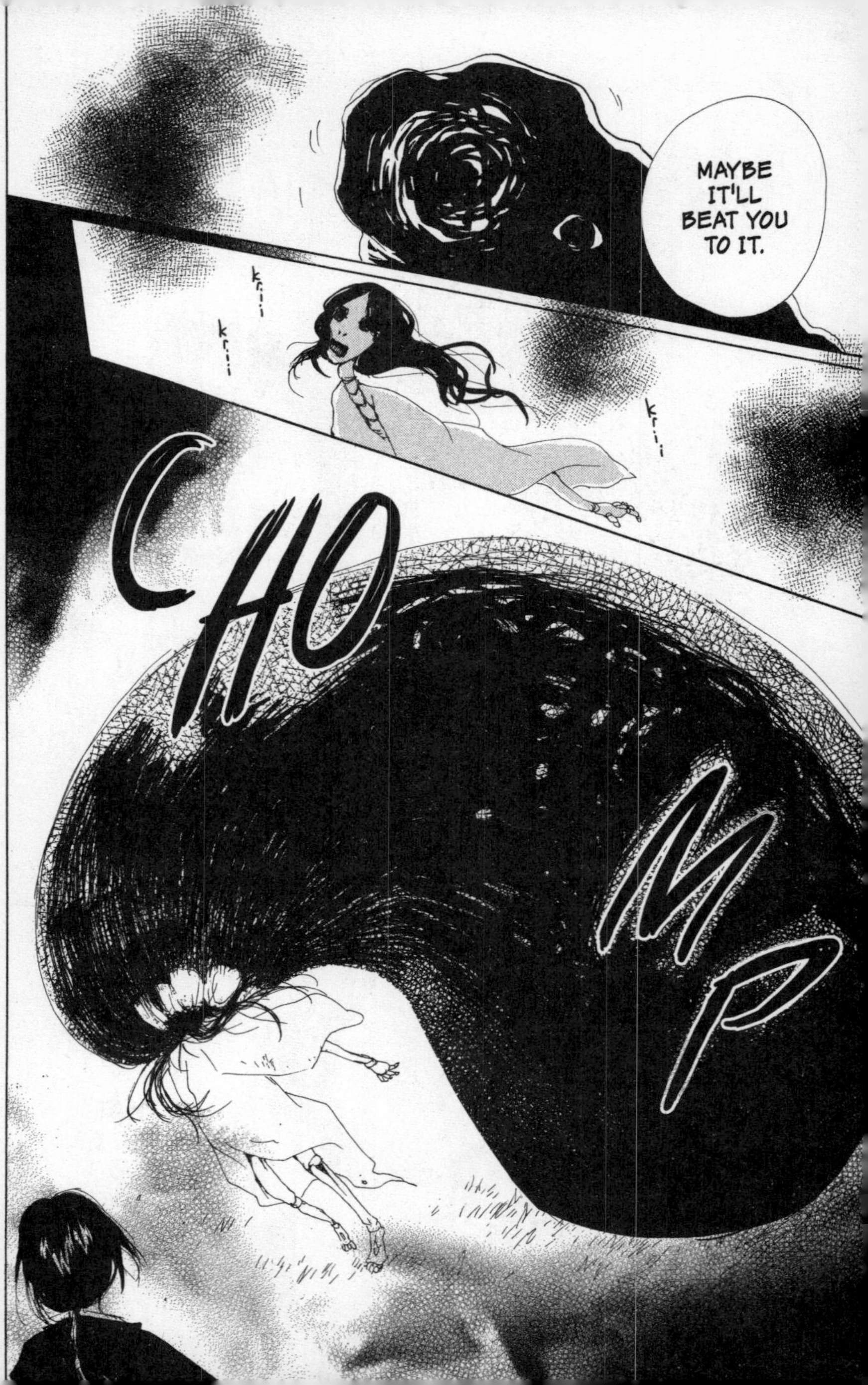
MAYBE IT'LL BEAT YOU TO IT.
kri i
kri i
kri i
CHOMP

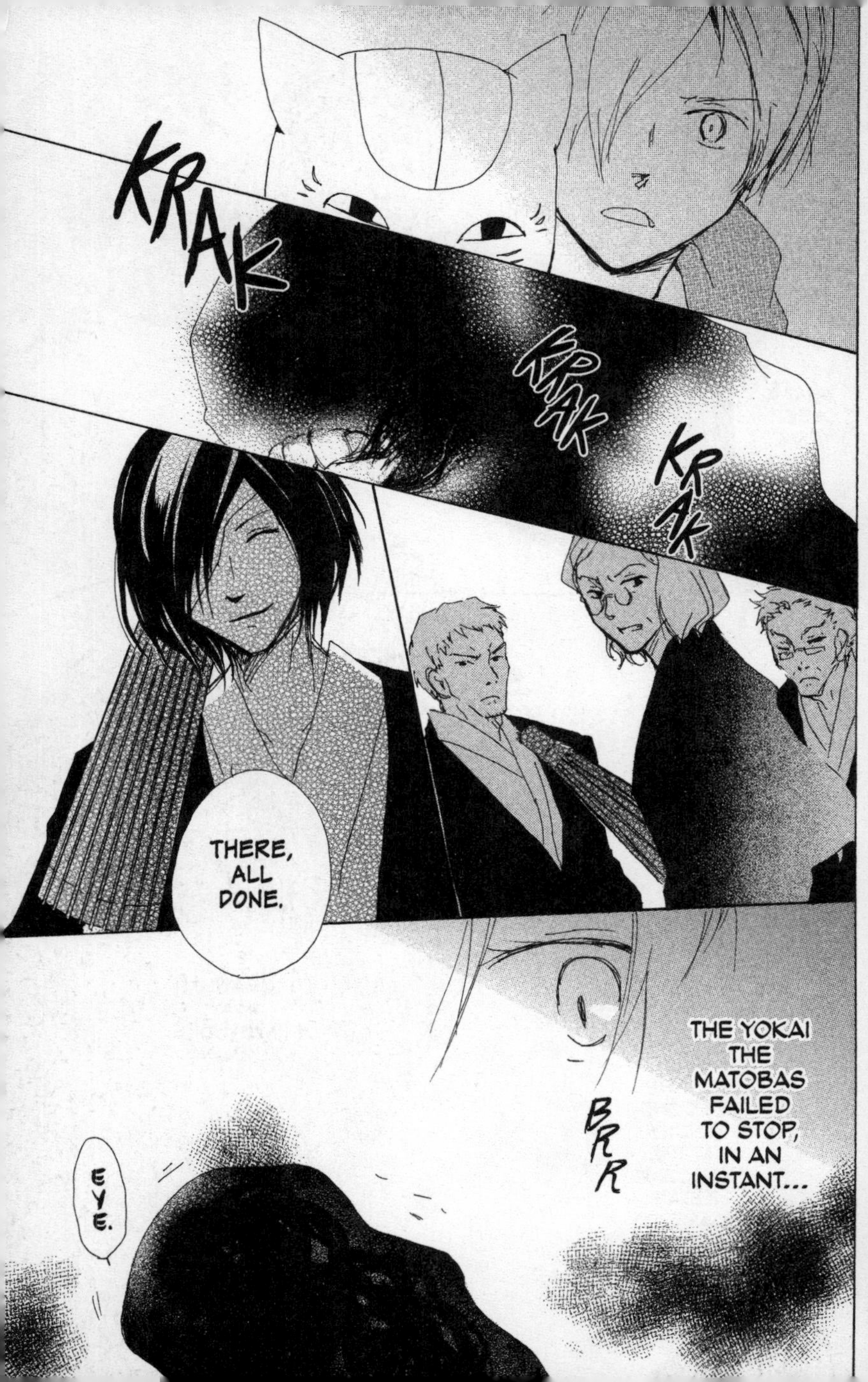
KRAK
KRAK
KRAK
THERE, ALL DONE.
THE YOKAI THE MATOBAS FAILED TO STOP, IN AN INSTANT...
BRR
EYE.

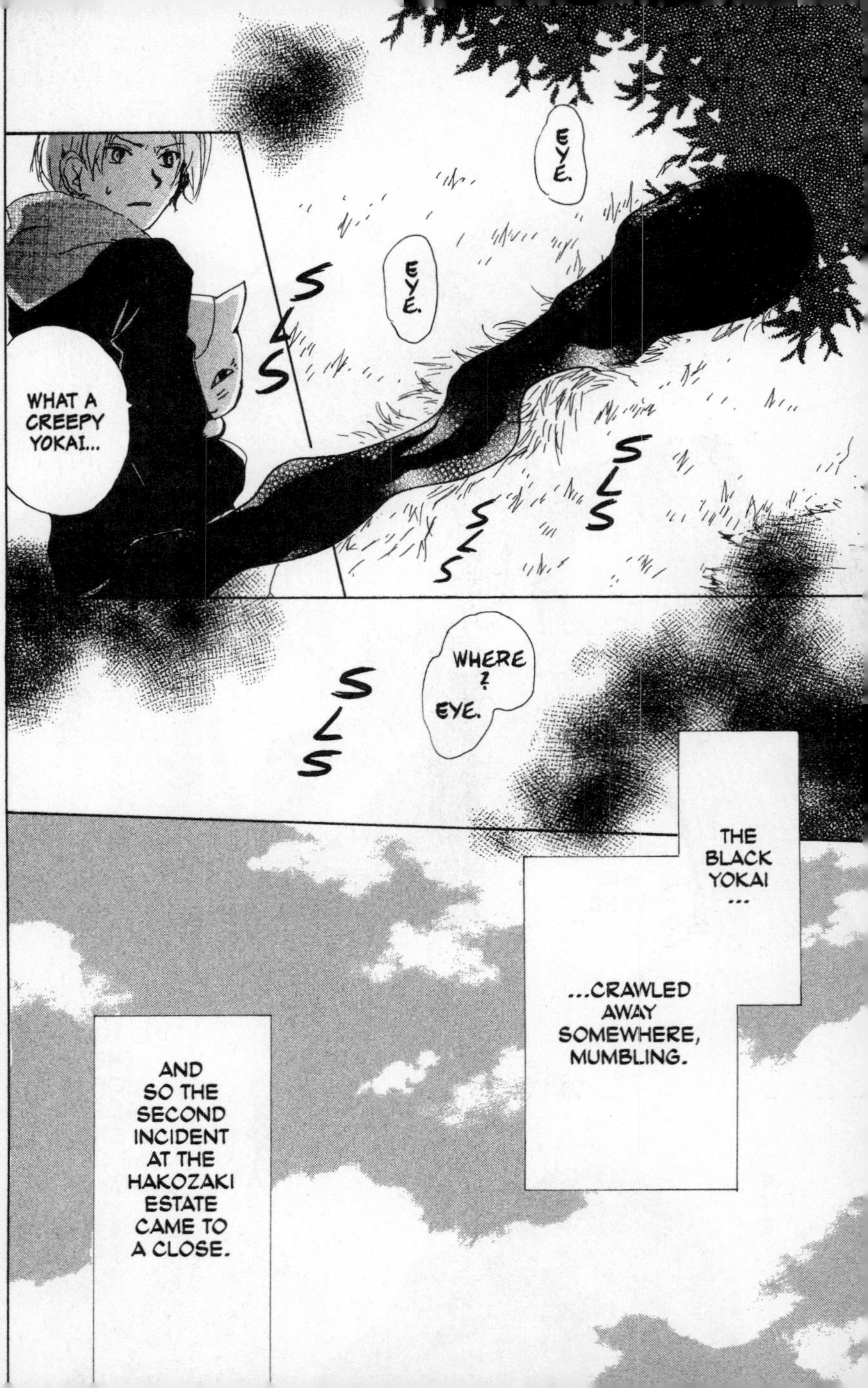
EYE.
EYE.
SLS
SLS
SLS
WHAT A CREEPY YOKAI...
WHERE? EYE.
SLS
THE BLACK YOKAI...
...CRAWLED AWAY SOMEWHERE, MUMBLING.
AND SO THE SECOND INCIDENT AT THE HAKOZAKI ESTATE CAME TO A CLOSE.

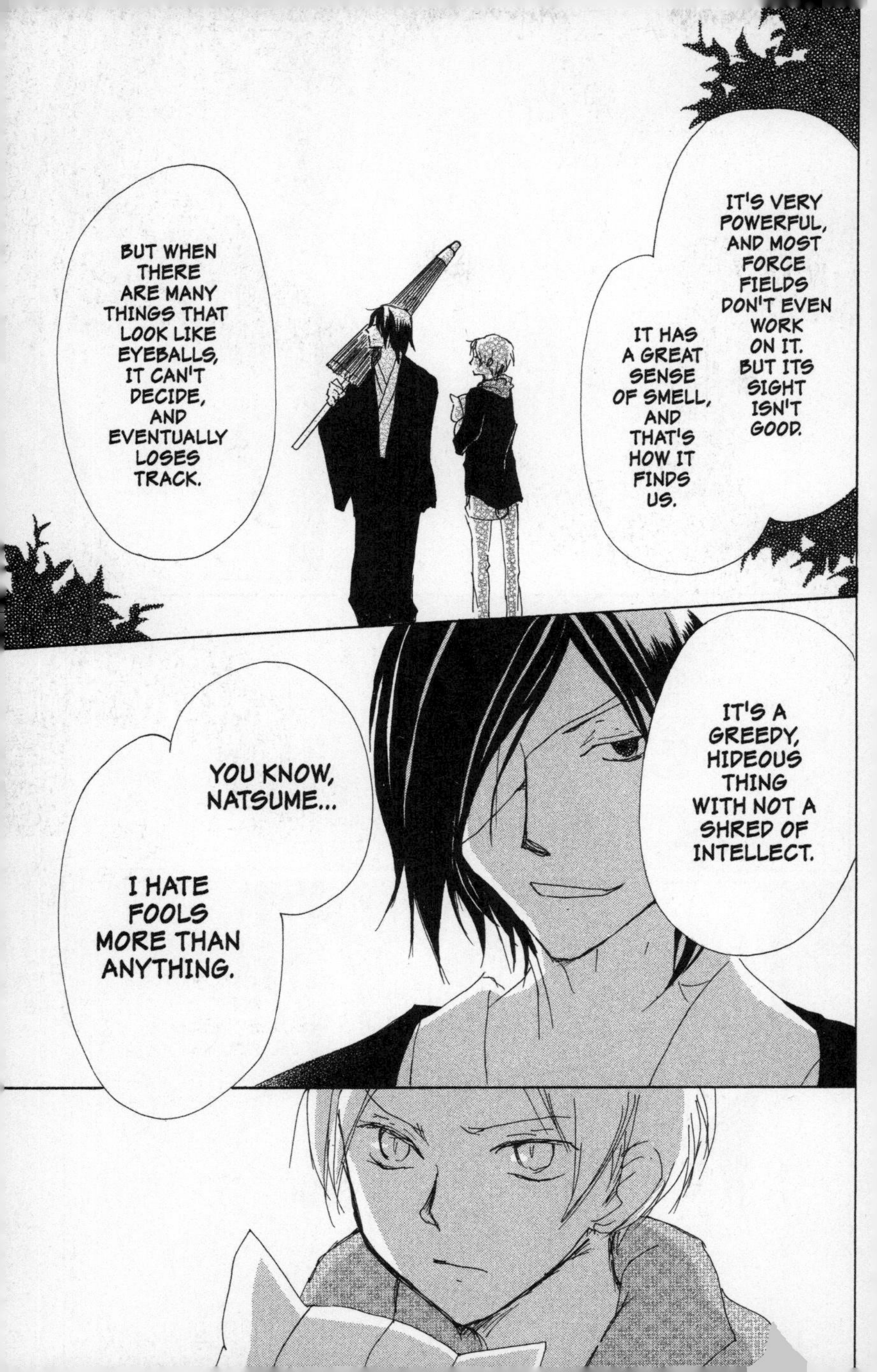
IT'S VERY POWERFUL, AND MOST FORCE FIELDS DON'T EVEN WORK ON IT. BUT ITS SIGHT ISN'T GOOD.
IT HAS A GREAT SENSE OF SMELL, AND THAT'S HOW IT FINDS US.
BUT WHEN THERE ARE MANY THINGS THAT LOOK LIKE EYEBALLS, IT CAN'T DECIDE, AND EVENTUALLY LOSES TRACK.
IT'S A GREEDY, HIDEOUS THING WITH NOT A SHRED OF INTELLECT.
YOU KNOW, NATSUME...
I HATE FOOLS MORE THAN ANYTHING.

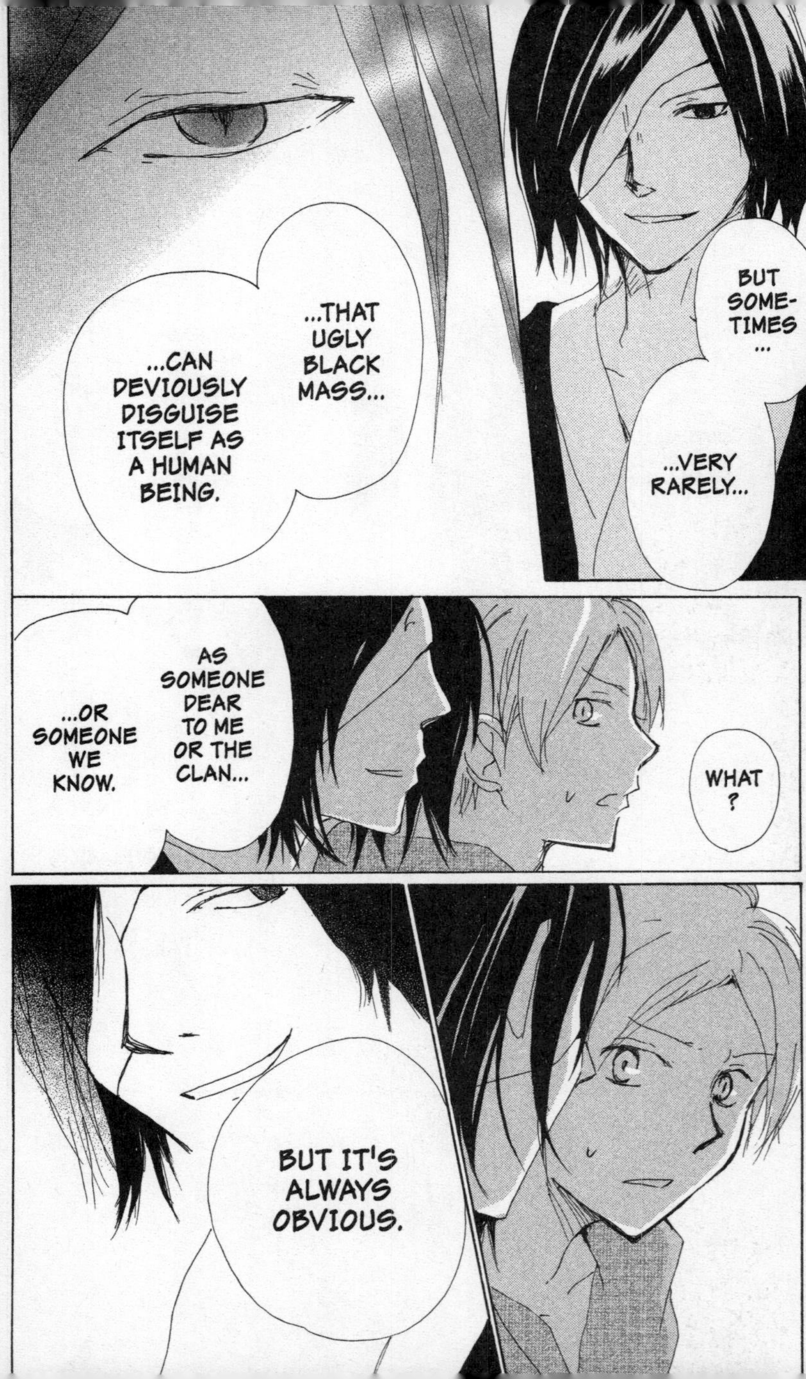
BUT SOME-TIMES...
...VERY RARELY...
...THAT UGLY BLACK MASS...
...CAN DEVIOUSLY DISGUISE ITSELF AS A HUMAN BEING.
AS SOMEONE DEAR TO ME OR THE CLAN...
...OR SOMEONE WE KNOW.
WHAT?
BUT IT'S ALWAYS OBVIOUS.

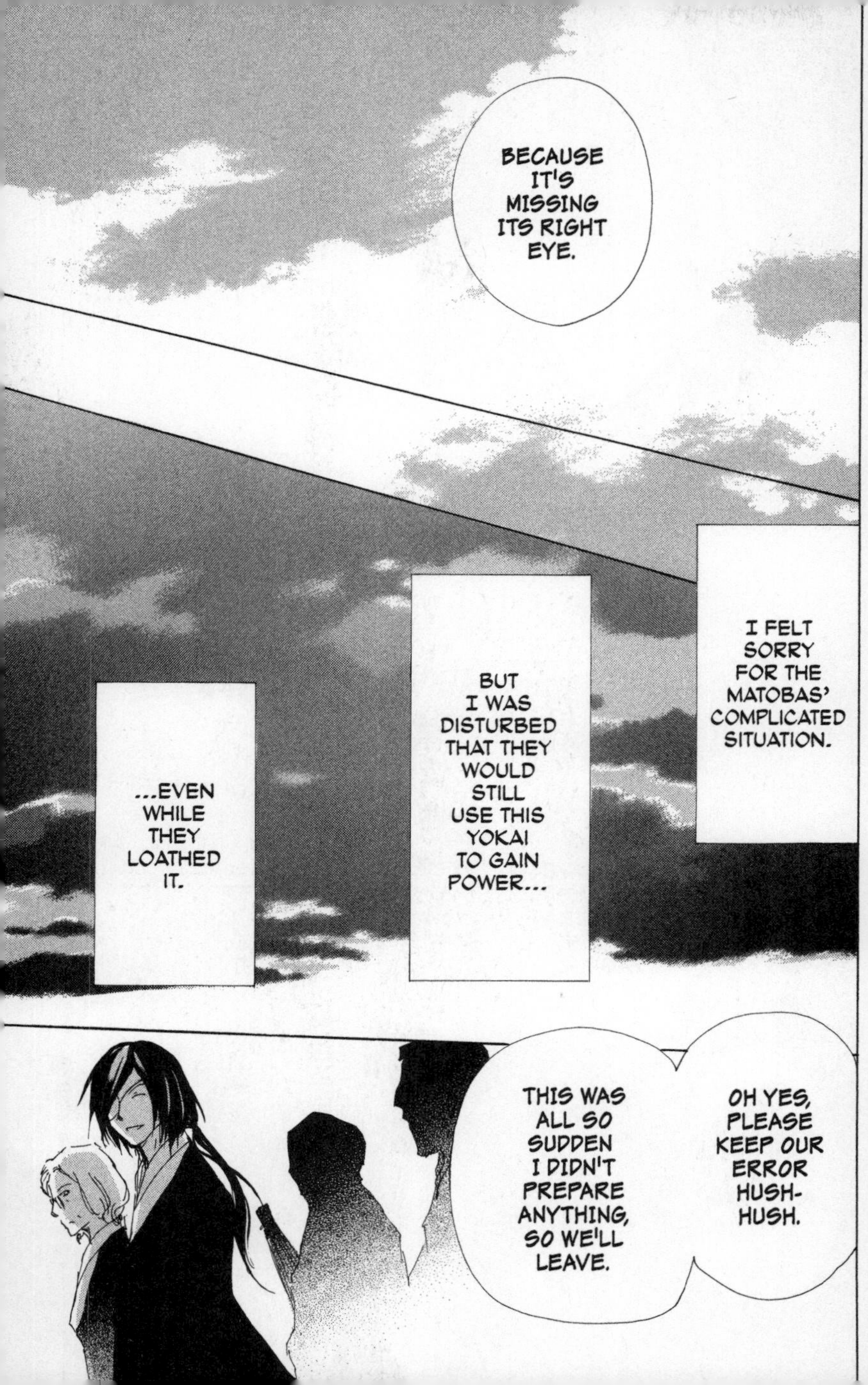
BECAUSE IT'S MISSING ITS RIGHT EYE.
I FELT SORRY FOR THE MATOBAS' COMPLICATED SITUATION.
BUT I WAS DISTURBED THAT THEY WOULD STILL USE THIS YOKAI TO GAIN POWER...
...EVEN WHILE THEY LOATHED IT.
OH YES, PLEASE KEEP OUR ERROR HUSH-HUSH.
THIS WAS ALL SO SUDDEN I DIDN'T PREPARE ANYTHING, SO WE'LL LEAVE.

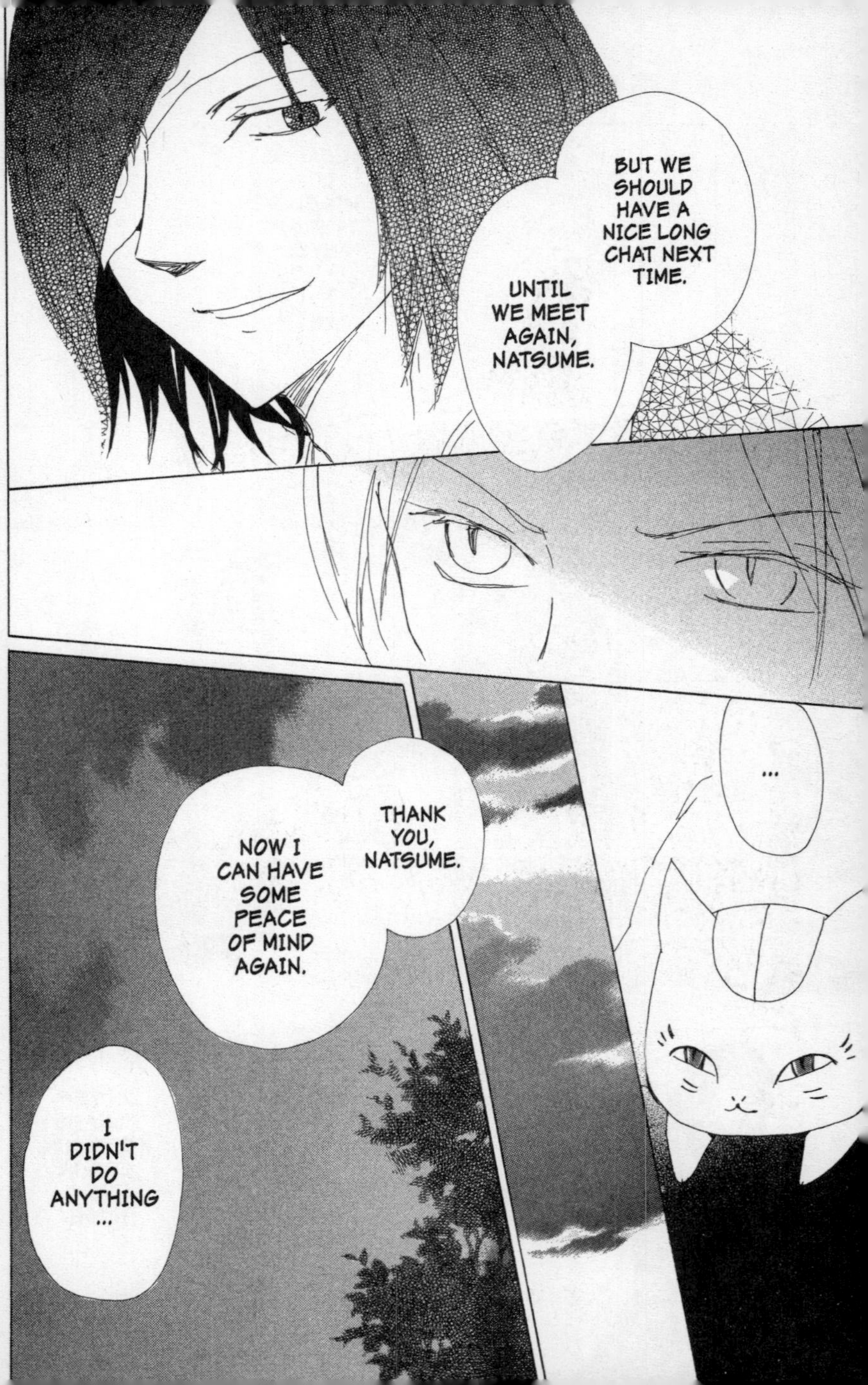
BUT WE SHOULD HAVE A NICE LONG CHAT NEXT TIME.
UNTIL WE MEET AGAIN, NATSUME.
...
THANK YOU, NATSUME.
NOW I CAN HAVE SOME PEACE OF MIND AGAIN.
I DIDN'T DO ANYTHING...

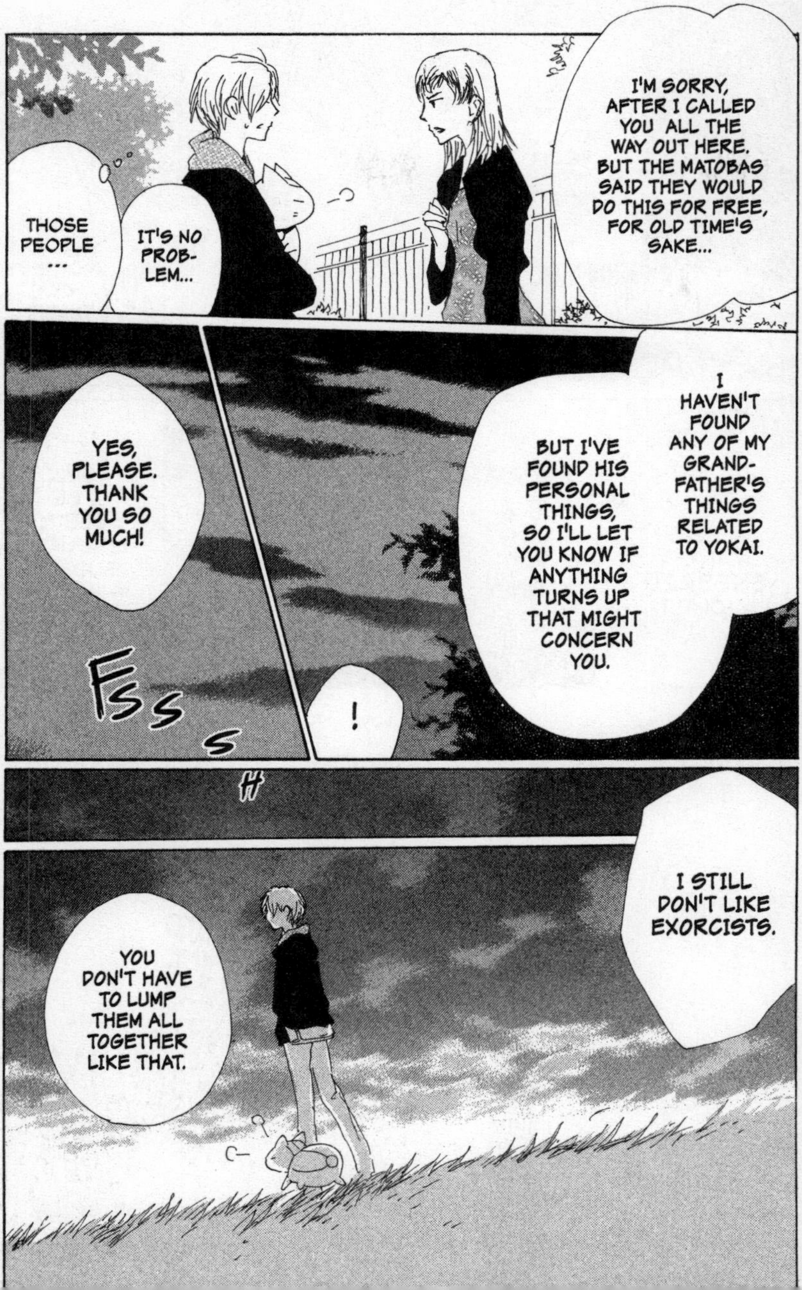
I'M SORRY, AFTER I CALLED YOU ALL THE WAY OUT HERE. BUT THE MATOBAS SAID THEY WOULD DO THIS FOR FREE, FOR OLD TIME'S SAKE...
IT'S NO PROB-LEM...
THOSE PEOPLE ...
I HAVEN'T FOUND ANY OF MY GRAND-FATHER'S THINGS RELATED TO YOKAI.
BUT I'VE FOUND HIS PERSONAL THINGS, SO I'LL LET YOU KNOW IF ANYTHING TURNS UP THAT MIGHT CONCERN YOU.
!
YES, PLEASE. THANK YOU SO MUCH!
FSSS
SH
I STILL DON'T LIKE EXORCISTS.
YOU DON'T HAVE TO LUMP THEM ALL TOGETHER LIKE THAT.

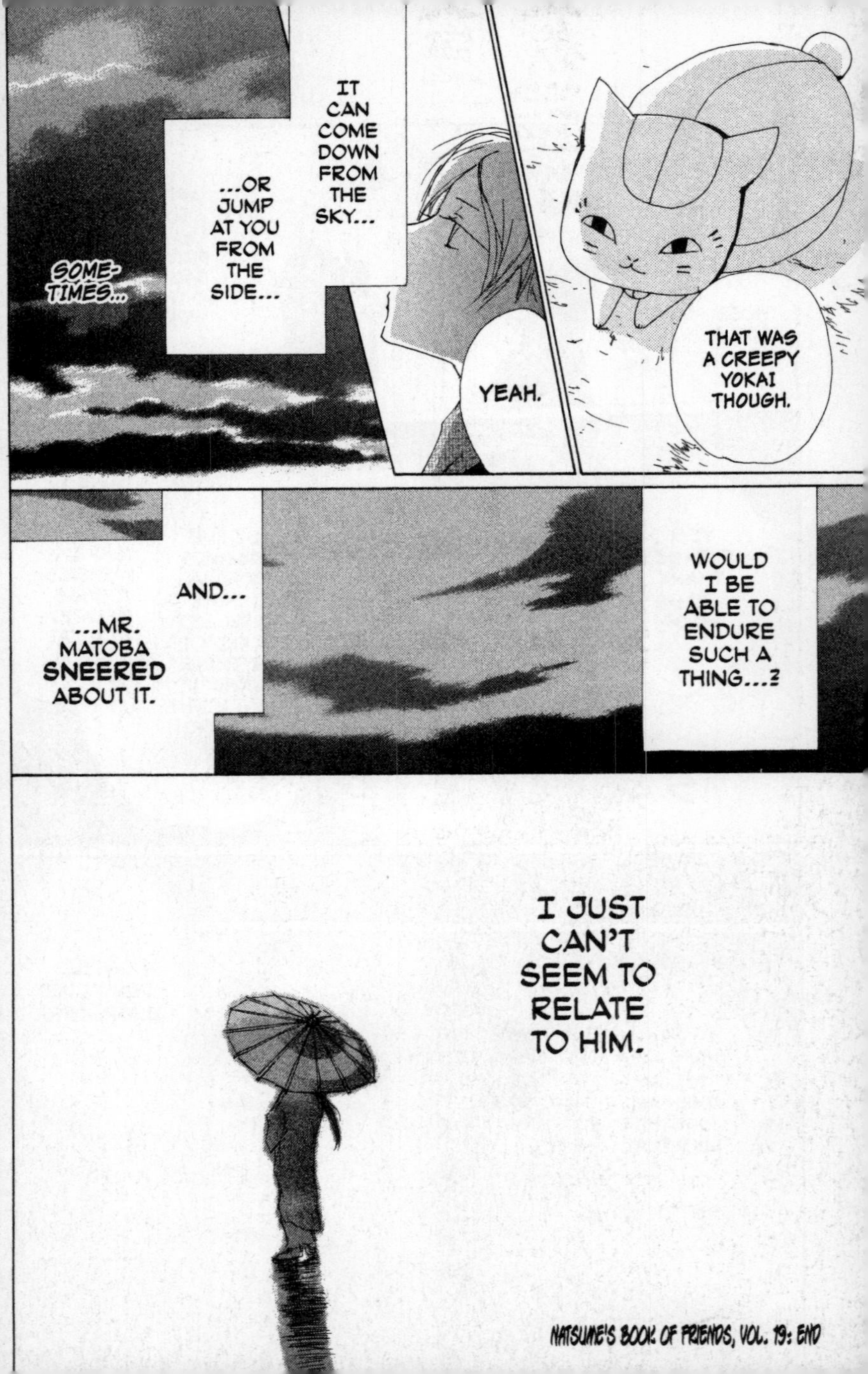
THAT WAS A CREEPY YOKAI THOUGH.
YEAH.
IT CAN COME DOWN FROM THE SKY...
...OR JUMP AT YOU FROM THE SIDE...
SOME-TIMES...
WOULD I BE ABLE TO ENDURE SUCH A THING...?
AND...
...MR. MATOBA SNEERED ABOUT IT.
I JUST CAN'T SEEM TO RELATE TO HIM.
NATSUME'S BOOK OF FRIENDS, VOL. 19: END

Thank you for reading.

With experience, Natsume is better able to move about like I u
to. These days, I notice the changes in him; of course, but now
main character is more secure in his surroundings, I also notice
instability and insecurities of the friends around him. When yo
is spinning and you're relying on others to keep you steady, you
not notice that the others are also unsure of themselves. I'd li
keep picking up on these subtle changes of maturity and human

Please read the rest of this afterword only after reading the

CHAPTER 74

The Two Terrors

I wanted to do an episode where Natsume takes a different tone of voice than usual, so I picked Shibata, since I consider him to be a semi-regular cast member. There are a lot of stories I want to do, or characters I want to revisit, but this is my first time working on such a long series, so I have no idea how to reintroduce characters and story lines or how to time it. So there are many ideas gathering dust, but I'd like to see how it goes and do another one like this.

I also want to draw more of Tanuma, but it's important for Natsume to not go to see Tanuma when there are yokai involved, so it's quite a dilemma. But I'd like to include the idea that they loaf around on those mundane days that can't be included in a manga. It was fun drawing Shibata in a panic.

CHAPTER 75

Bloom Tomorrow

I've always wanted to do a story about art on rocks, and I finally figured out how to do it. There was more I wanted to include, but I made the pace more leisurely. It's a bit plain, but I hope you enjoy it.

CHAPTER 76

Gomochi's Benefactor

I wanted to do a story of a regular day in Reiko's life—one where she neither gains nor advances anything. It was difficult and I wish I could've done it better.

CHAPTER 77

The Two Rings

This was another story I had always wanted to do, but the timing never worked out, so I was very happy to get to it now. When I'm drawing Natsume, I always agonize over his dialogue and pick his words carefully. But when I'm drawing the Matoba clan, I don't have to think about the impression they're making, and I just use words that pop up in my head. Mr. Natori is somewhere in between. It's always a bit refreshing to draw the exorcists. I hope people form their opinions of Mr. Matoba based on what's on the page. In good ways and bad, he's a character who lies but is also uninhibited.

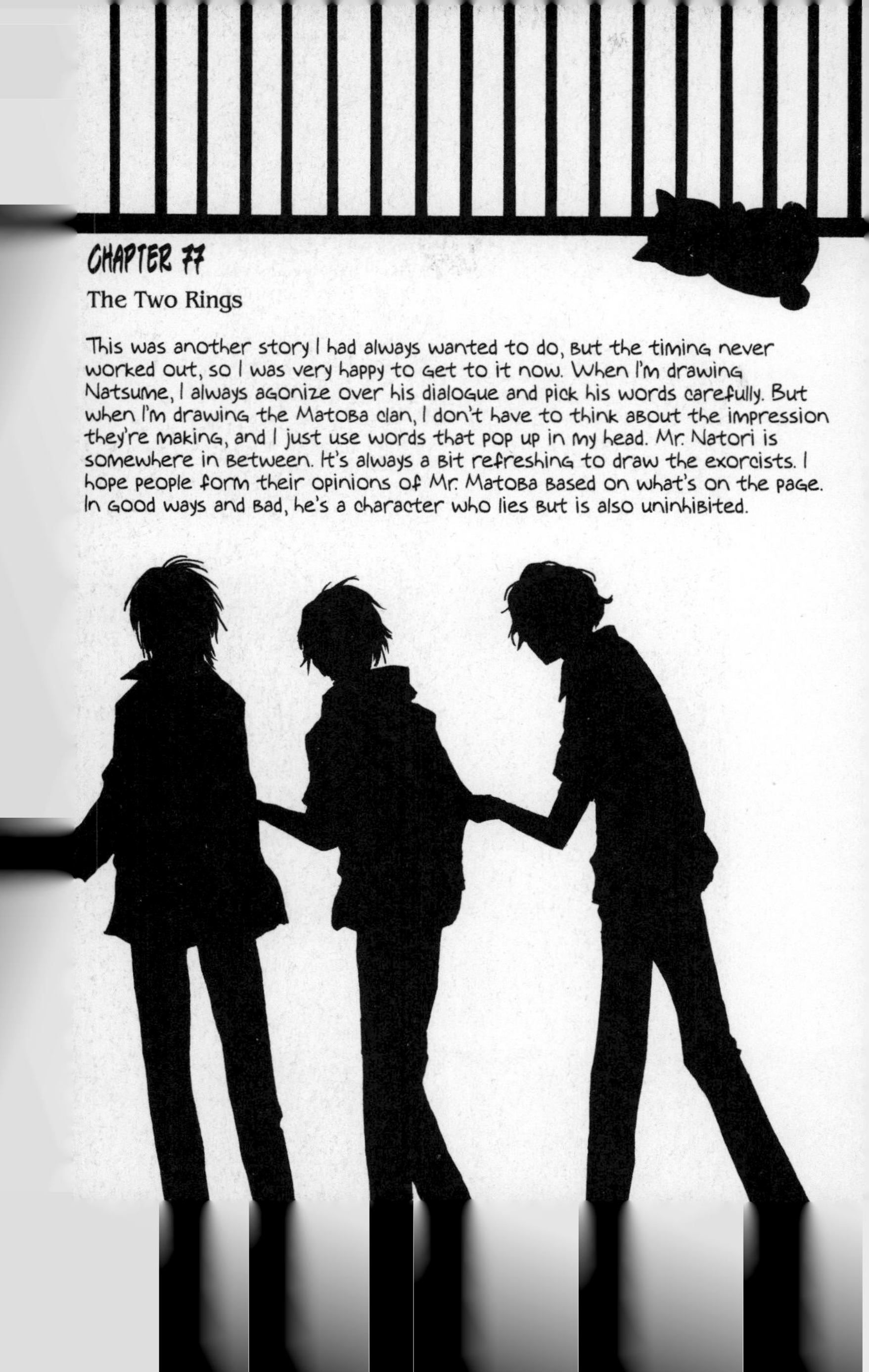

I've reached volume 19! I feel so happy that I've gotten to work on this for so long and also nervous that I have to be careful. I've received so much support and made so many new connections with people. I'll work hard without getting careless so that you'll pick this series up again.

Thanks to:

Tamao Ohki
Chika
Mika
Mr. Fujita
My sister
Mr. Sato
Hoen Kikaku, Ltd.
    Thank you.

AFTERWORD: END

Natsume's BOOK of FRIENDS
VOLUME 19 END NOTES

PAGE 49, PANEL 4: *Kuzu-kiri sweet noodles*
Sweetened noodles made from *kuzuko* (kudzu starch), usually served cold with *kuromitsu* (Okinawan black sugar syrup).

Yuki Midorikawa
is the creator of *Natsume's Book
of Friends*, which was nominated
for the Manga Taisho (Cartoon
Grand Prize). Her other titles
published in Japan include
Hotarubi no Mori e (Into the
Forest of Fireflies), *Hiiro no Isu*
(The Scarlet Chair) and *Akaku
Saku Koe* (The Voice That
Blooms Red).

NATSUME'S BOOK OF FRIENDS
Vol. 19
Shojo Beat Edition

STORY AND ART BY *Yuki Midorikawa*

Translation & Adaptation *Lillian Olsen*
Touch-up Art & Lettering *Sabrina Heep*
Design *Fawn Lau*
Editor *Pancha Diaz*

Natsume Yujincho by Yuki Midorikawa
© Yuki Midorikawa 2015
All rights reserved.
First published in Japan in 2015 by HAKUSENSHA, Inc., Tokyo.
English language translation rights arranged with HAKUSENSHA, Inc., Tokyo.

The stories, characters and incidents mentioned in this publication are entirely fictional.

Printed in the U.S.A.

Published by VIZ Media, LLC
P.O. Box 77010
San Francisco, CA 94107

10 9 8 7 6 5 4 3 2 1
First printing, January 2016

www.shojobeat.com

SURPRISE!

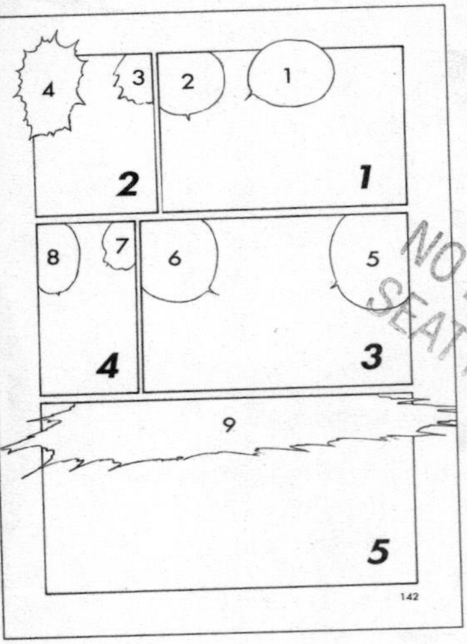
1
2
1
3
4
2
5
6
3
7
8
4
9
5
142

You may be reading the wrong way!

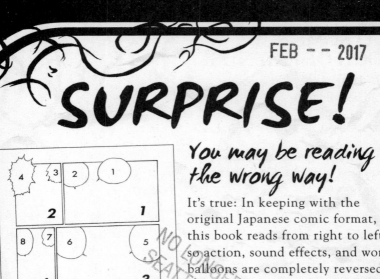

It's true: In keeping with the original Japanese comic format, this book reads from right to left—so action, sound effects, and word balloons are completely reversed. This preserves the orientation of the original artwork—plus, it's fun! Check out the diagram shown here to get the hang of things, and then turn to the other side of the book to get started!

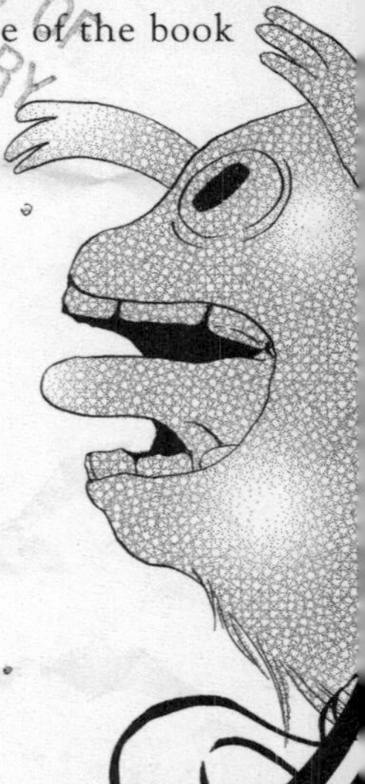

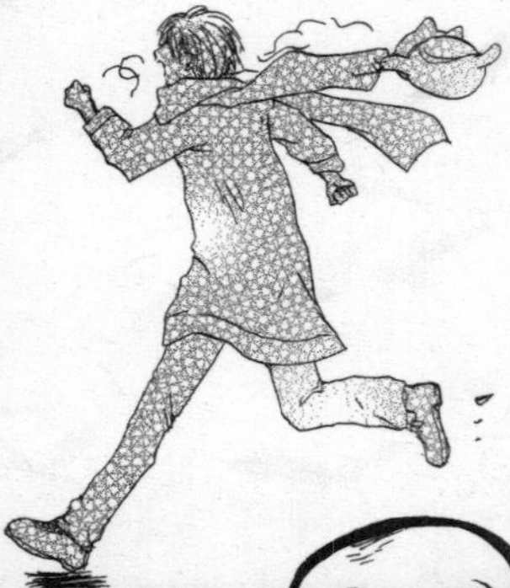

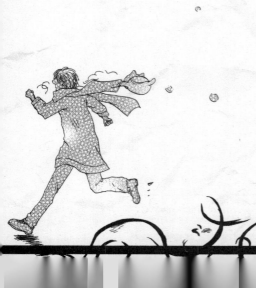